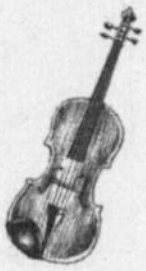

Your Lie in April

I met the girl
under full-bloomed cherry blossoms,
and my fate has begun to change.

1

Naoshi Arakawa

contents

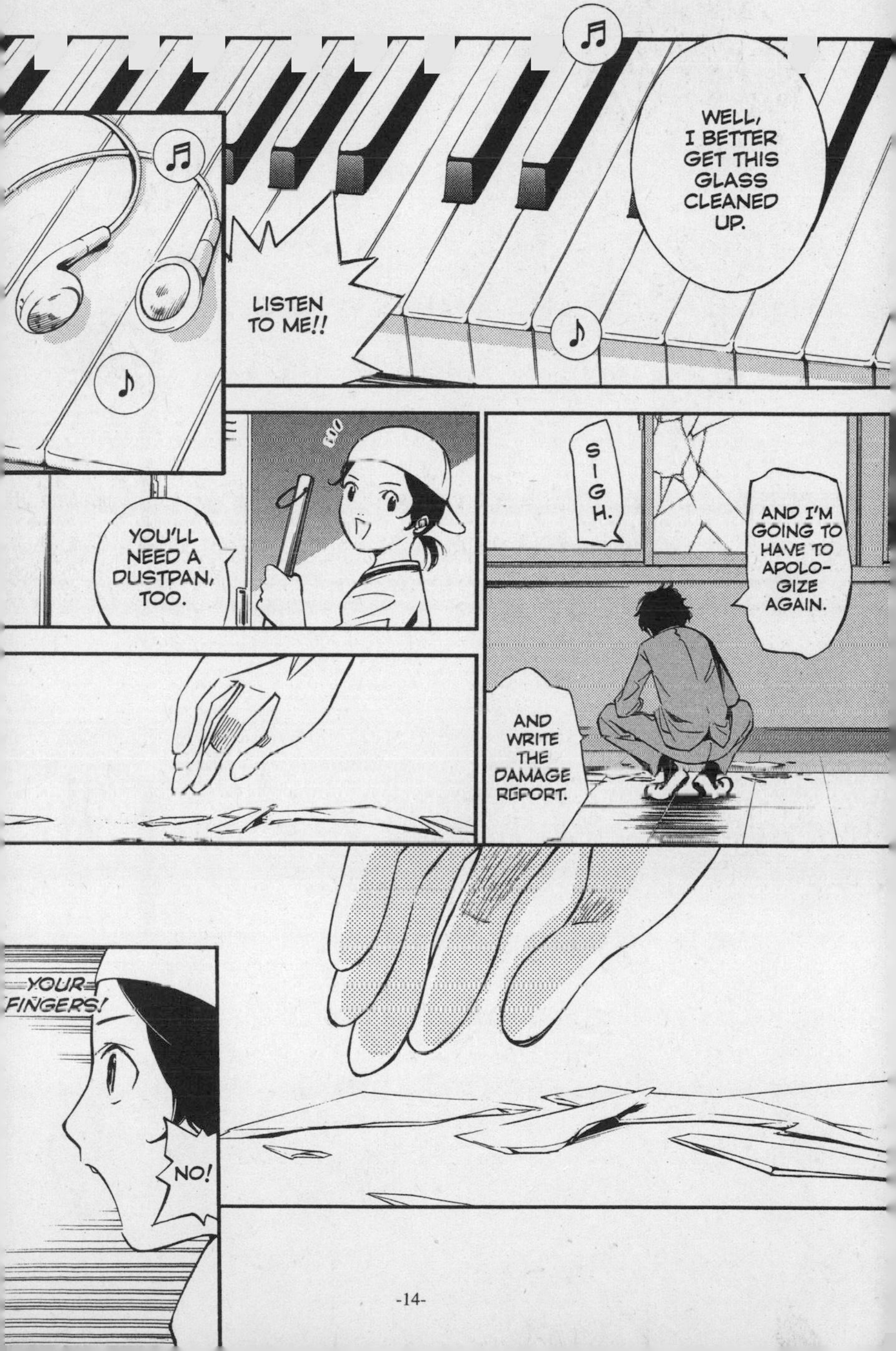
WELL, I BETTER GET THIS GLASS CLEANED UP.
LISTEN TO ME!!
SIGH.
AND I'M GOING TO HAVE TO APOLOGIZE AGAIN.
AND WRITE THE DAMAGE REPORT.
YOU'LL NEED A DUSTPAN, TOO.
YOUR FINGERS!
NO!

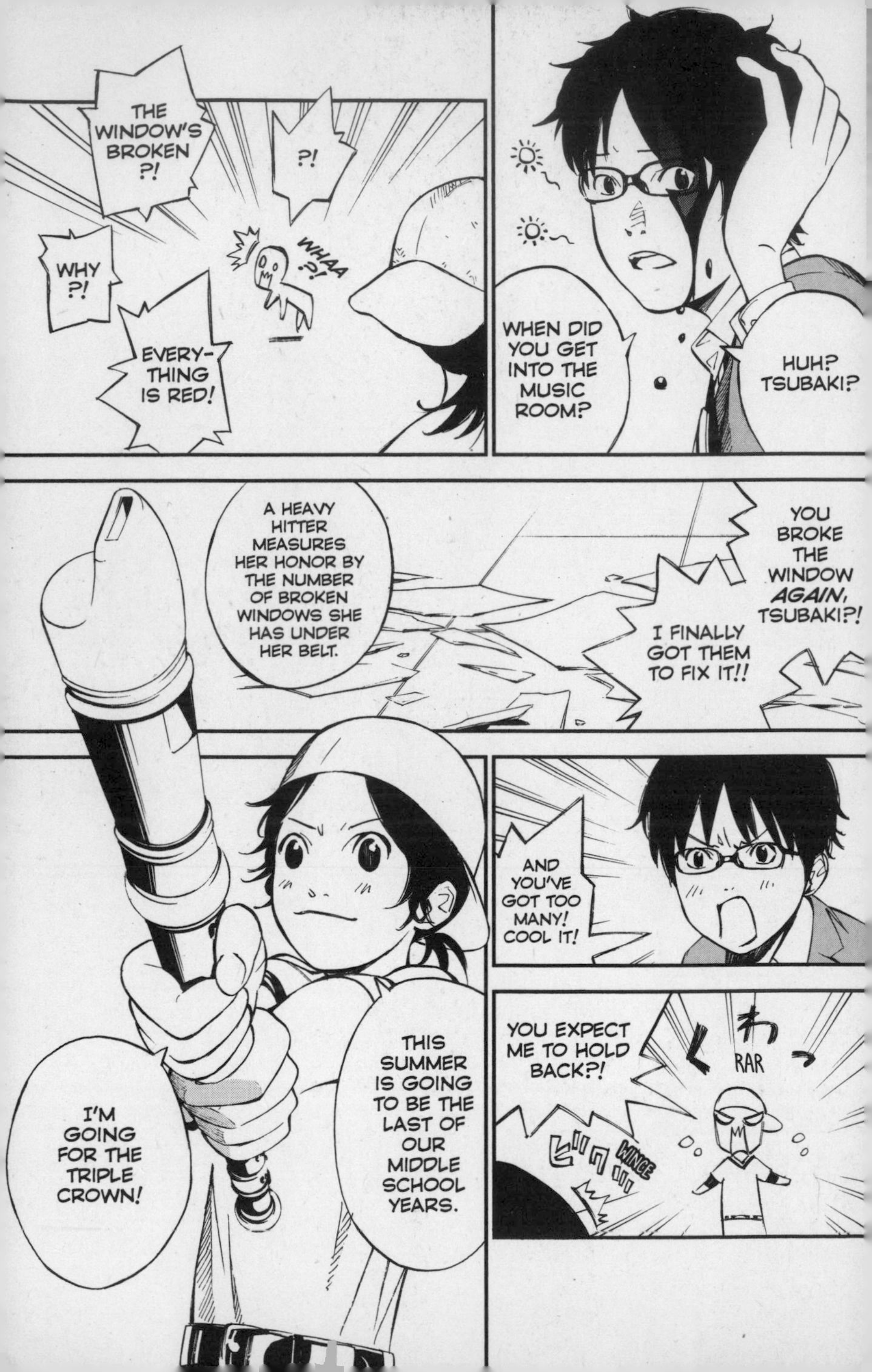
HUH? TSUBAKI?!
WHEN DID YOU GET INTO THE MUSIC ROOM?
?!
THE WINDOW'S BROKEN ?!
WHAA ?!
WHY ?!
EVERY-THING IS RED!
YOU BROKE THE WINDOW *AGAIN*, TSUBAKI?!
I FINALLY GOT THEM TO FIX IT!!
A HEAVY HITTER MEASURES HER HONOR BY THE NUMBER OF BROKEN WINDOWS SHE HAS UNDER HER BELT.
AND YOU'VE GOT TOO MANY! COOL IT!
YOU EXPECT ME TO HOLD BACK?!
RAR
WINCE
THIS SUMMER IS GOING TO BE THE LAST OF OUR MIDDLE SCHOOL YEARS.
I'M GOING FOR THE TRIPLE CROWN!

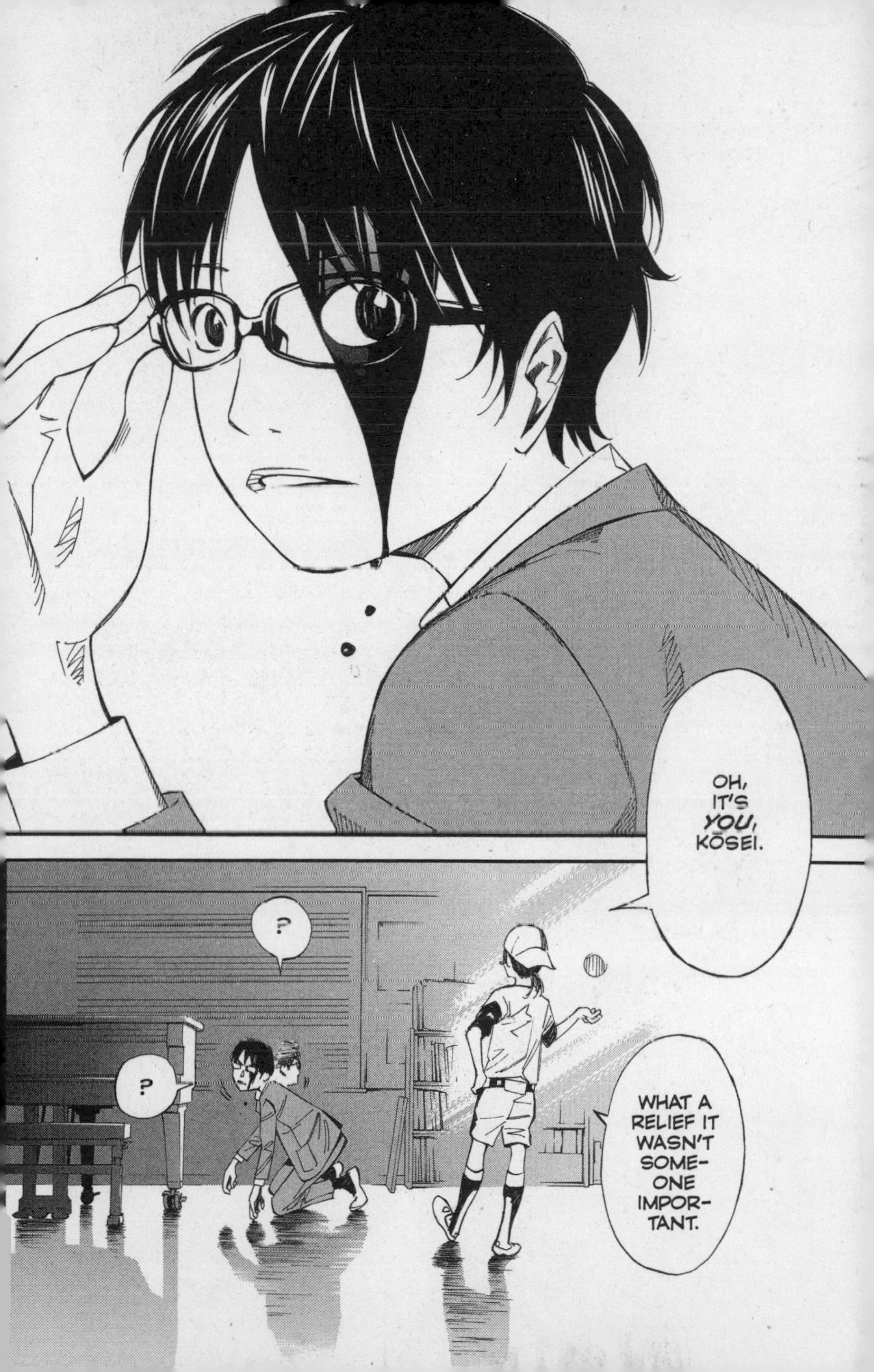
OH, IT'S *YOU*, KOSEI.
WHAT A RELIEF IT WASN'T SOME-ONE IMPOR-TANT.
?
?

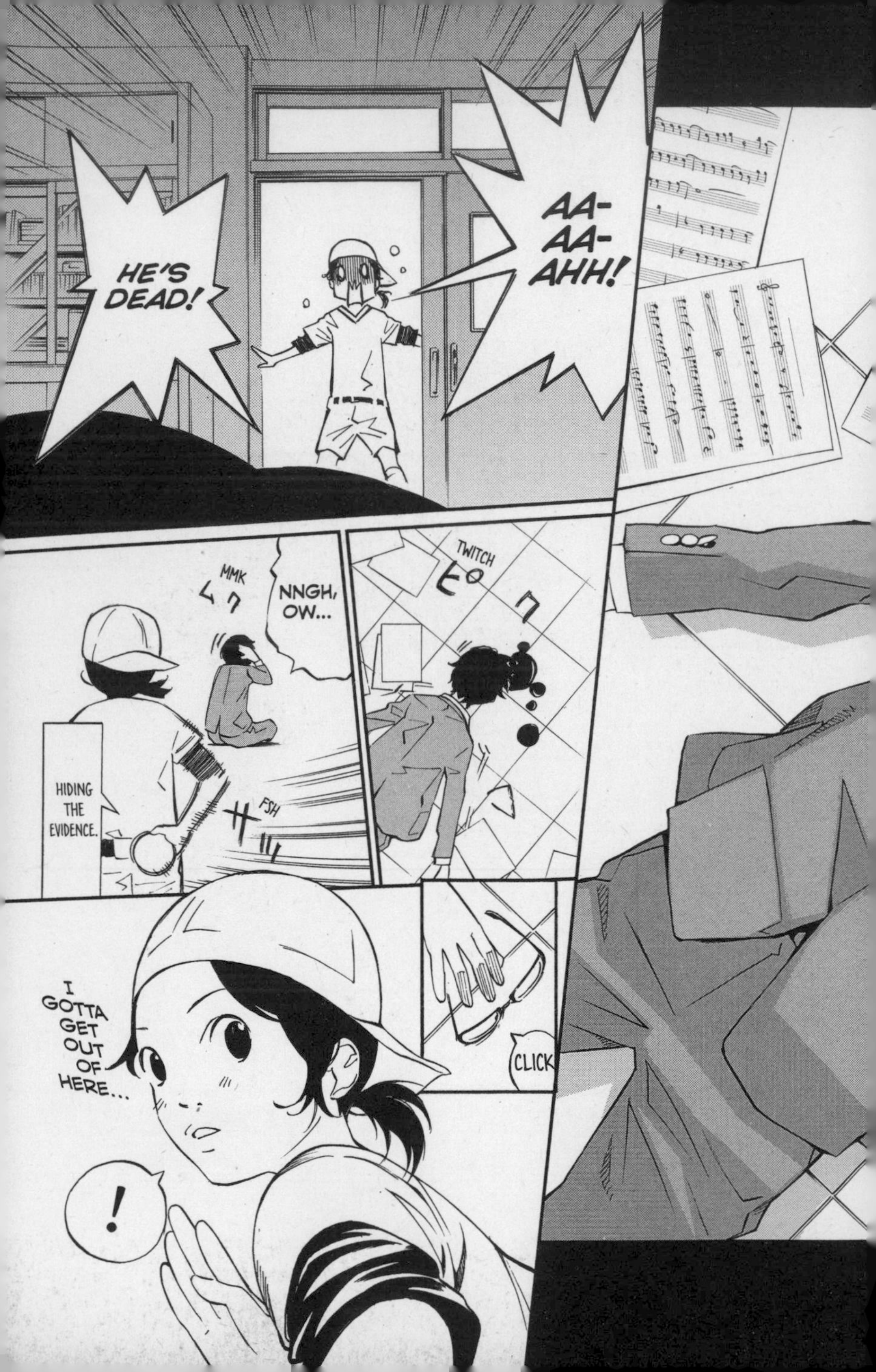
AA-AA-AHH!
HE'S DEAD!
TWITCH
ピク
NNGH, OW...
MMK
ムク
FSH
HIDING THE EVIDENCE.
CLICK
I GOTTA GET OUT OF HERE...
!

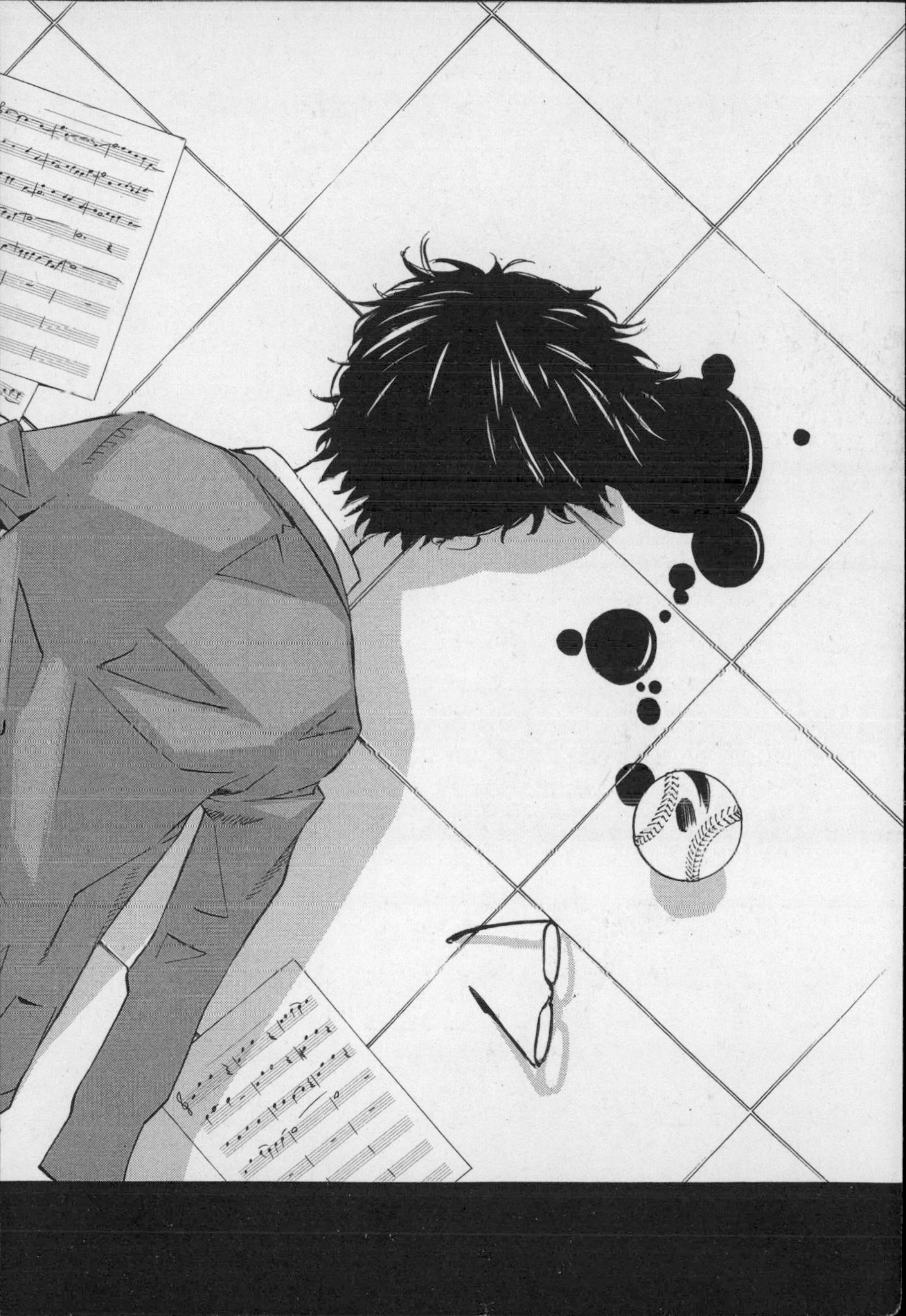

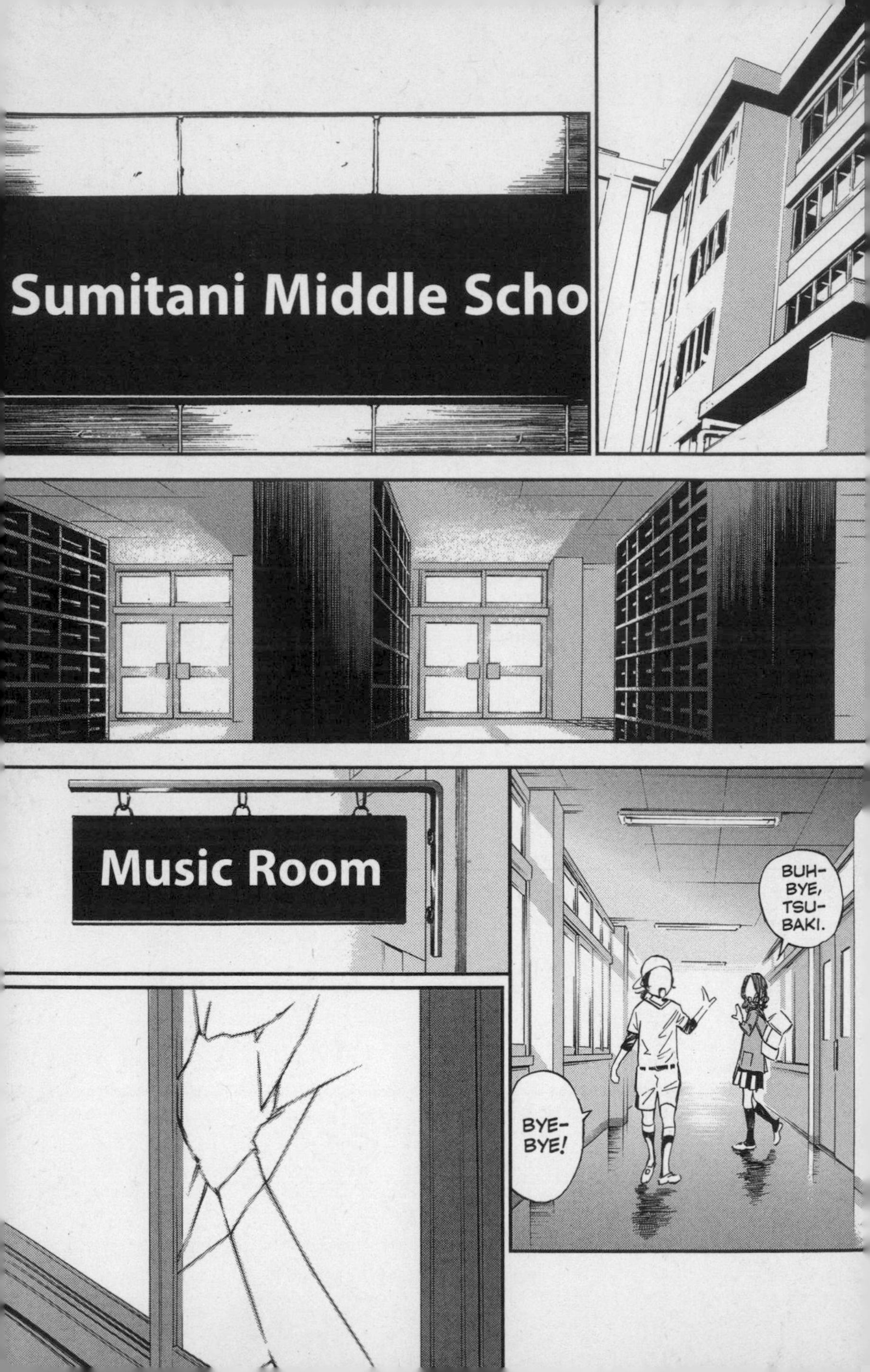
Sumitani Middle Scho
BUH-BYE, TSUBAKI.
BYE-BYE!
Music Room

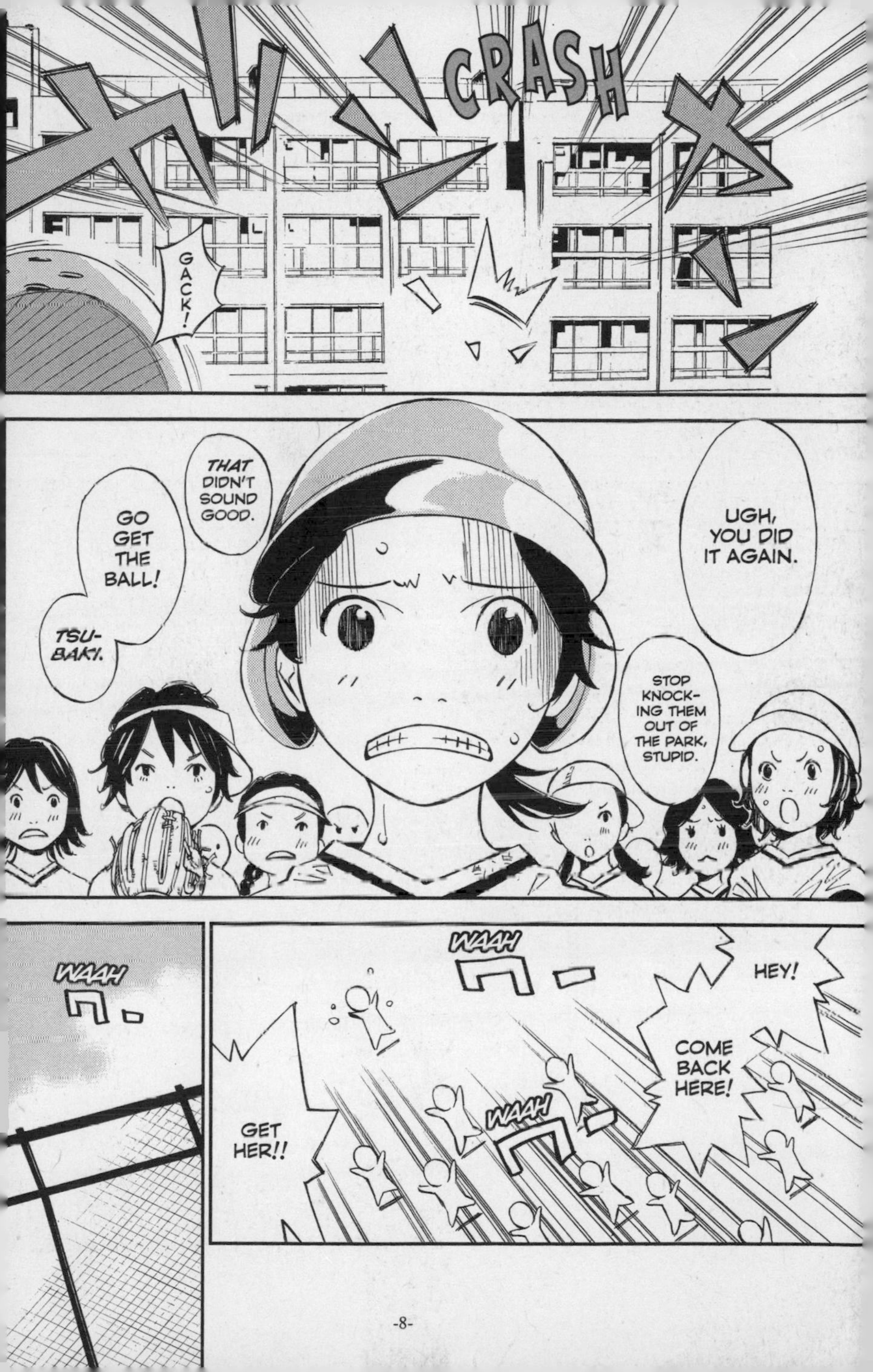
CRASH
GACK!
UGH, YOU DID IT AGAIN.
STOP KNOCKING THEM OUT OF THE PARK, STUPID.
THAT DIDN'T SOUND GOOD.
GO GET THE BALL!
TSUBAKI.
HEY!
COME BACK HERE!
WAAH
WAAH
GET HER!!
WAAH

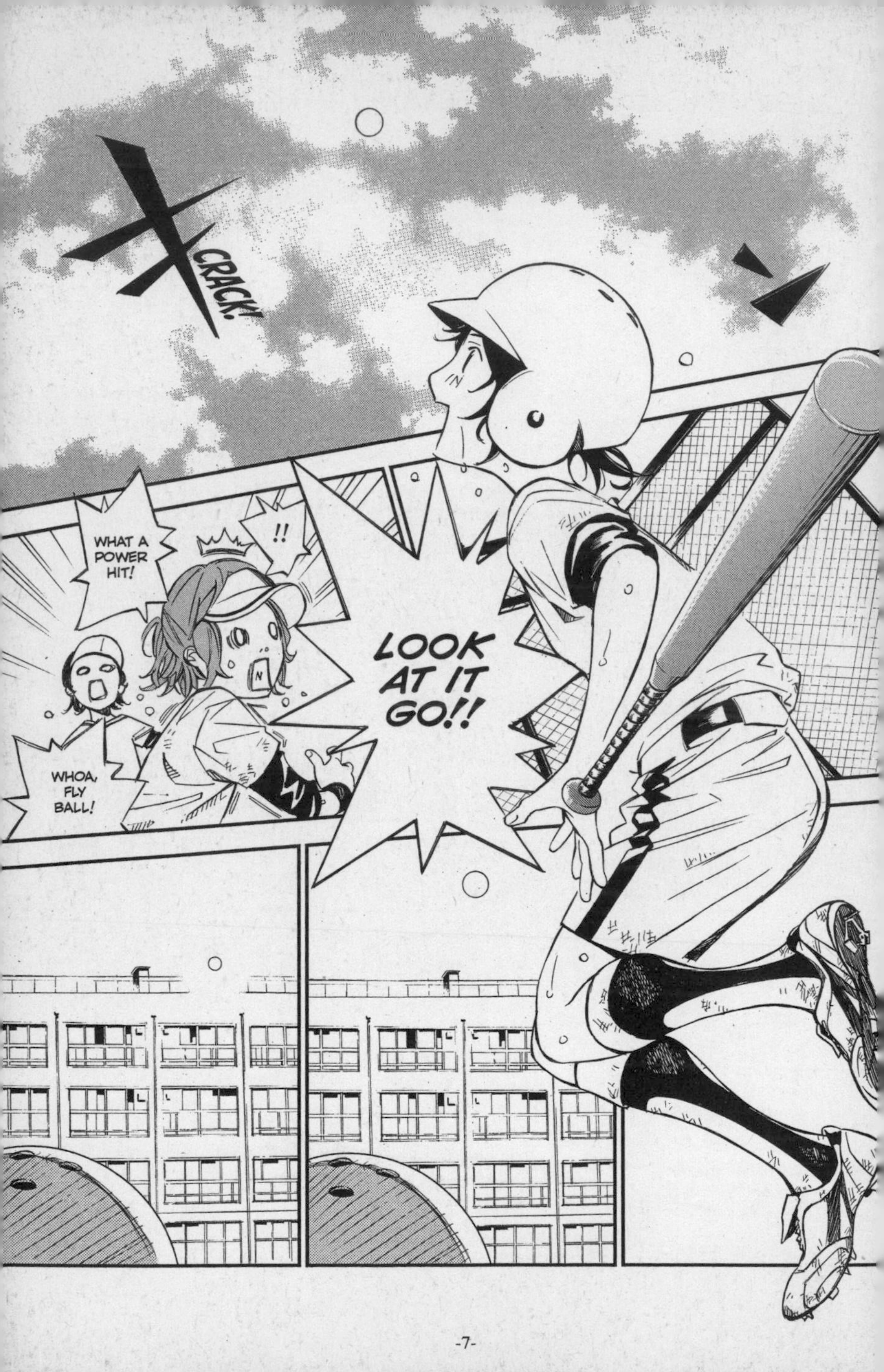
CRACK!
LOOK AT IT GO!!
!!
WHAT A POWER HIT!
WHOA, FLY BALL!

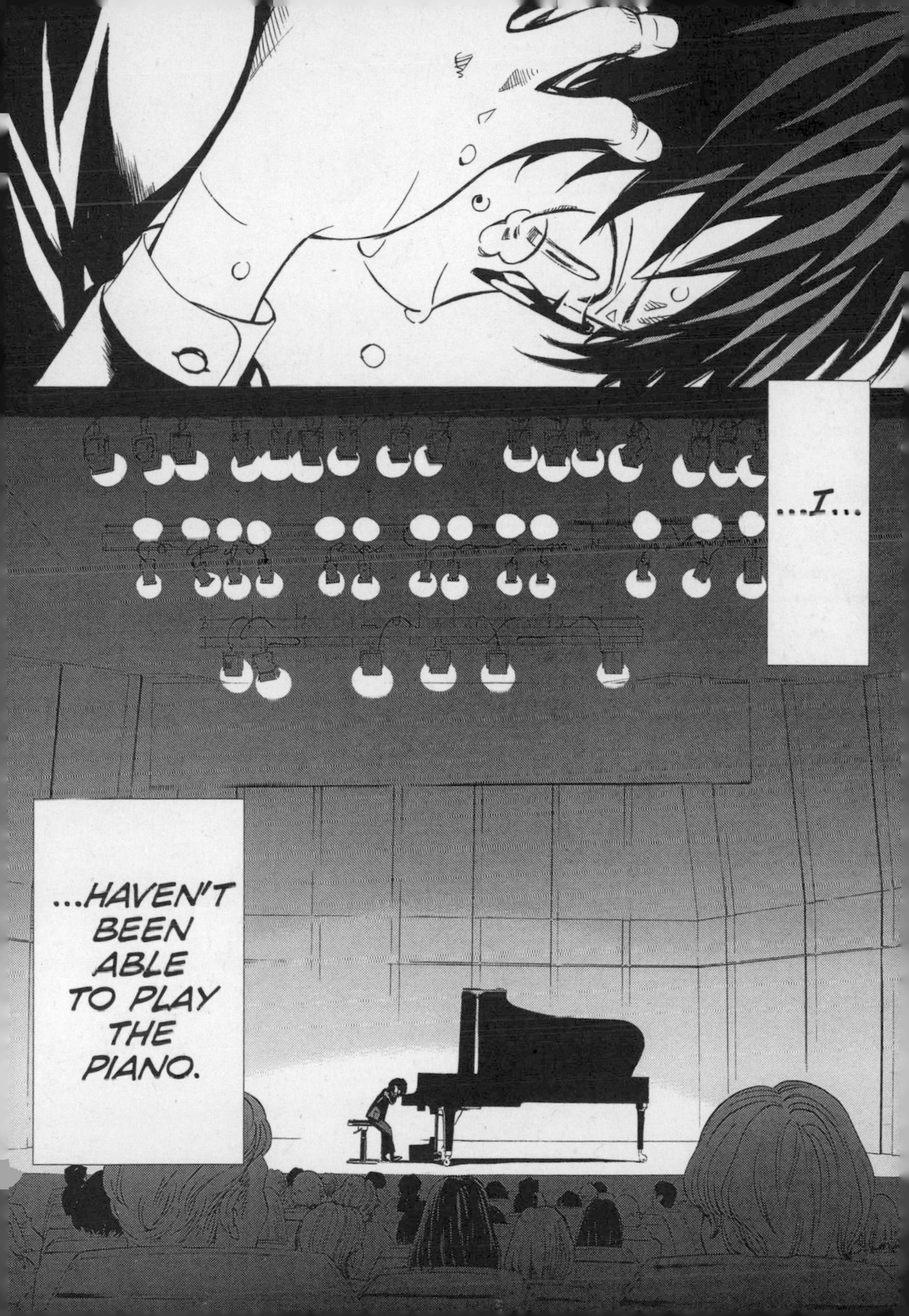
...I...
...HAVEN'T BEEN ABLE TO PLAY THE PIANO.

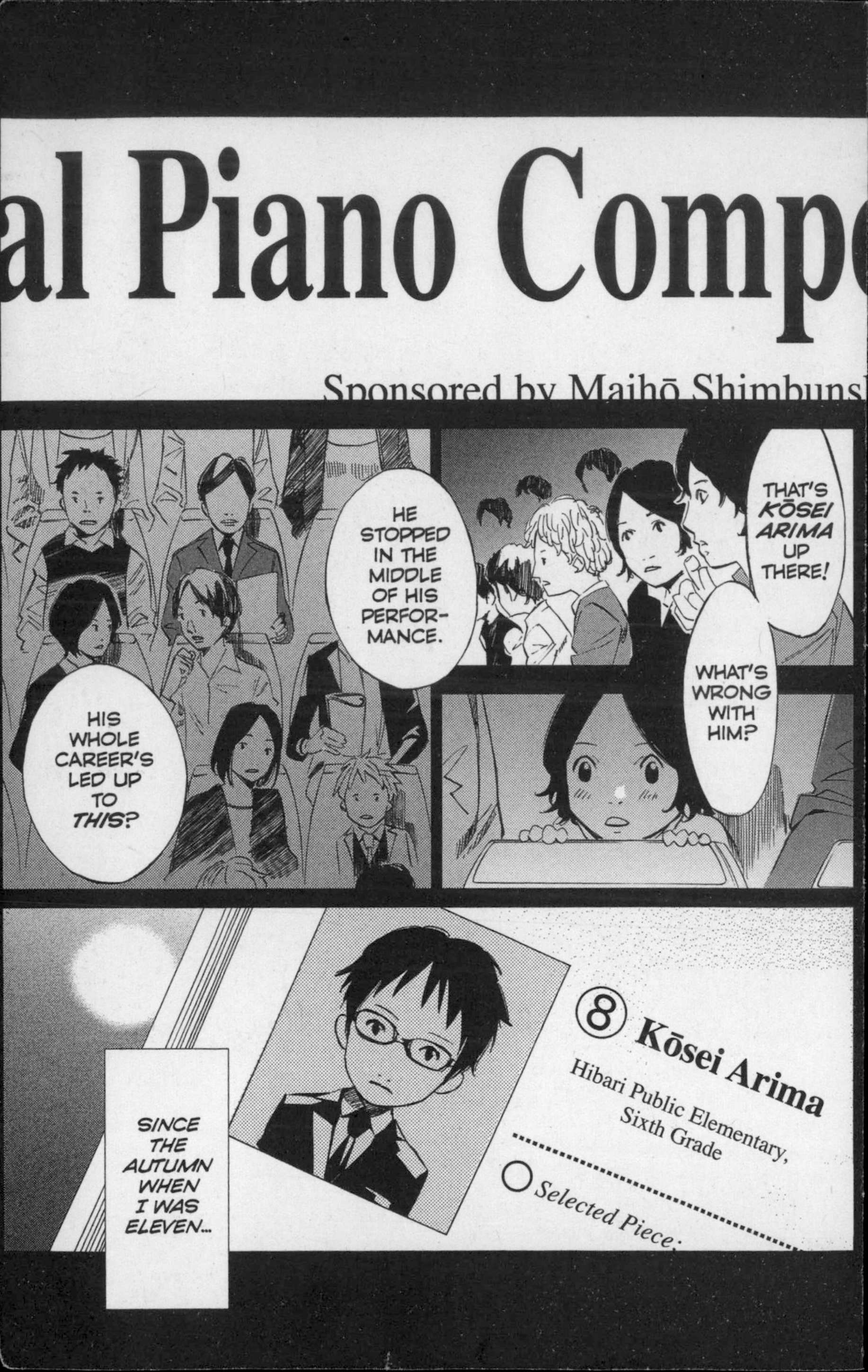
al Piano Comp
Sponsored by Maihō Shimbuns
THAT'S KŌSEI ARIMA UP THERE!
WHAT'S WRONG WITH HIM?
HE STOPPED IN THE MIDDLE OF HIS PERFORMANCE.
HIS WHOLE CAREER'S LED UP TO THIS?
8 Kōsei Arima
Hibari Public Elementary, Sixth Grade
Selected Piece:
SINCE THE AUTUMN WHEN I WAS ELEVEN...

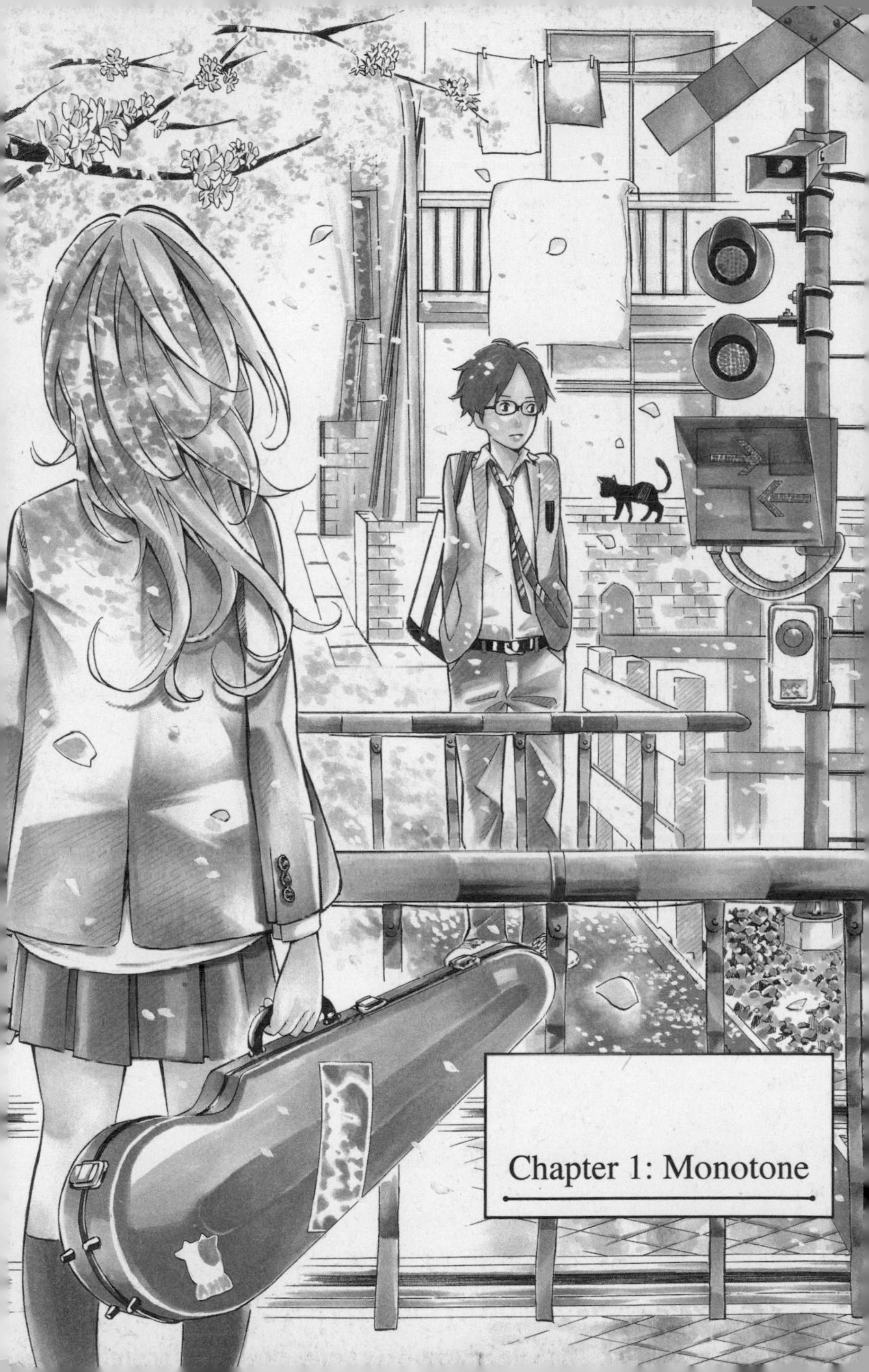
Chapter 1: Monotone

Your Lie in April

I met the girl under full-bloomed cherry blossoms, and my fate has begun to change.

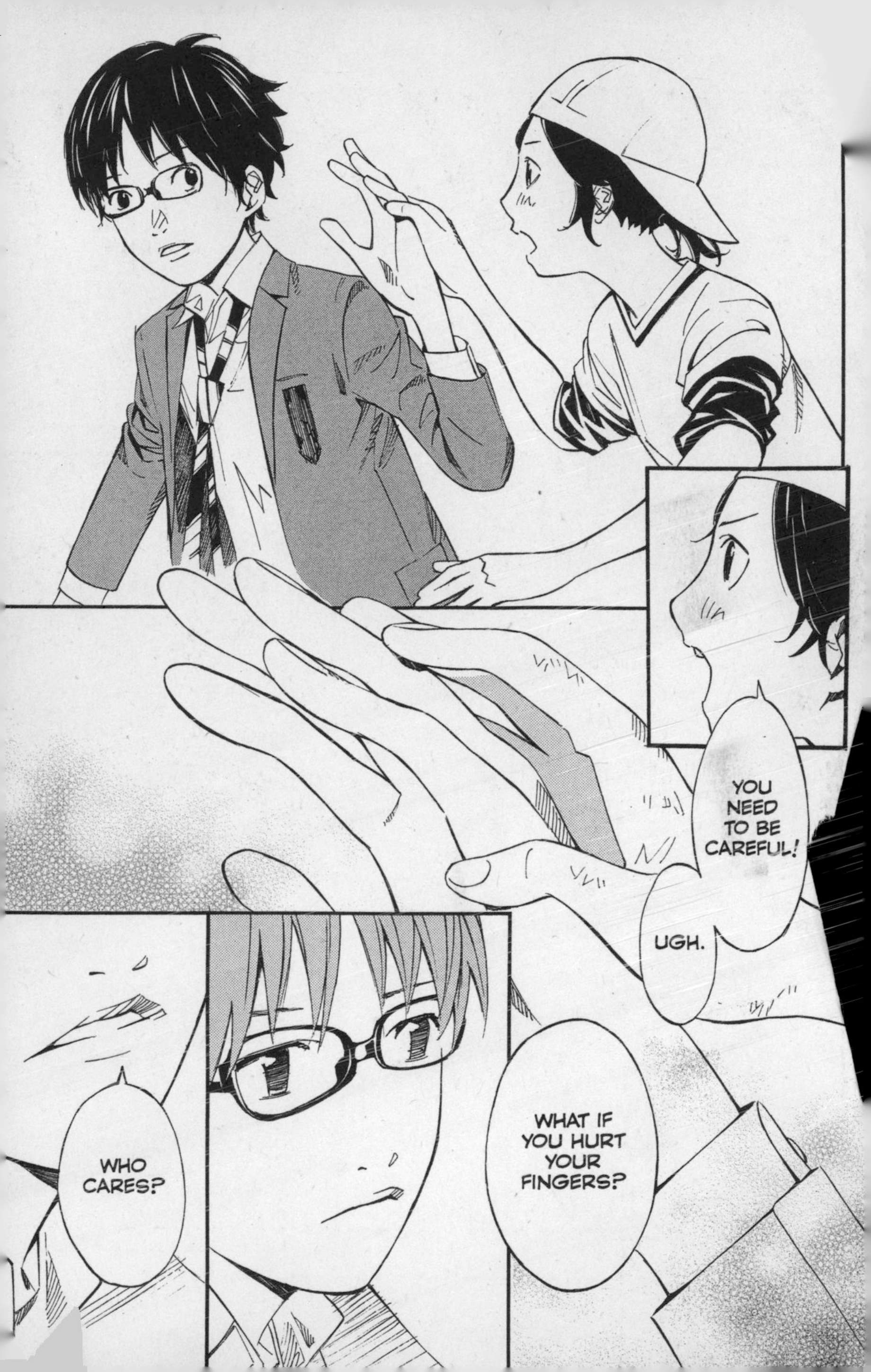
YOU NEED TO BE CAREFUL!
UGH.
WHAT IF YOU HURT YOUR FINGERS?
WHO CARES?

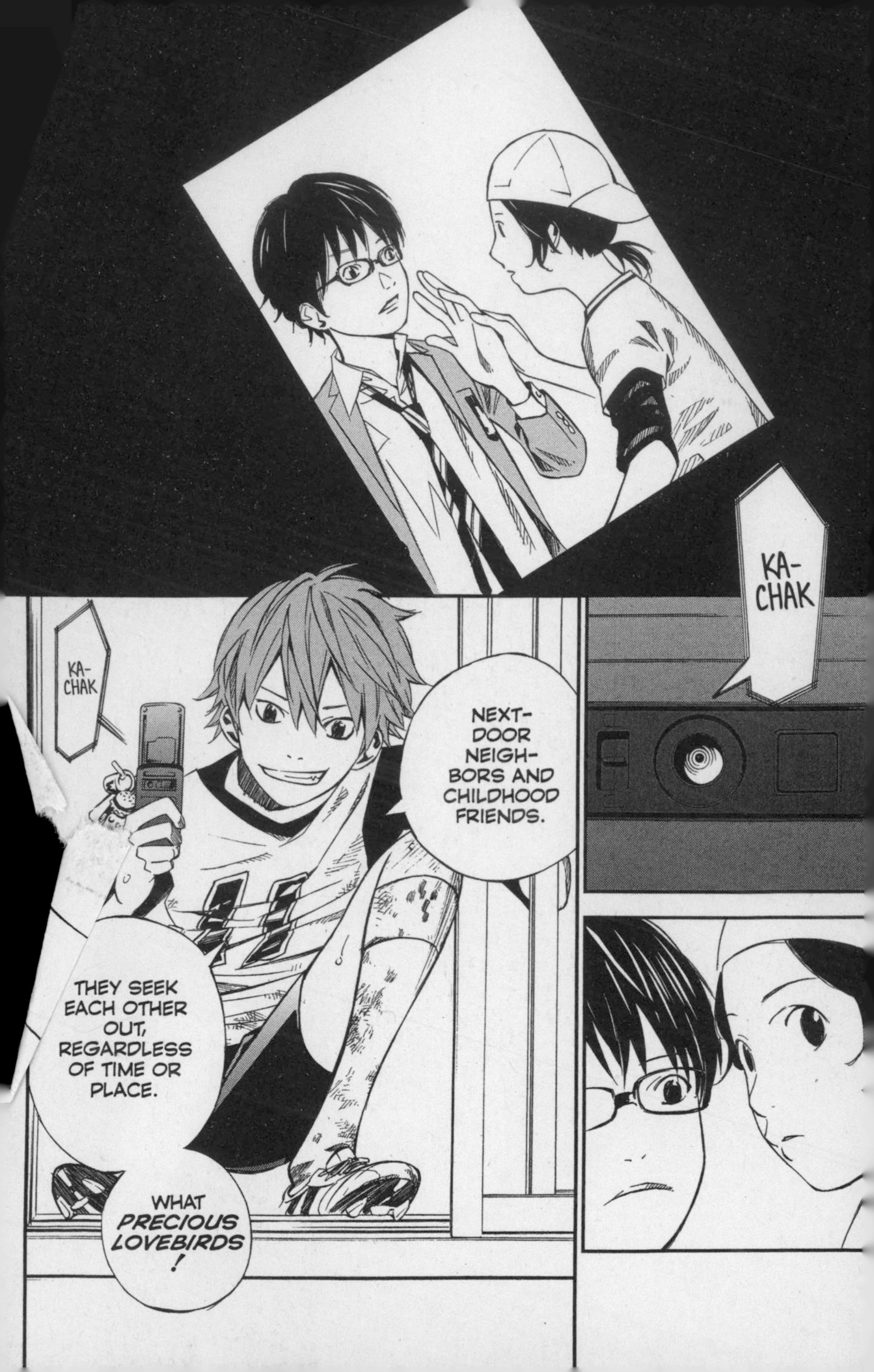
KA-CHAK
KA-CHAK
NEXT-DOOR NEIGHBORS AND CHILDHOOD FRIENDS.
THEY SEEK EACH OTHER OUT, REGARDLESS OF TIME OR PLACE.
WHAT *PRECIOUS LOVEBIRDS*!

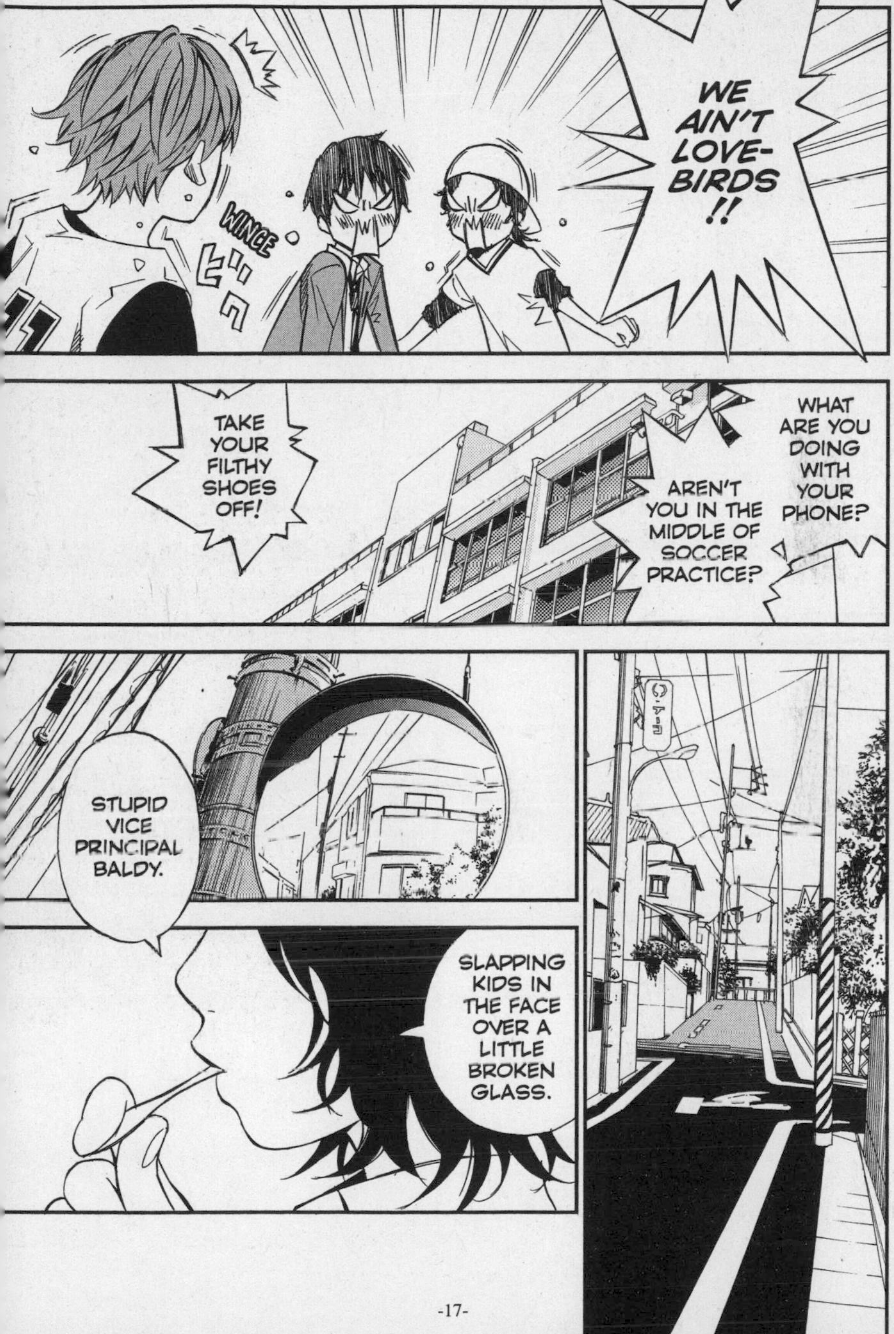
WE AIN'T LOVE-BIRDS!!
WINCE
WHAT ARE YOU DOING WITH YOUR PHONE?
AREN'T YOU IN THE MIDDLE OF SOCCER PRACTICE?
TAKE YOUR FILTHY SHOES OFF!
STUPID VICE PRINCIPAL BALDY.
SLAPPING KIDS IN THE FACE OVER A LITTLE BROKEN GLASS.

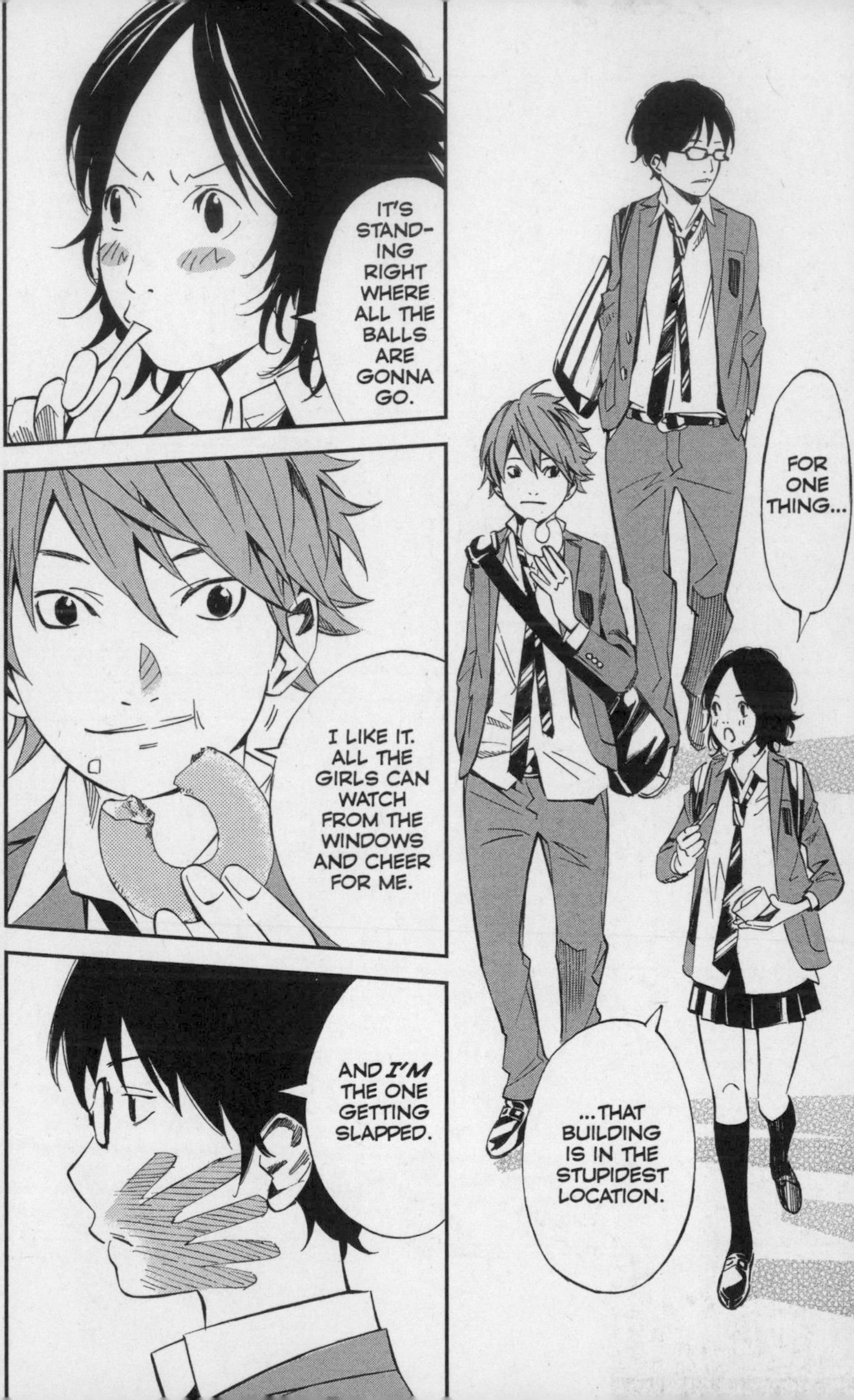
FOR ONE THING...
...THAT BUILDING IS IN THE STUPIDEST LOCATION.
IT'S STANDING RIGHT WHERE ALL THE BALLS ARE GONNA GO.
I LIKE IT. ALL THE GIRLS CAN WATCH FROM THE WINDOWS AND CHEER FOR ME.
AND *I'M* THE ONE GETTING SLAPPED.

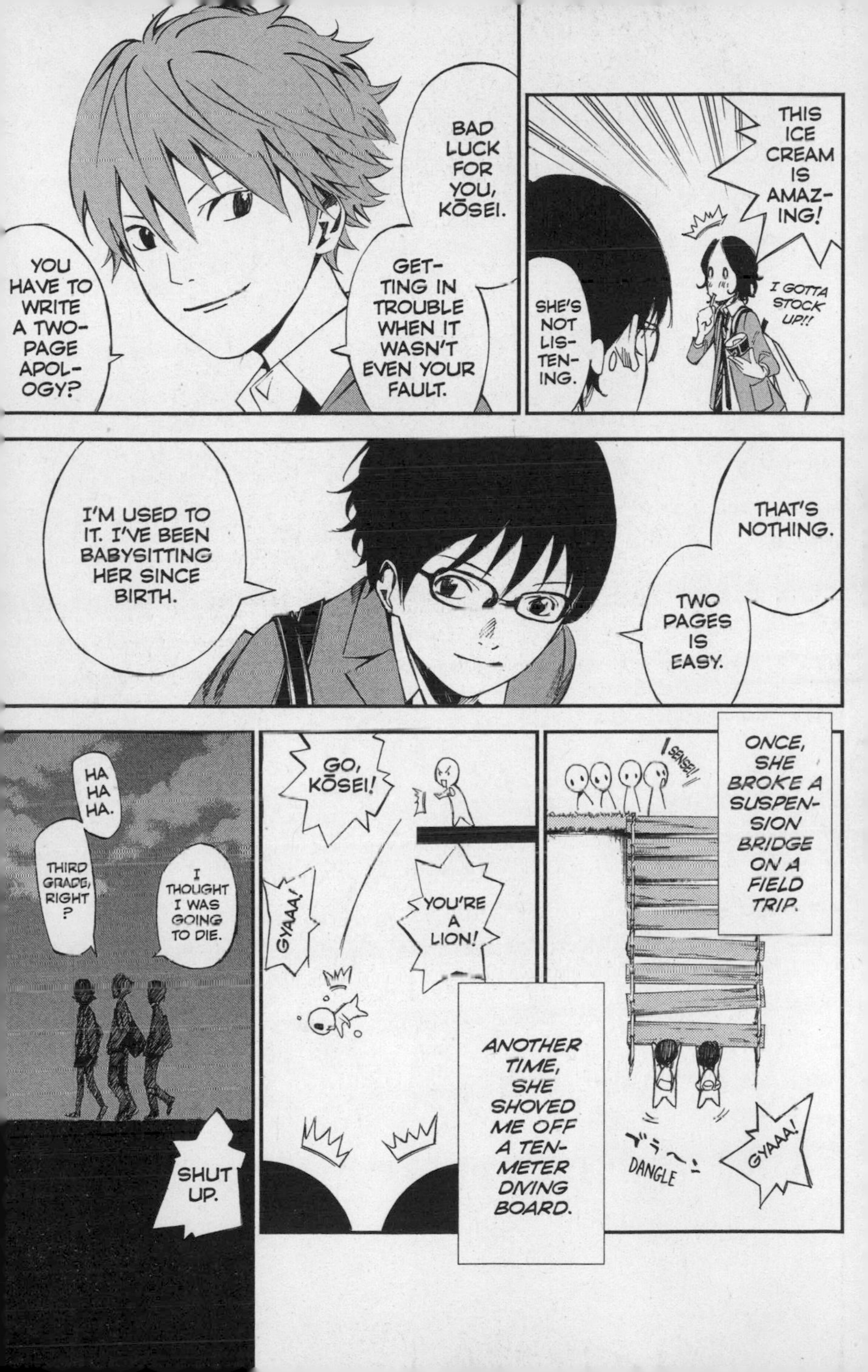
THIS ICE CREAM IS AMAZING!
I GOTTA STOCK UP!!
SHE'S NOT LISTENING.
BAD LUCK FOR YOU, KŌSEI.
GETTING IN TROUBLE WHEN IT WASN'T EVEN YOUR FAULT.
YOU HAVE TO WRITE A TWO-PAGE APOLOGY?
THAT'S NOTHING.
TWO PAGES IS EASY.
I'M USED TO IT. I'VE BEEN BABYSITTING HER SINCE BIRTH.
ONCE, SHE BROKE A SUSPENSION BRIDGE ON A FIELD TRIP.
SENSEI!!
GYAAA!
DANGLE
GO, KŌSEI!
YOU'RE A LION!
GYAAA!
ANOTHER TIME, SHE SHOVED ME OFF A TEN-METER DIVING BOARD.
HA HA HA.
I THOUGHT I WAS GOING TO DIE.
THIRD GRADE, RIGHT?
SHUT UP.

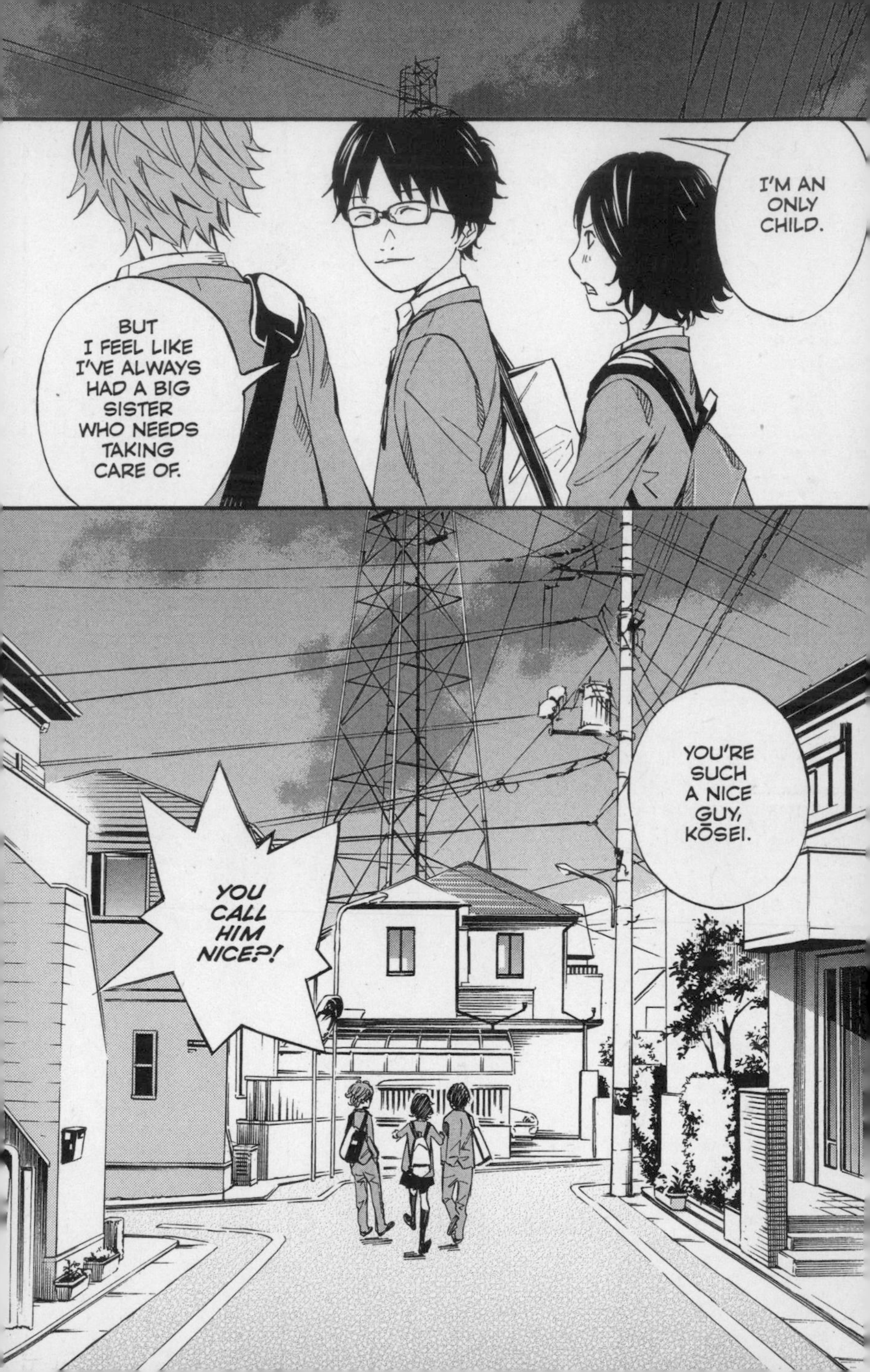
I'M AN ONLY CHILD.
BUT I FEEL LIKE I'VE ALWAYS HAD A BIG SISTER WHO NEEDS TAKING CARE OF.
YOU'RE SUCH A NICE GUY, KŌSEI.
YOU CALL HIM NICE?!

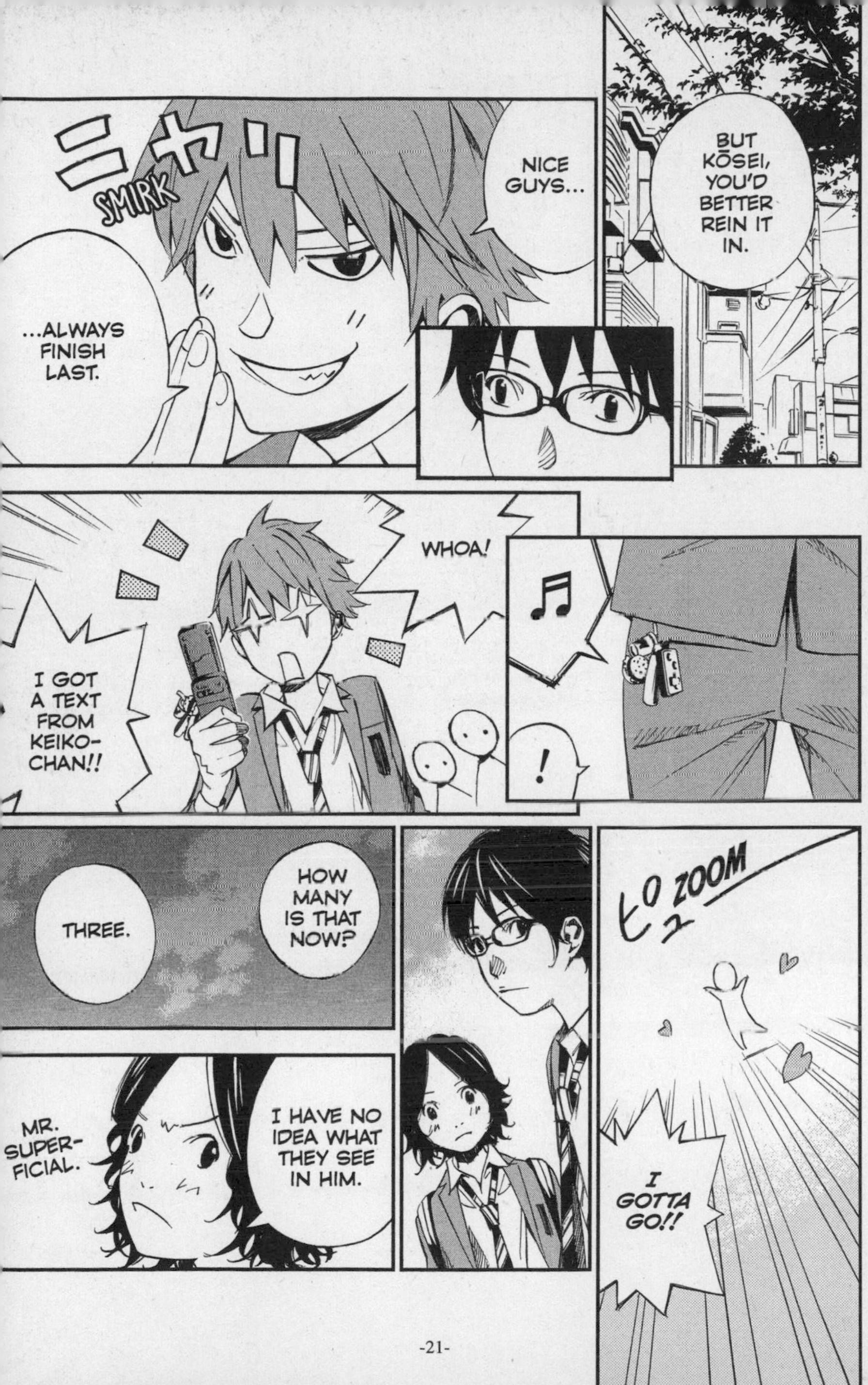
BUT KŌSEI, YOU'D BETTER REIN IT IN.
NICE GUYS...
SMIRK
...ALWAYS FINISH LAST.
♫
!
WHOA!
I GOT A TEXT FROM KEIKO-CHAN!!
ZOOM
I GOTTA GO!!
HOW MANY IS THAT NOW?
THREE.
I HAVE NO IDEA WHAT THEY SEE IN HIM.
MR. SUPER-FICIAL.

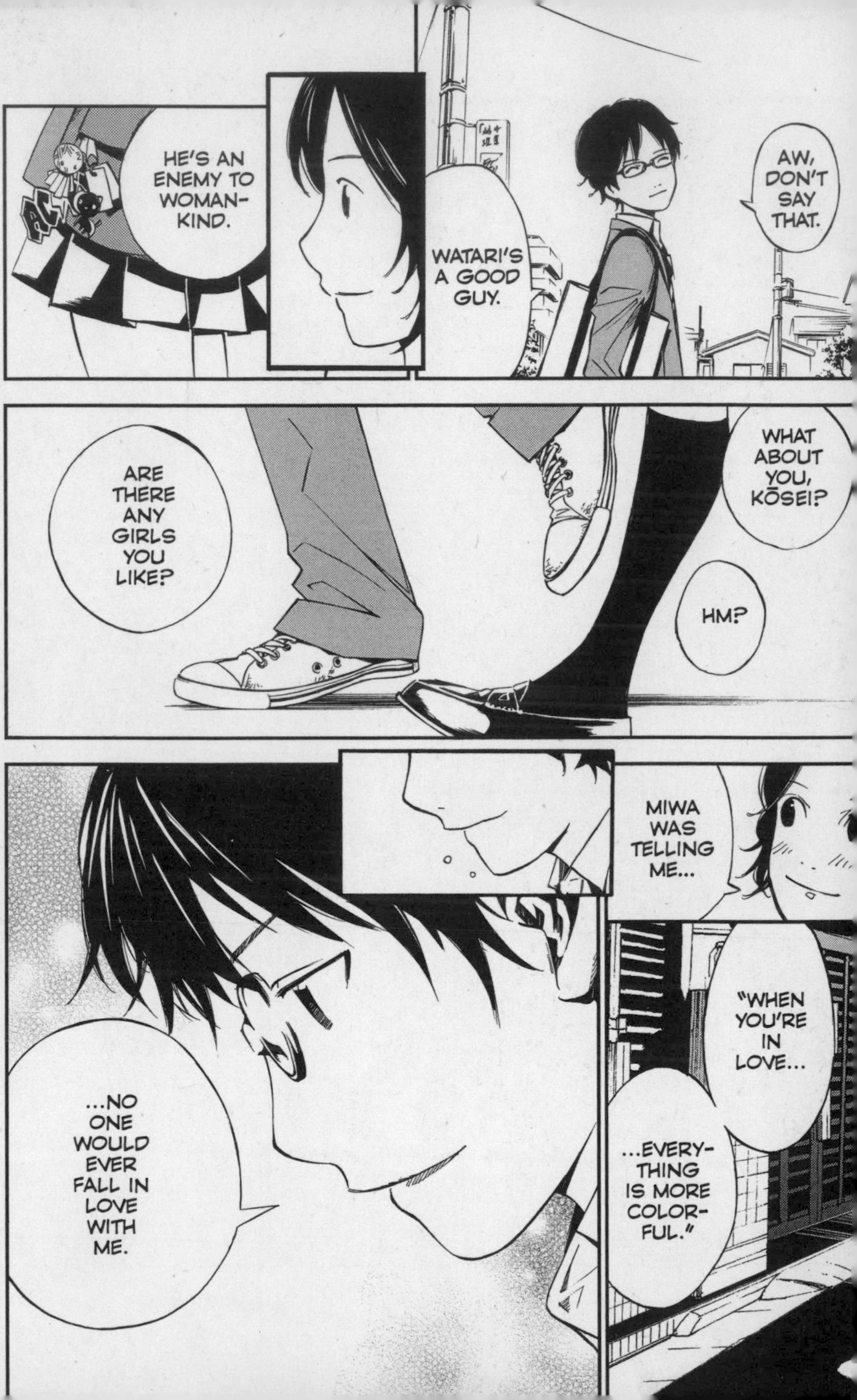
AW, DON'T SAY THAT.
WATARI'S A GOOD GUY.
HE'S AN ENEMY TO WOMAN-KIND.
WHAT ABOUT YOU, KŌSEI?
HM?
ARE THERE ANY GIRLS YOU LIKE?
MIWA WAS TELLING ME...
"WHEN YOU'RE IN LOVE...
...EVERY-THING IS MORE COLOR-FUL."
...NO ONE WOULD EVER FALL IN LOVE WITH ME.

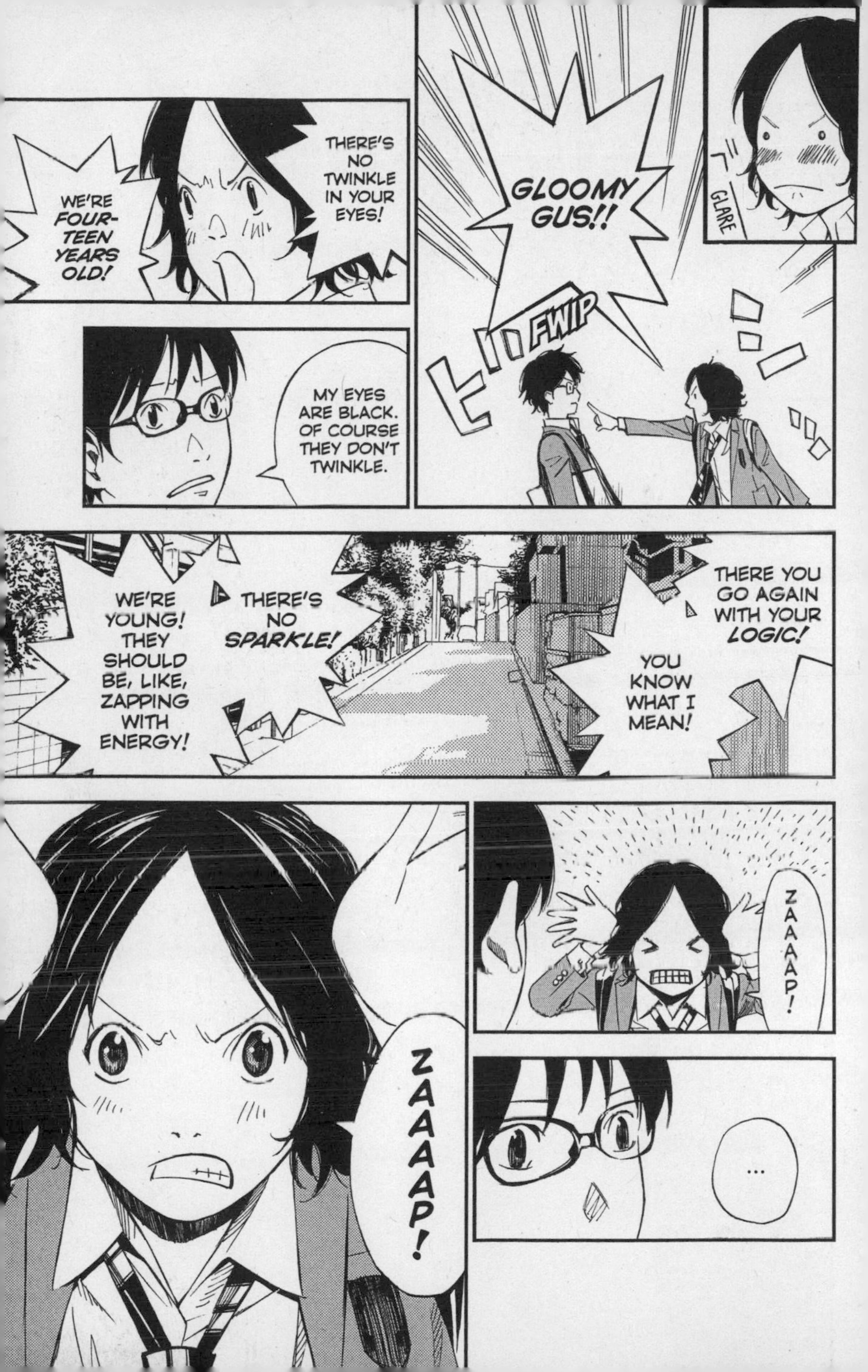
GLARE
GLOOMY GUS!!
FWIP
THERE'S NO TWINKLE IN YOUR EYES!
WE'RE FOURTEEN YEARS OLD!
MY EYES ARE BLACK. OF COURSE THEY DON'T TWINKLE.
THERE YOU GO AGAIN WITH YOUR LOGIC!
YOU KNOW WHAT I MEAN!
THERE'S NO SPARKLE!
WE'RE YOUNG! THEY SHOULD BE, LIKE, ZAPPING WITH ENERGY!
ZAAAAP!
...
ZAAAAP!

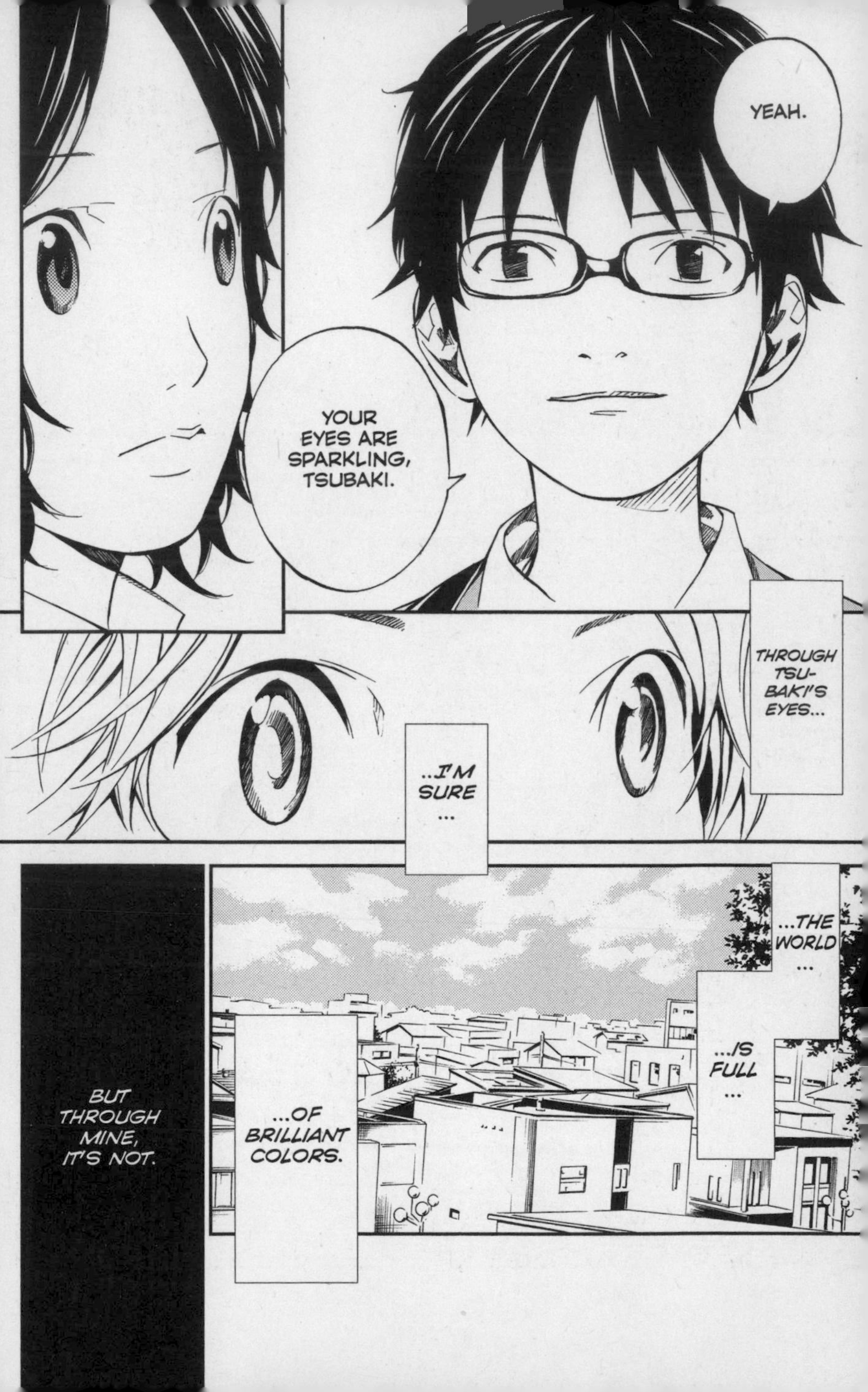
YEAH.
YOUR EYES ARE SPARKLING, TSUBAKI.
THROUGH TSU-BAKI'S EYES...
...I'M SURE ...
...THE WORLD ...
...IS FULL ...
...OF BRILLIANT COLORS.
BUT THROUGH MINE, IT'S NOT.

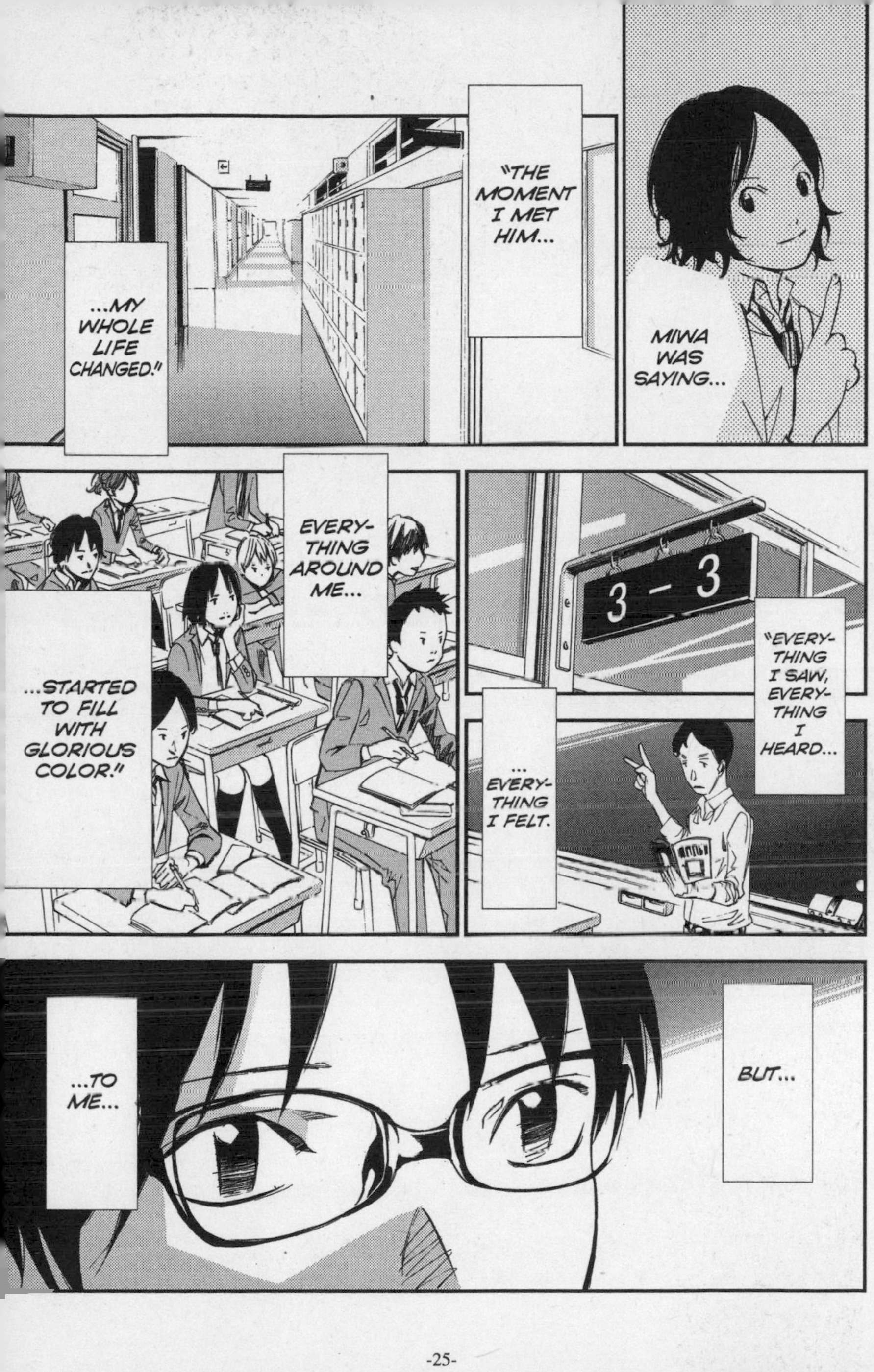
MIWA WAS SAYING...
"THE MOMENT I MET HIM...
...MY WHOLE LIFE CHANGED."
"EVERY-THING I SAW, EVERY-THING I HEARD...
...EVERY-THING I FELT.
EVERY-THING AROUND ME...
...STARTED TO FILL WITH GLORIOUS COLOR."
3 – 3
BUT...
...TO ME...

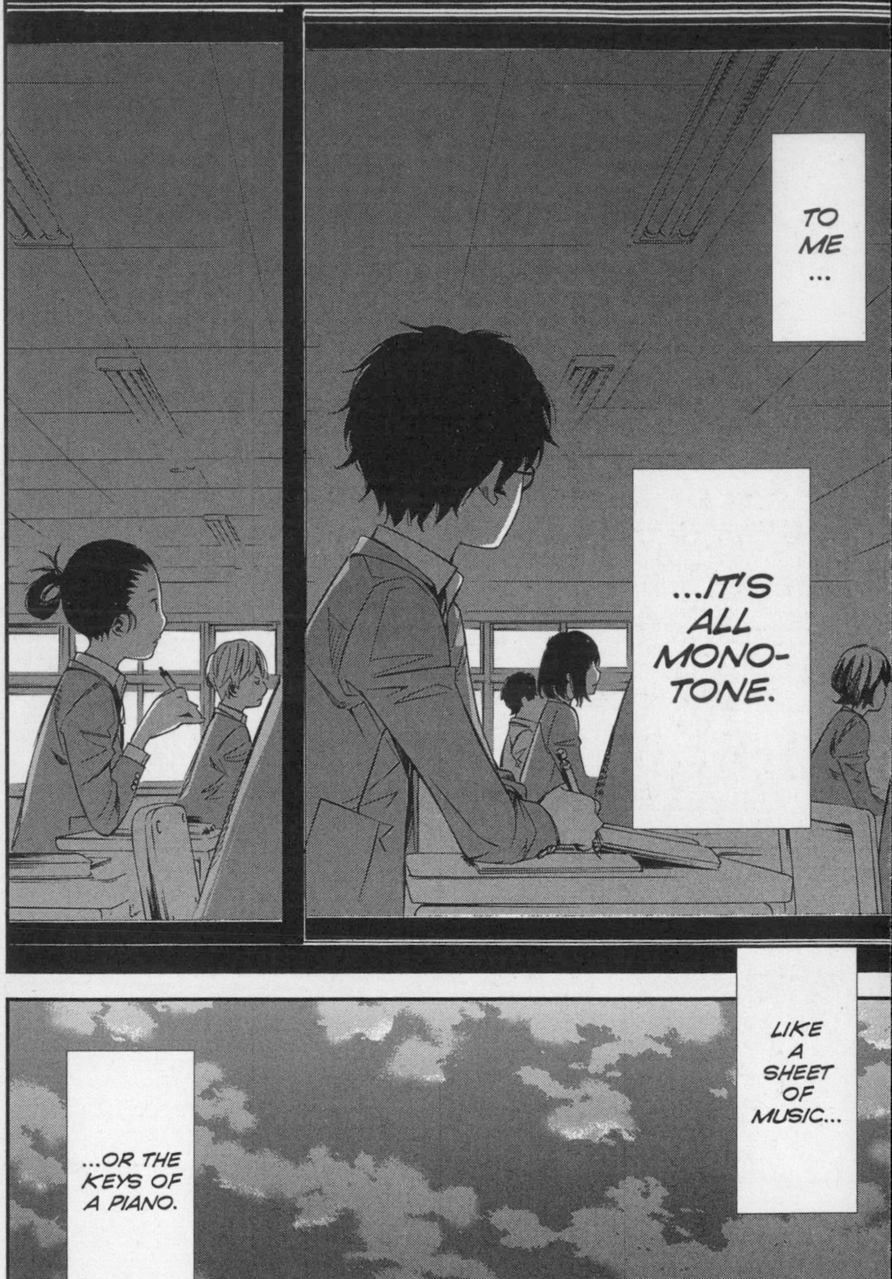
TO ME ...
...IT'S ALL MONO-TONE.
LIKE A SHEET OF MUSIC...
...OR THE KEYS OF A PIANO.

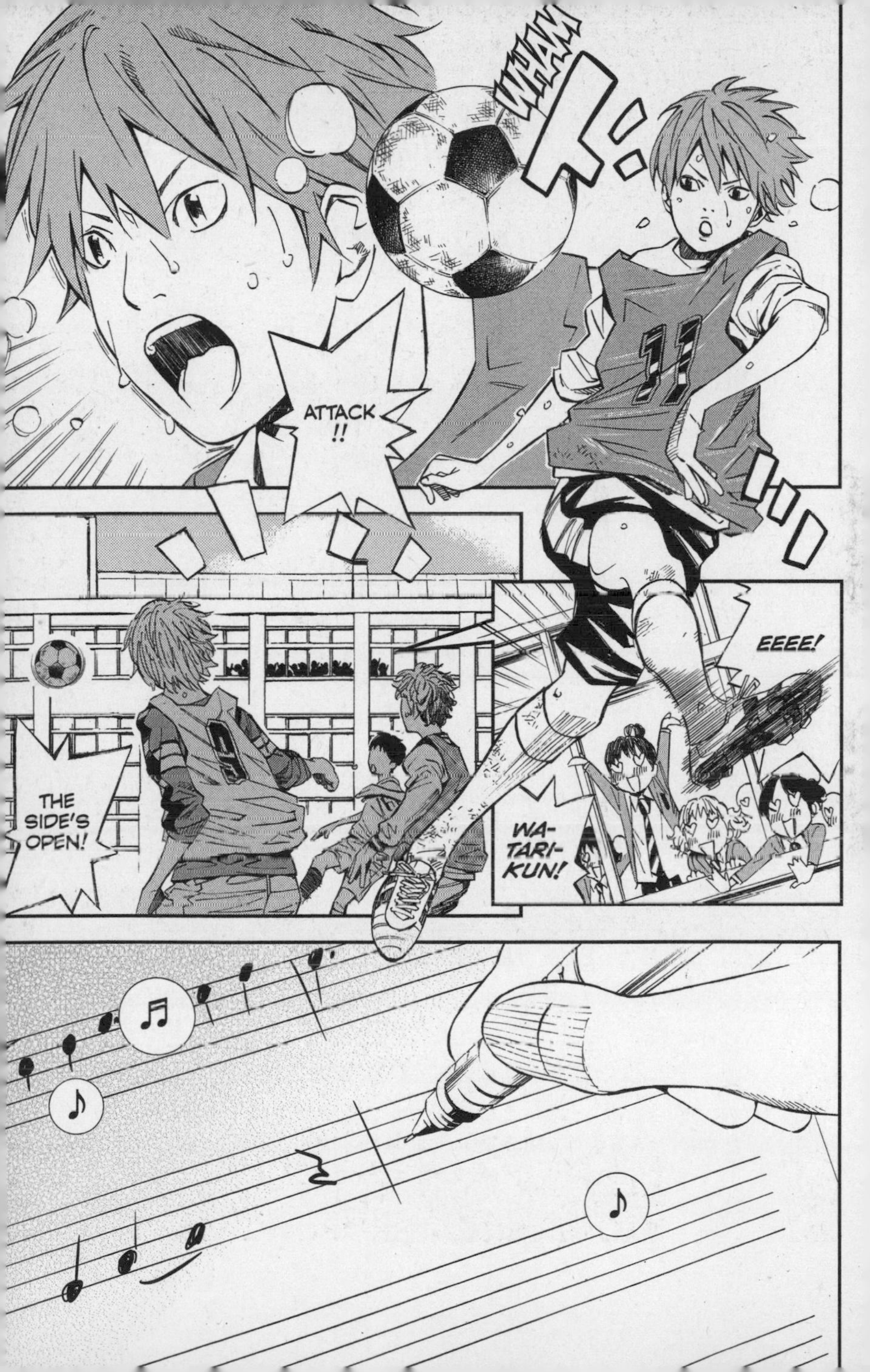
WHAM!
ATTACK!!
EEEE!
WA-TARI-KUN!
THE SIDE'S OPEN!

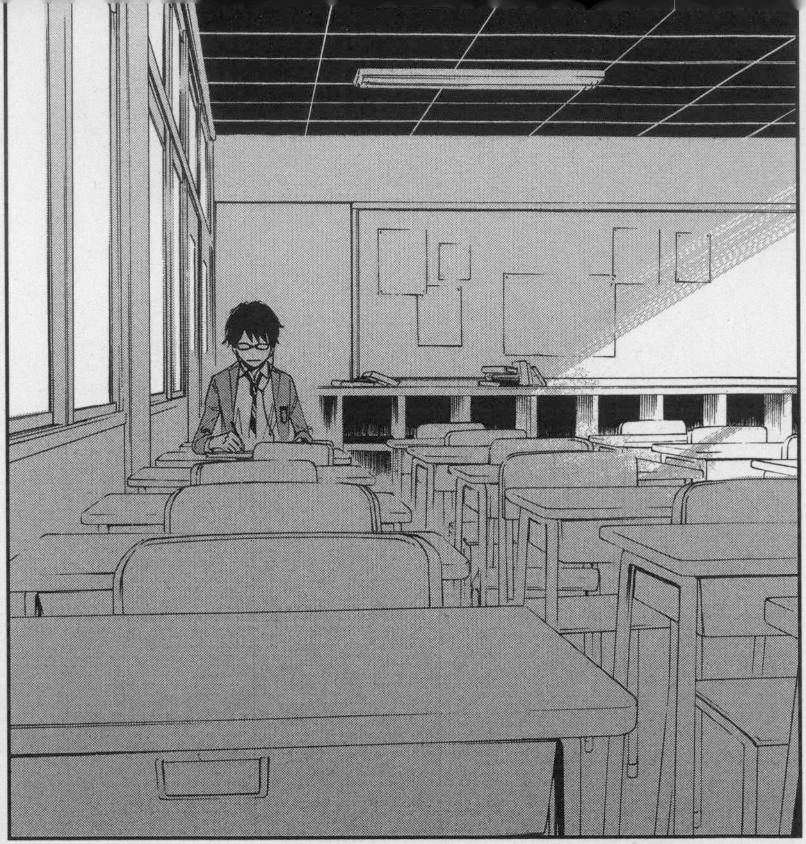

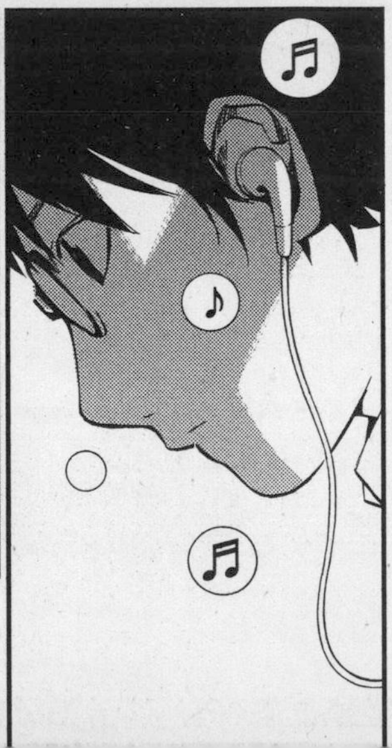

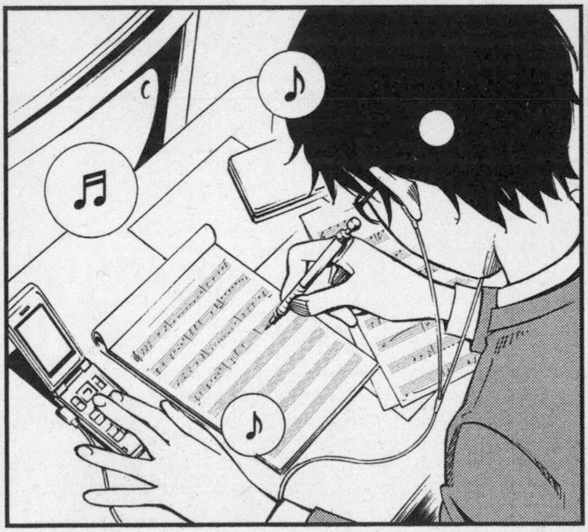

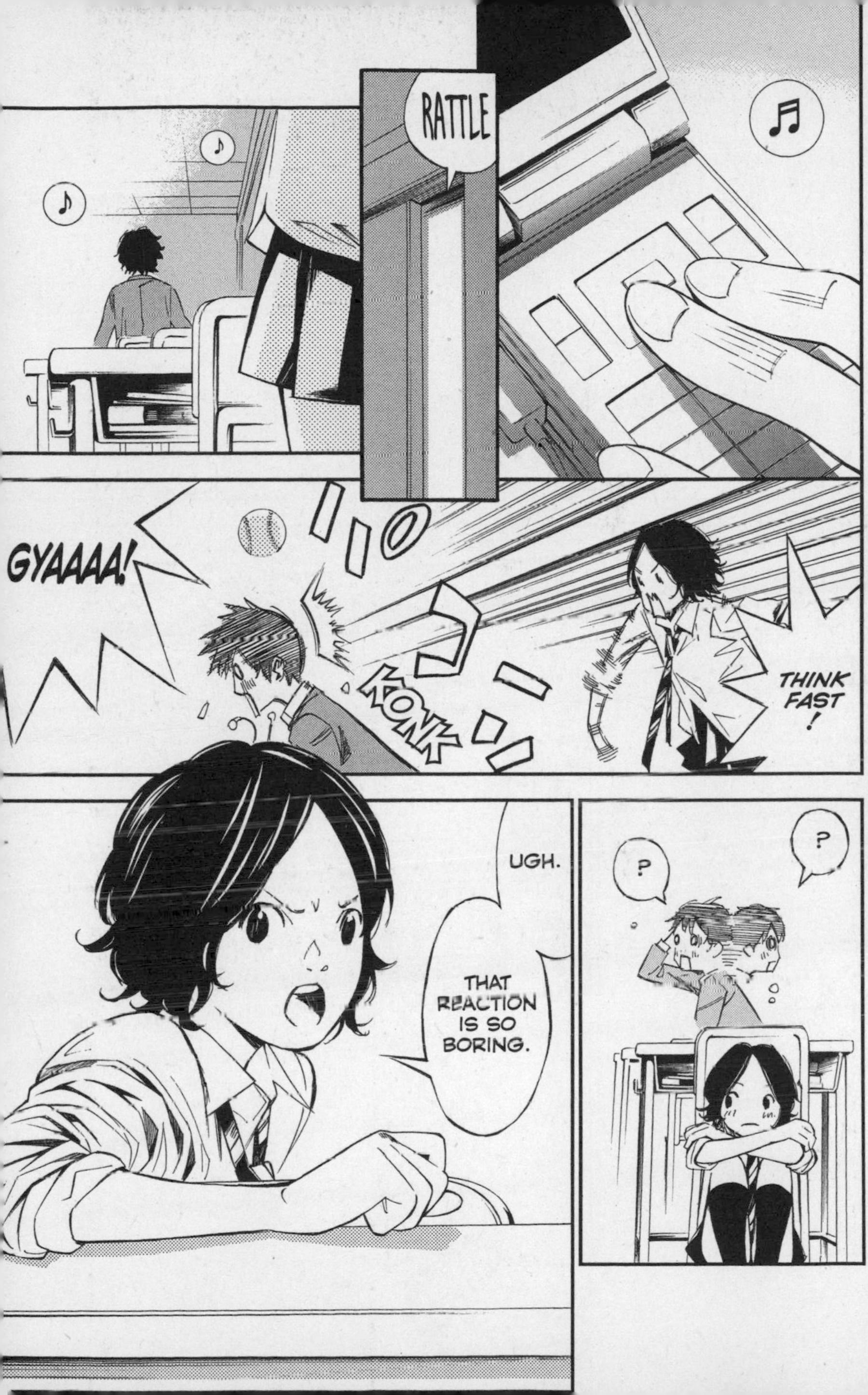
♬
RATTLE
♪
♪
THINK FAST!
KONK
GYAAAA!
?
?
UGH.
THAT REACTION IS SO BORING.

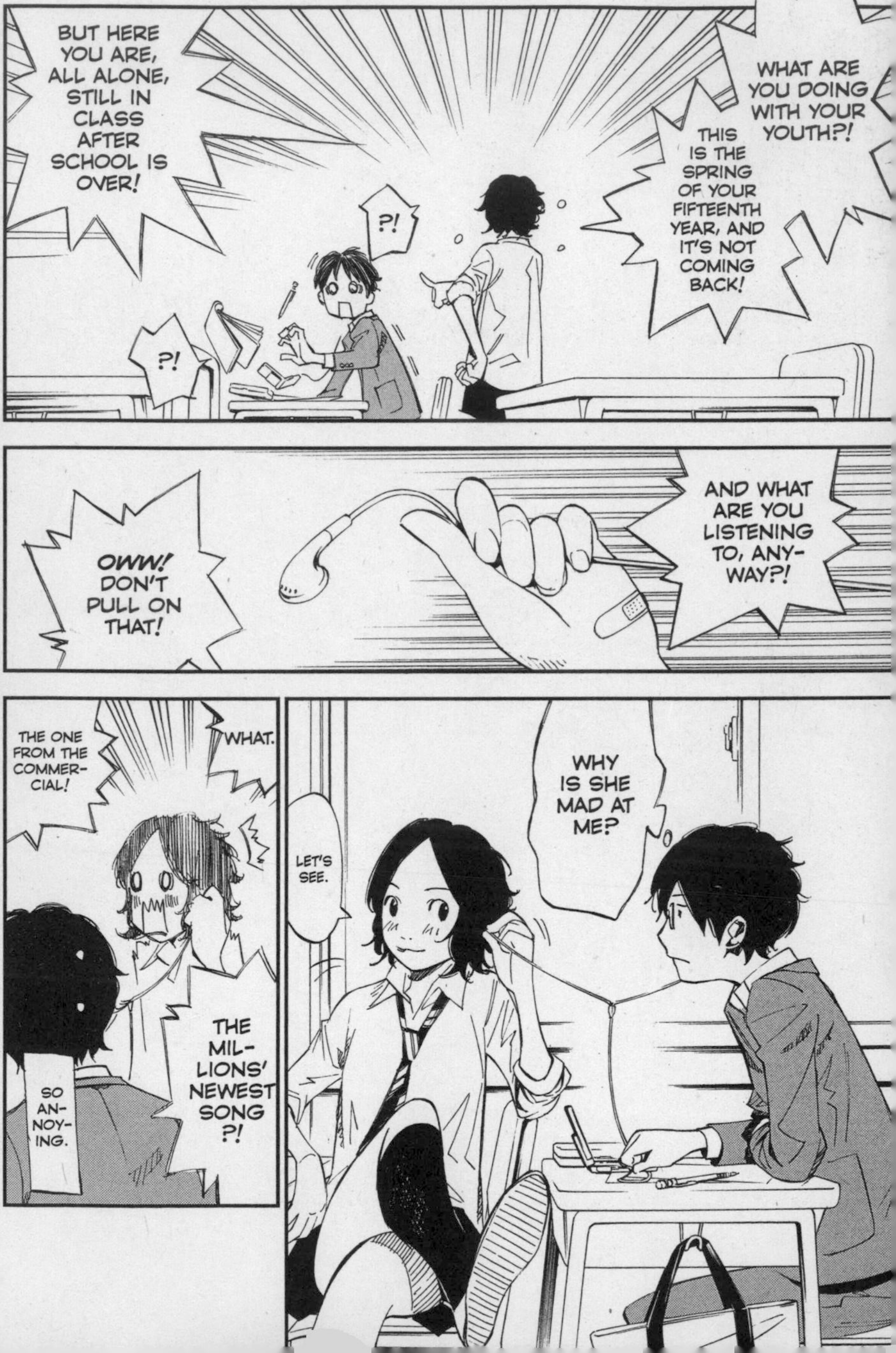
WHAT ARE YOU DOING WITH YOUR YOUTH?!
THIS IS THE SPRING OF YOUR FIFTEENTH YEAR, AND IT'S NOT COMING BACK!
BUT HERE YOU ARE, ALL ALONE, STILL IN CLASS AFTER SCHOOL IS OVER!
?!
?!
AND WHAT ARE YOU LISTENING TO, ANY-WAY?!
OWW! DON'T PULL ON THAT!
WHY IS SHE MAD AT ME?
LET'S SEE.
WHAT.
THE ONE FROM THE COMMER-CIAL!
THE MIL-LIONS' NEWEST SONG ?!
SO AN-NOY-ING.

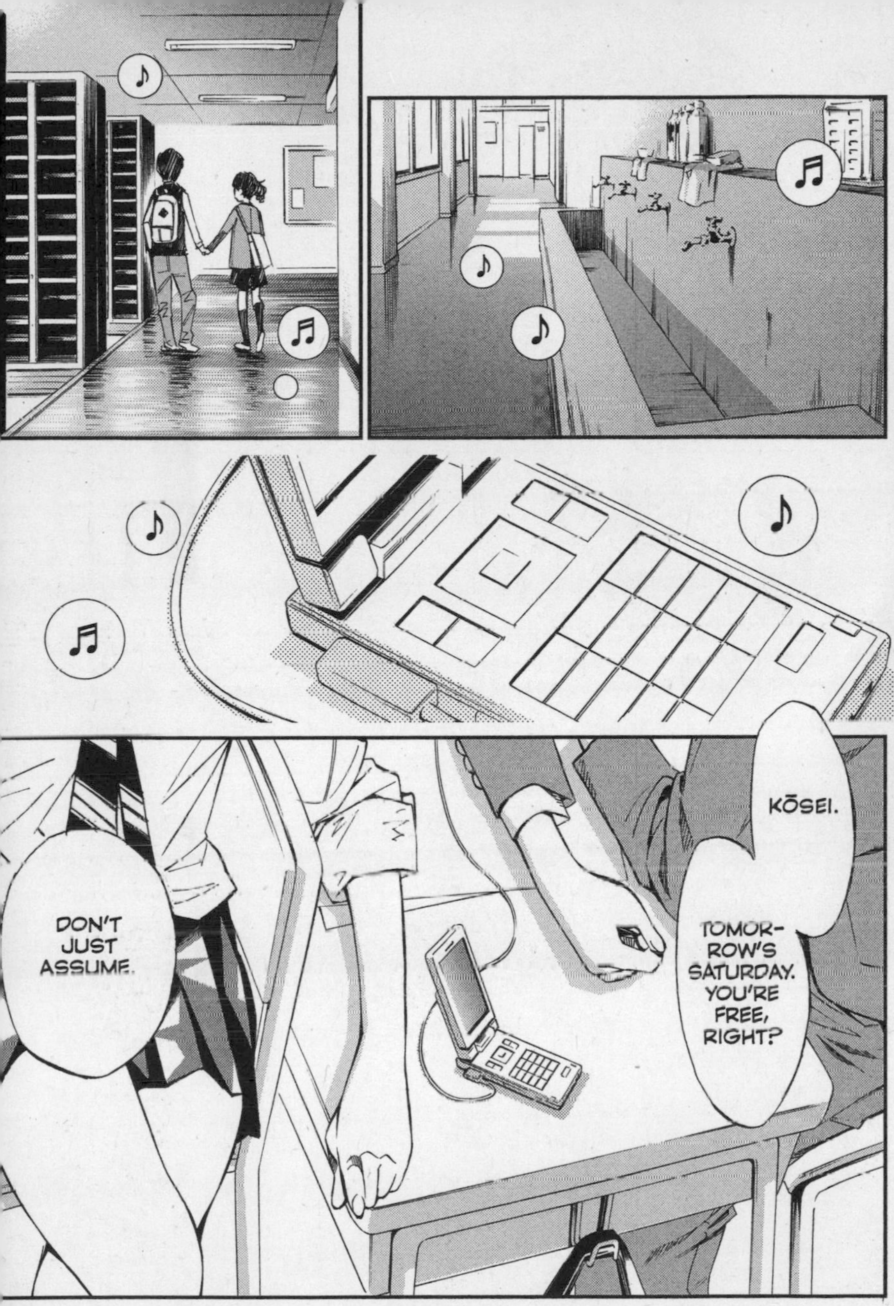
KŌSEI.
TOMOR-ROW'S SATURDAY. YOU'RE FREE, RIGHT?
DON'T JUST ASSUME.

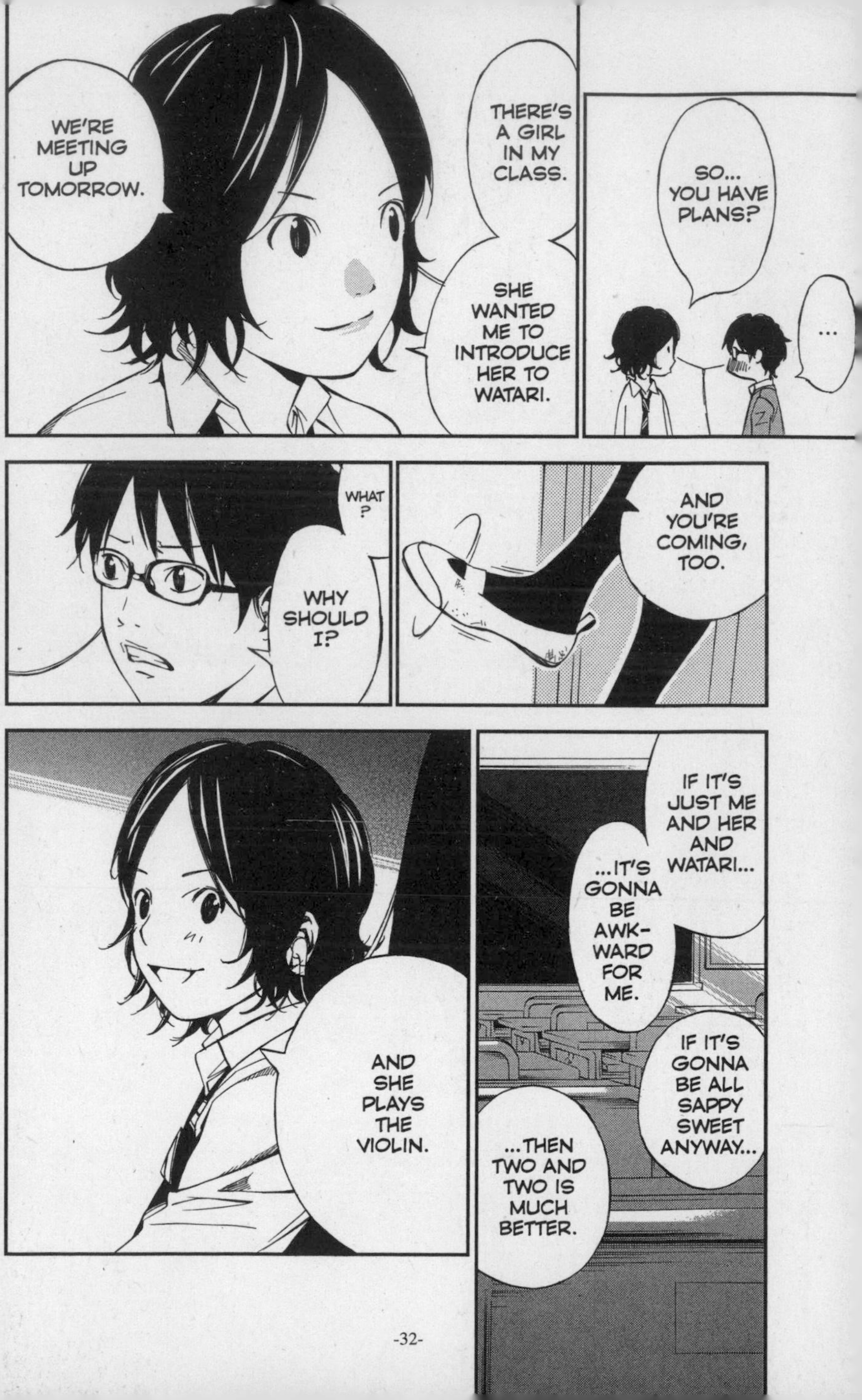
SO... YOU HAVE PLANS?
...
THERE'S A GIRL IN MY CLASS.
SHE WANTED ME TO INTRODUCE HER TO WATARI.
WE'RE MEETING UP TOMORROW.
AND YOU'RE COMING, TOO.
WHAT?
WHY SHOULD I?
IF IT'S JUST ME AND HER AND WATARI...
...IT'S GONNA BE AWK-WARD FOR ME.
IF IT'S GONNA BE ALL SAPPY SWEET ANYWAY...
...THEN TWO AND TWO IS MUCH BETTER.
AND SHE PLAYS THE VIOLIN.

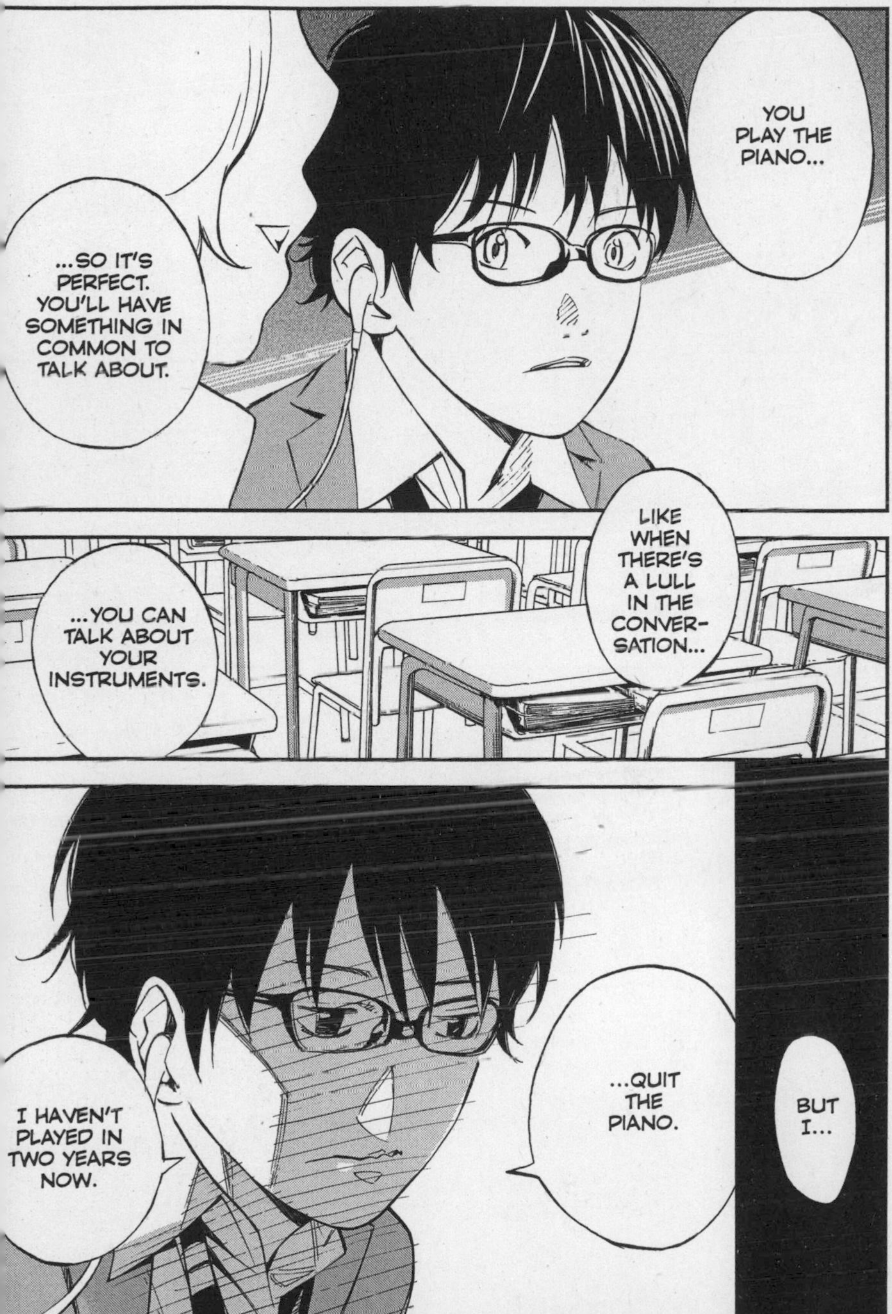
YOU PLAY THE PIANO...
...SO IT'S PERFECT. YOU'LL HAVE SOMETHING IN COMMON TO TALK ABOUT.
LIKE WHEN THERE'S A LULL IN THE CONVER-SATION...
...YOU CAN TALK ABOUT YOUR INSTRUMENTS.
BUT I...
...QUIT THE PIANO.
I HAVEN'T PLAYED IN TWO YEARS NOW.

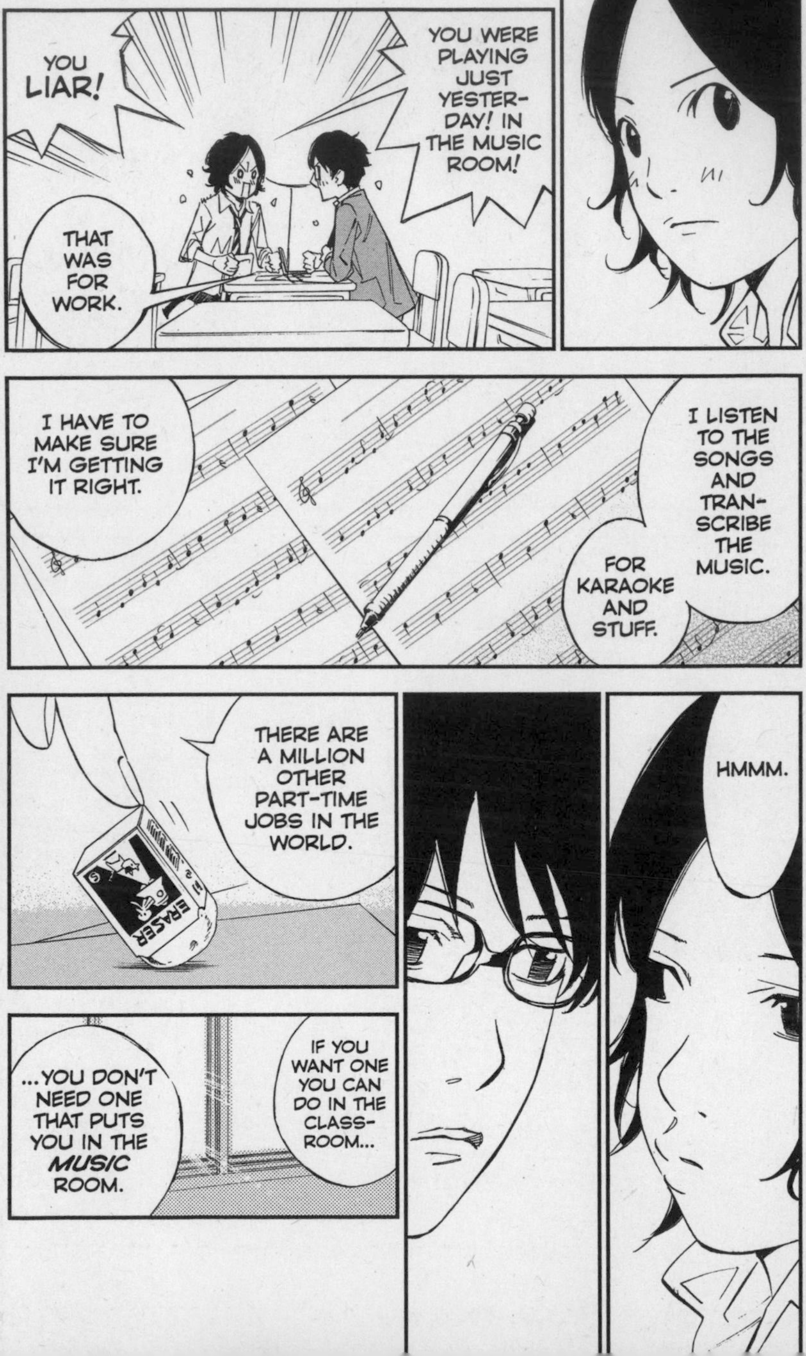
YOU WERE PLAYING JUST YESTER-DAY! IN THE MUSIC ROOM!
YOU LIAR!
THAT WAS FOR WORK.
I LISTEN TO THE SONGS AND TRAN-SCRIBE THE MUSIC.
FOR KARAOKE AND STUFF.
I HAVE TO MAKE SURE I'M GETTING IT RIGHT.
HMMM.
THERE ARE A MILLION OTHER PART-TIME JOBS IN THE WORLD.
ERASER
IF YOU WANT ONE YOU CAN DO IN THE CLASS-ROOM...
...YOU DON'T NEED ONE THAT PUTS YOU IN THE *MUSIC* ROOM.

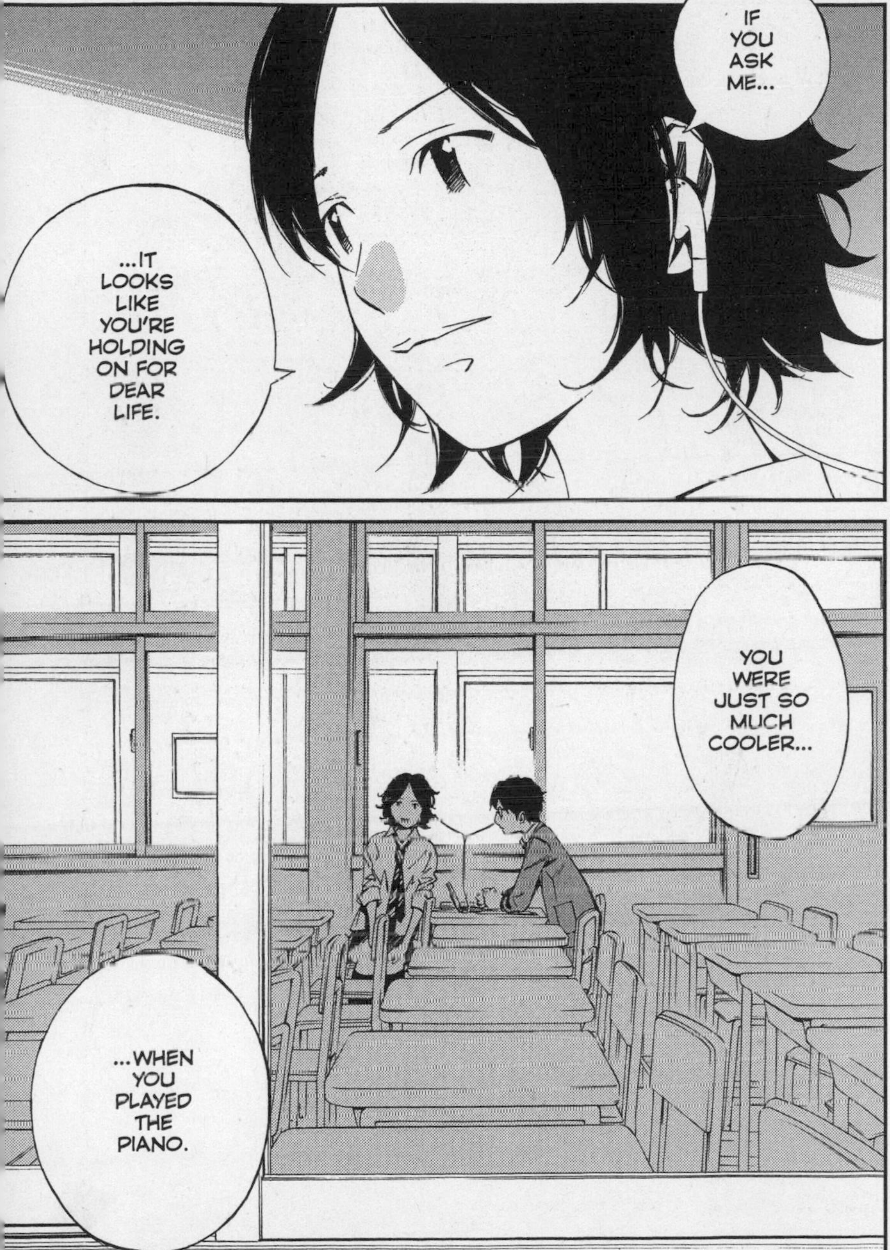
IF YOU ASK ME...
...IT LOOKS LIKE YOU'RE HOLDING ON FOR DEAR LIFE.
YOU WERE JUST SO MUCH COOLER...
...WHEN YOU PLAYED THE PIANO.

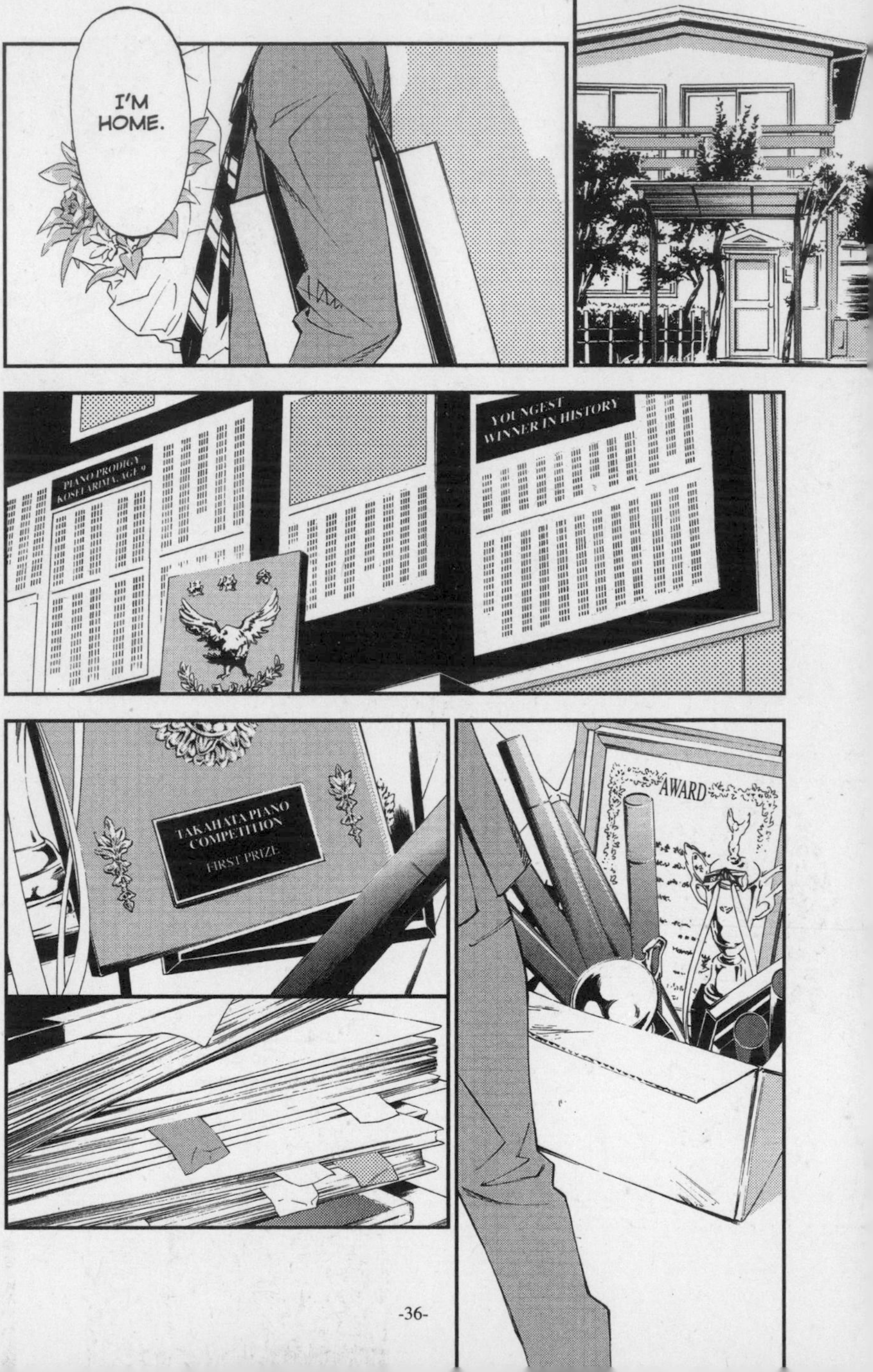
I'M HOME.
YOUNGEST WINNER IN HISTORY
PIANO PRODIGY KOSEI ARIMA, AGE 9
AWARD
TAKAHATA PIANO COMPETITION FIRST PRIZE

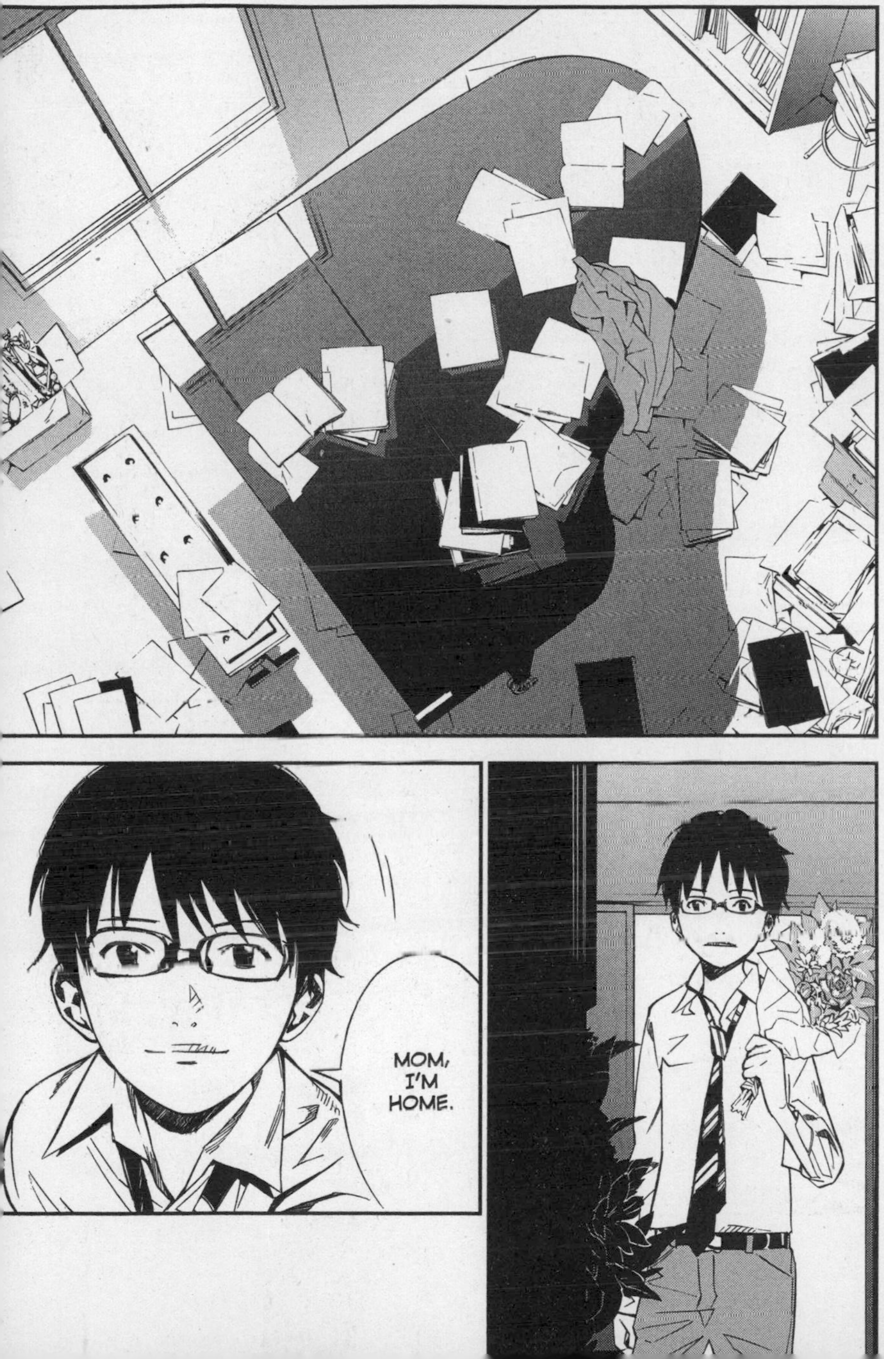
MOM, I'M HOME.

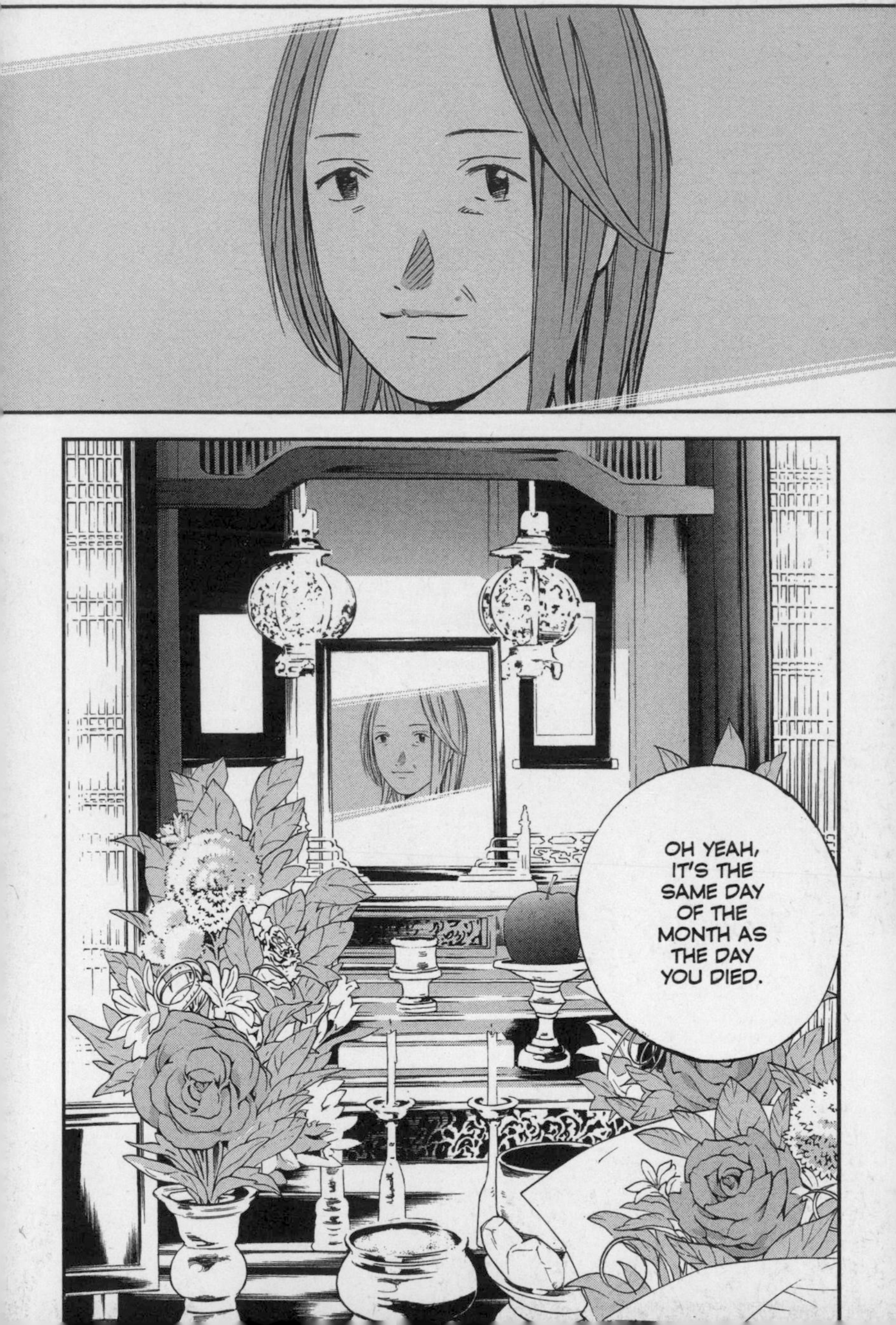
OH YEAH, IT'S THE SAME DAY OF THE MONTH AS THE DAY YOU DIED.

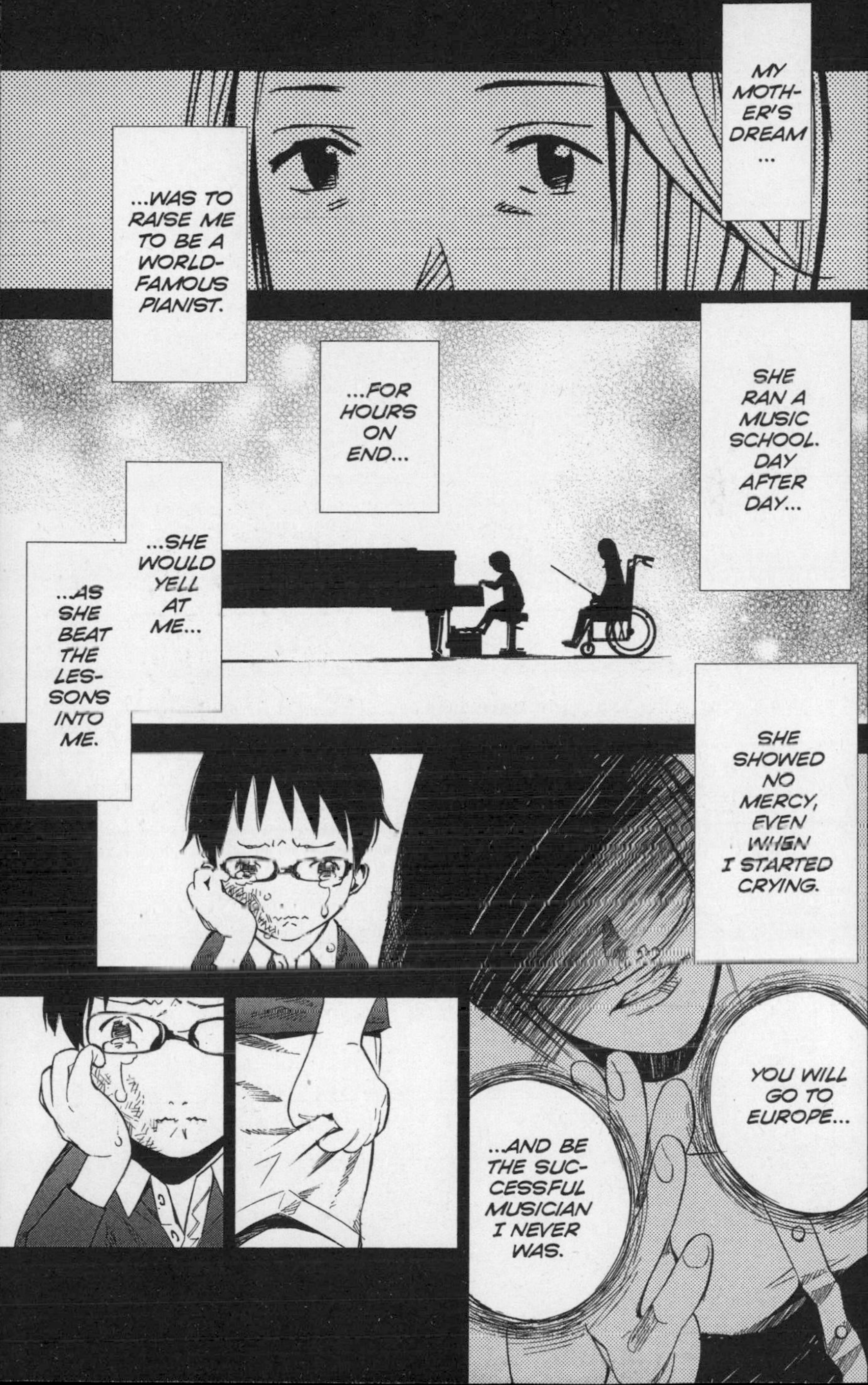
MY MOTHER'S DREAM...
...WAS TO RAISE ME TO BE A WORLD-FAMOUS PIANIST.
SHE RAN A MUSIC SCHOOL. DAY AFTER DAY...
...FOR HOURS ON END...
...SHE WOULD YELL AT ME...
...AS SHE BEAT THE LESSONS INTO ME.
SHE SHOWED NO MERCY, EVEN WHEN I STARTED CRYING.
YOU WILL GO TO EUROPE...
...AND BE THE SUCCESSFUL MUSICIAN I NEVER WAS.

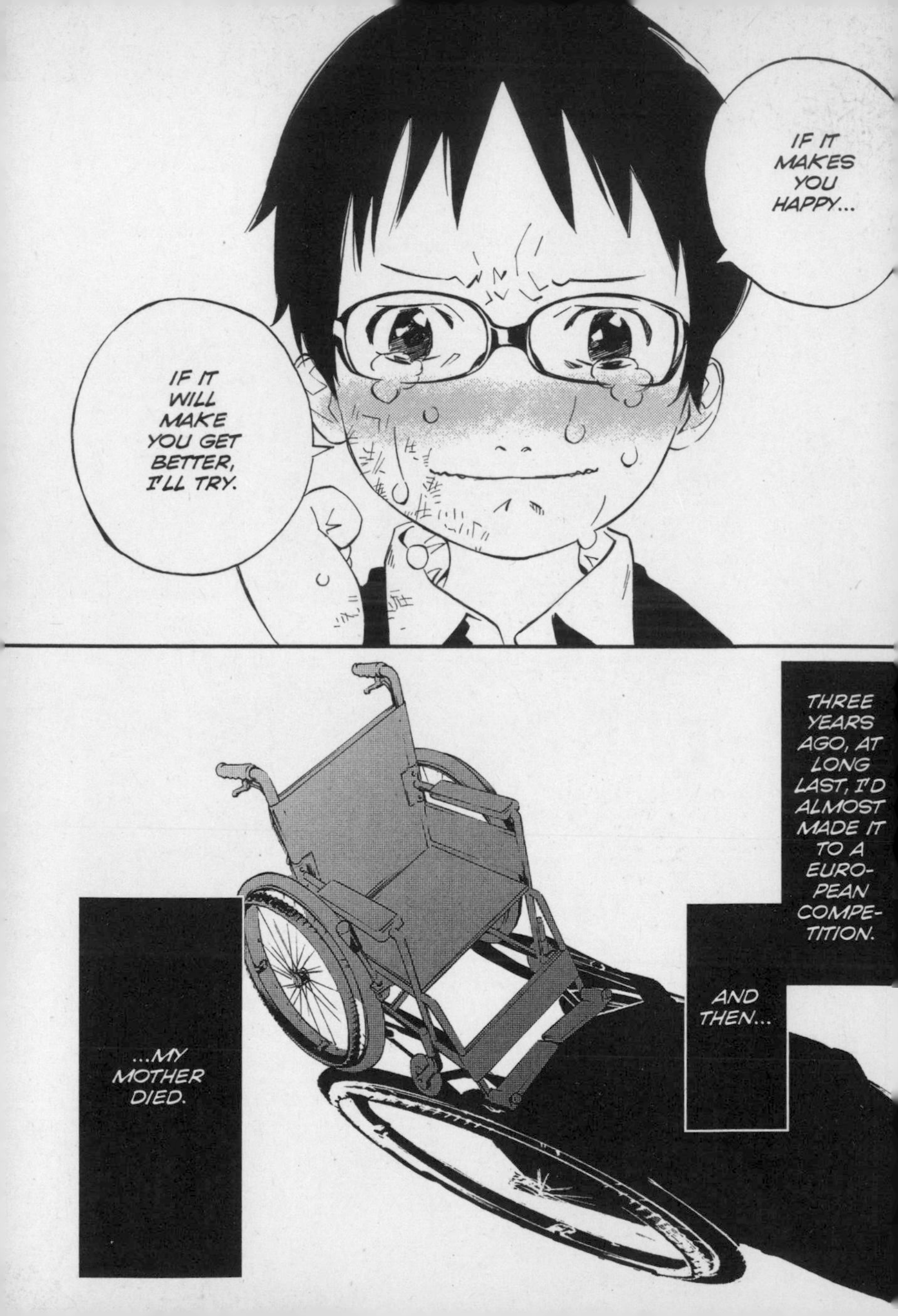
IF IT MAKES YOU HAPPY...
IF IT WILL MAKE YOU GET BETTER, I'LL TRY.
THREE YEARS AGO, AT LONG LAST, I'D ALMOST MADE IT TO A EURO-PEAN COMPE-TITION.
AND THEN...
...MY MOTHER DIED.

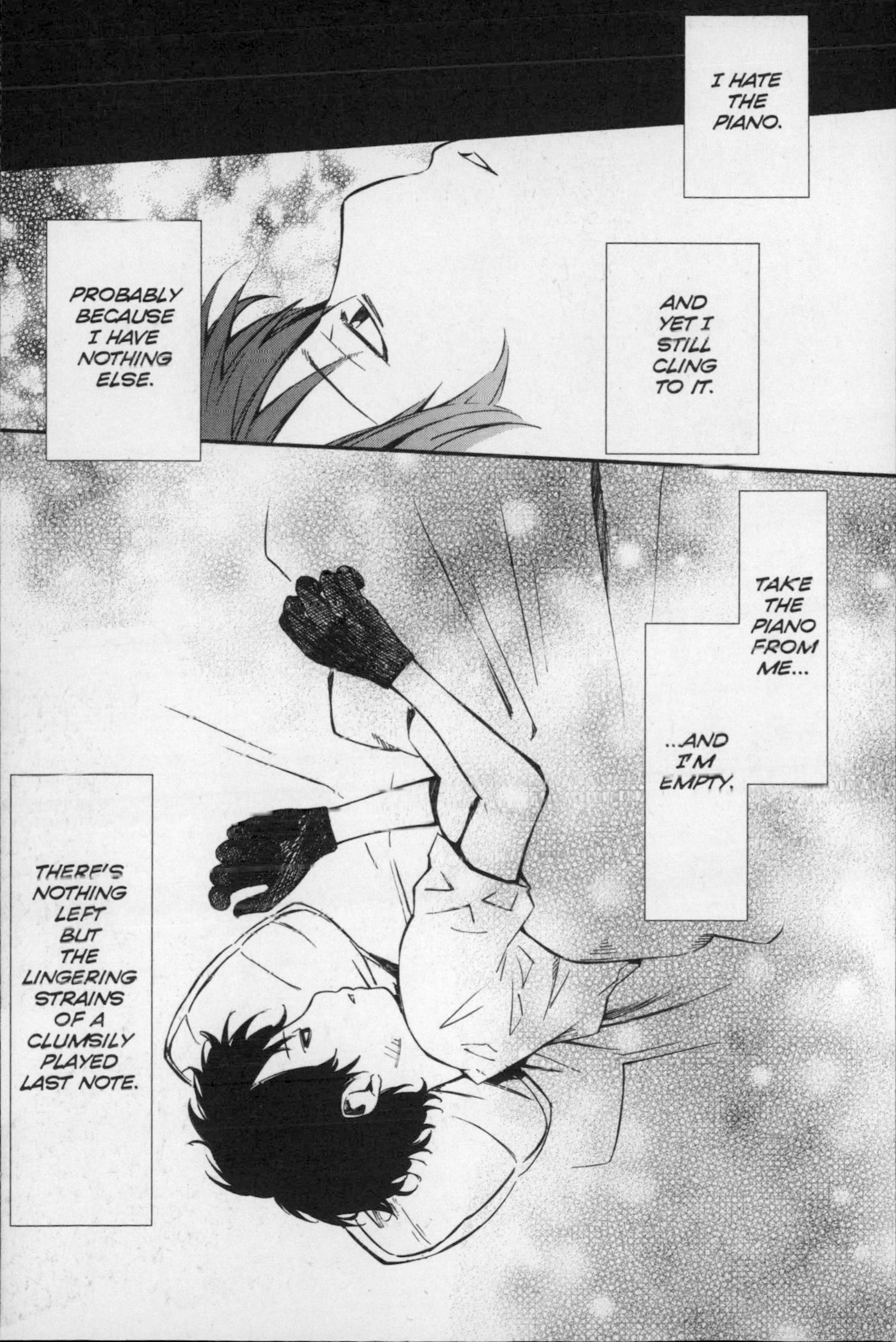
I HATE THE PIANO.
AND YET I STILL CLING TO IT.
PROBABLY BECAUSE I HAVE NOTHING ELSE.
TAKE THE PIANO FROM ME...
...AND I'M EMPTY.
THERE'S NOTHING LEFT BUT THE LINGERING STRAINS OF A CLUMSILY PLAYED LAST NOTE.

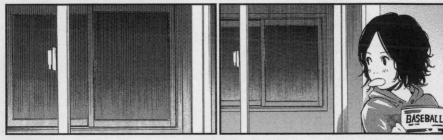

CRUNCH

NO
PIANO
FROM
NEXT
DOOR
TODAY,
EITHER.

POFF

BASEBALL

SENBEI

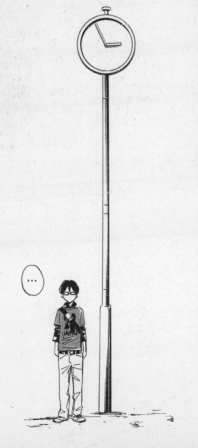

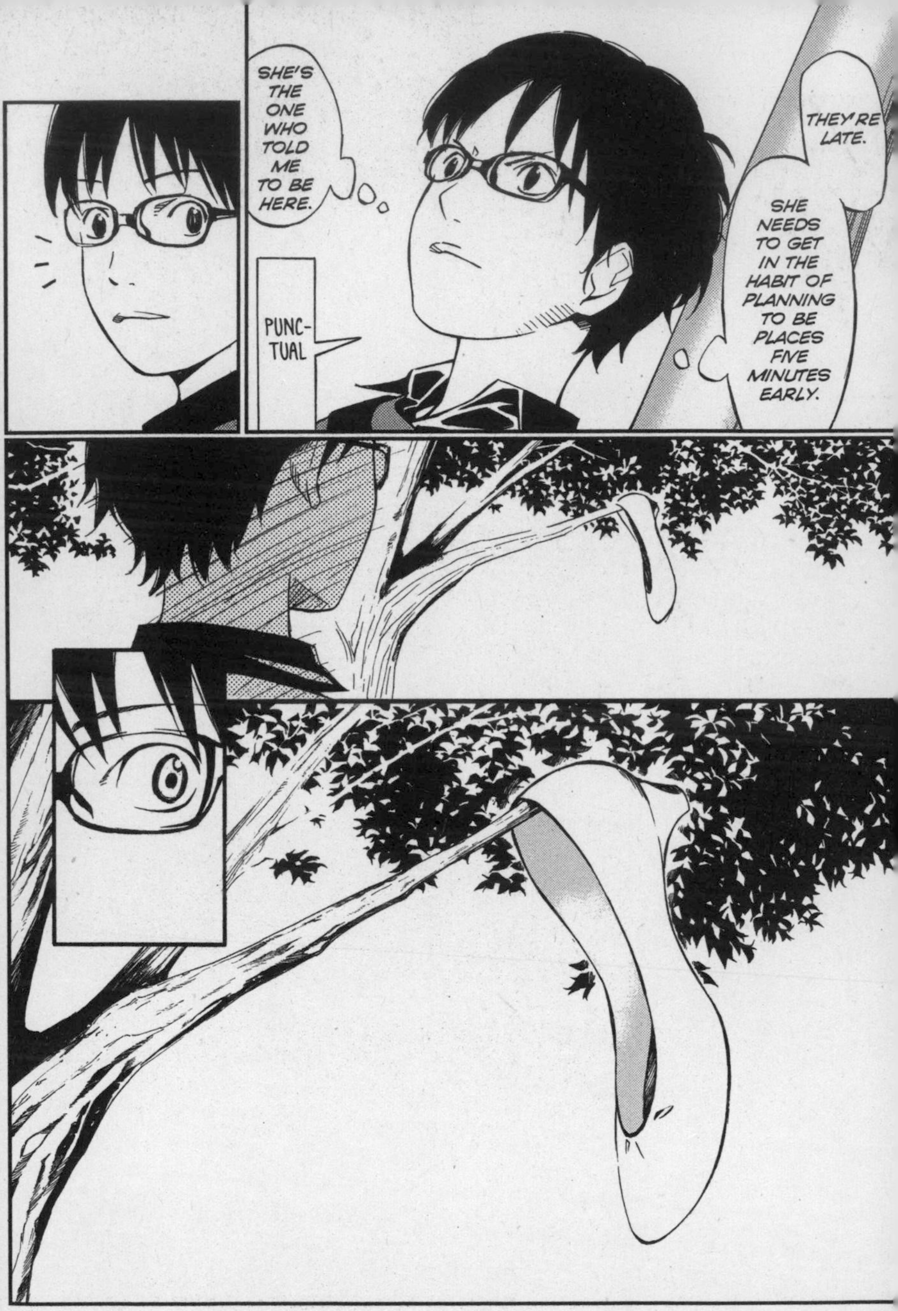
THEY'RE LATE.
SHE NEEDS TO GET IN THE HABIT OF PLANNING TO BE PLACES FIVE MINUTES EARLY.
SHE'S THE ONE WHO TOLD ME TO BE HERE.
PUNC-TUAL

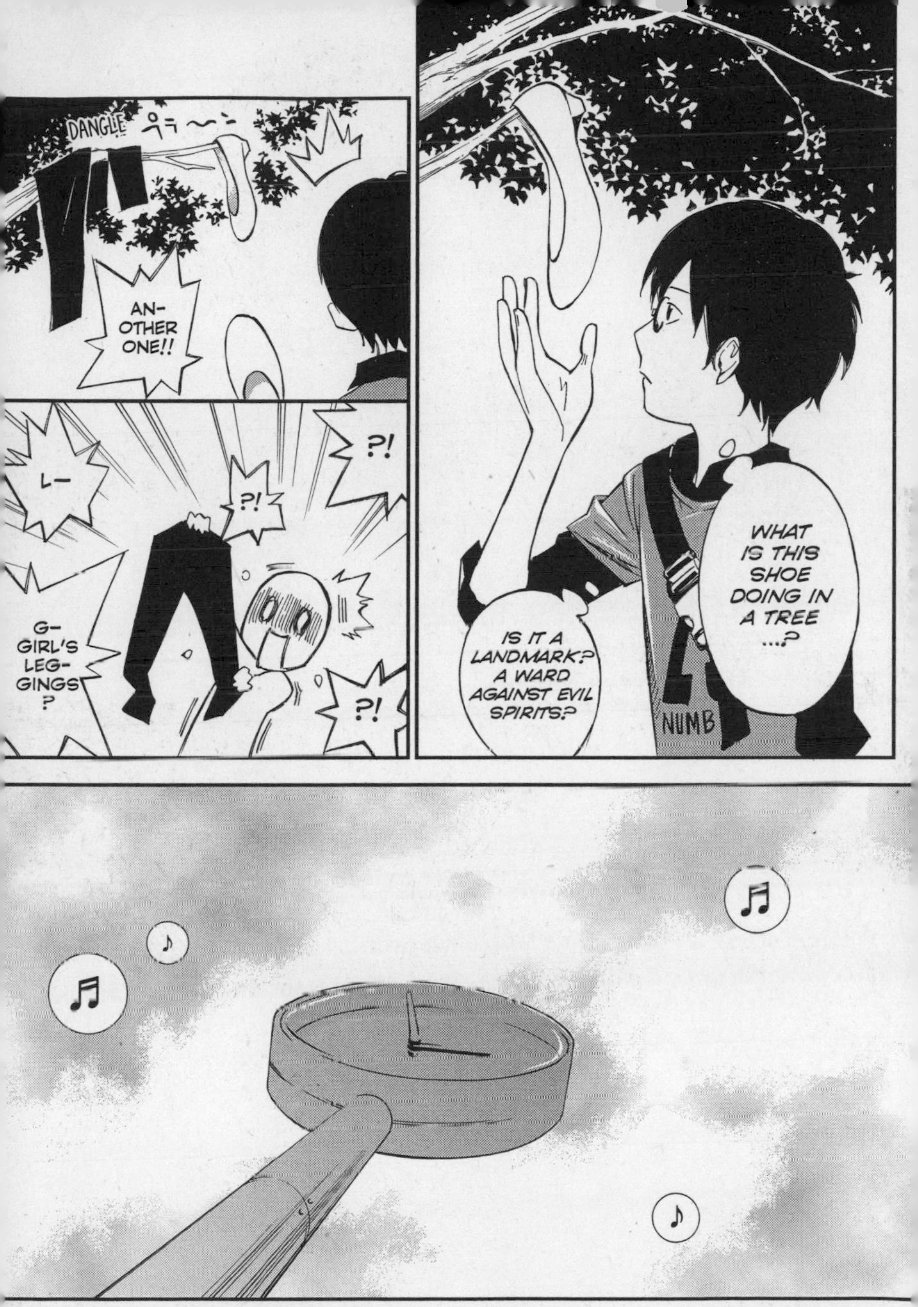
WHAT IS THIS SHOE DOING IN A TREE ...?
IS IT A LANDMARK? A WARD AGAINST EVIL SPIRITS?
DANGLE
AN-OTHER ONE!!
?!
?!
G-GIRL'S LEG-GINGS?
?!
NUMB

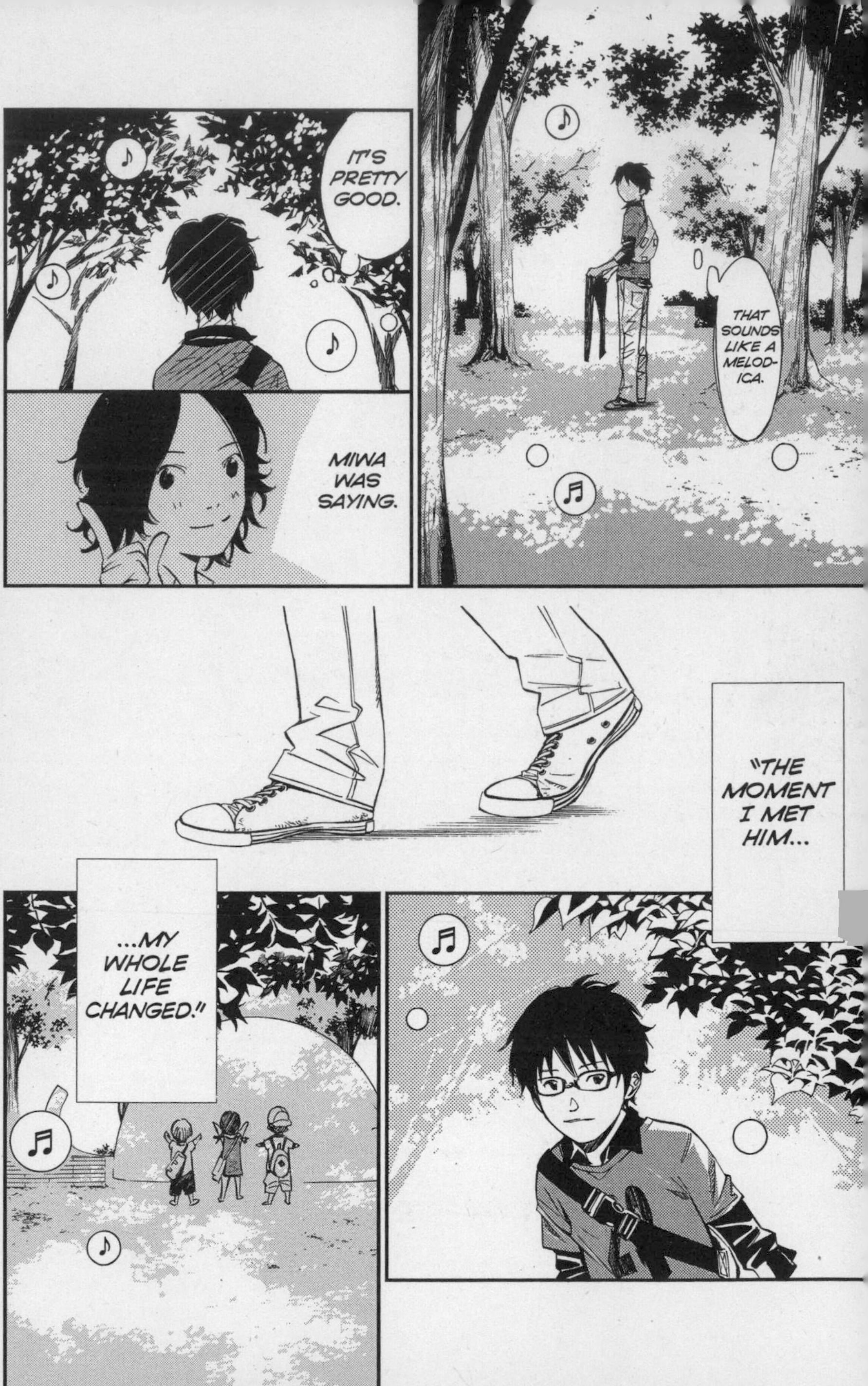
THAT SOUNDS LIKE A MELOD-ICA.
IT'S PRETTY GOOD.
MIWA WAS SAYING.
"THE MOMENT I MET HIM...
...MY WHOLE LIFE CHANGED."

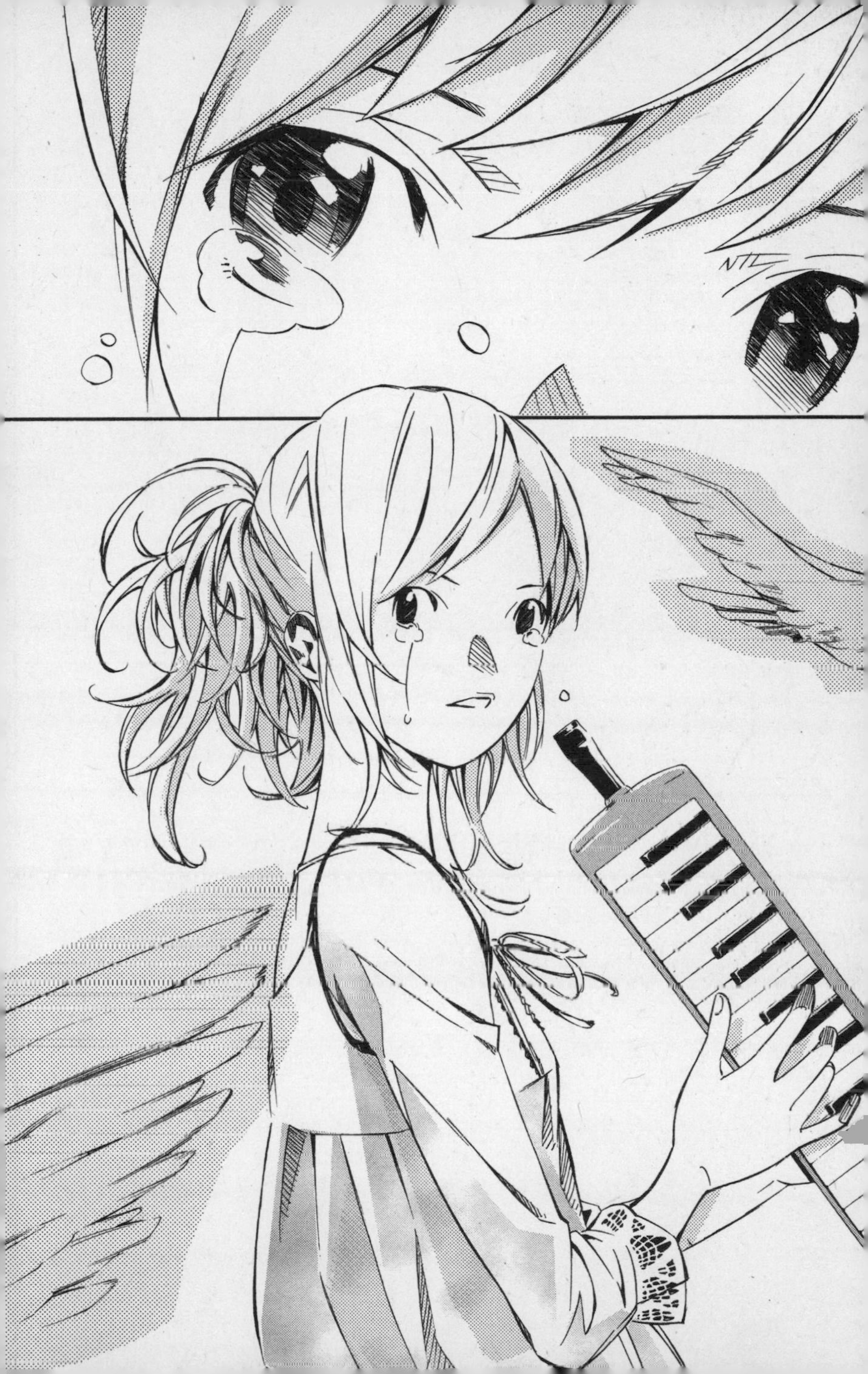

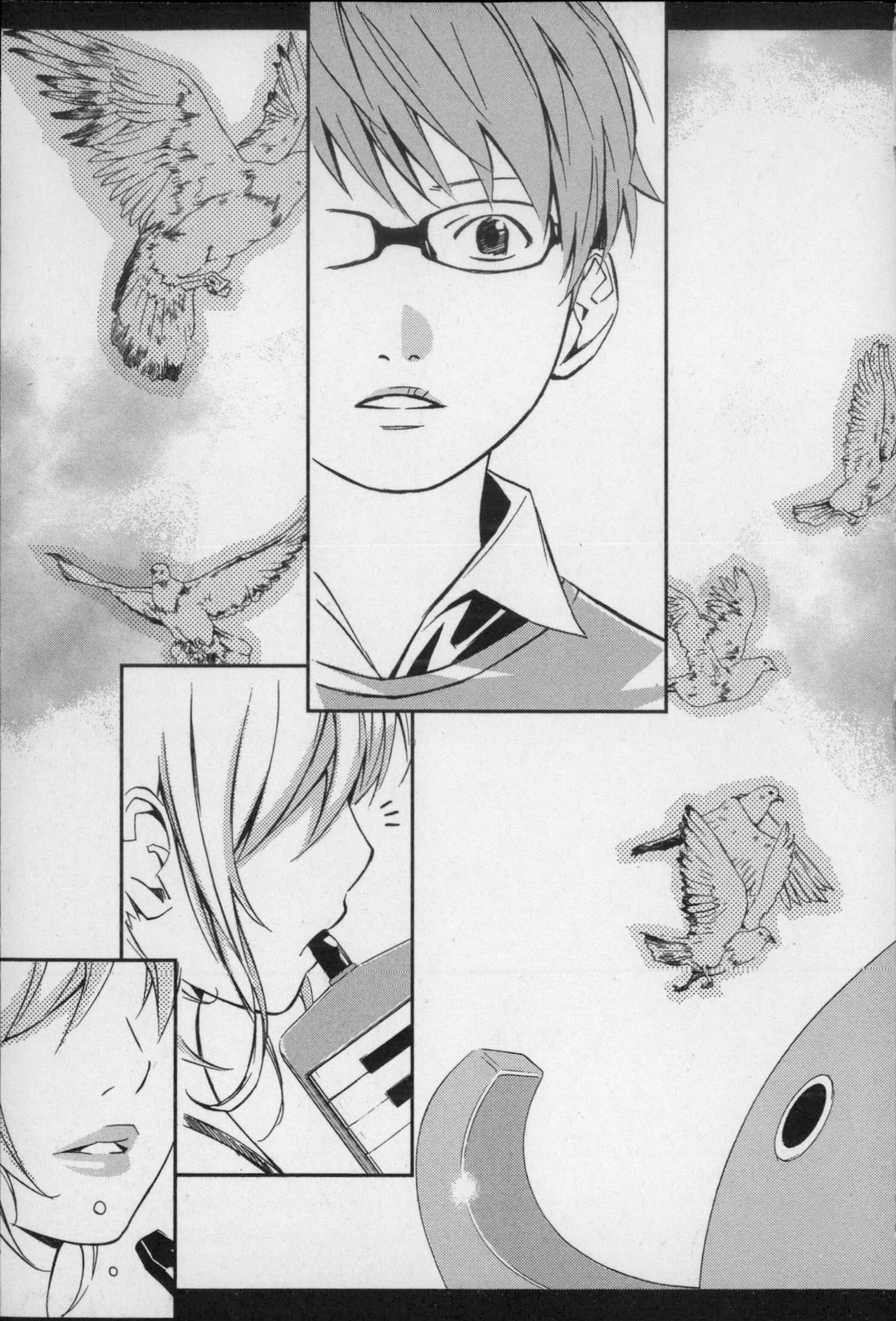

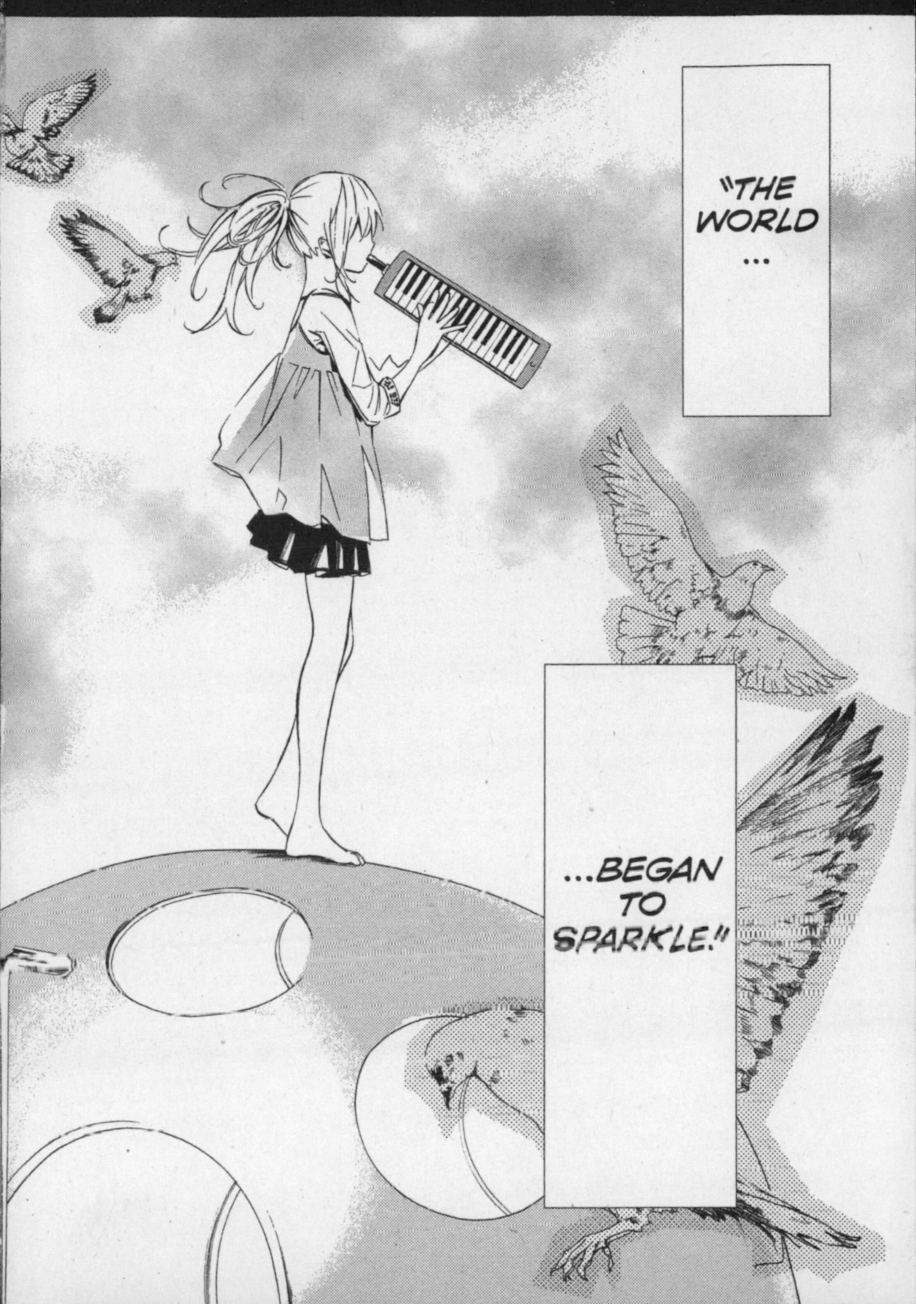
"THE WORLD ...
...BEGAN TO SPARKLE!"

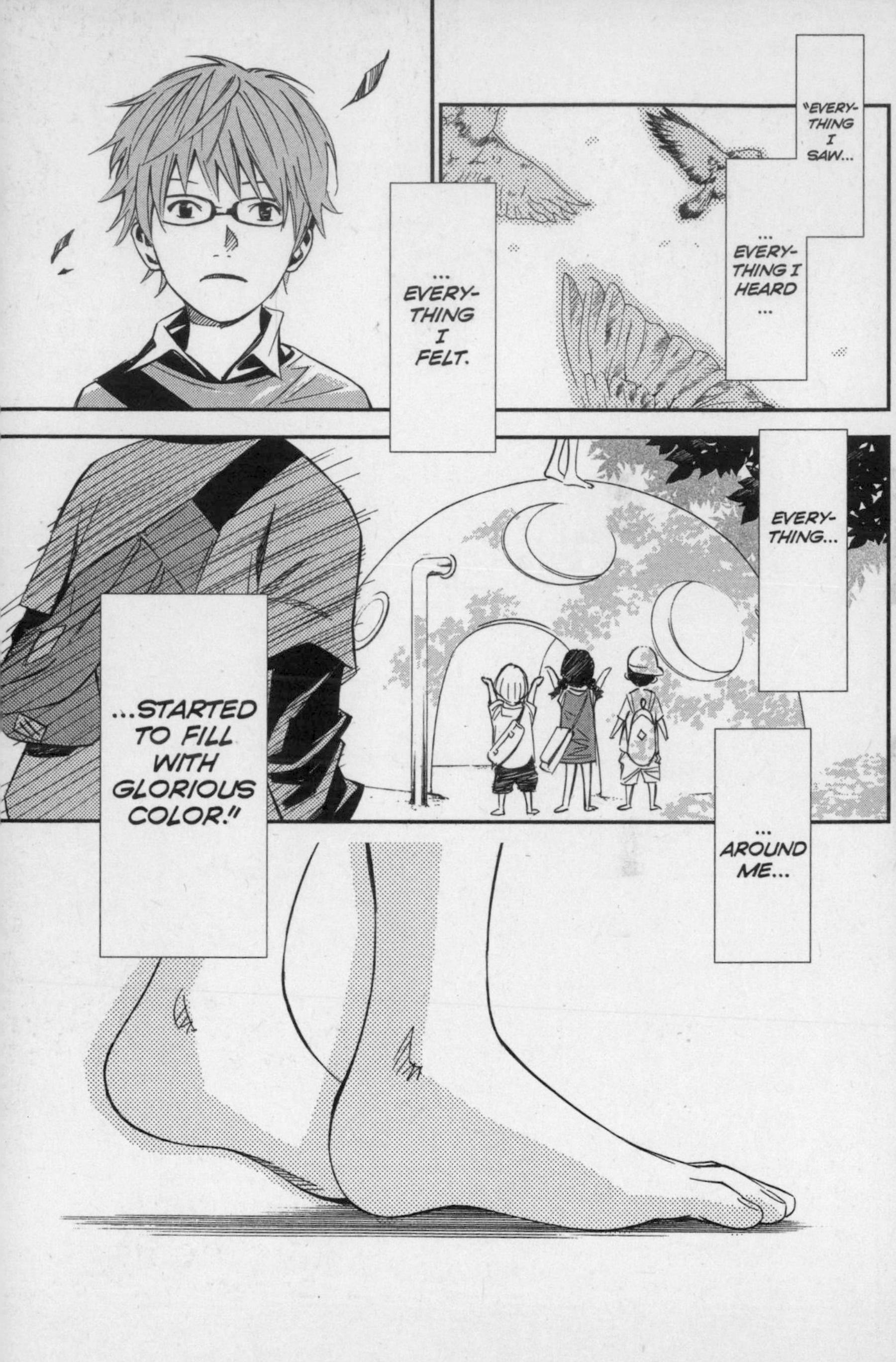
"EVERY-THING I SAW...
...EVERY-THING I HEARD...
...EVERY-THING I FELT.
EVERY-THING...
...AROUND ME...
...STARTED TO FILL WITH GLORIOUS COLOR."

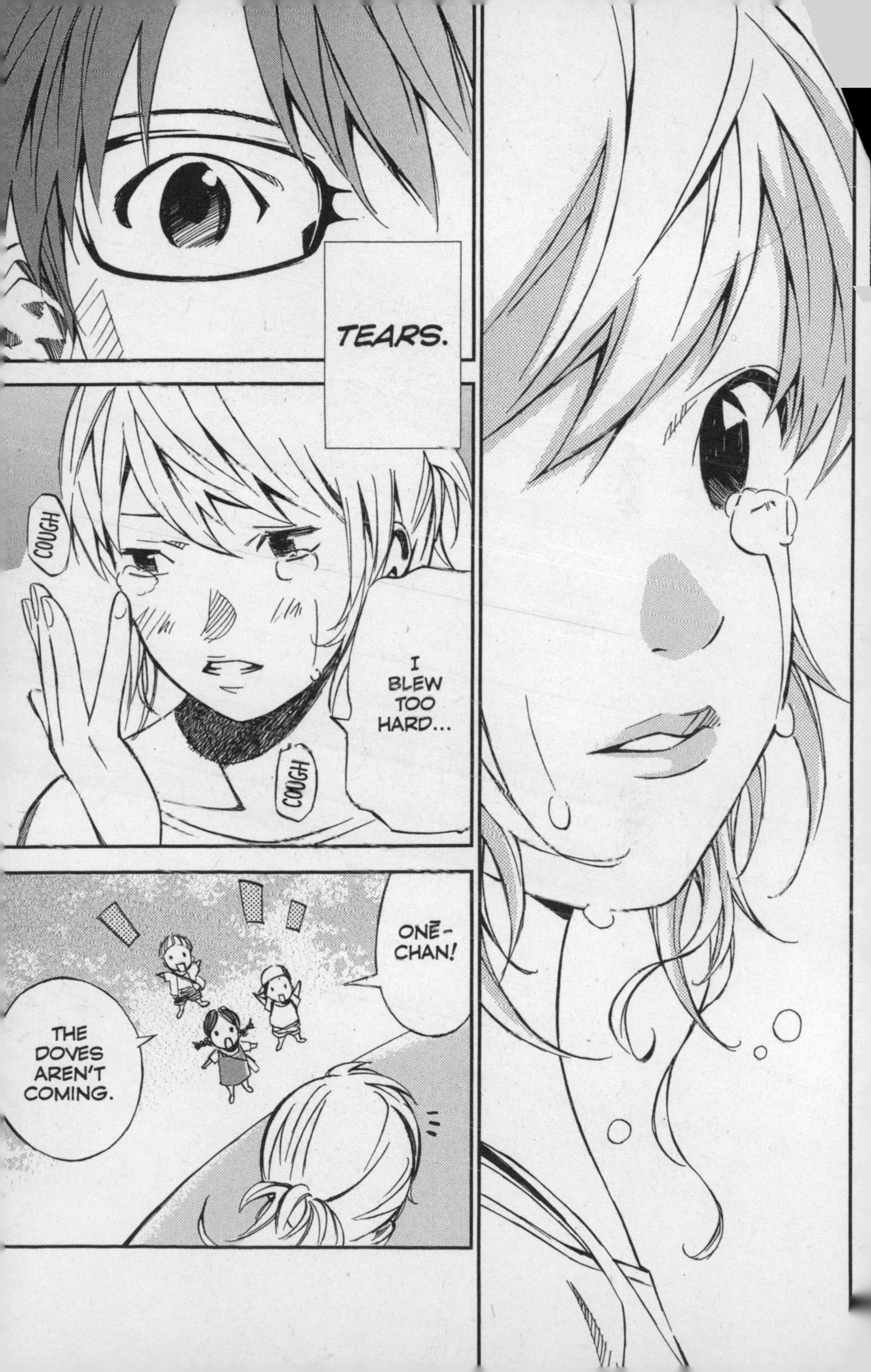
TEARS.
COUGH
I BLEW TOO HARD...
COUGH
ONĒ-CHAN!
THE DOVES AREN'T COMING.

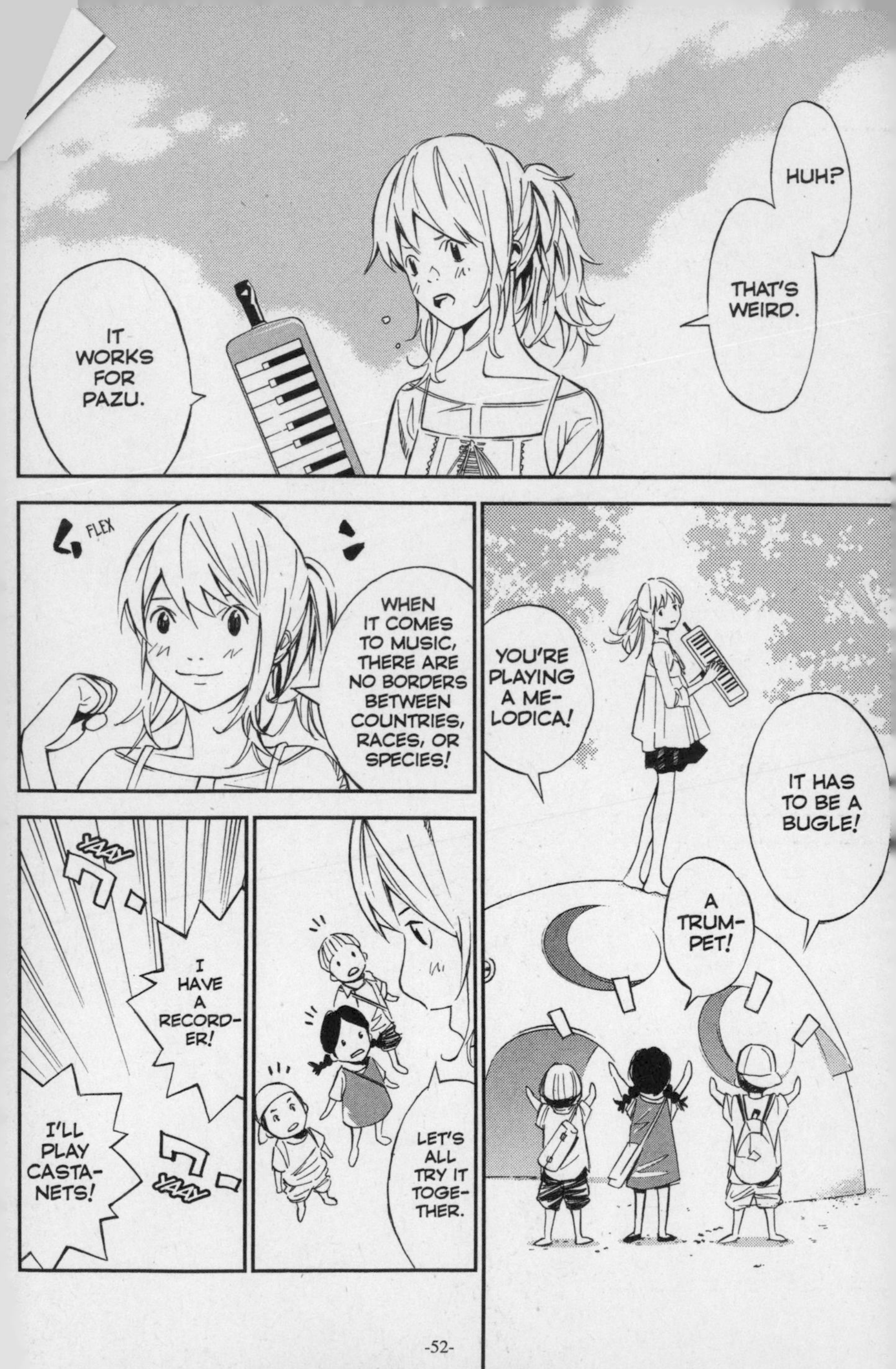
HUH?
THAT'S WEIRD.
IT WORKS FOR PAZU.
YOU'RE PLAYING A ME-LODICA!
IT HAS TO BE A BUGLE!
A TRUM-PET!
FLEX
WHEN IT COMES TO MUSIC, THERE ARE NO BORDERS BETWEEN COUNTRIES, RACES, OR SPECIES!
LET'S ALL TRY IT TOGE-THER.
YAAY
I HAVE A RECORD-ER!
I'LL PLAY CASTA-NETS!
YAAY

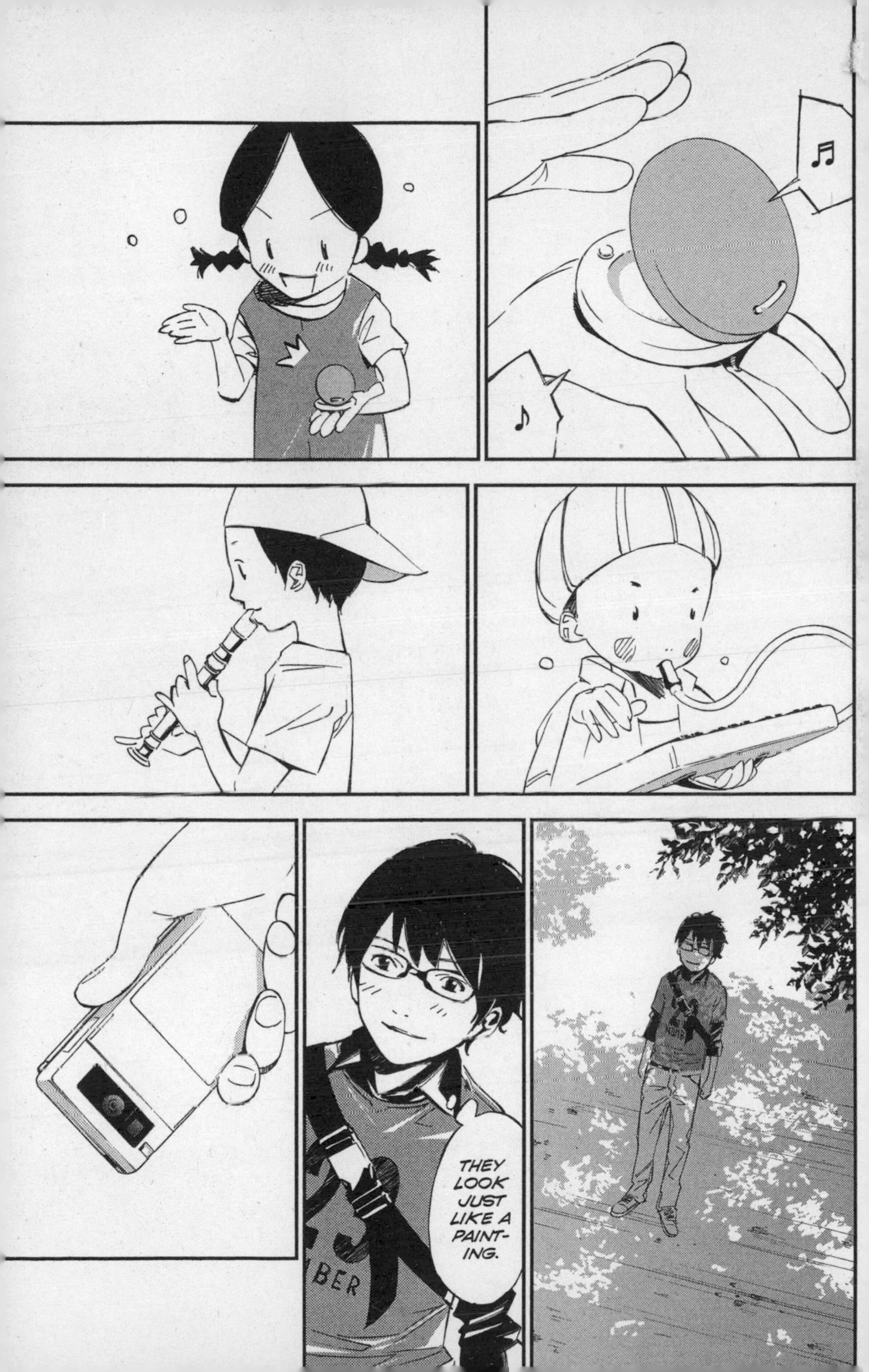
THEY LOOK JUST LIKE A PAINT-ING.

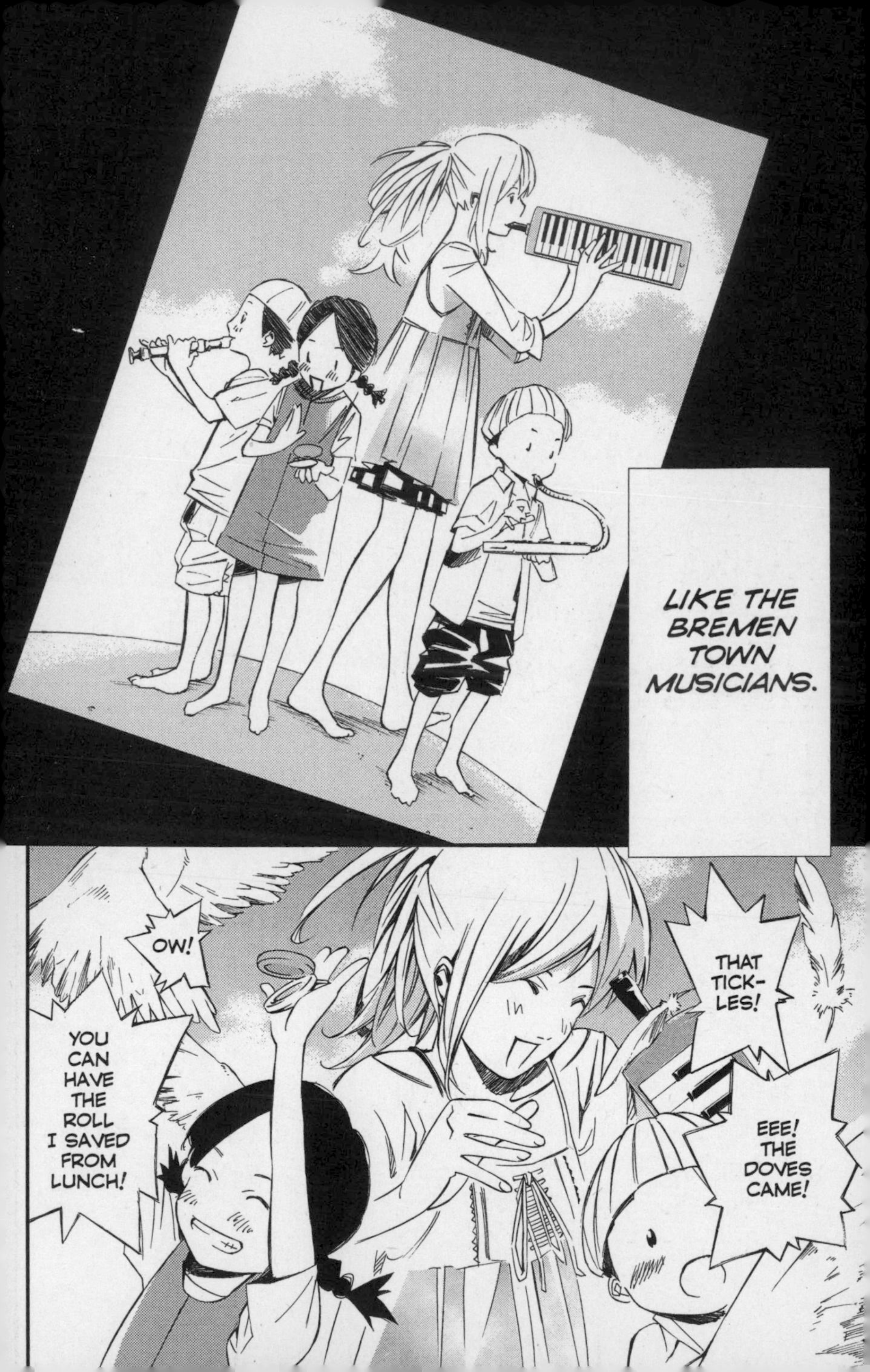
LIKE THE BREMEN TOWN MUSICIANS.
THAT TICKLES!
EEE! THE DOVES CAME!
OW!
YOU CAN HAVE THE ROLL I SAVED FROM LUNCH!

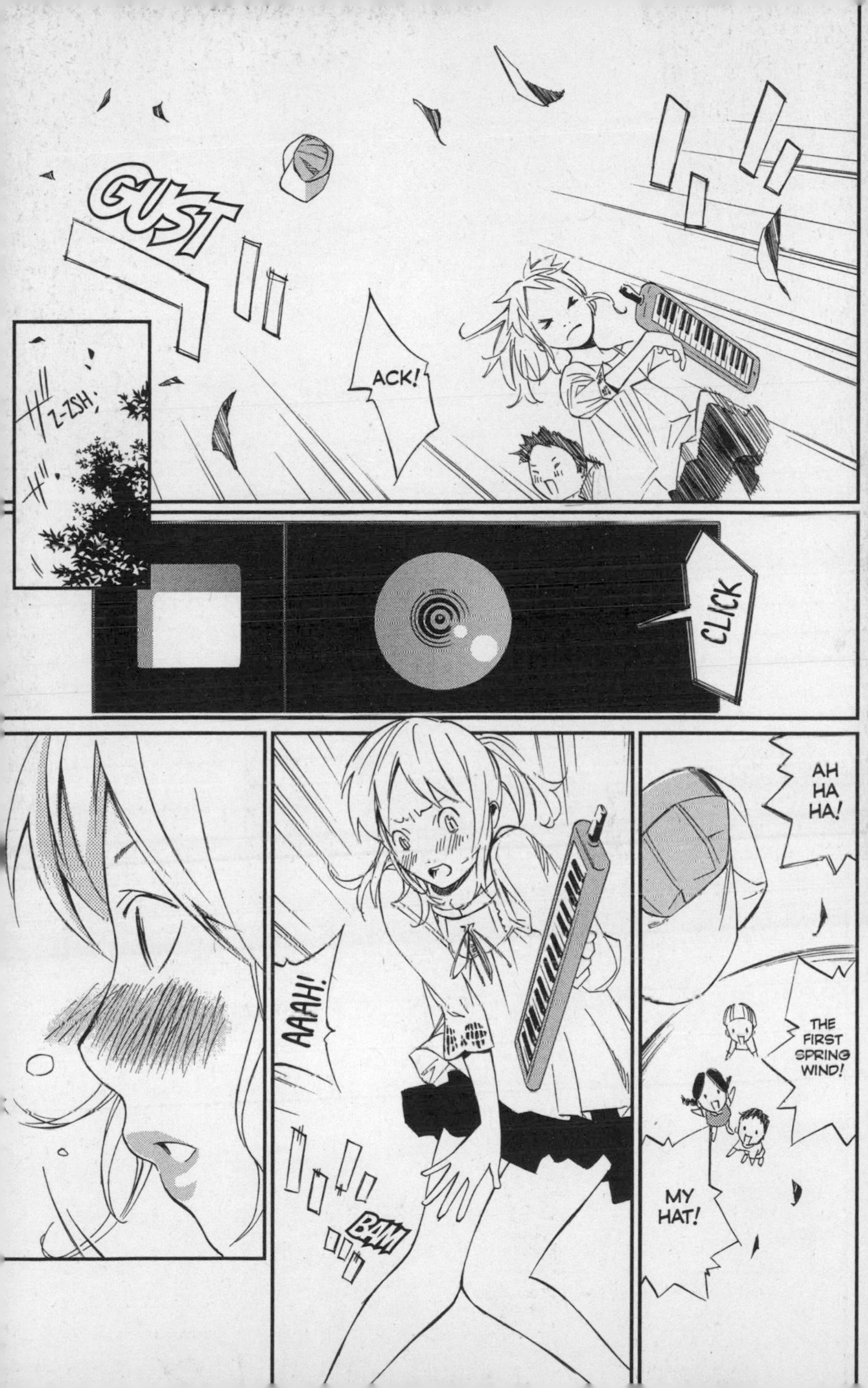
GUST
ACK!
Z-ZSH
CLICK
AH HA HA!
THE FIRST SPRING WIND!
MY HAT!
AAAH!
BAM

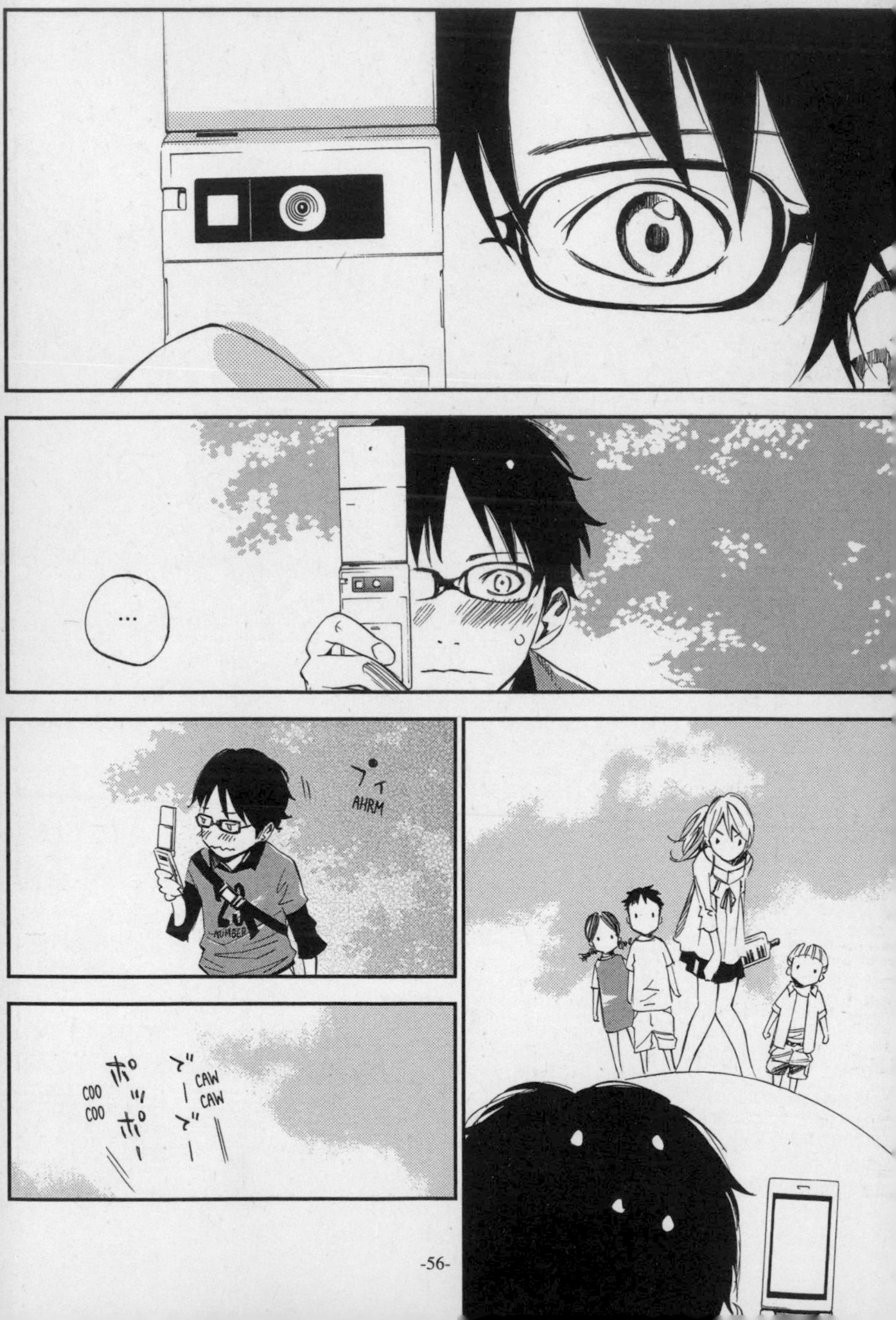
...
AHRM
でーでー
CAW CAW
ポッポー
COO COO

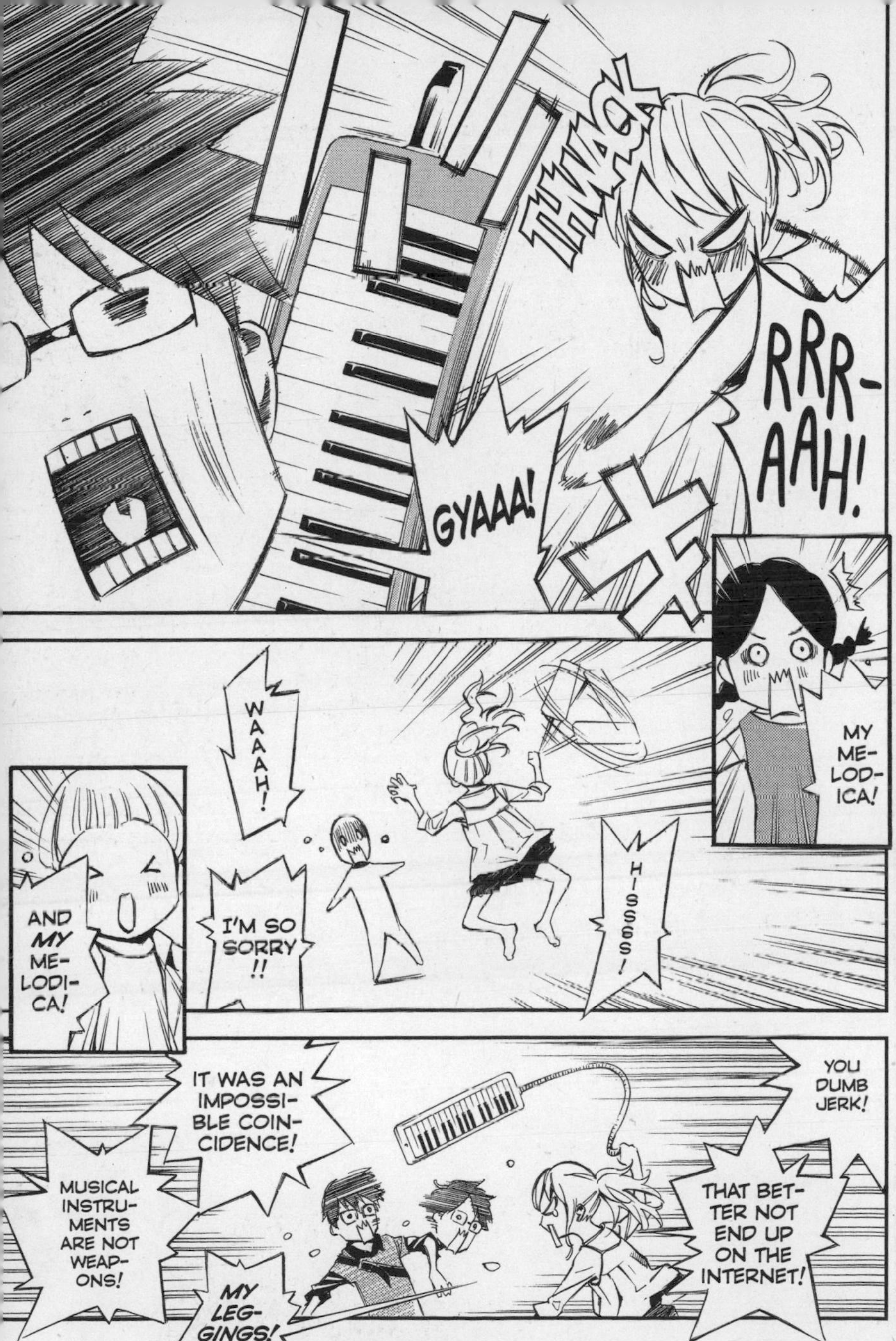
THWACK
RRR-AAH!
GYAAA!
MY MELODICA!
HISSSS!
WAAAH!
I'M SO SORRY!!
AND MY MELODICA!
YOU DUMB JERK!
THAT BETTER NOT END UP ON THE INTERNET!
IT WAS AN IMPOSSIBLE COINCIDENCE!
MY LEGGINGS!
MUSICAL INSTRUMENTS ARE NOT WEAPONS!

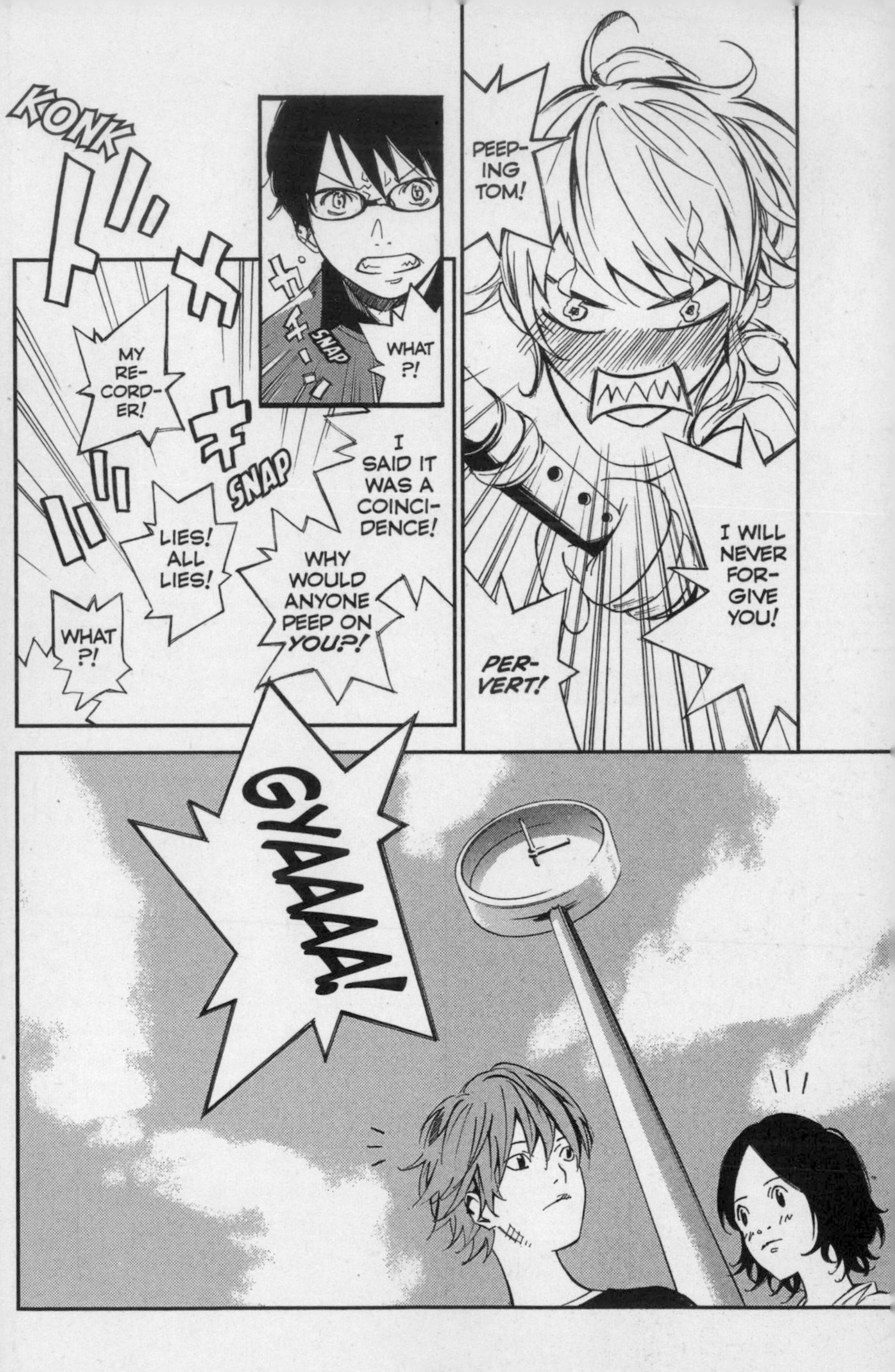
PEEP-ING TOM!
I WILL NEVER FOR-GIVE YOU!
PER-VERT!
KONK
WHAT?!
SNAP
MY RE-CORD-ER!
SNAP
I SAID IT WAS A COINCI-DENCE!
LIES! ALL LIES!
WHY WOULD ANYONE PEEP ON YOU?!
WHAT?!
GYAAAA!

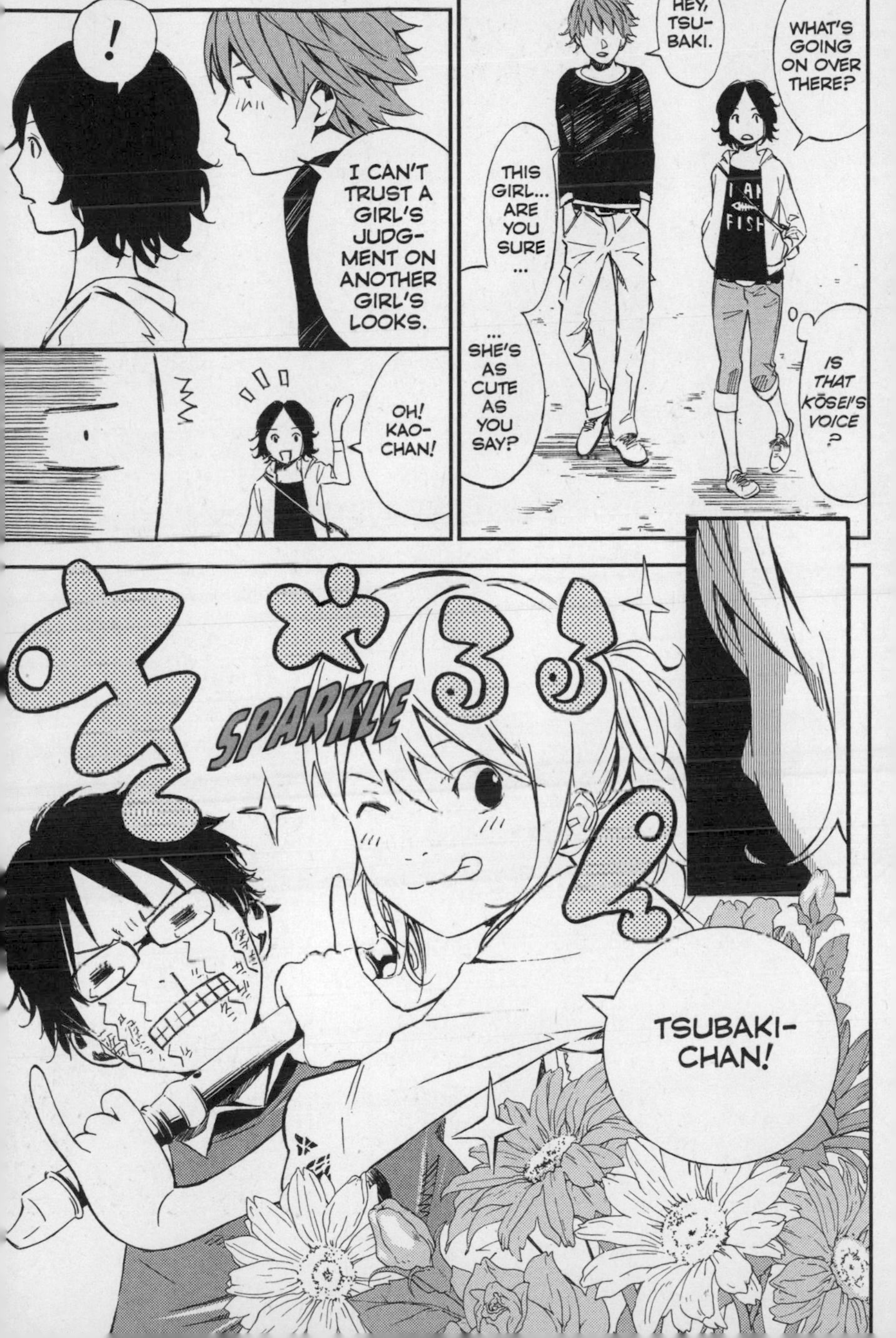
WHAT'S GOING ON OVER THERE?
HEY, TSUBAKI.
IS THAT KŌSEI'S VOICE?
THIS GIRL... ARE YOU SURE ...
... SHE'S AS CUTE AS YOU SAY?
!
I CAN'T TRUST A GIRL'S JUDGMENT ON ANOTHER GIRL'S LOOKS.
OH! KAO-CHAN!
SPARKLE
TSUBAKI-CHAN!

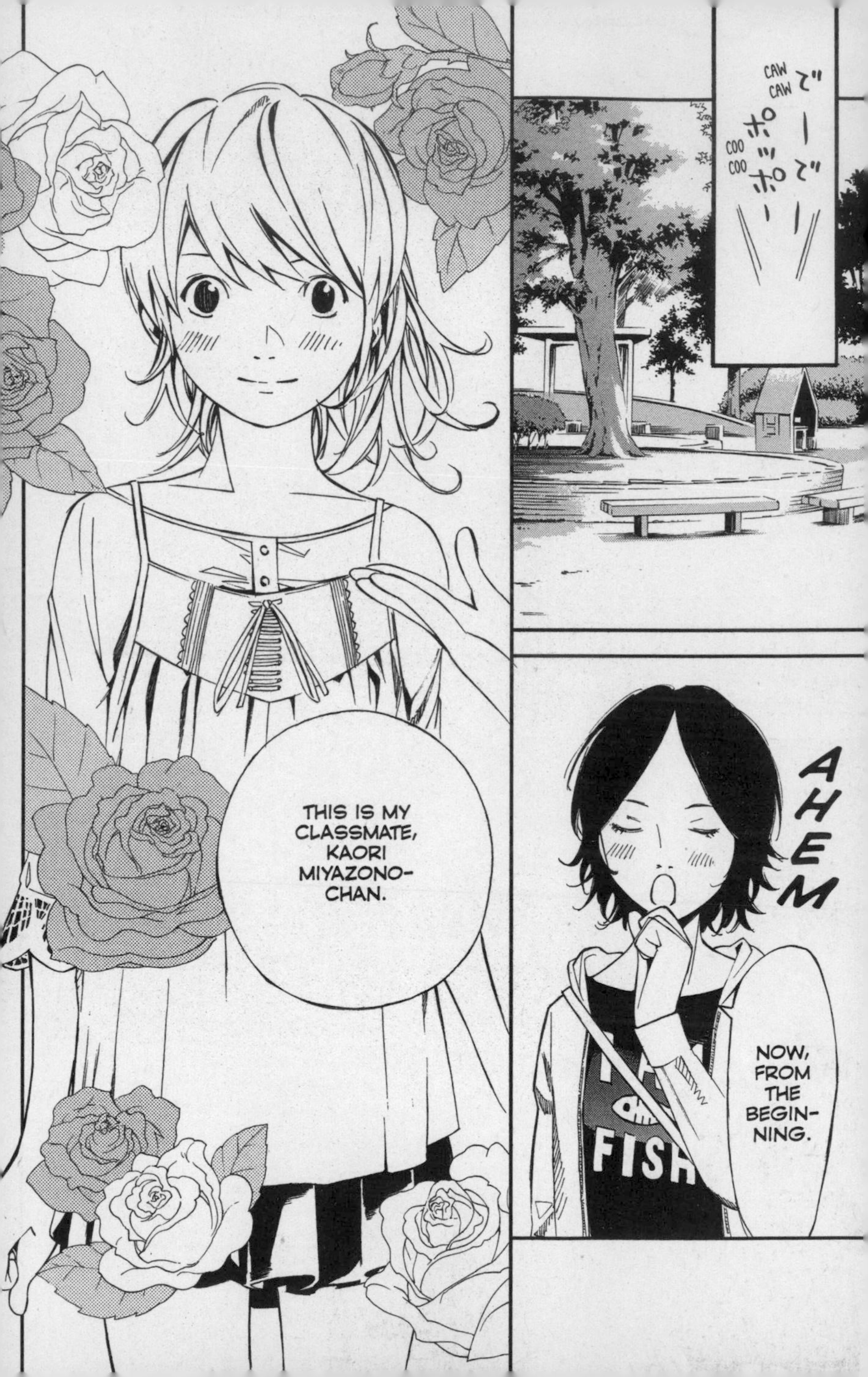
CAW CAW
でーでー
COO COO
ポッポー
AHEM
NOW, FROM THE BEGIN-NING.
THIS IS MY CLASSMATE, KAORI MIYAZONO-CHAN.

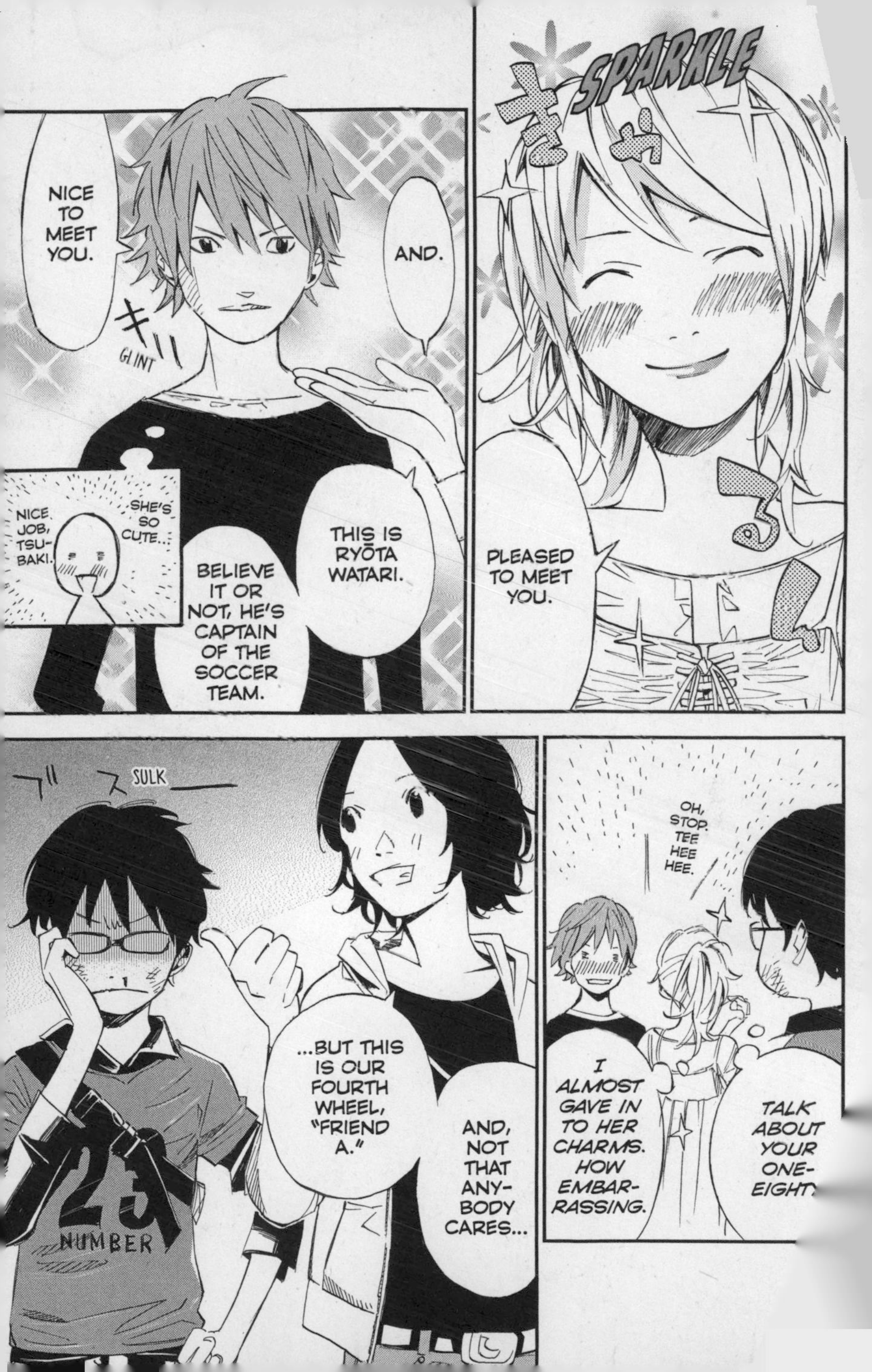
SPARKLE
PLEASED TO MEET YOU.
AND.
THIS IS RYŌTA WATARI.
BELIEVE IT OR NOT, HE'S CAPTAIN OF THE SOCCER TEAM.
NICE TO MEET YOU.
GLINT
SHE'S SO CUTE...
NICE JOB, TSUBAKI.
OH, STOP. TEE HEE HEE.
TALK ABOUT YOUR ONE-EIGHTY.
I ALMOST GAVE IN TO HER CHARMS. HOW EMBARRASSING.
SULK
...BUT THIS IS OUR FOURTH WHEEL, "FRIEND A."
AND, NOT THAT ANYBODY CARES...
23
NUMBER

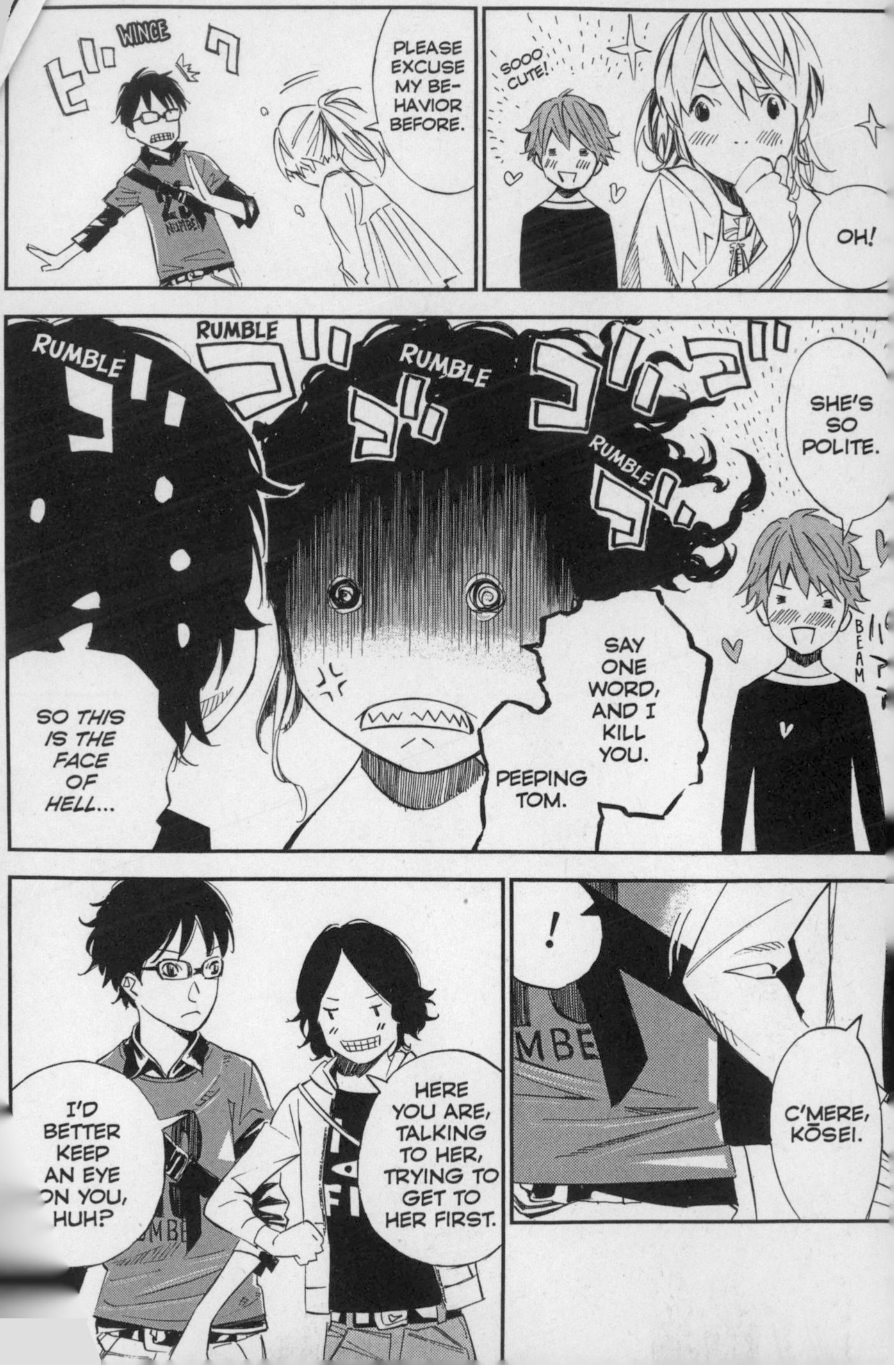
SOOO CUTE!
OH!
PLEASE EXCUSE MY BE-HAVIOR BEFORE.
WINCE
SHE'S SO POLITE.
BEAM
RUMBLE
RUMBLE
RUMBLE
RUMBLE
SAY ONE WORD, AND I KILL YOU.
PEEPING TOM.
SO THIS IS THE FACE OF HELL...
!
C'MERE, KŌSEI.
HERE YOU ARE, TALKING TO HER, TRYING TO GET TO HER FIRST.
I'D BETTER KEEP AN EYE ON YOU, HUH?

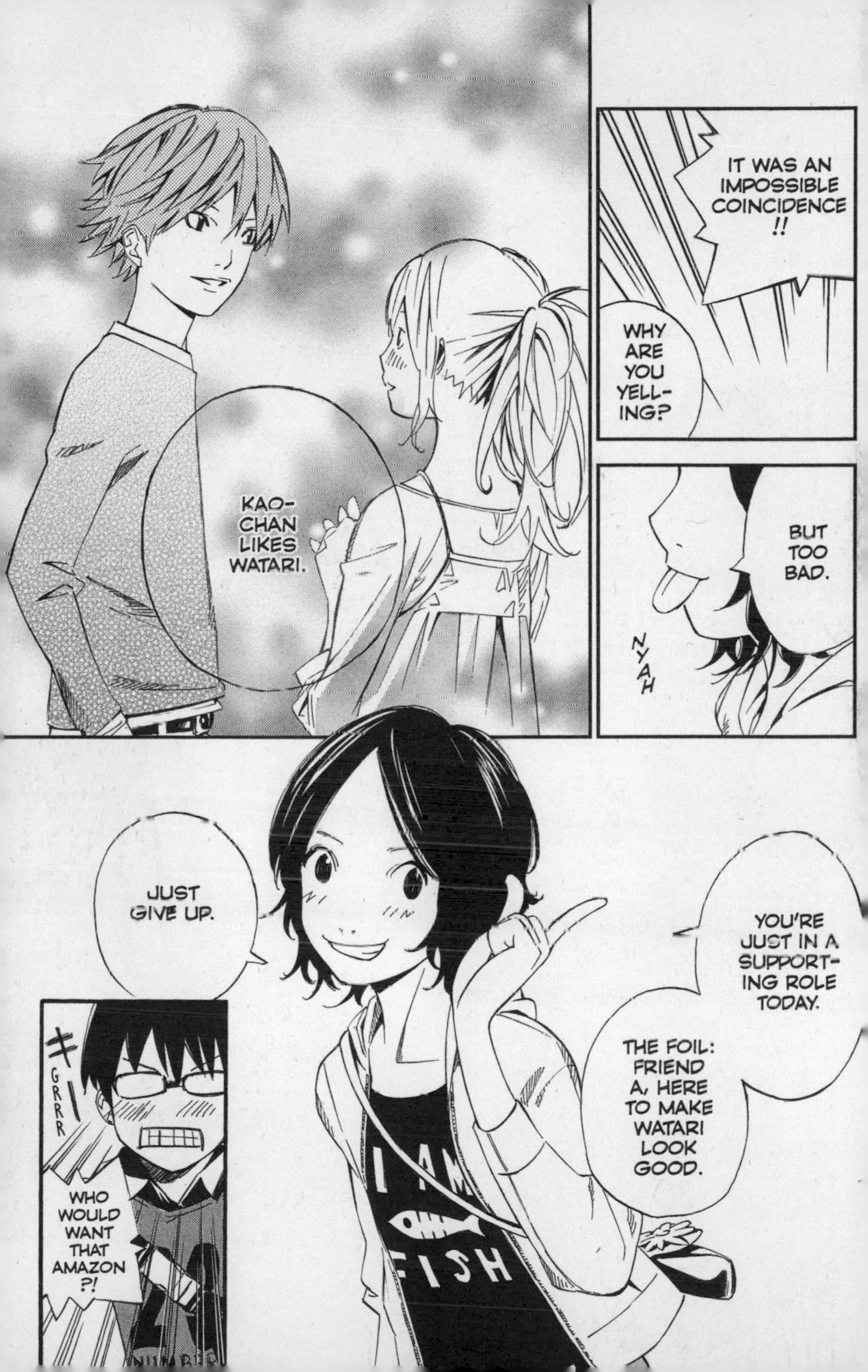
IT WAS AN IMPOSSIBLE COINCIDENCE!!
WHY ARE YOU YELL-ING?
BUT TOO BAD.
NYAH
KAO-CHAN LIKES WATARI.
YOU'RE JUST IN A SUPPORT-ING ROLE TODAY.
THE FOIL: FRIEND A, HERE TO MAKE WATARI LOOK GOOD.
JUST GIVE UP.
I AM FISH
GRRR
WHO WOULD WANT THAT AMAZON?!

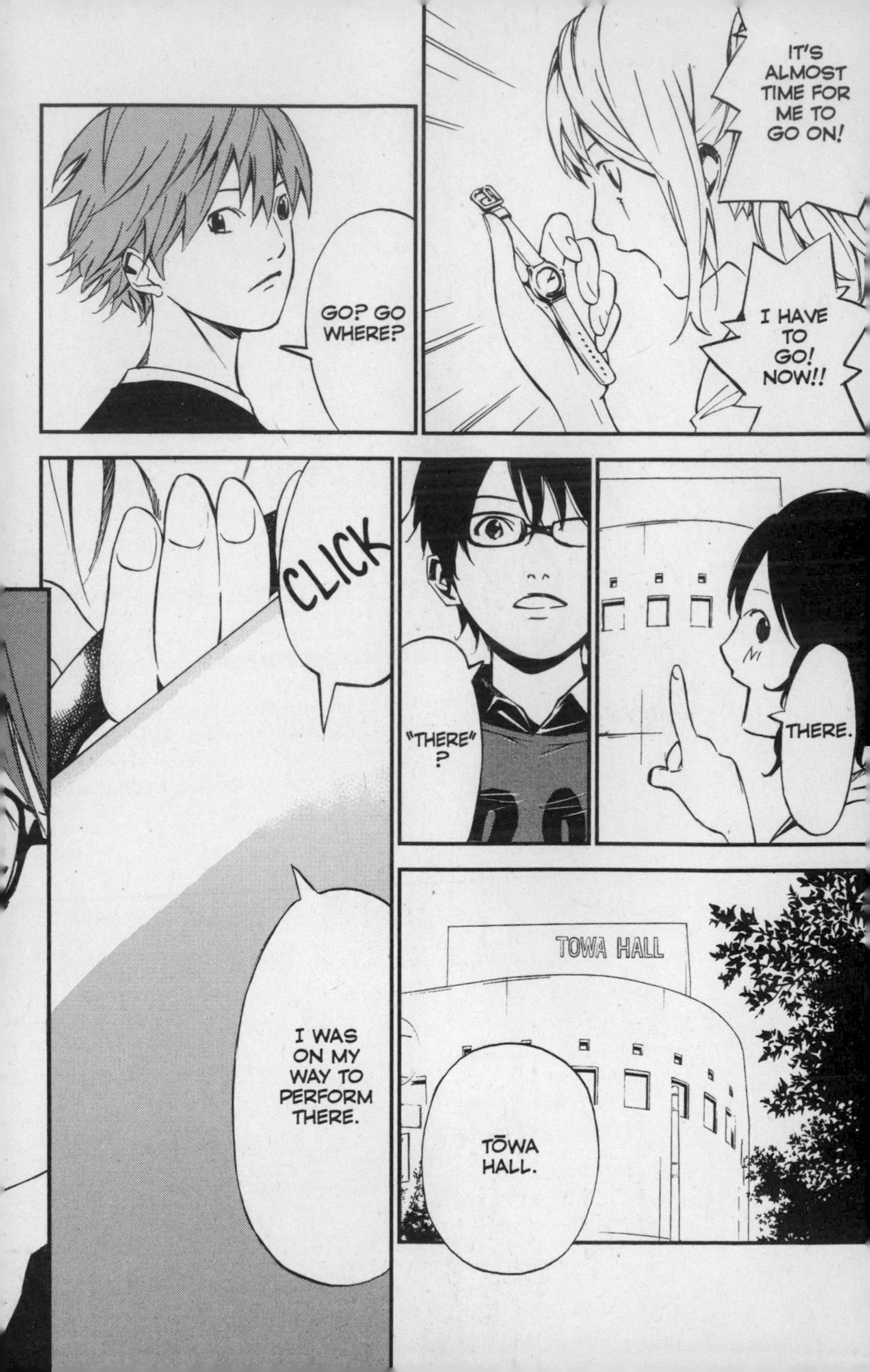
IT'S ALMOST TIME FOR ME TO GO ON!
I HAVE TO GO! NOW!!
GO? GO WHERE?
THERE.
"THERE"?
TOWA HALL
TŌWA HALL.
CLICK
I WAS ON MY WAY TO PERFORM THERE.

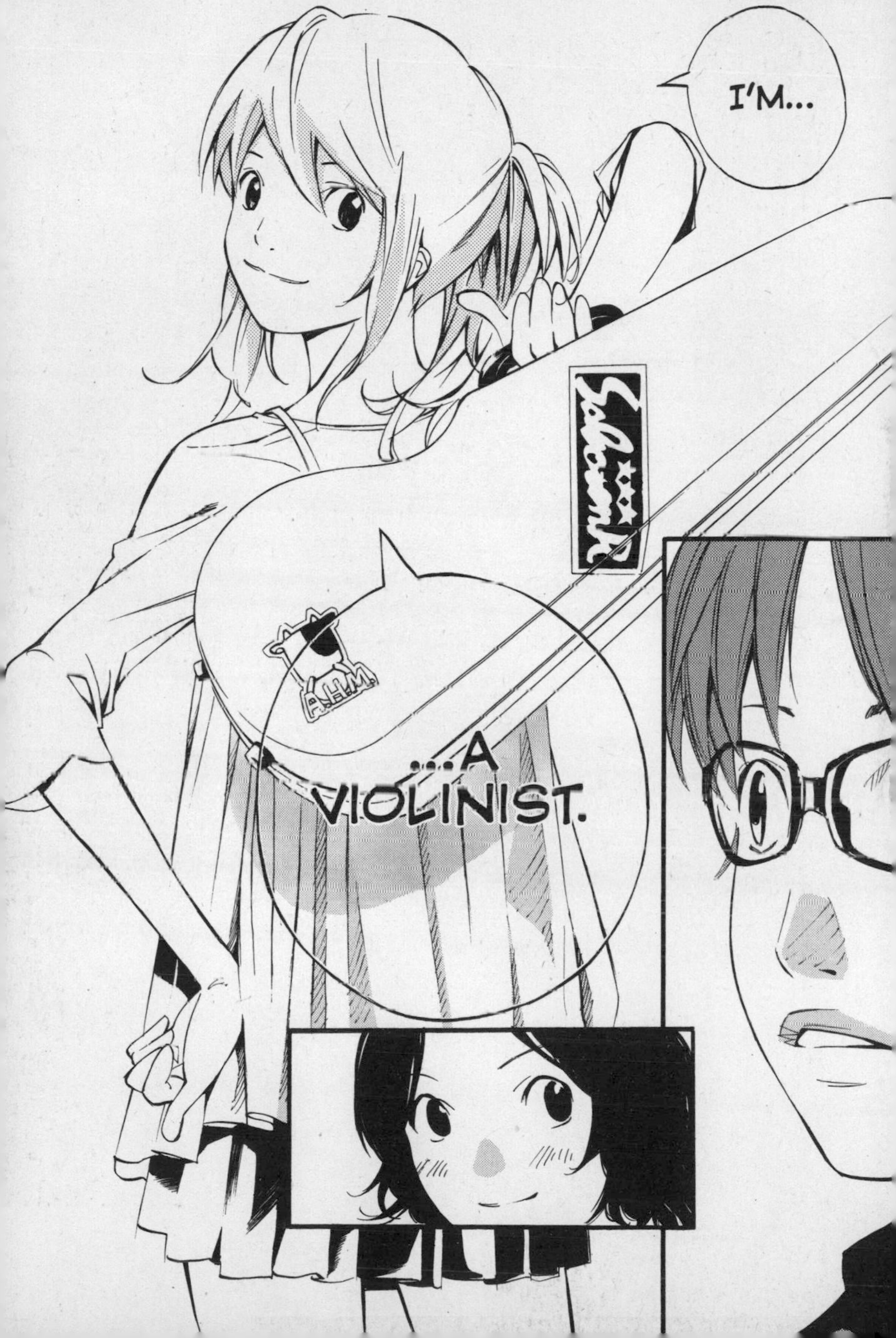
I'M...
...A VIOLINIST.

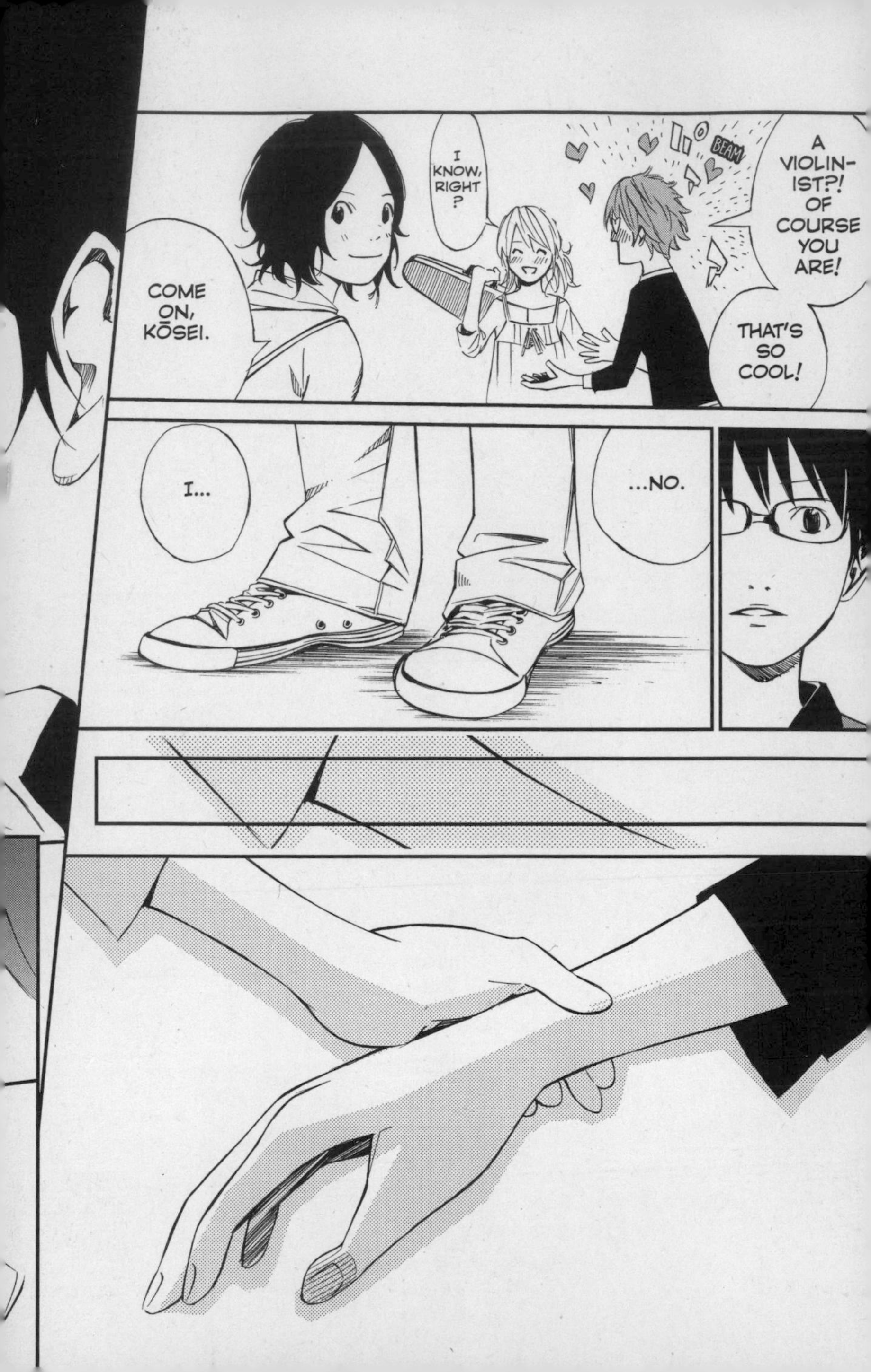
A VIOLIN-IST?! OF COURSE YOU ARE!
THAT'S SO COOL!
BEAM
I KNOW, RIGHT?
COME ON, KŌSEI.
I...
...NO.

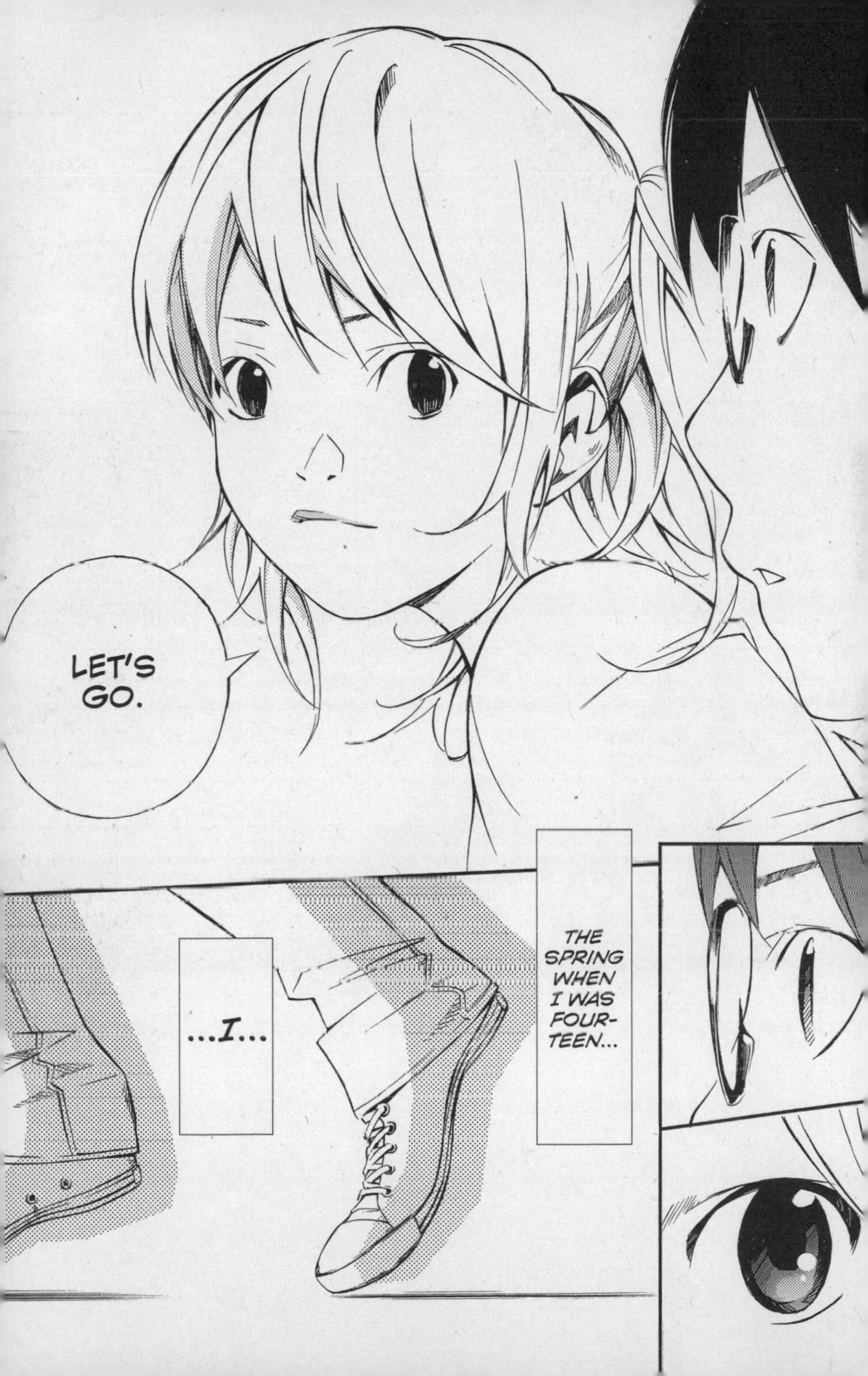
LET'S GO.
THE SPRING WHEN I WAS FOURTEEN...
...I...

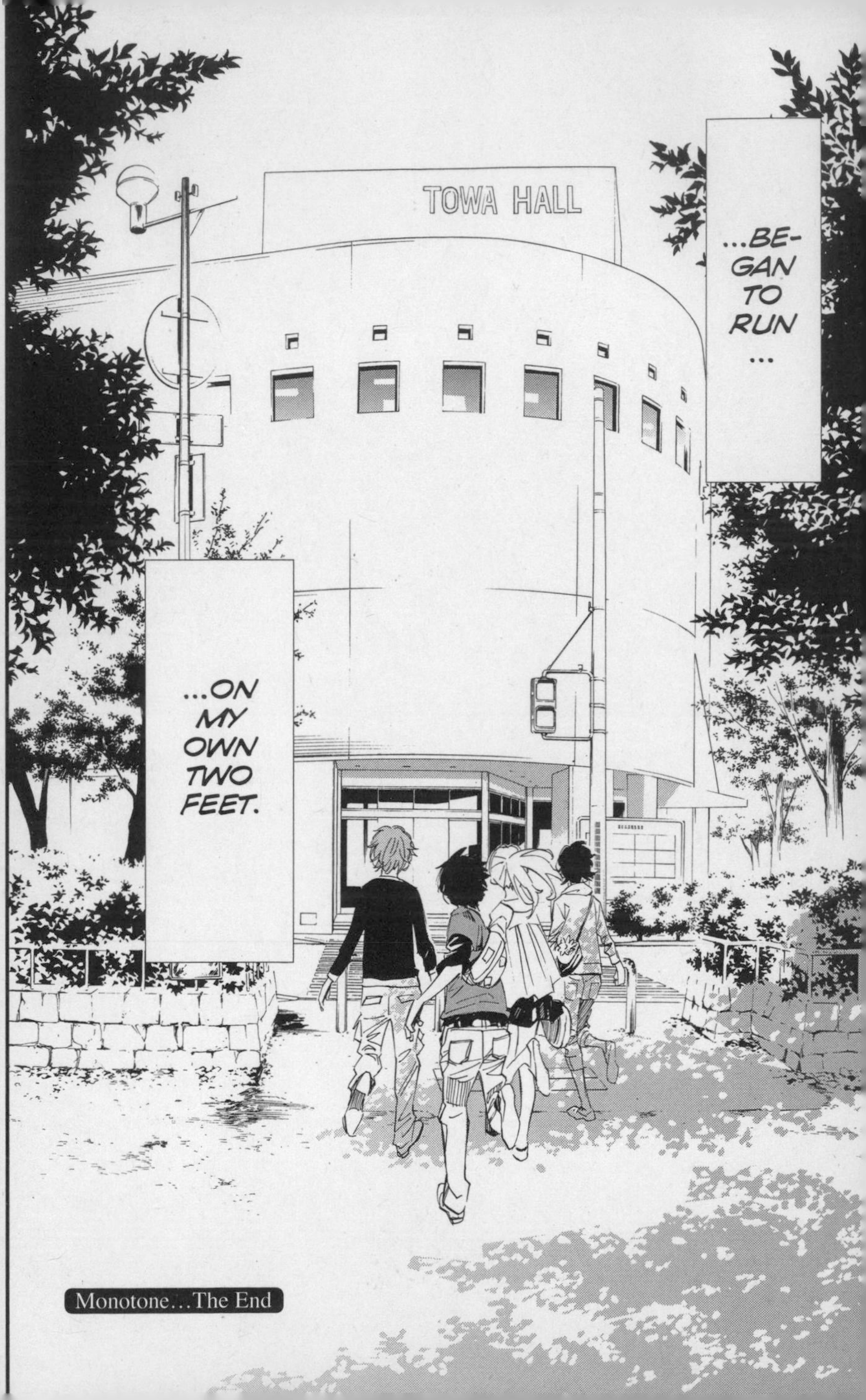
...BEGAN TO RUN...
TOWA HALL
...ON MY OWN TWO FEET.
Monotone...The End

Your Lie in April

I met the girl under full-bloomed cherry blossoms, and my fate has begun to change.

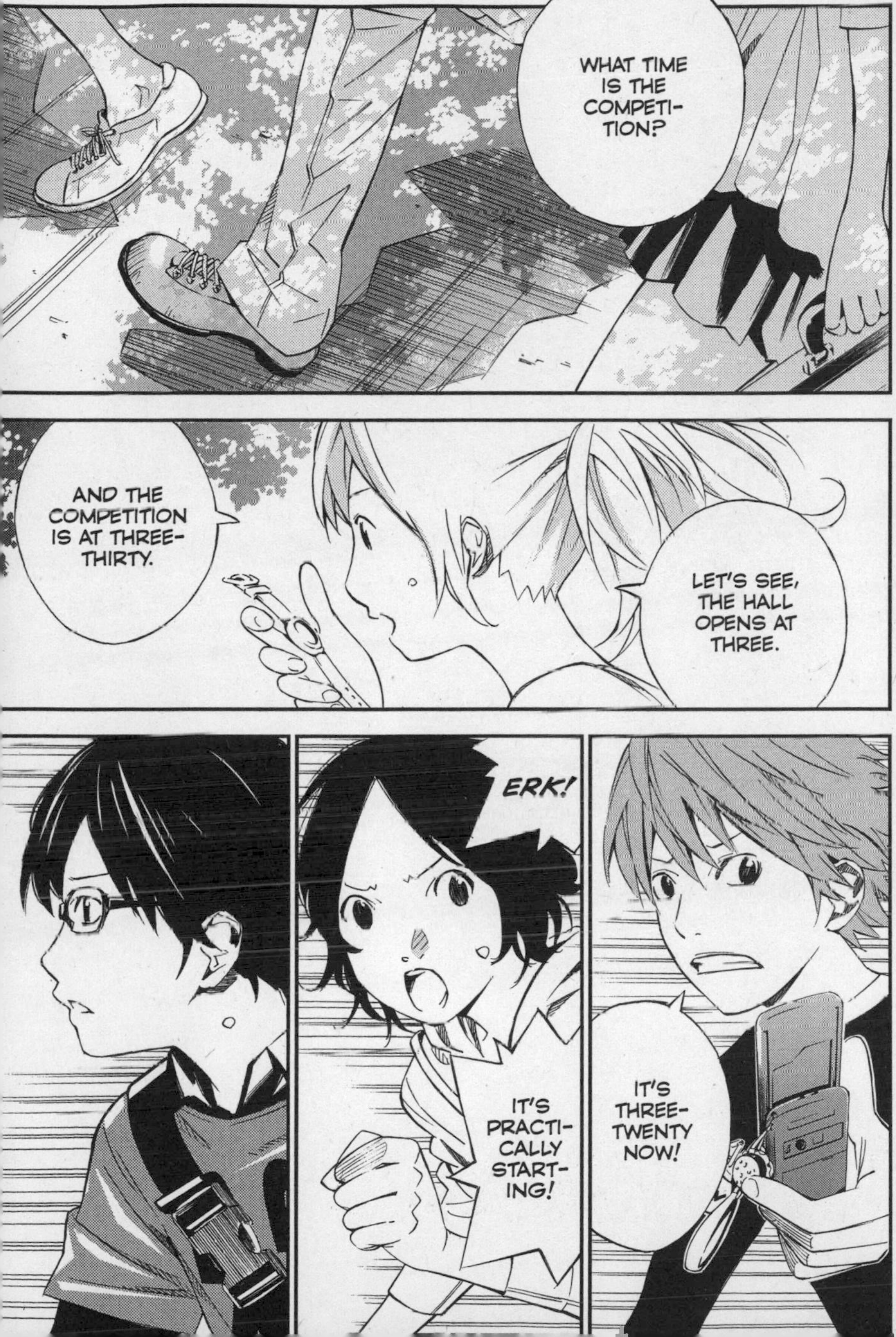
WHAT TIME IS THE COMPETITION?
LET'S SEE, THE HALL OPENS AT THREE.
AND THE COMPETITION IS AT THREE-THIRTY.
IT'S THREE-TWENTY NOW!
ERK!
IT'S PRACTICALLY STARTING!

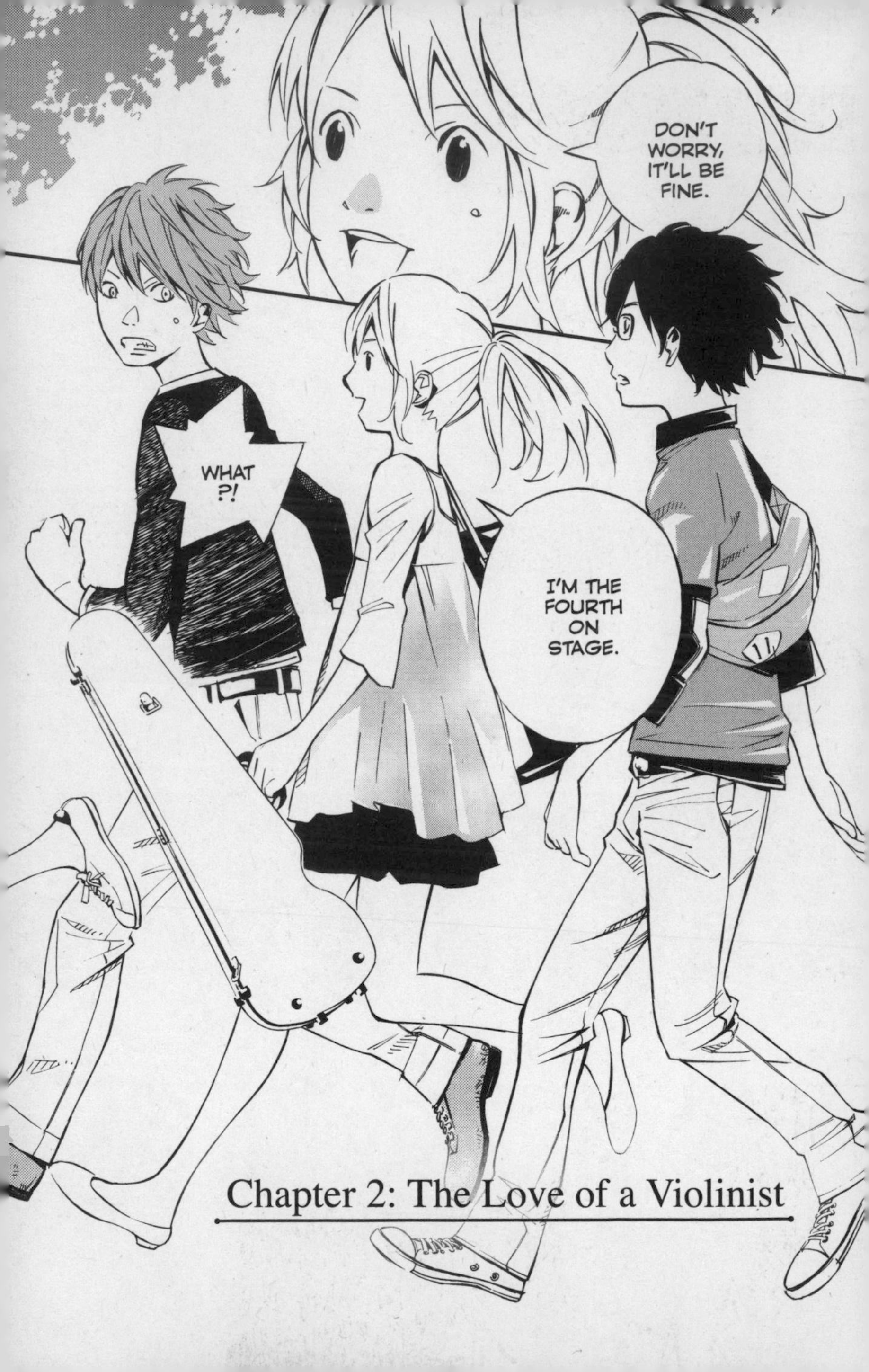
DON'T WORRY, IT'LL BE FINE.
I'M THE FOURTH ON STAGE.
WHAT ?!

Chapter 2: The Love of a Violinist

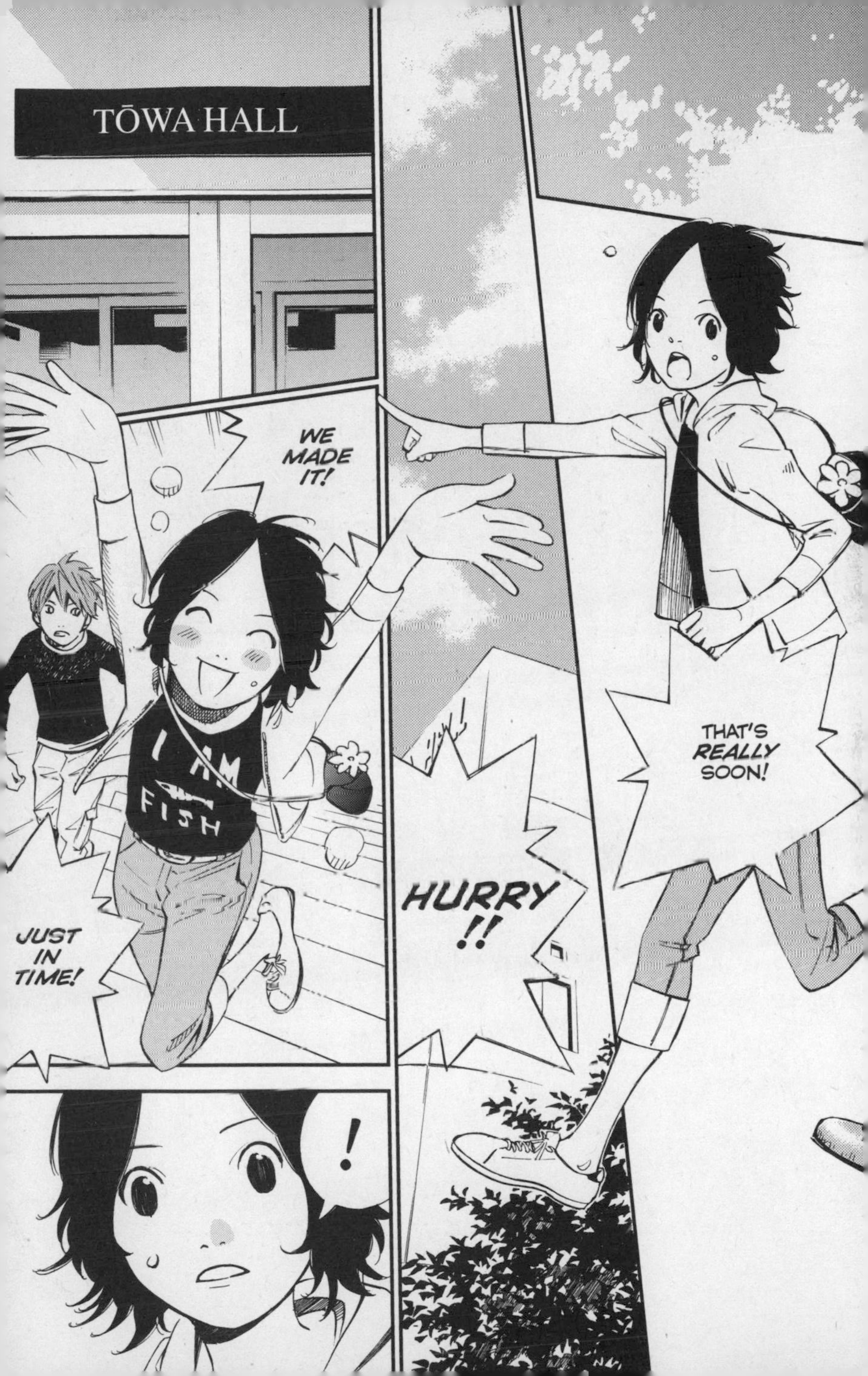
THAT'S REALLY SOON!
HURRY !!
TŌWA HALL
WE MADE IT!
JUST IN TIME!
!

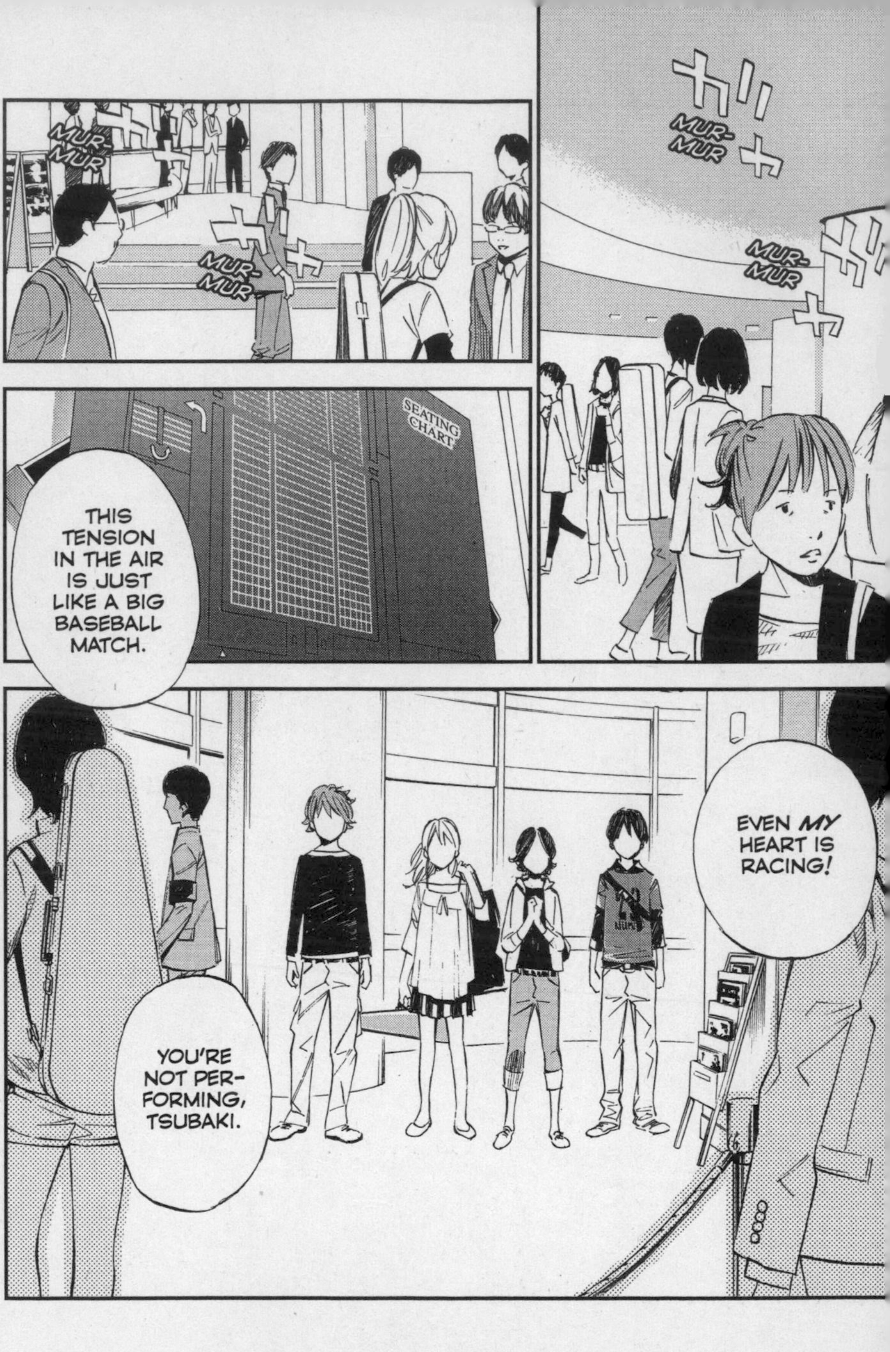
MUR-MUR
MUR-MUR
MUR-MUR
MUR-MUR
SEATING CHART
THIS TENSION IN THE AIR IS JUST LIKE A BIG BASEBALL MATCH.
EVEN MY HEART IS RACING!
YOU'RE NOT PER-FORMING, TSUBAKI.

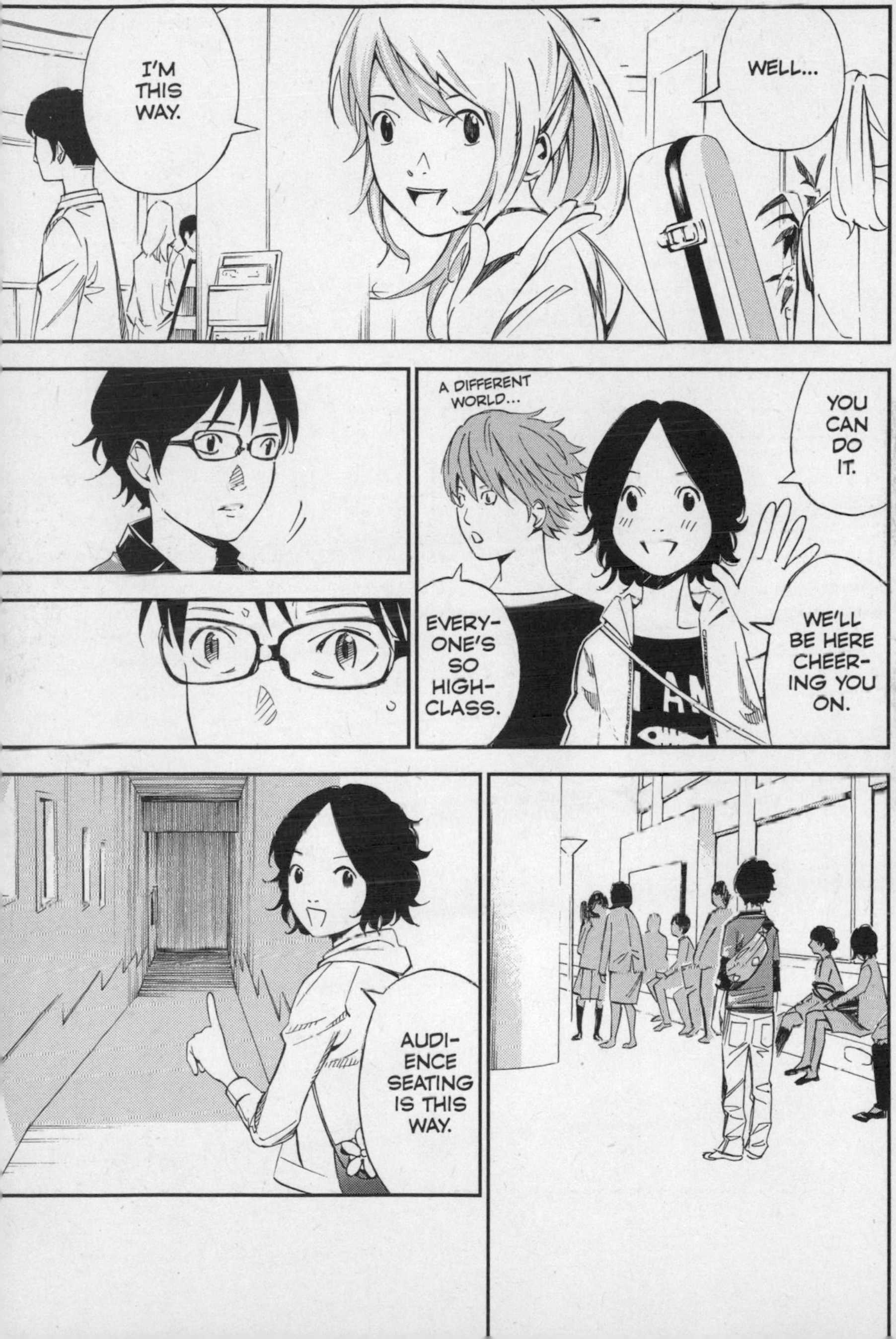
WELL...
I'M THIS WAY.
YOU CAN DO IT.
WE'LL BE HERE CHEER-ING YOU ON.
A DIFFERENT WORLD...
EVERY-ONE'S SO HIGH-CLASS.
AUDI-ENCE SEATING IS THIS WAY.

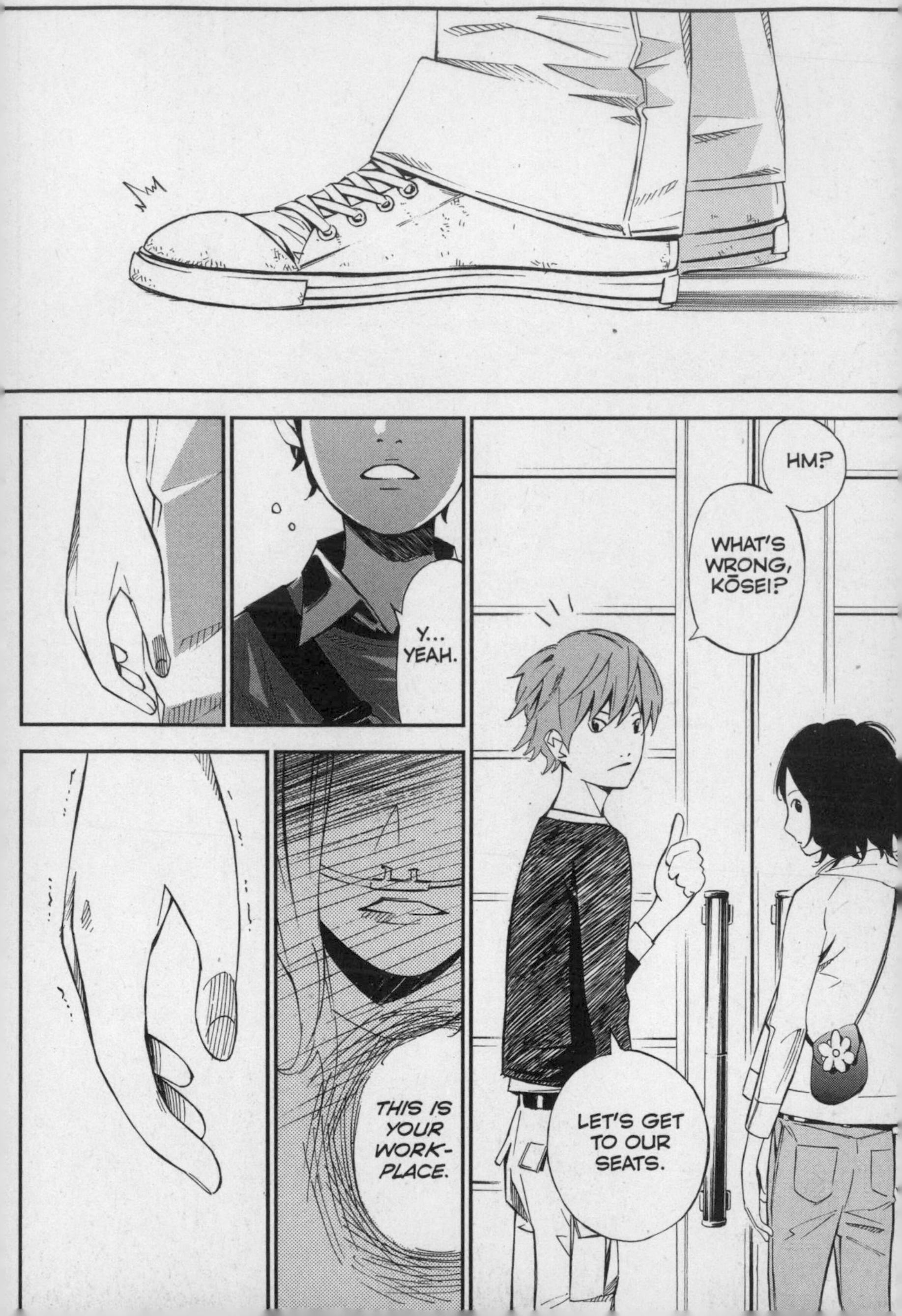
HM?
WHAT'S WRONG, KŌSEI?
LET'S GET TO OUR SEATS.
Y... YEAH.
THIS IS YOUR WORK-PLACE.

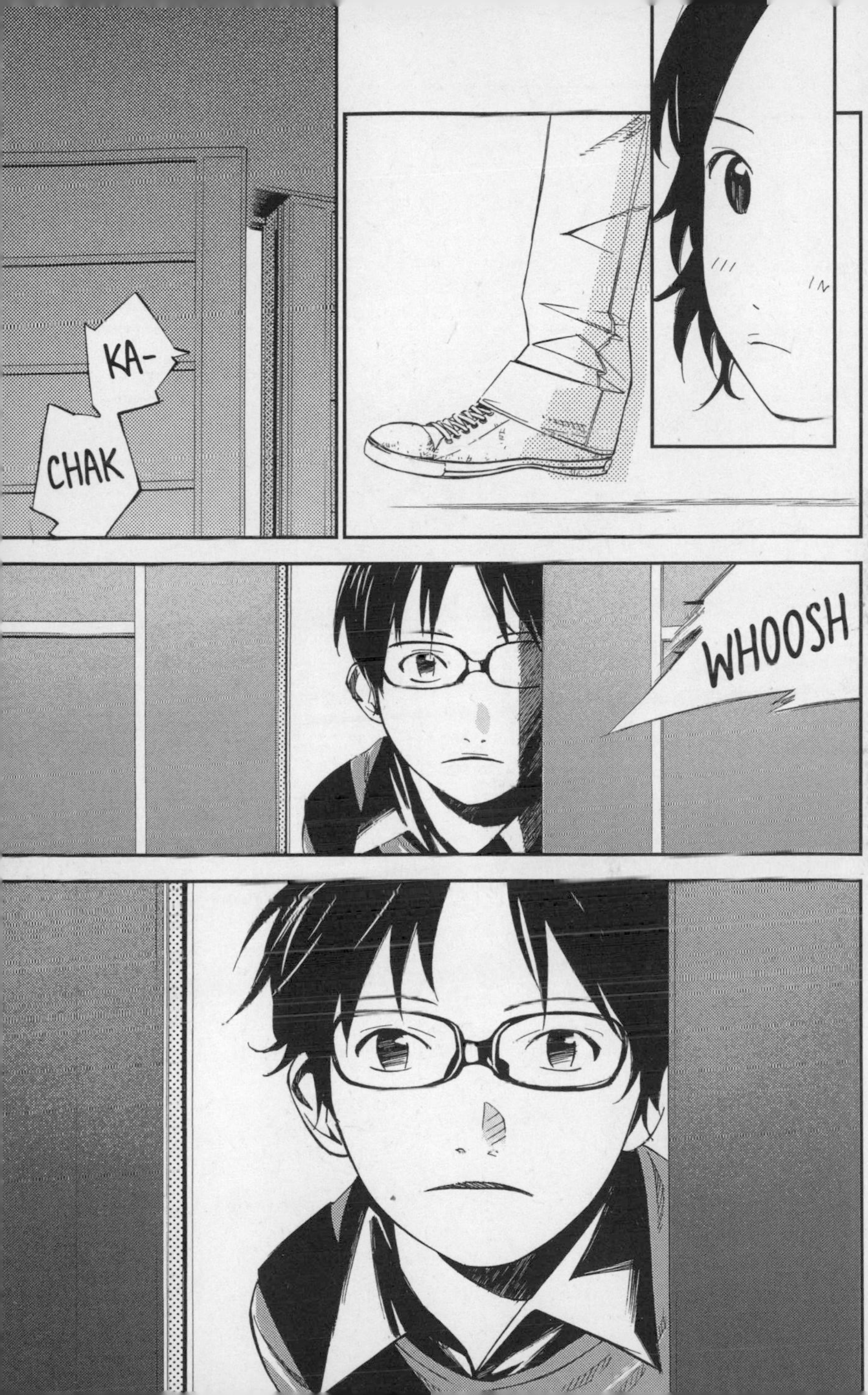
KA-
CHAK
WHOOSH

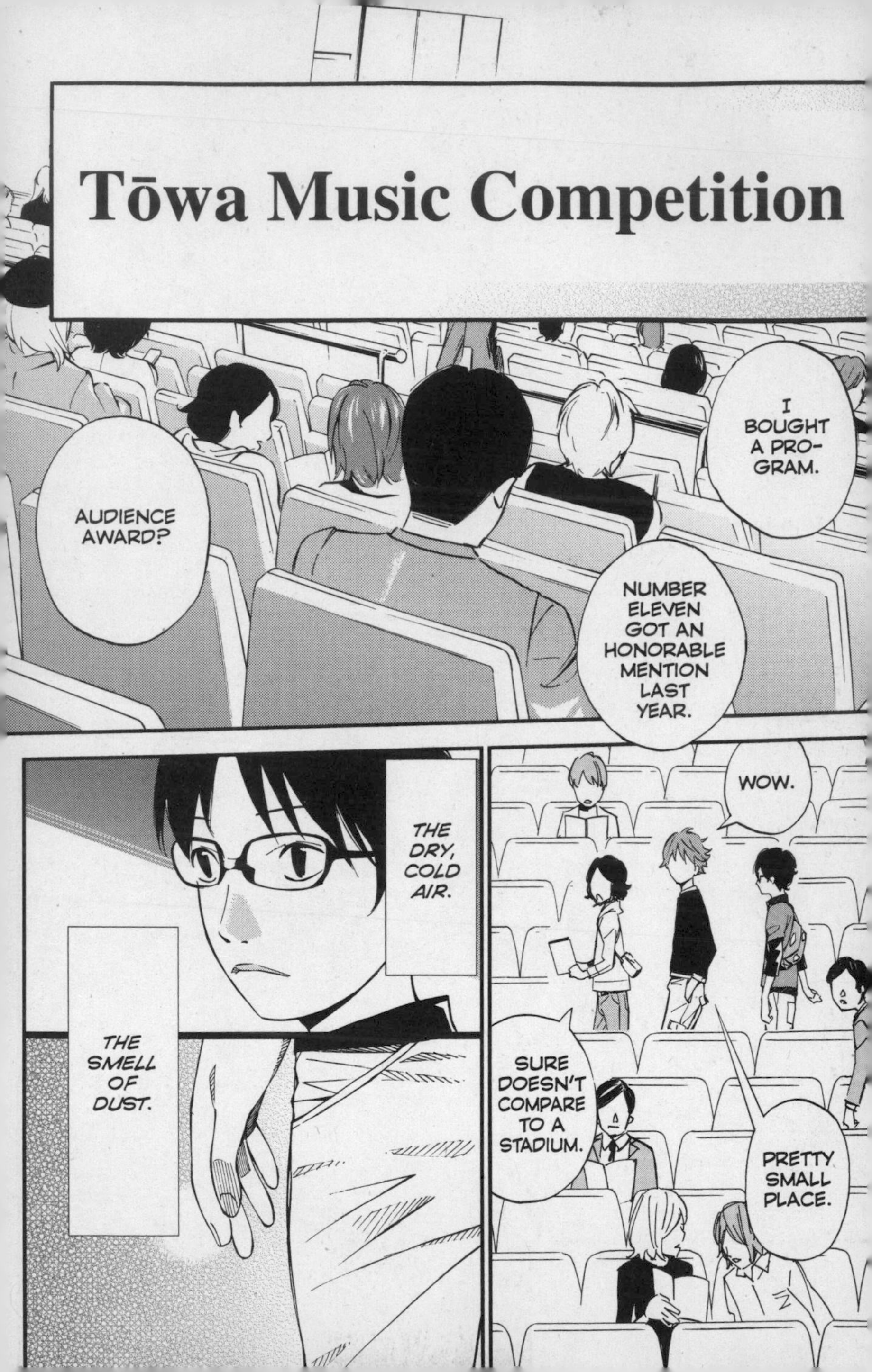
Tōwa Music Competition
I BOUGHT A PRO-GRAM.
NUMBER ELEVEN GOT AN HONORABLE MENTION LAST YEAR.
AUDIENCE AWARD?
WOW.
SURE DOESN'T COMPARE TO A STADIUM.
PRETTY SMALL PLACE.
THE DRY, COLD AIR.
THE SMELL OF DUST.

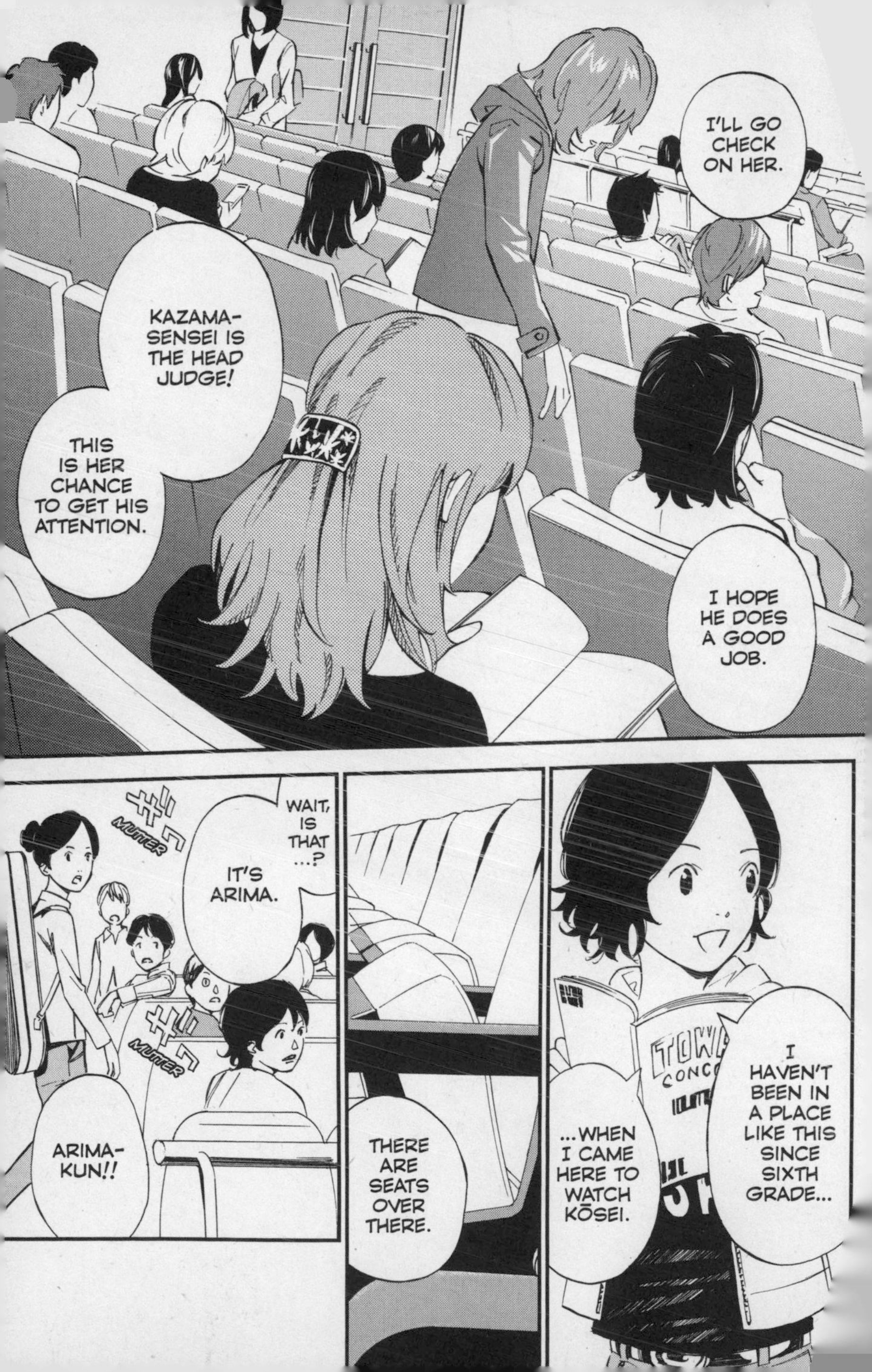
I'LL GO CHECK ON HER.
KAZAMA-SENSEI IS THE HEAD JUDGE!
THIS IS HER CHANCE TO GET HIS ATTENTION.
I HOPE HE DOES A GOOD JOB.
I HAVEN'T BEEN IN A PLACE LIKE THIS SINCE SIXTH GRADE...
...WHEN I CAME HERE TO WATCH KŌSEI.
THERE ARE SEATS OVER THERE.
WAIT, IS THAT ...?
IT'S ARIMA.
MUTTER
MUTTER
ARIMA-KUN!!

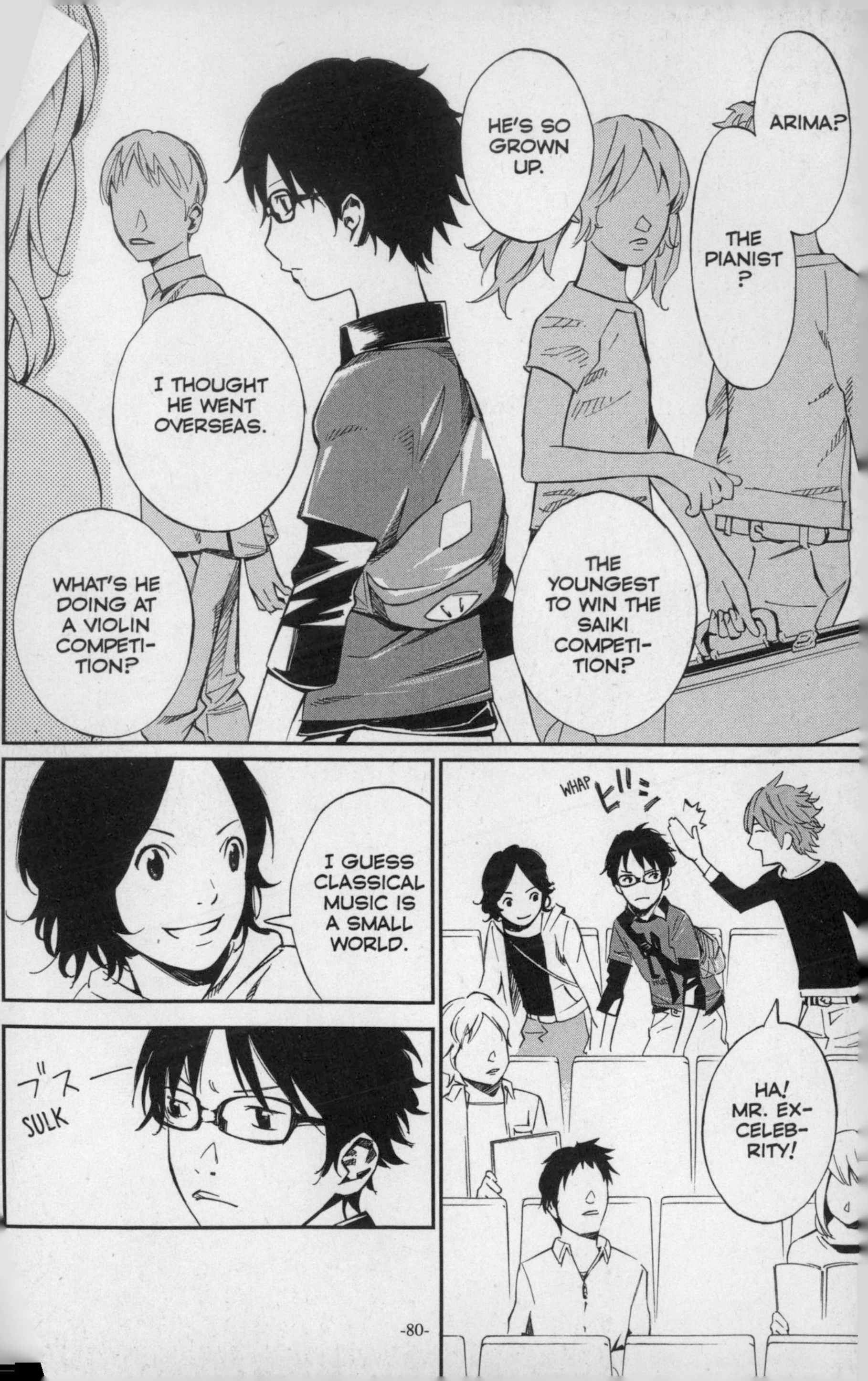
ARIMA?
THE PIANIST?
HE'S SO GROWN UP.
THE YOUNGEST TO WIN THE SAIKI COMPETITION?
I THOUGHT HE WENT OVERSEAS.
WHAT'S HE DOING AT A VIOLIN COMPETITION?
WHAP
HA! MR. EX-CELEBRITY!
I GUESS CLASSICAL MUSIC IS A SMALL WORLD.
SULK

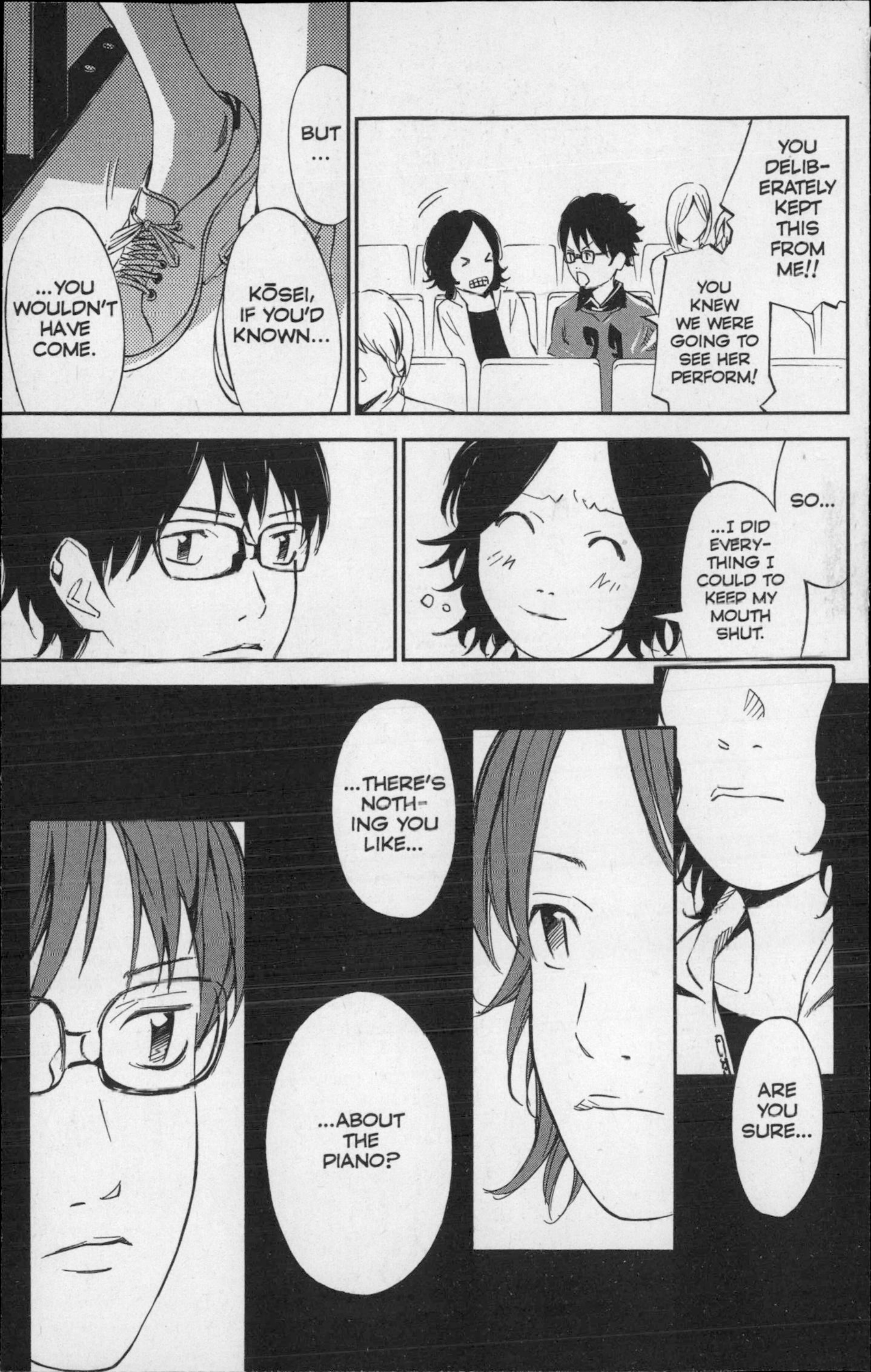
YOU DELIBERATELY KEPT THIS FROM ME!!
YOU KNEW WE WERE GOING TO SEE HER PERFORM!
BUT ...
KŌSEI, IF YOU'D KNOWN...
...YOU WOULDN'T HAVE COME.
SO...
...I DID EVERYTHING I COULD TO KEEP MY MOUTH SHUT.
ARE YOU SURE...
...THERE'S NOTHING YOU LIKE...
...ABOUT THE PIANO?

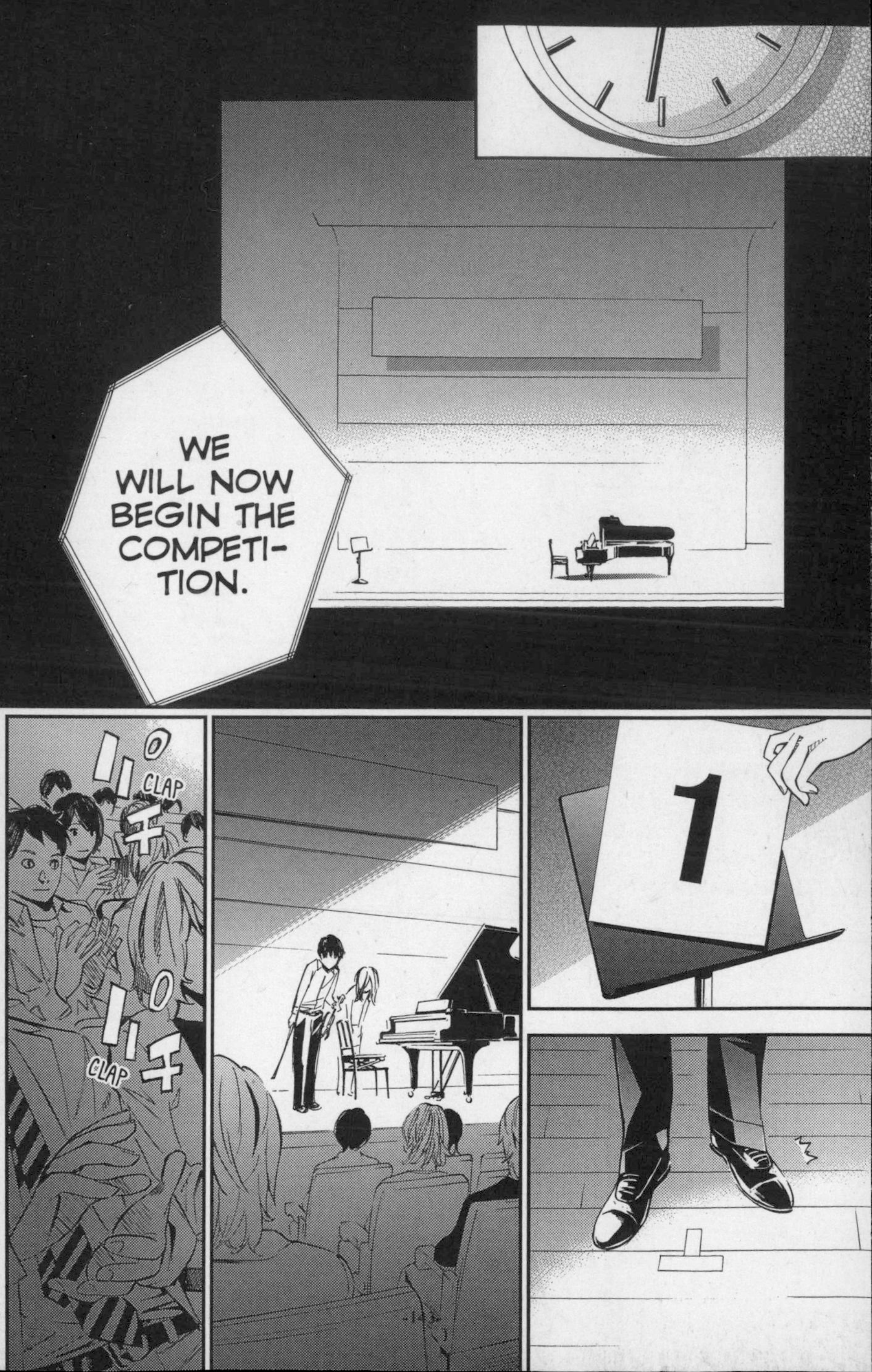
WE WILL NOW BEGIN THE COMPETITION.
1
パチ
CLAP
パチ
CLAP

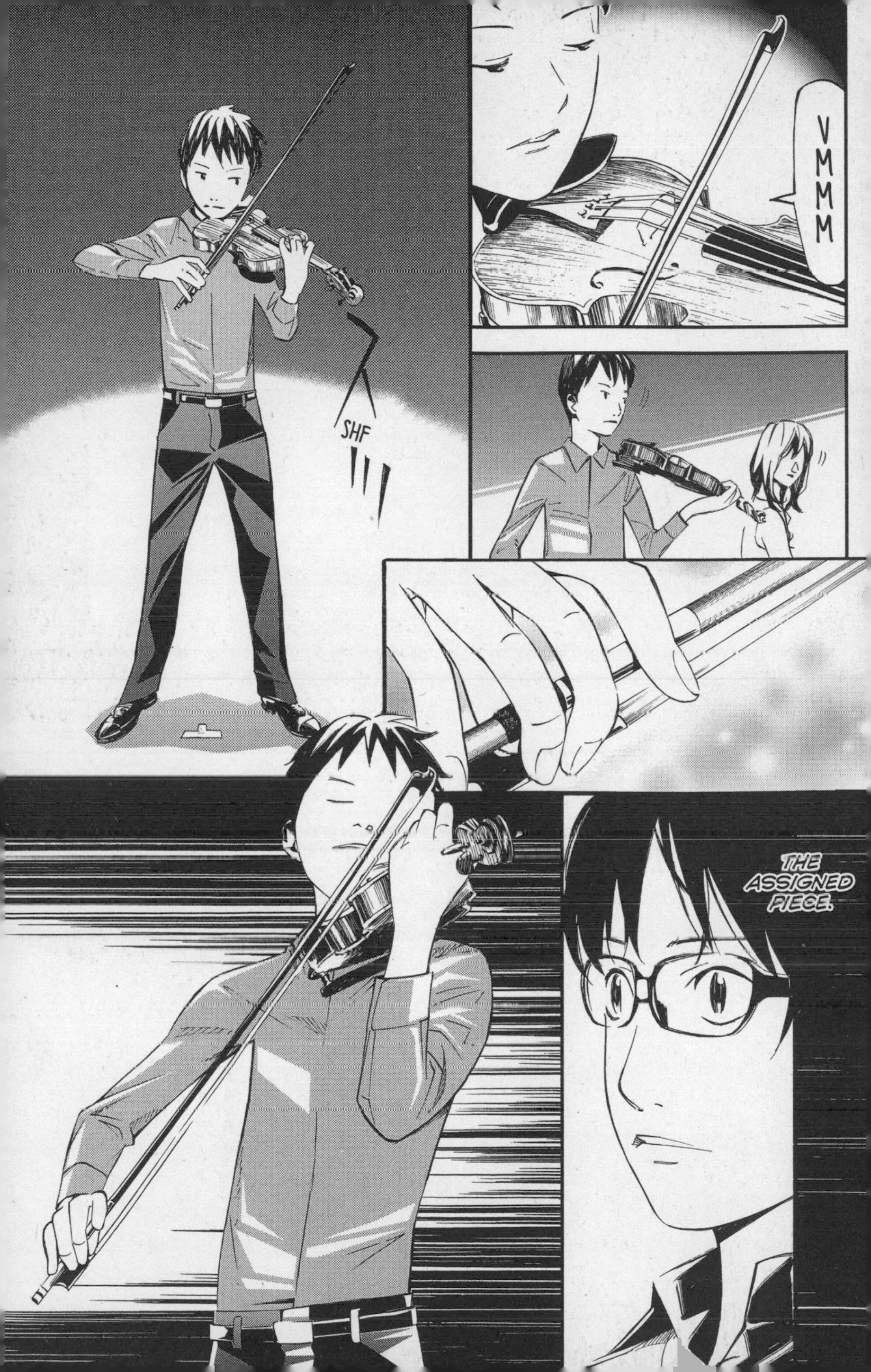
VMMM
SHF
THE ASSIGNED PIECE.

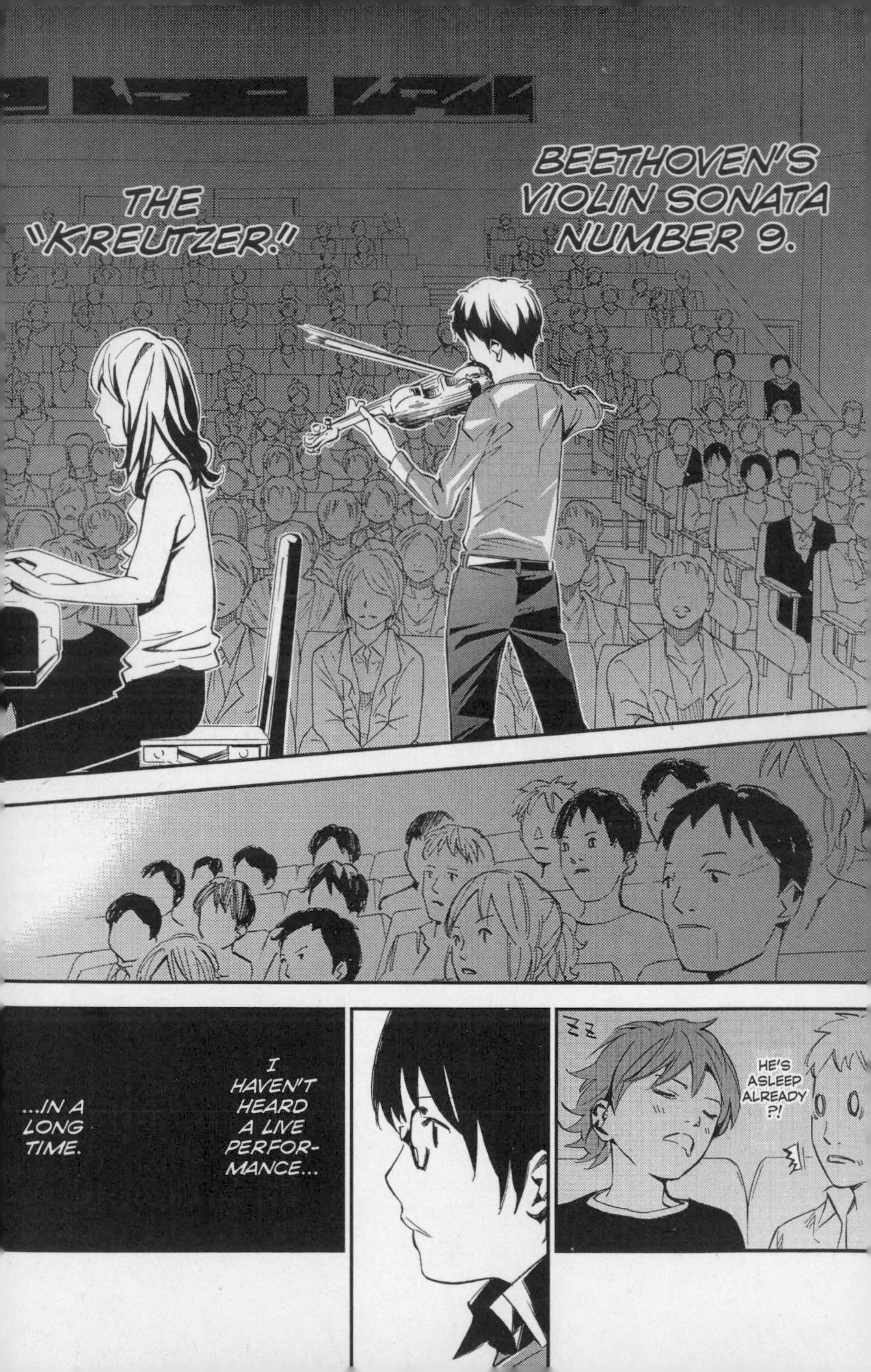
BEETHOVEN'S VIOLIN SONATA NUMBER 9.
THE "KREUTZER."
Z Z
HE'S ASLEEP ALREADY ?!
I HAVEN'T HEARD A LIVE PERFOR-MANCE...
...IN A LONG TIME.

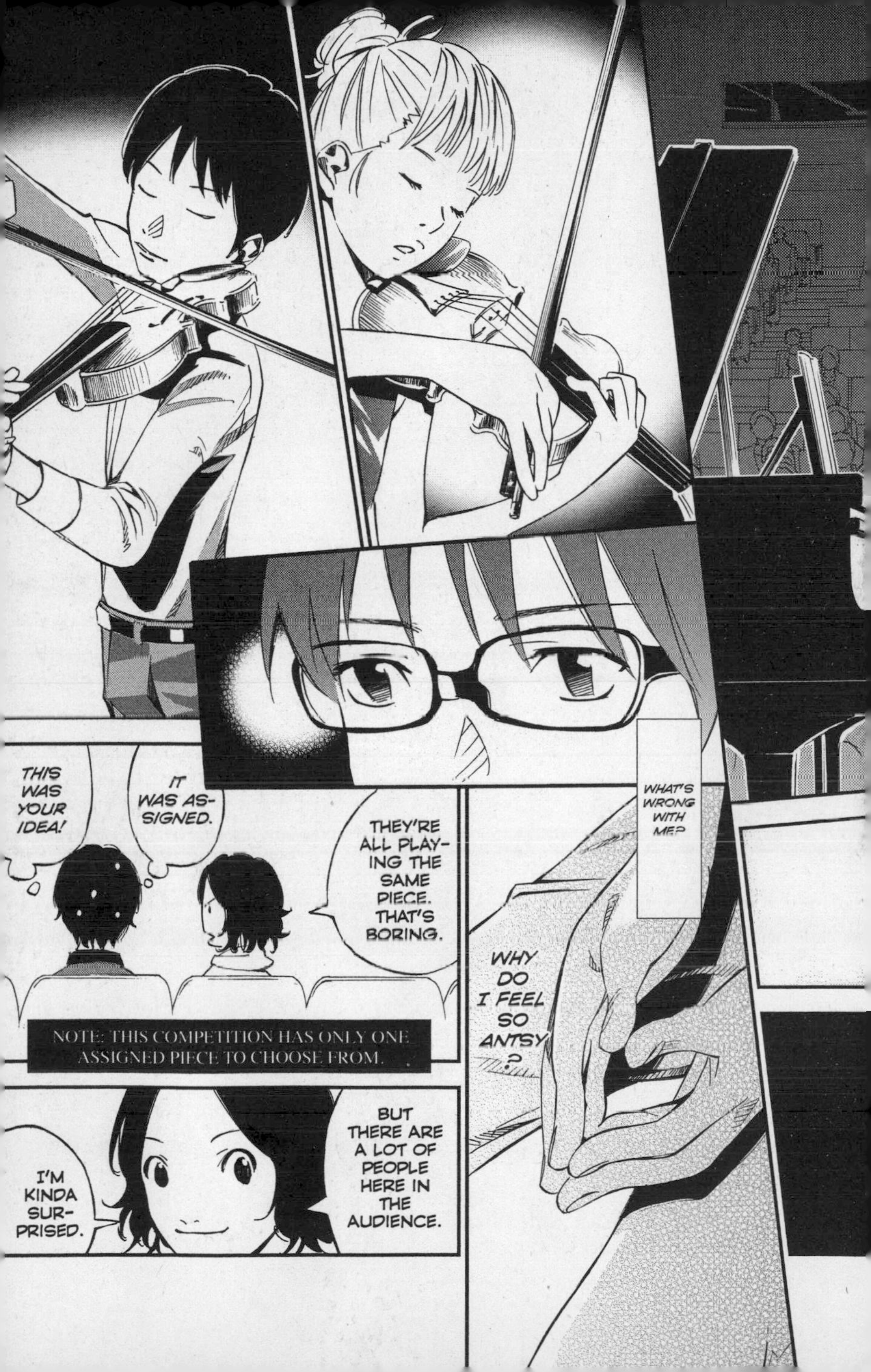
WHAT'S WRONG WITH ME?
WHY DO I FEEL SO ANTSY?
THEY'RE ALL PLAYING THE SAME PIECE. THAT'S BORING.
IT WAS ASSIGNED.
THIS WAS YOUR IDEA!
NOTE: THIS COMPETITION HAS ONLY ONE ASSIGNED PIECE TO CHOOSE FROM.
BUT THERE ARE A LOT OF PEOPLE HERE IN THE AUDIENCE.
I'M KINDA SURPRISED.

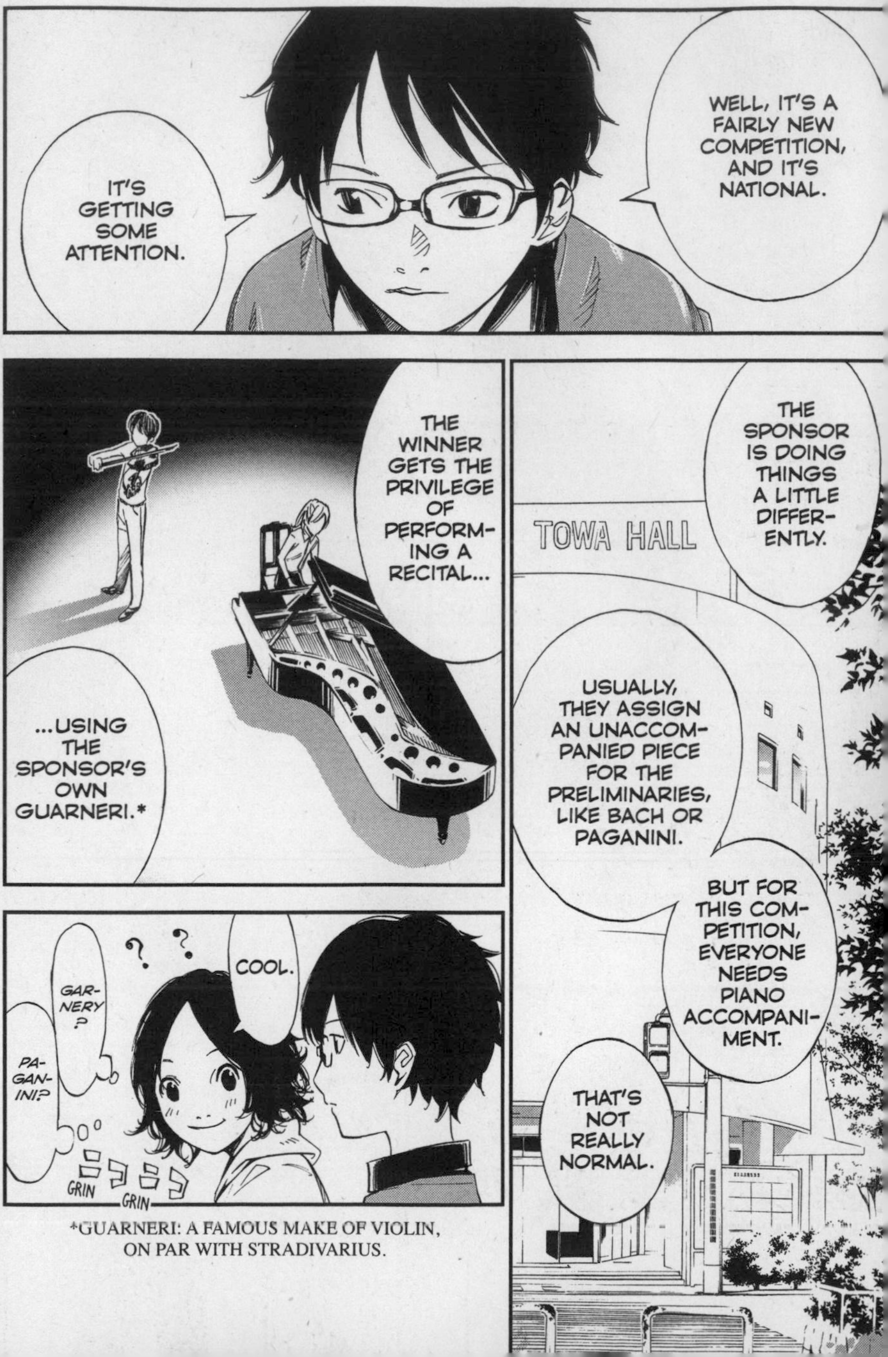
WELL, IT'S A FAIRLY NEW COMPETITION, AND IT'S NATIONAL.
IT'S GETTING SOME ATTENTION.
THE SPONSOR IS DOING THINGS A LITTLE DIFFERENTLY.
TOWA HALL
USUALLY, THEY ASSIGN AN UNACCOMPANIED PIECE FOR THE PRELIMINARIES, LIKE BACH OR PAGANINI.
BUT FOR THIS COMPETITION, EVERYONE NEEDS PIANO ACCOMPANIMENT.
THAT'S NOT REALLY NORMAL.
THE WINNER GETS THE PRIVILEGE OF PERFORMING A RECITAL...
...USING THE SPONSOR'S OWN GUARNERI.*
COOL.
GARNERY?
PAGANINI?
GRIN
GRIN

*GUARNERI: A FAMOUS MAKE OF VIOLIN, ON PAR WITH STRADIVARIUS.

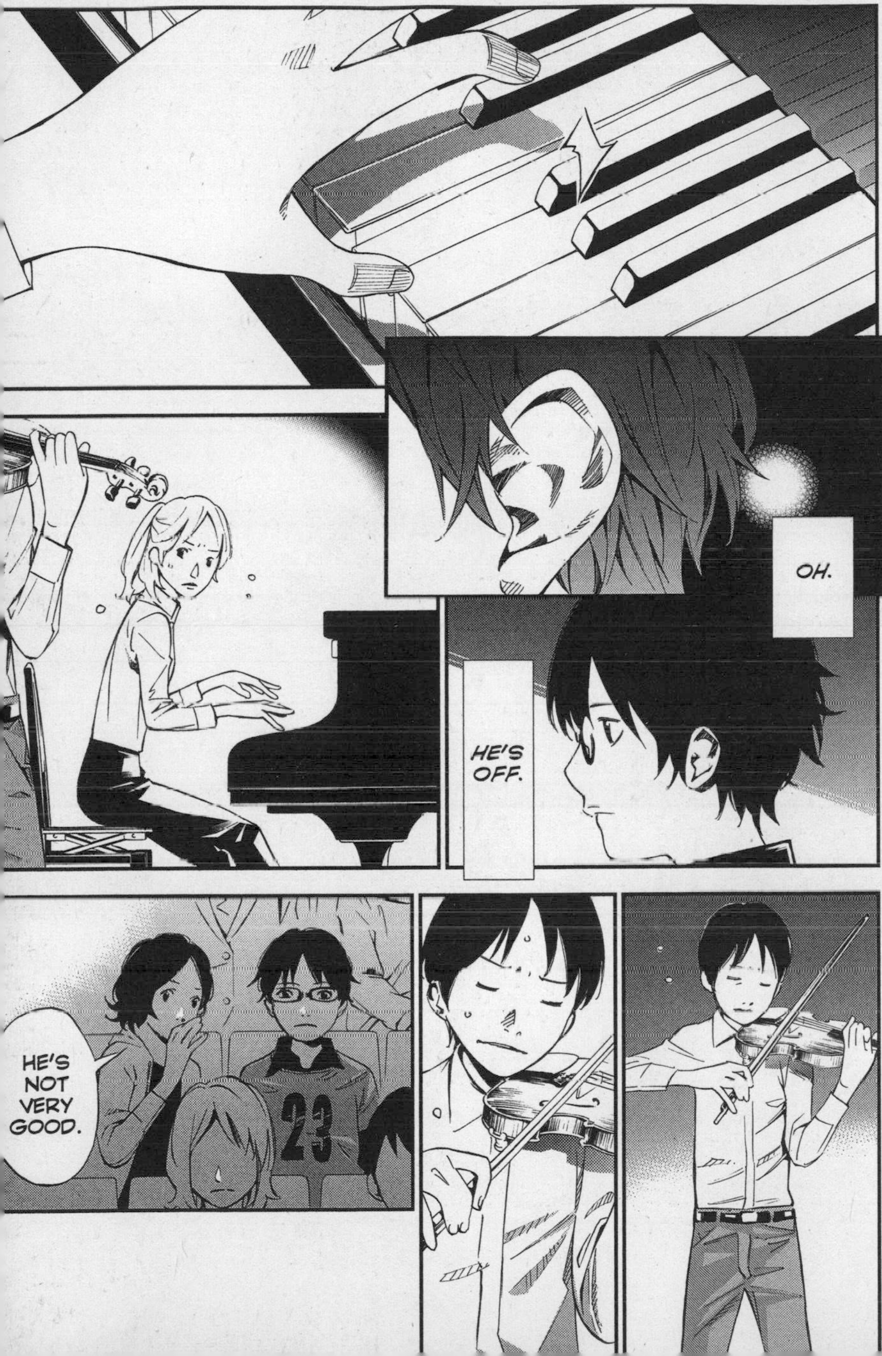
OH.
HE'S OFF.
HE'S NOT VERY GOOD.

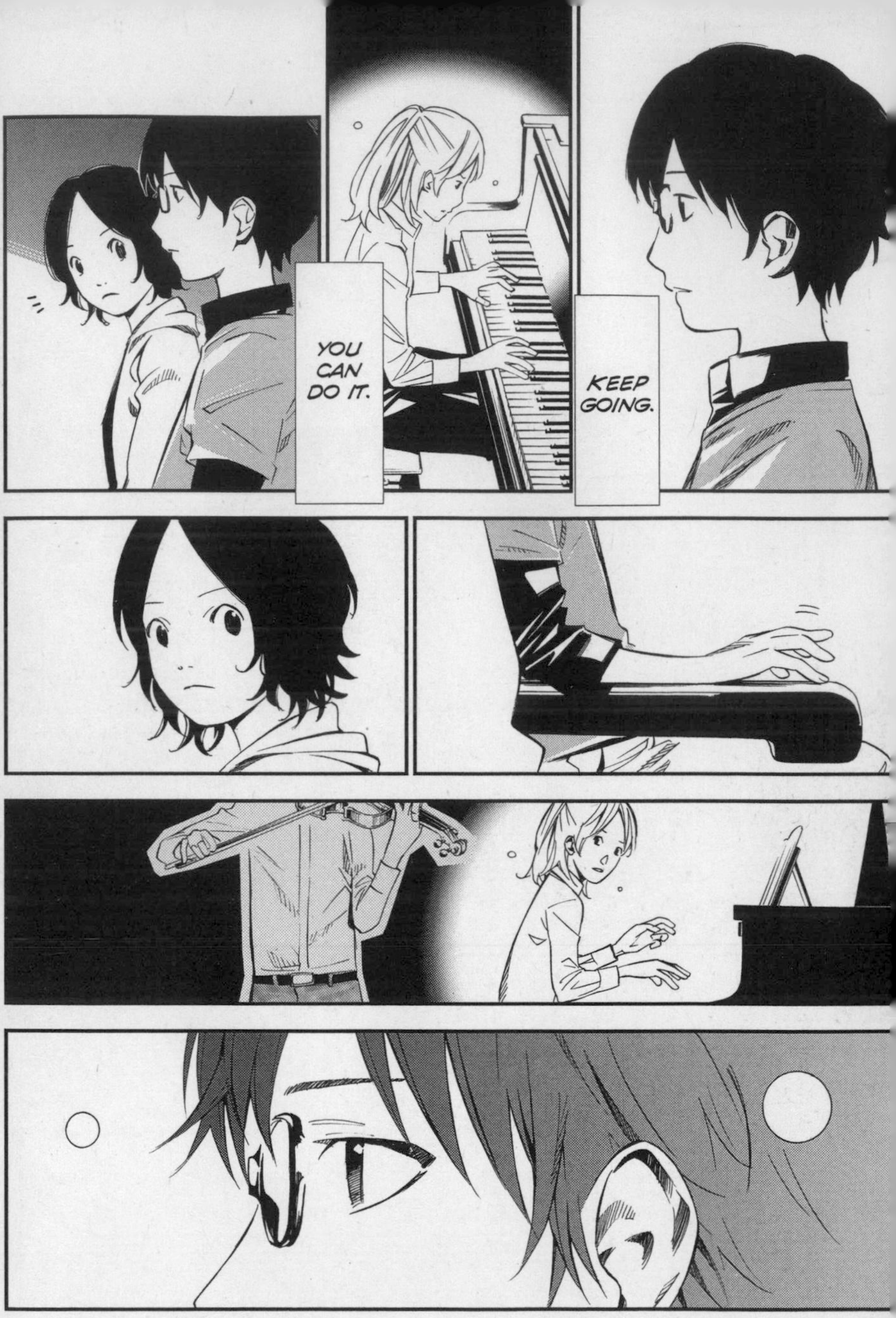
KEEP GOING.
YOU CAN DO IT.

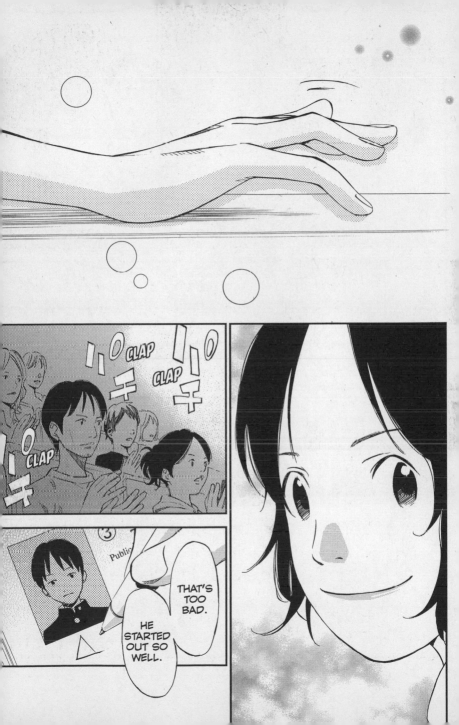

CLAP

CLAP

CLAP

③
Public

THAT'S TOO BAD.

HE STARTED OUT SO WELL.

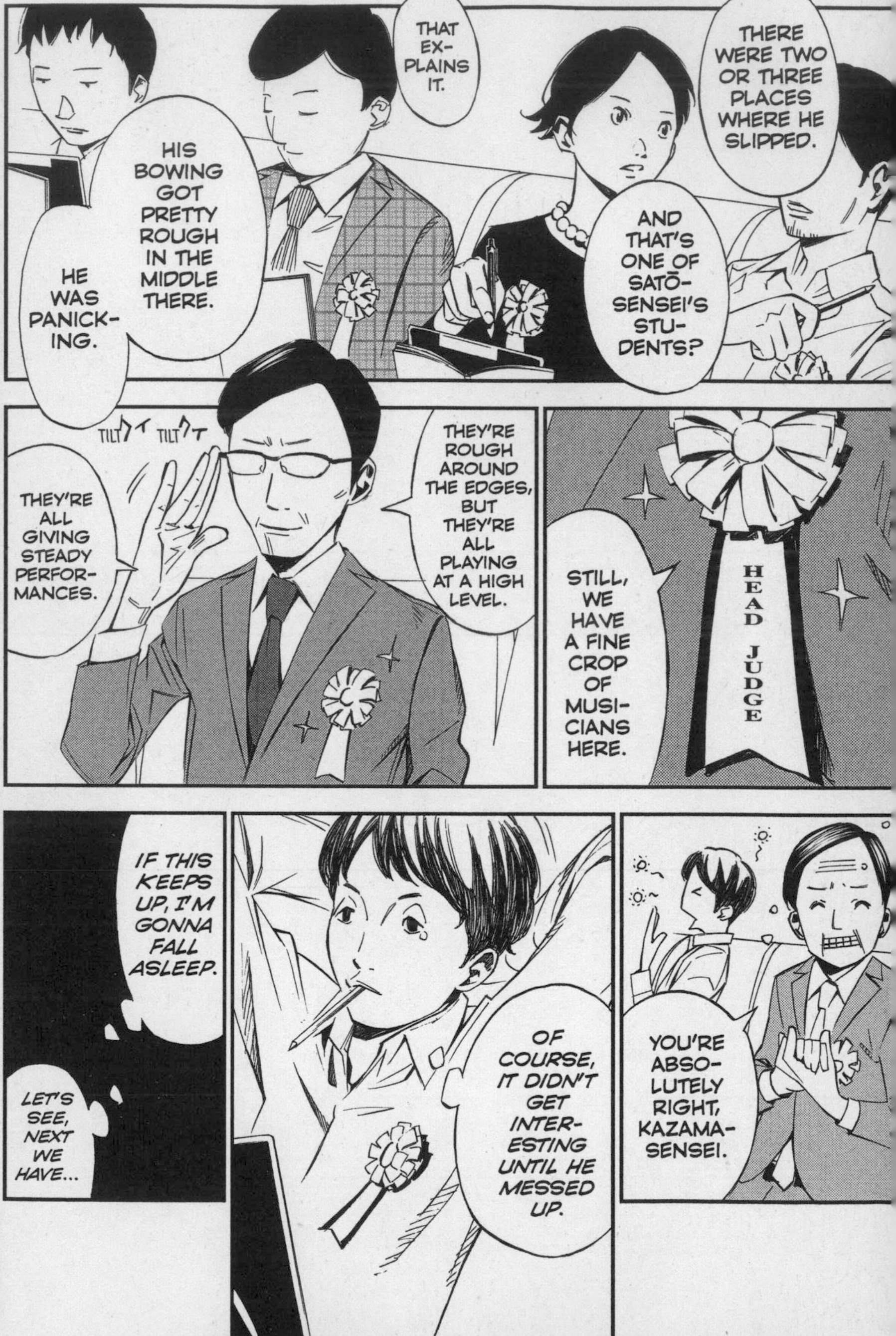
THERE WERE TWO OR THREE PLACES WHERE HE SLIPPED.
AND THAT'S ONE OF SATŌ-SENSEI'S STUDENTS?
THAT EX-PLAINS IT.
HIS BOWING GOT PRETTY ROUGH IN THE MIDDLE THERE.
HE WAS PANICK-ING.
STILL, WE HAVE A FINE CROP OF MUSI-CIANS HERE.
HEAD JUDGE
TILT TILT
THEY'RE ROUGH AROUND THE EDGES, BUT THEY'RE ALL PLAYING AT A HIGH LEVEL.
THEY'RE ALL GIVING STEADY PERFOR-MANCES.
YOU'RE ABSO-LUTELY RIGHT, KAZAMA-SENSEI.
OF COURSE, IT DIDN'T GET INTER-ESTING UNTIL HE MESSED UP.
IF THIS KEEPS UP, I'M GONNA FALL ASLEEP.
LET'S SEE, NEXT WE HAVE...

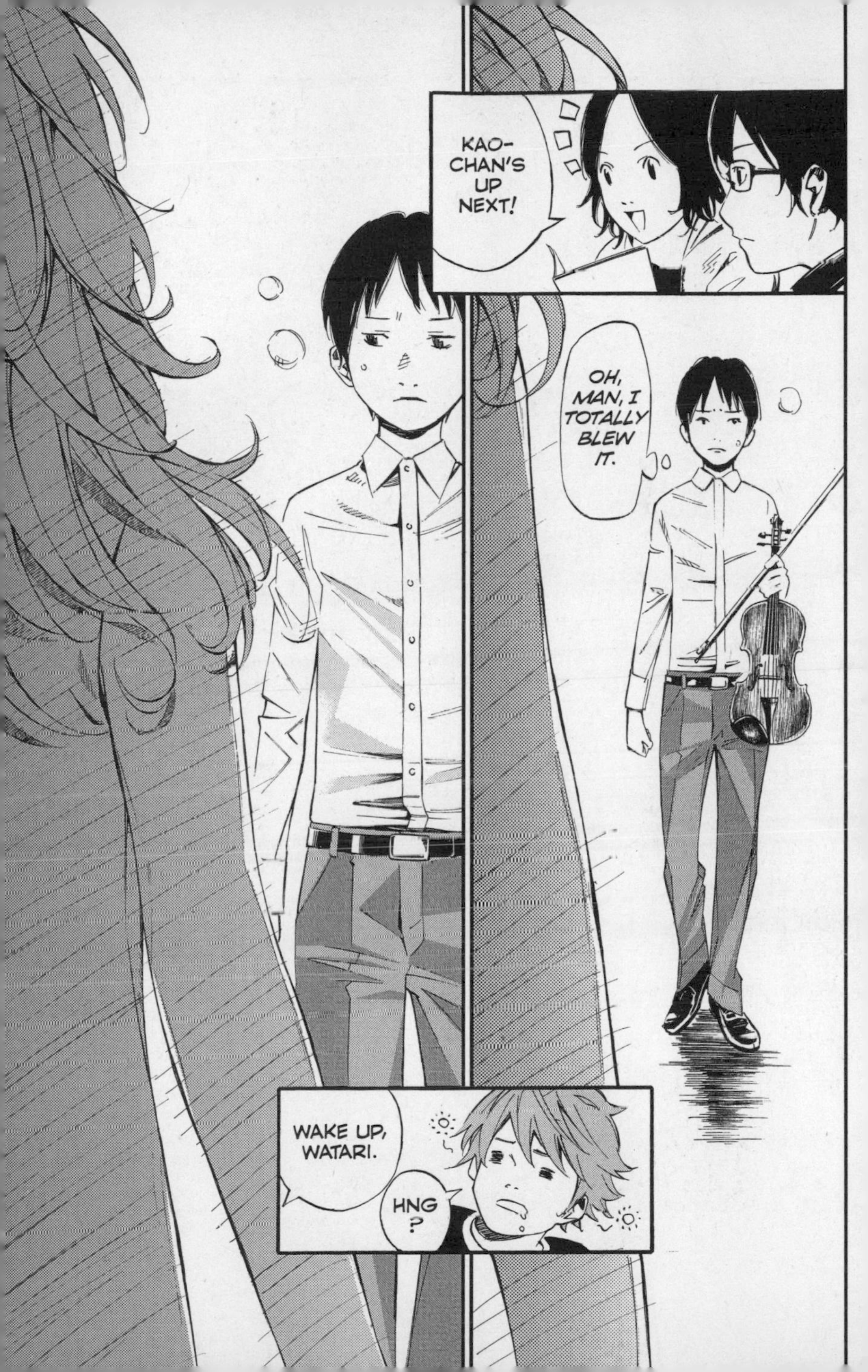
KAO-CHAN'S UP NEXT!
OH, MAN, I TOTALLY BLEW IT.
WAKE UP, WATARI.
HNG?

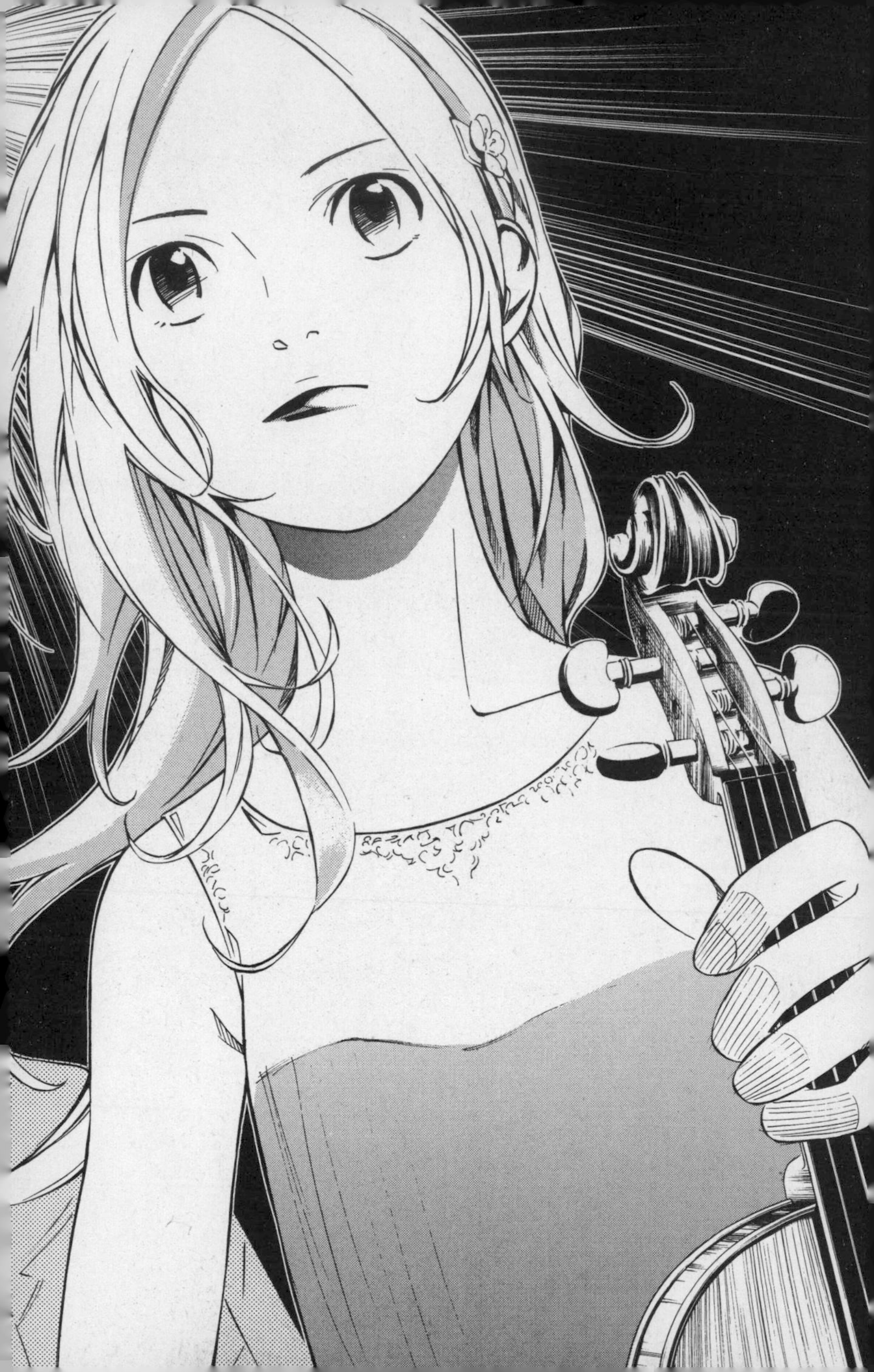

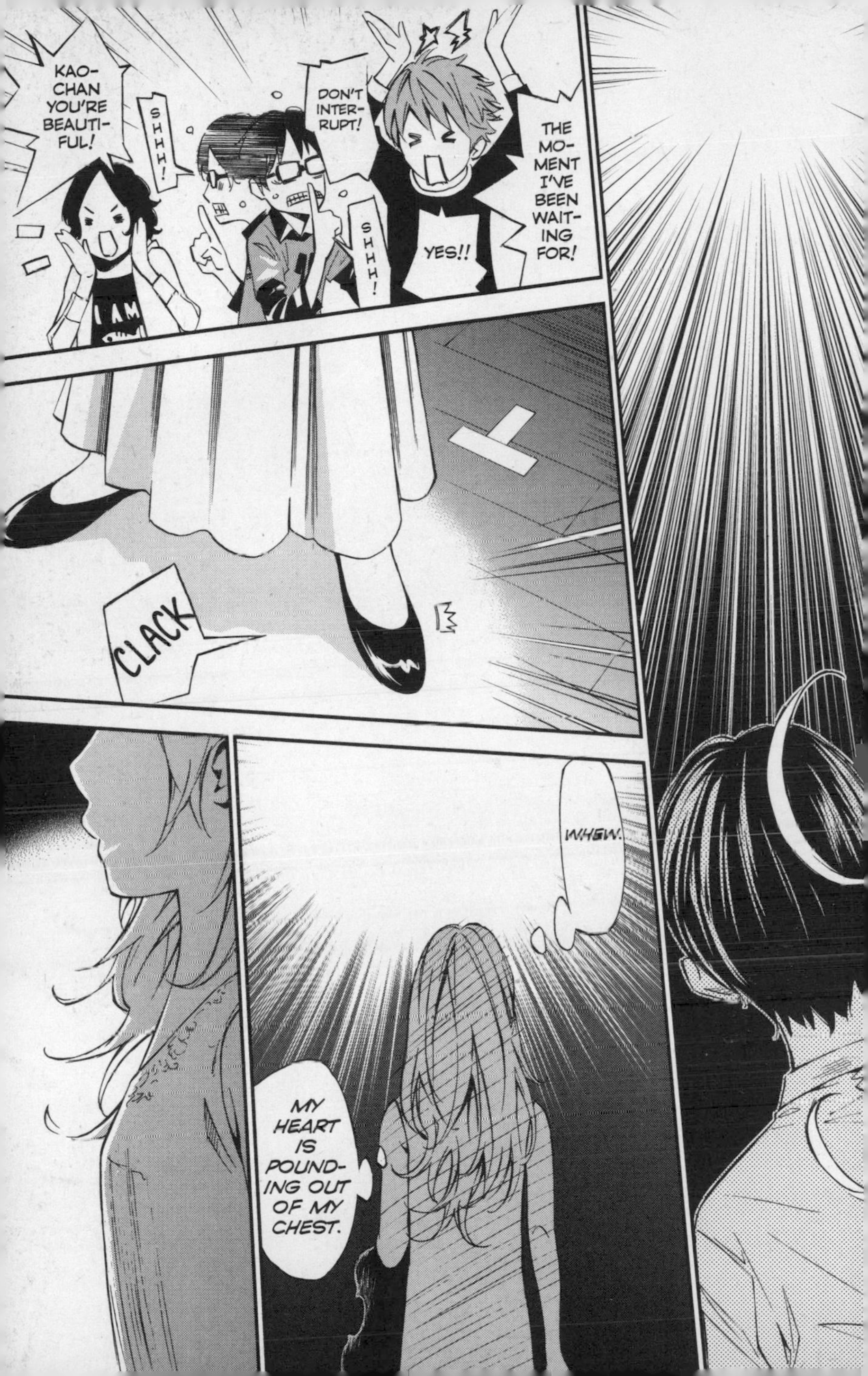
THE MOMENT I'VE BEEN WAITING FOR!
DON'T INTERRUPT!
YES!!
KAO-CHAN YOU'RE BEAUTIFUL!
SHHH!
SHHH!
CLACK
WHEW.
MY HEART IS POUNDING OUT OF MY CHEST.

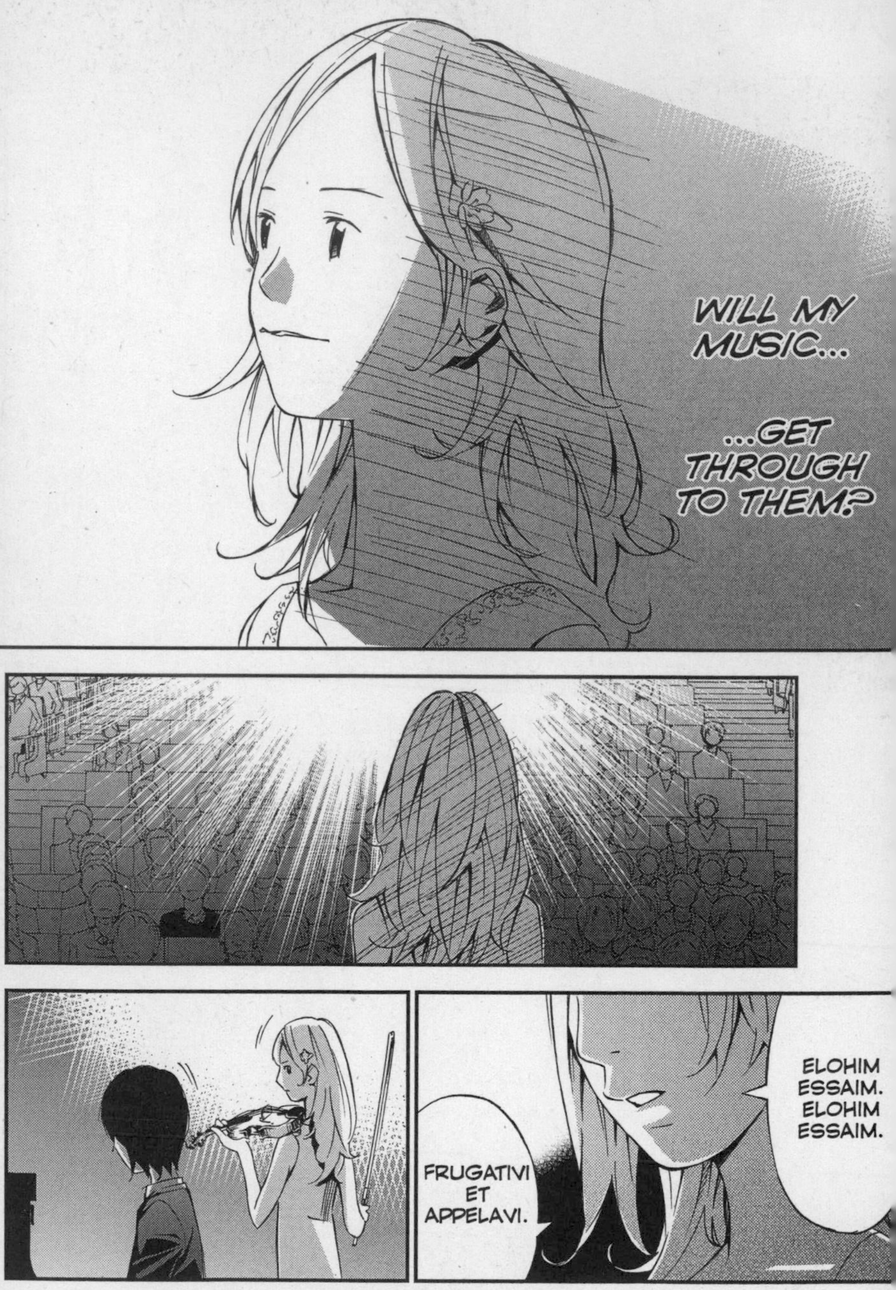
WILL MY MUSIC...
...GET THROUGH TO THEM?
ELOHIM ESSAIM. ELOHIM ESSAIM.
FRUGATIVI ET APPELAVI.

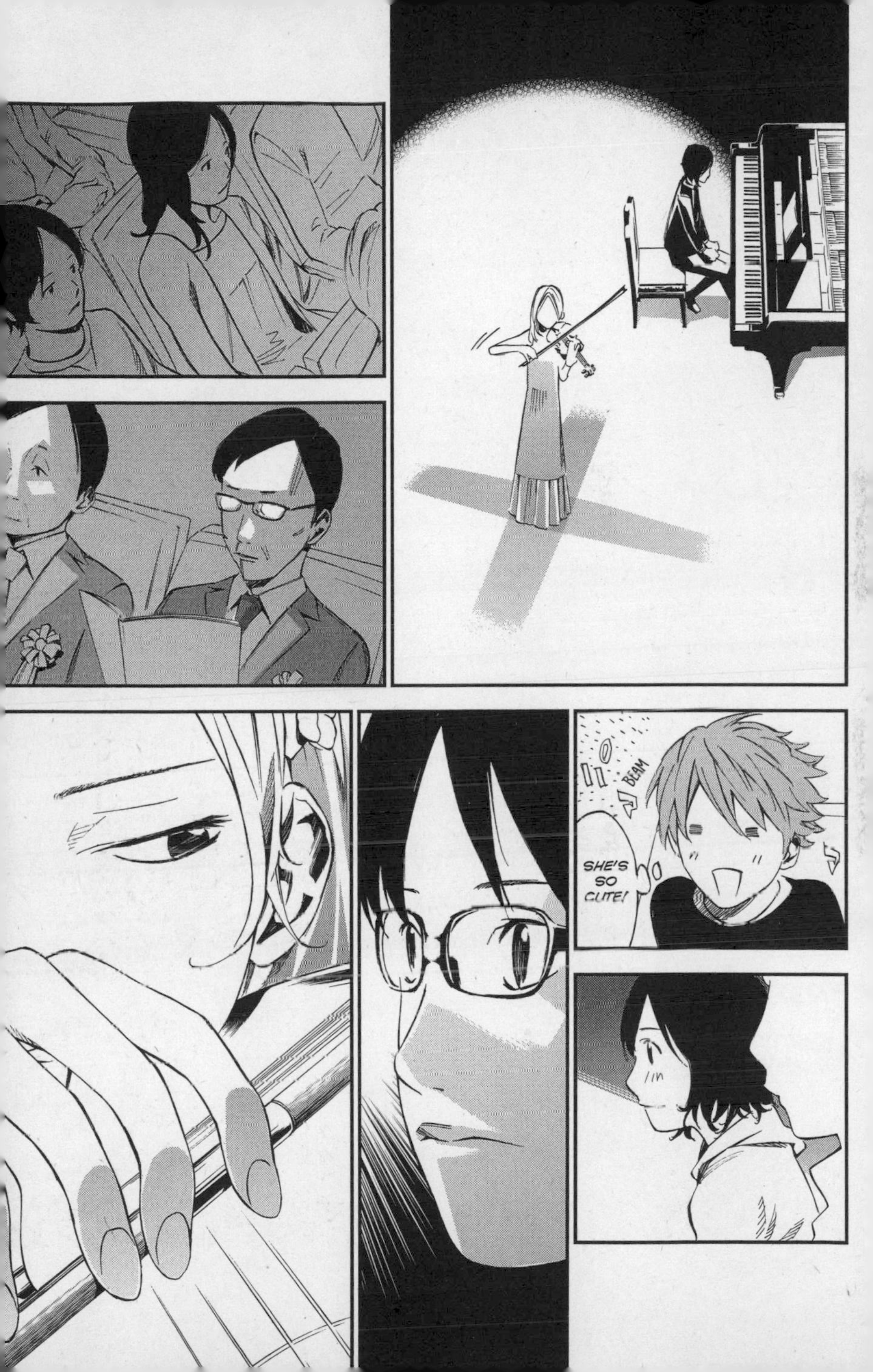
BEAM
SHE'S SO CUTE!

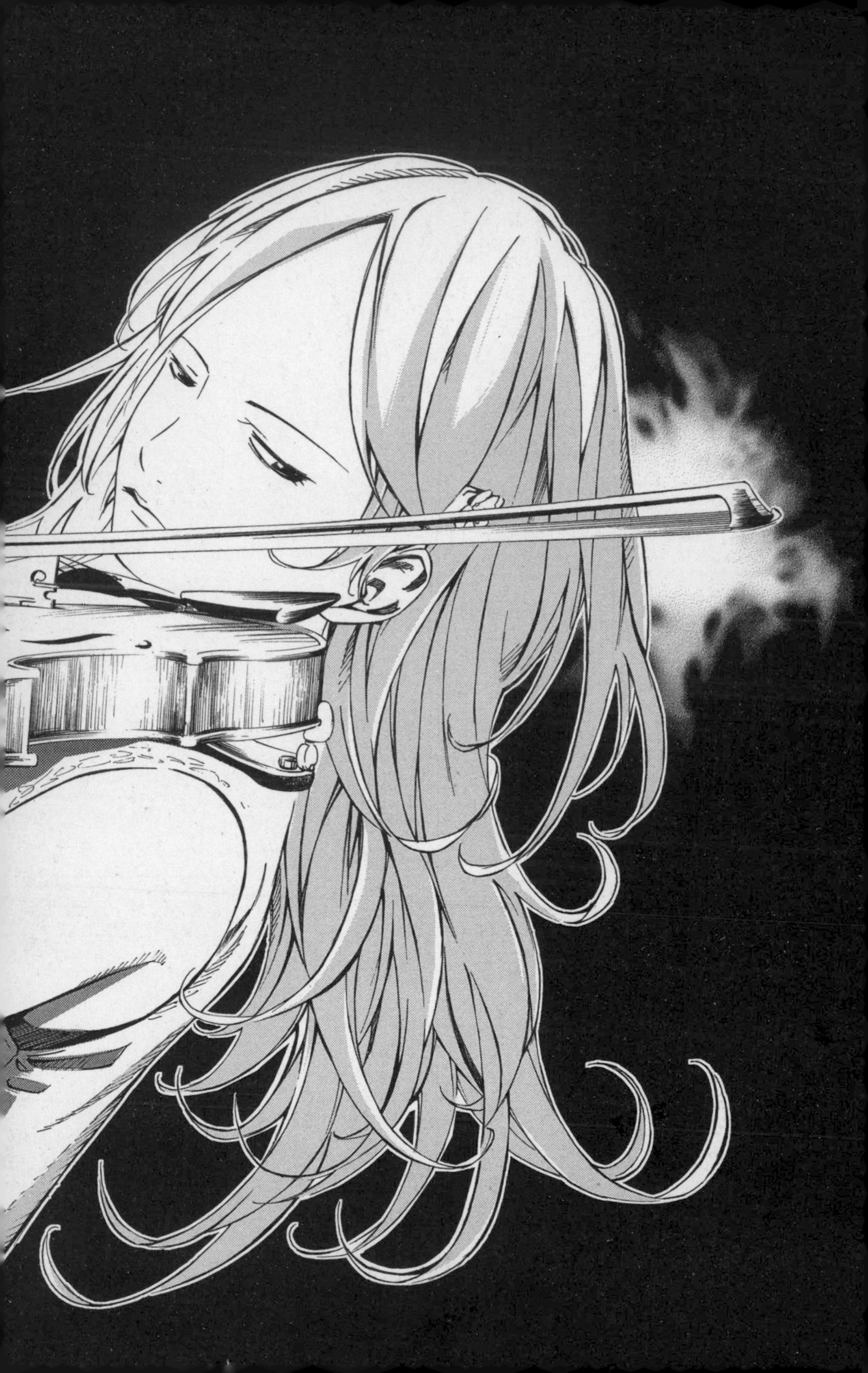

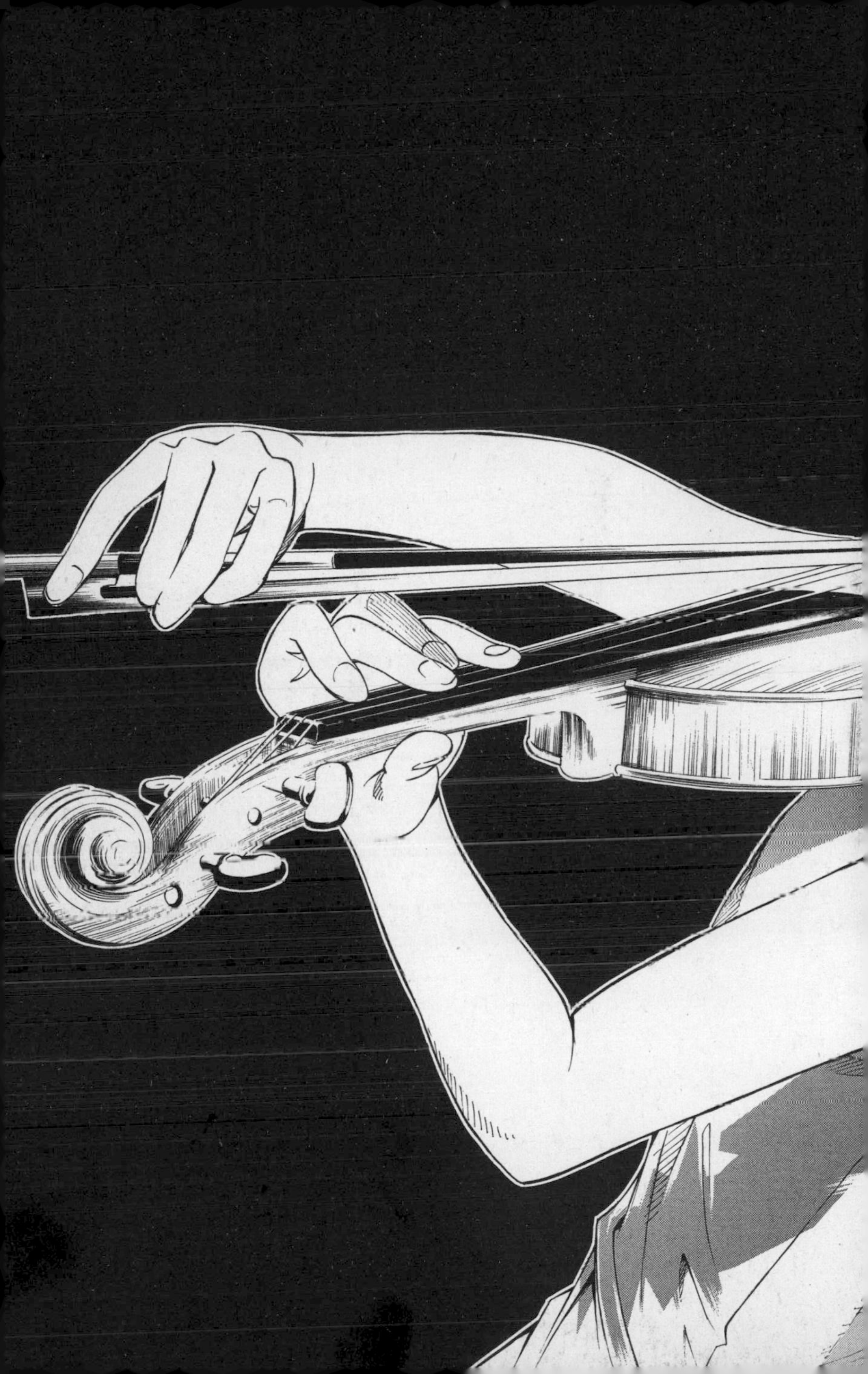

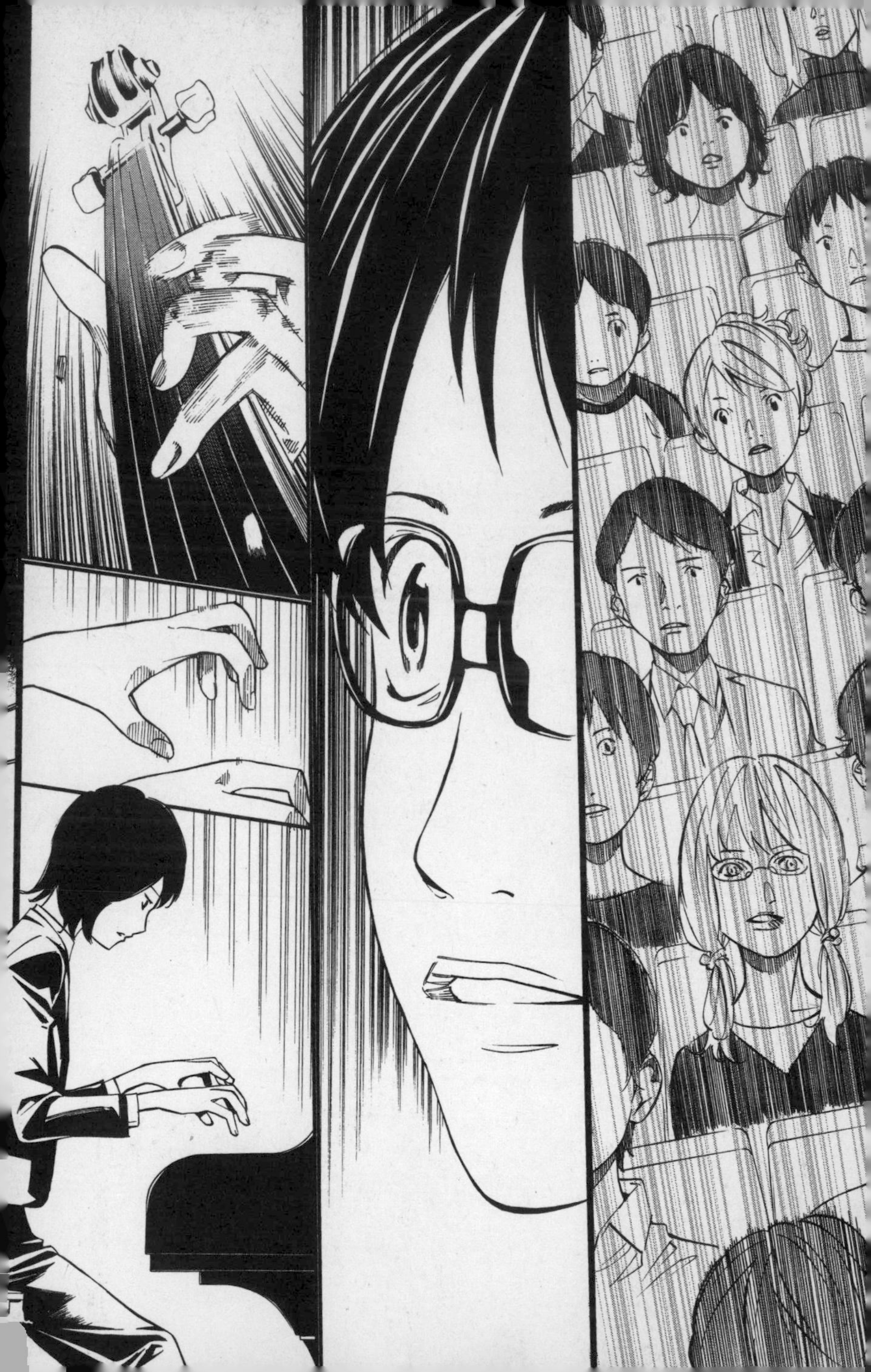

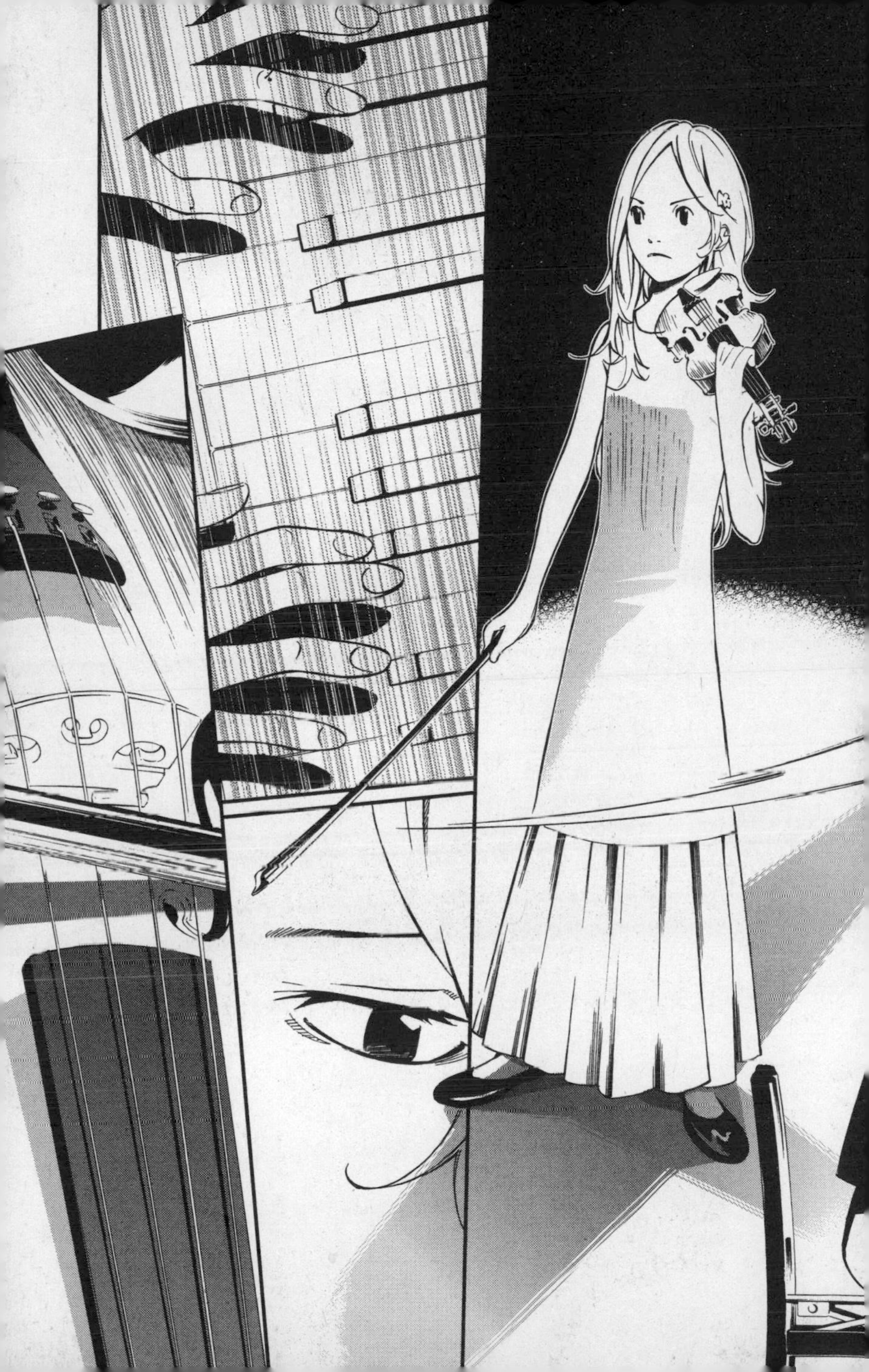

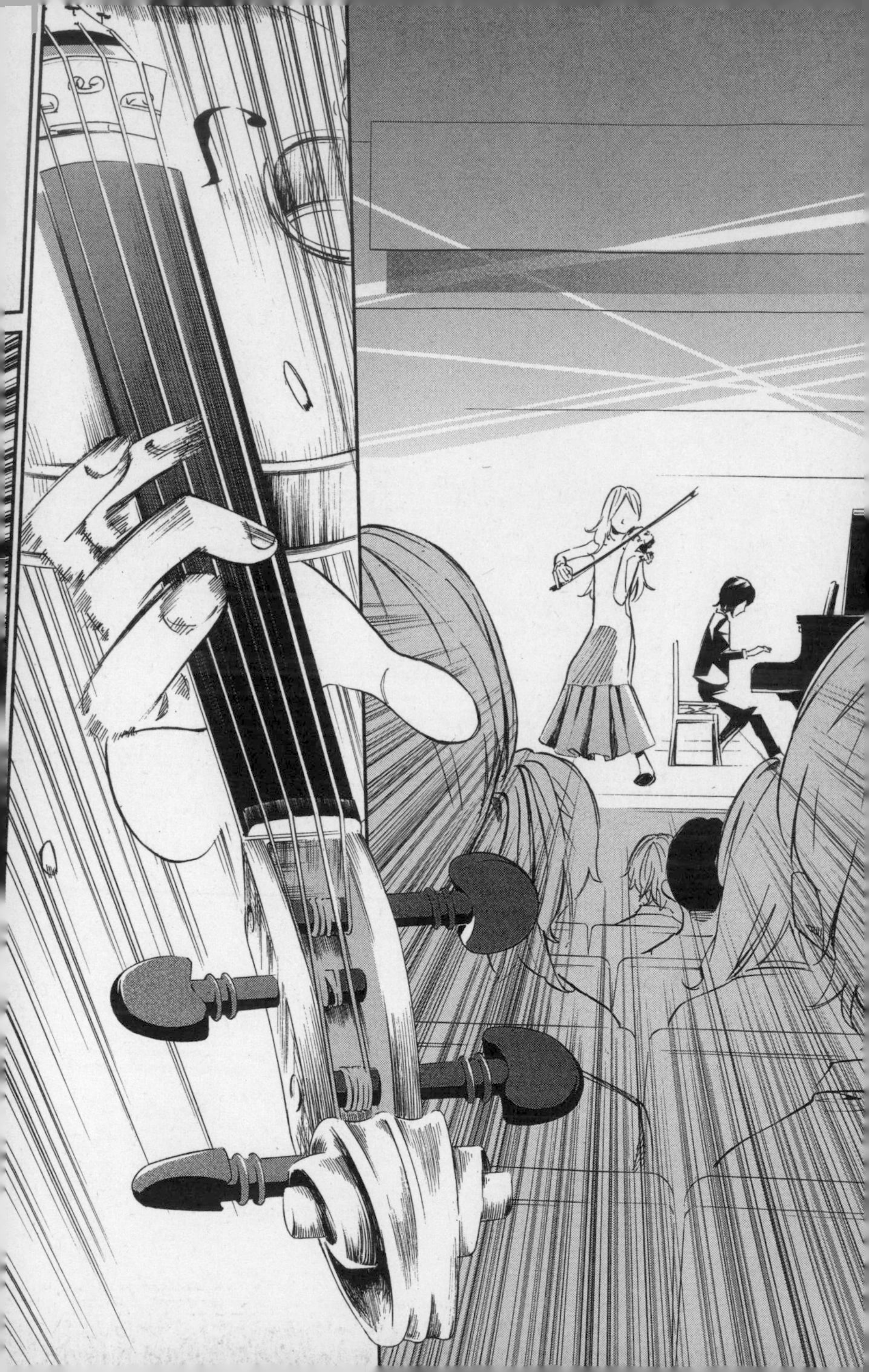

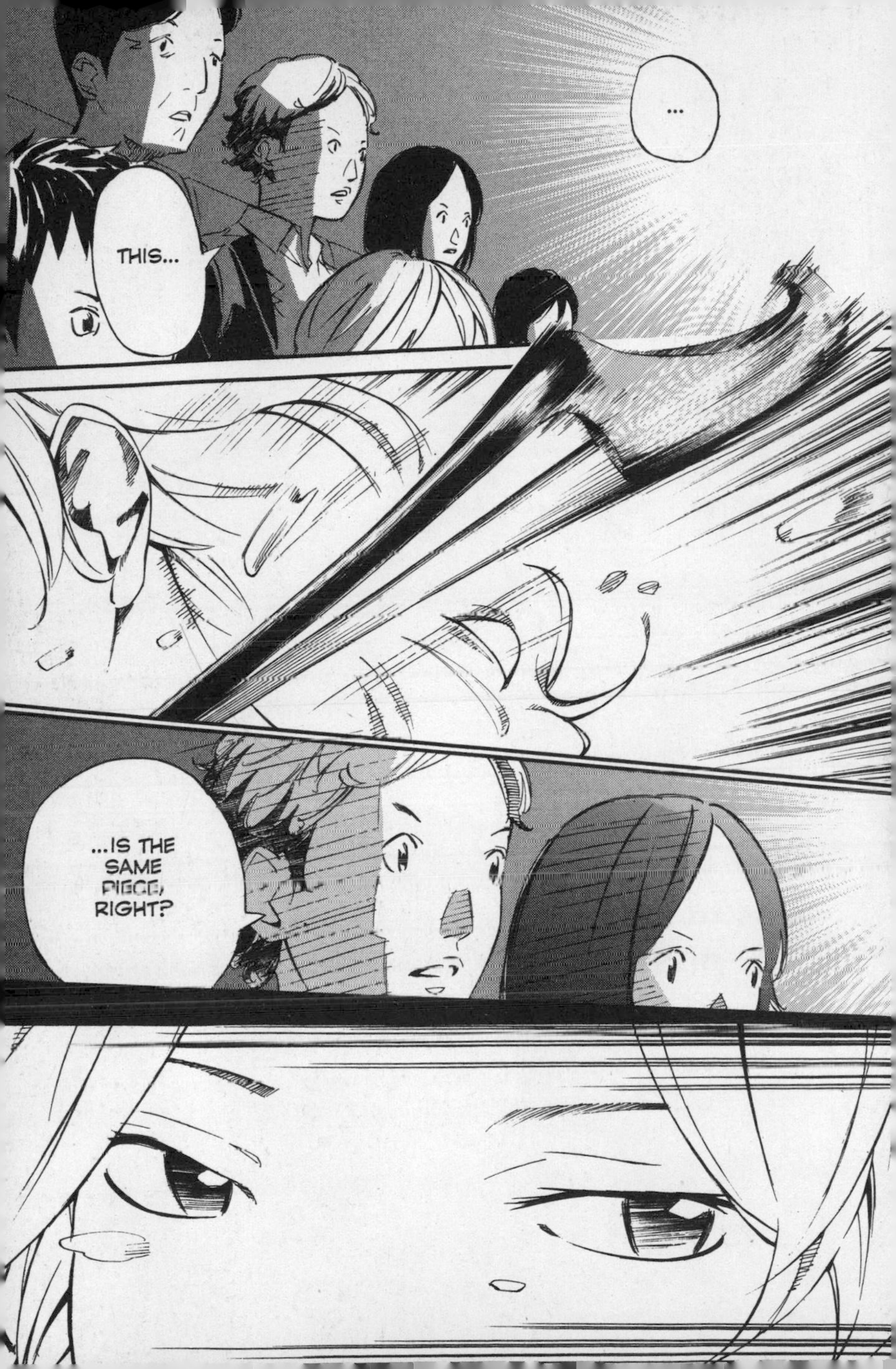
...
THIS...
...IS THE SAME PIECE, RIGHT?

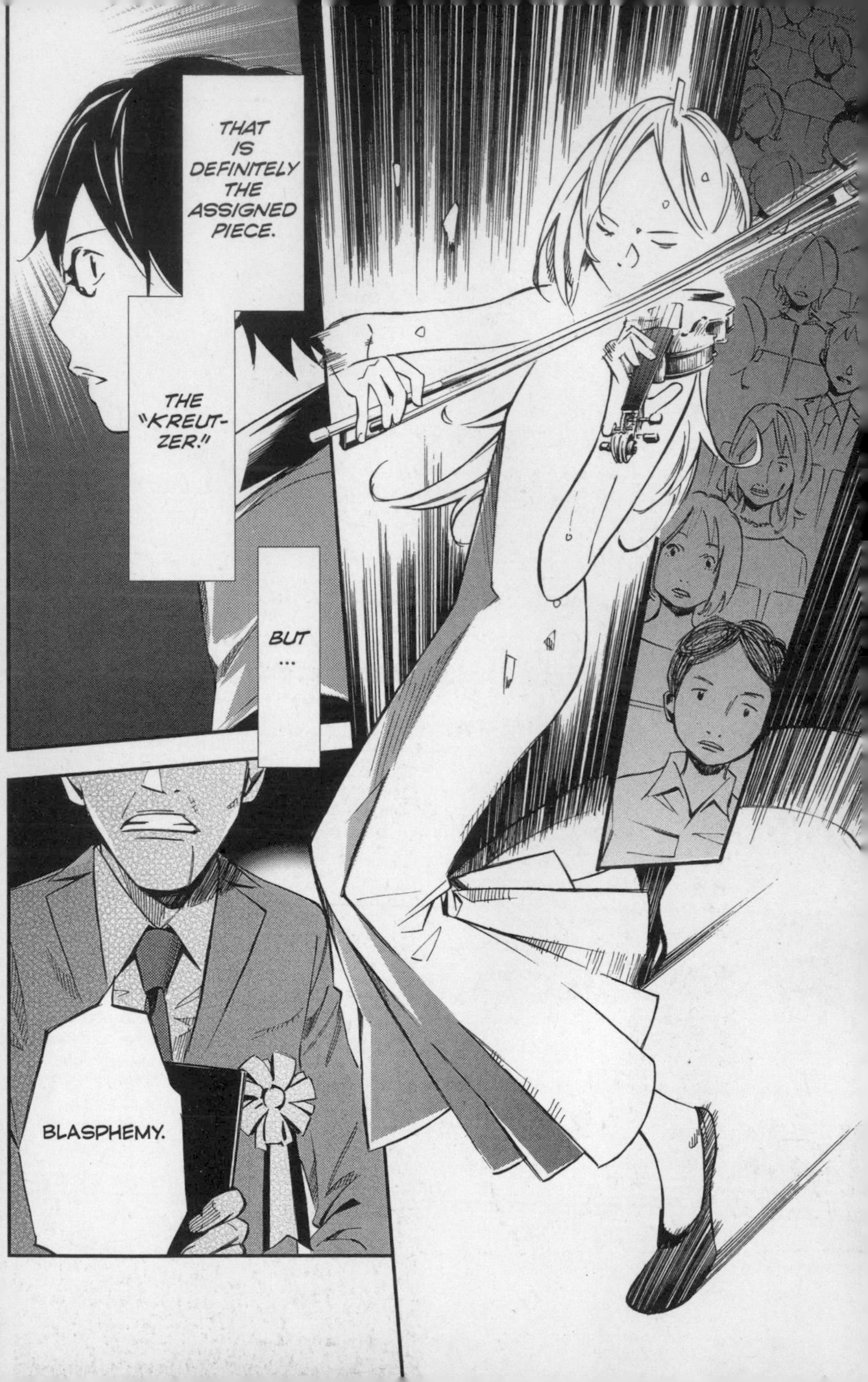
THAT IS DEFINITELY THE ASSIGNED PIECE.
THE "KREUTZER."
BUT ...
BLASPHEMY.

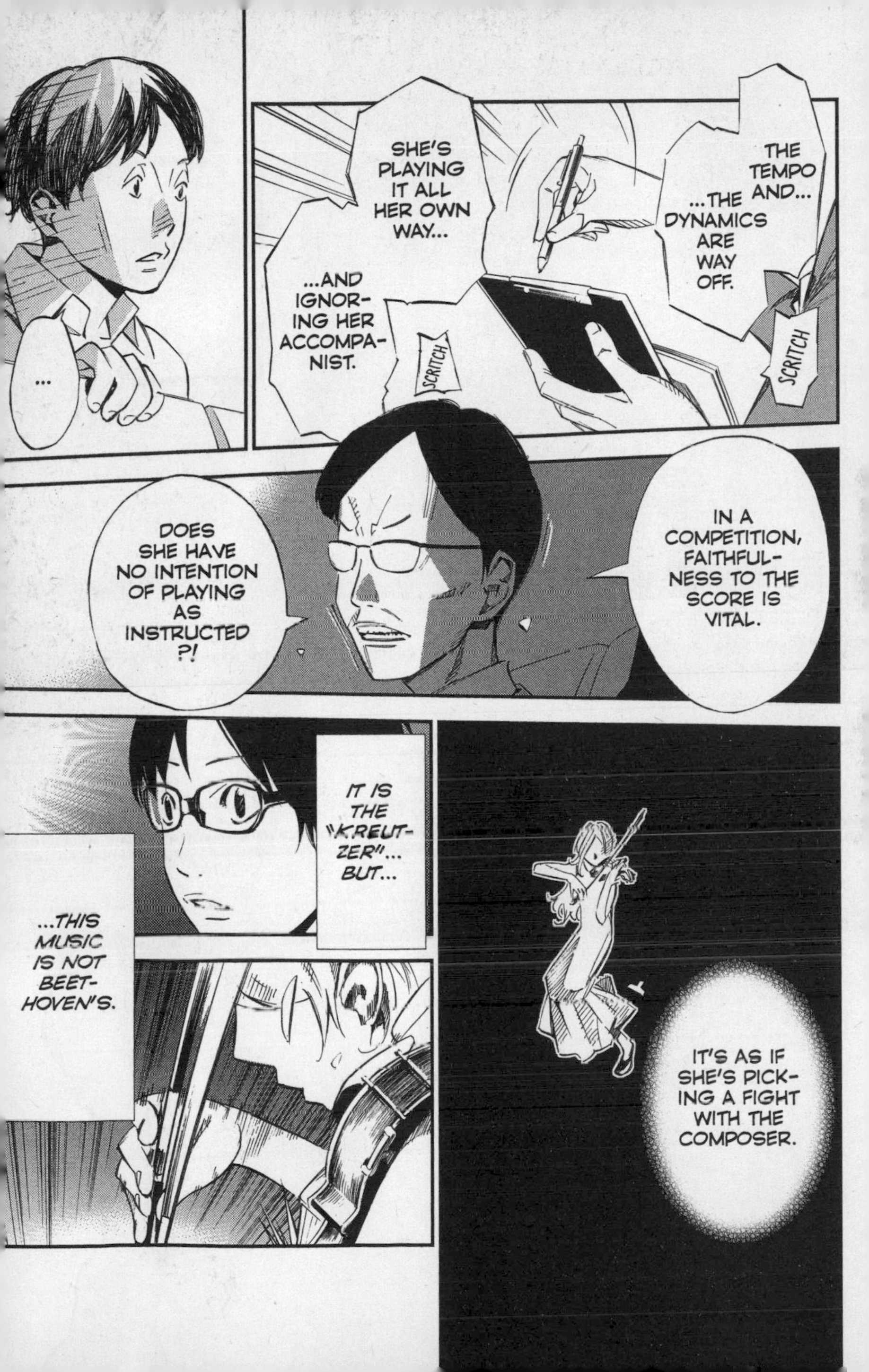
THE TEMPO AND...
...THE DYNAMICS ARE WAY OFF.
SCRITCH
SHE'S PLAYING IT ALL HER OWN WAY...
...AND IGNORING HER ACCOMPANIST.
SCRITCH
...
IN A COMPETITION, FAITHFULNESS TO THE SCORE IS VITAL.
DOES SHE HAVE NO INTENTION OF PLAYING AS INSTRUCTED?!
IT'S AS IF SHE'S PICKING A FIGHT WITH THE COMPOSER.
IT IS THE "KREUTZER"... BUT...
...THIS MUSIC IS NOT BEETHOVEN'S.

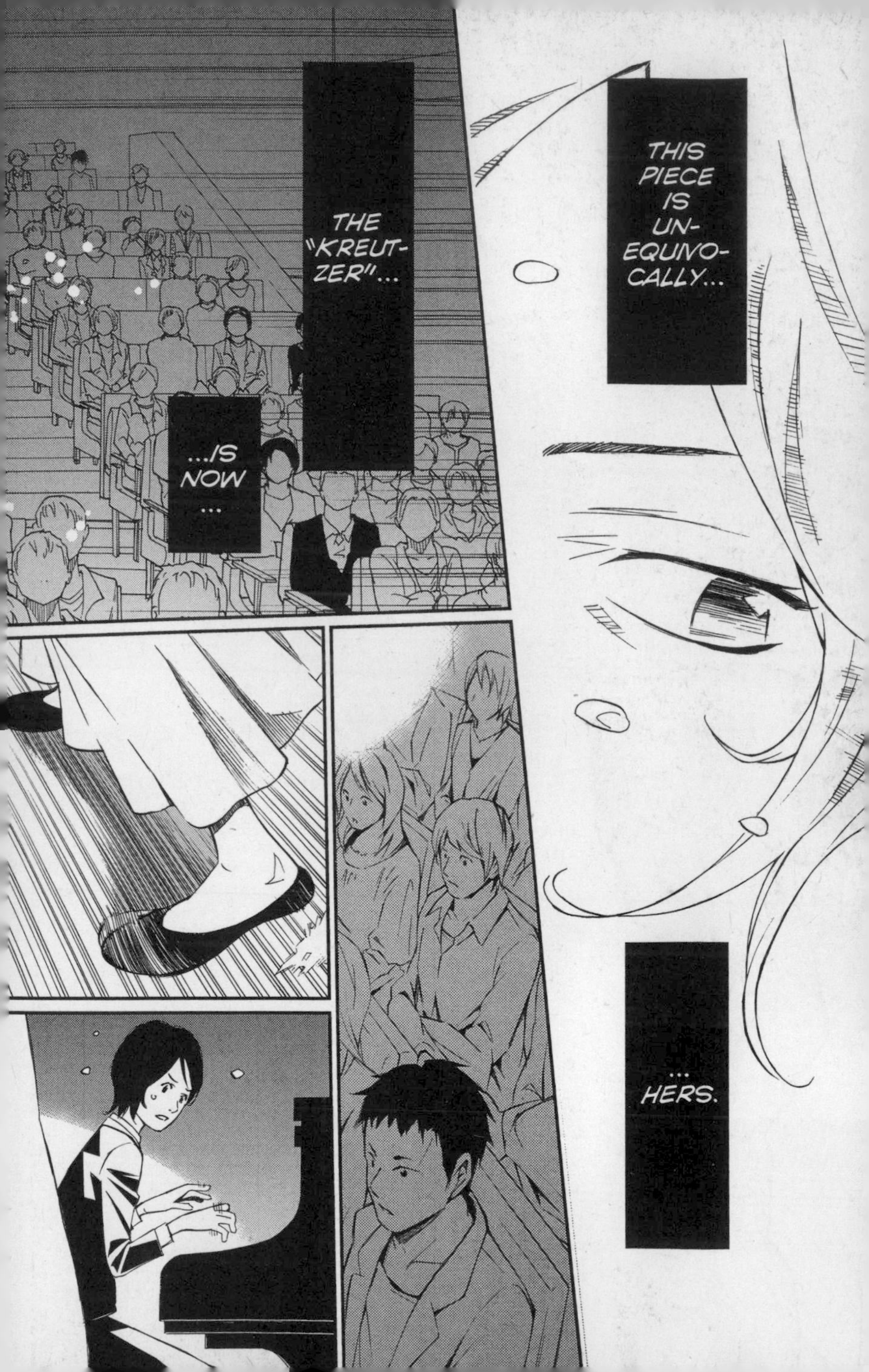
THIS PIECE IS UN-EQUIVO-CALLY...
...HERS.
THE "KREUT-ZER"...
...IS NOW ...

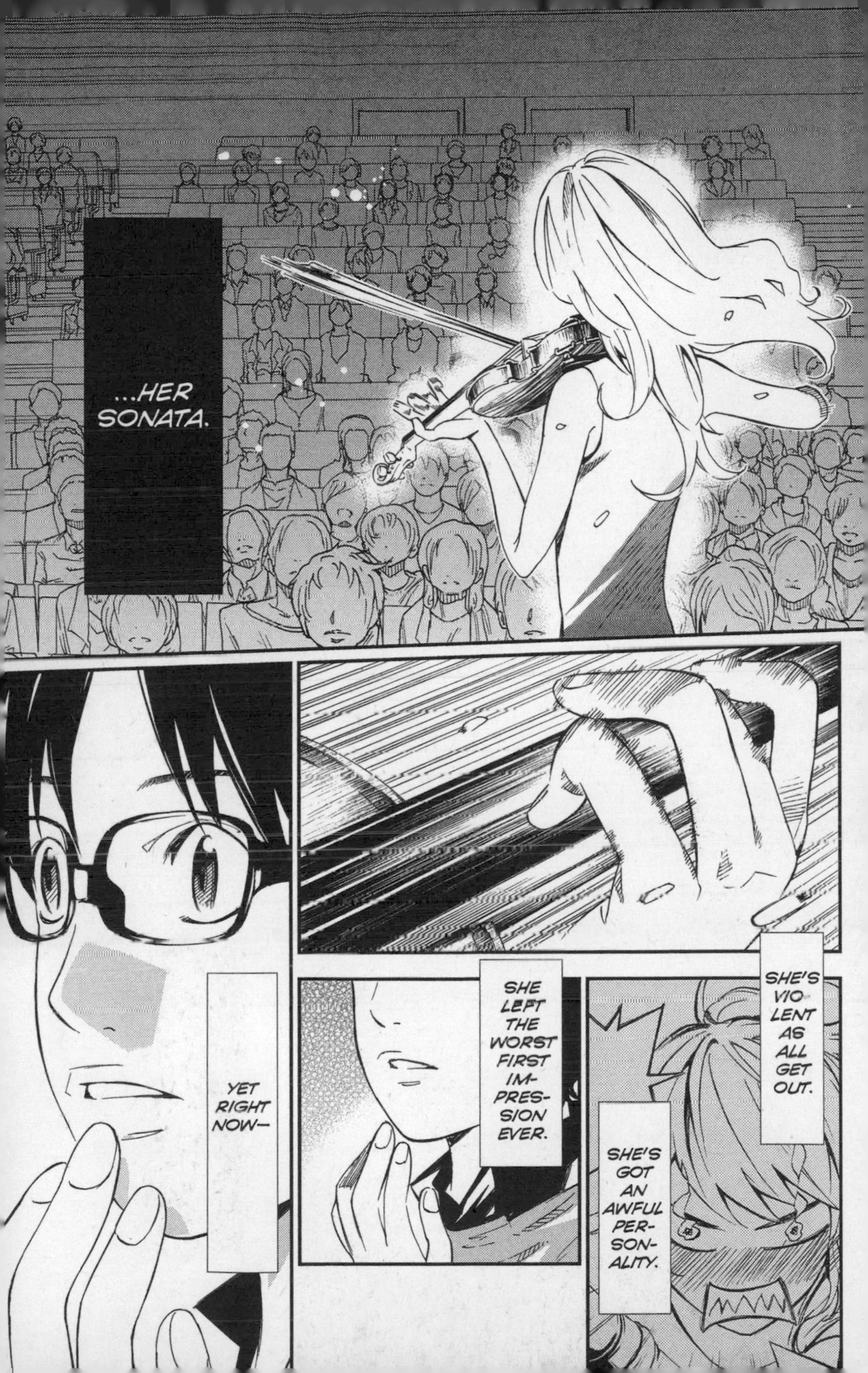
...HER SONATA.
SHE'S VIO-LENT AS ALL GET OUT.
SHE'S GOT AN AWFUL PER-SON-ALITY.
SHE LEFT THE WORST FIRST IM-PRES-SION EVER.
YET RIGHT NOW—

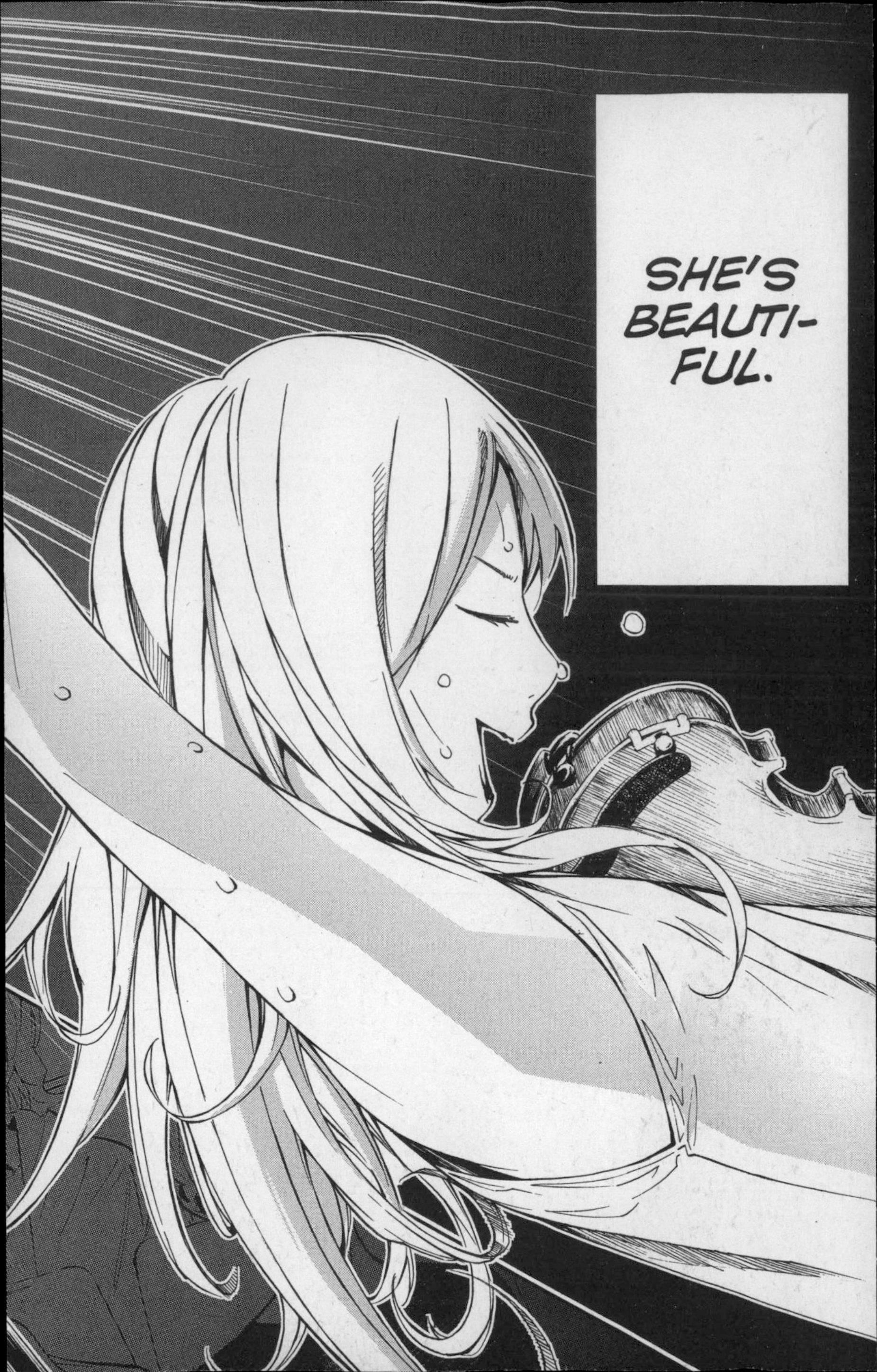
SHE'S BEAUTI-FUL.

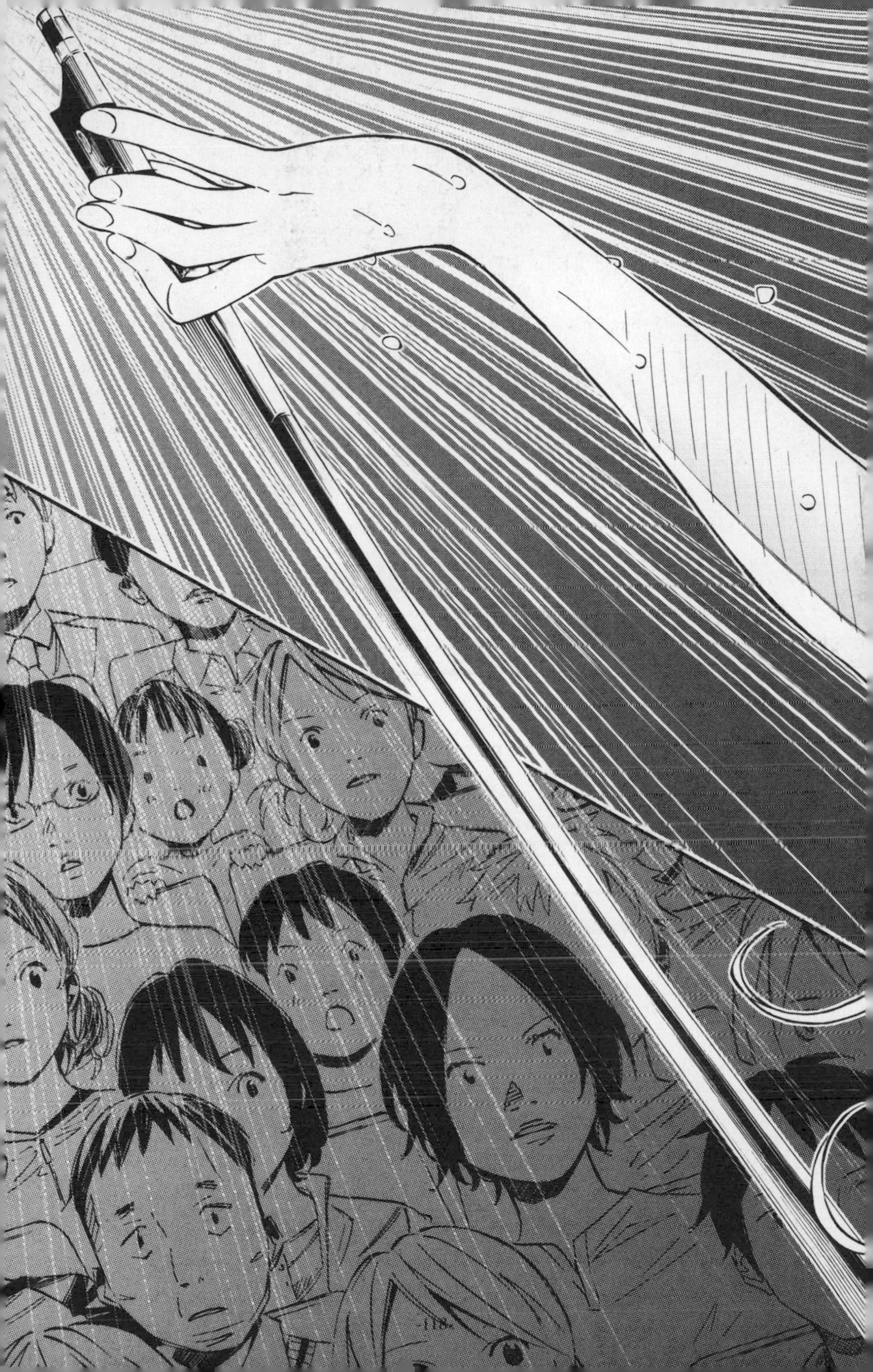

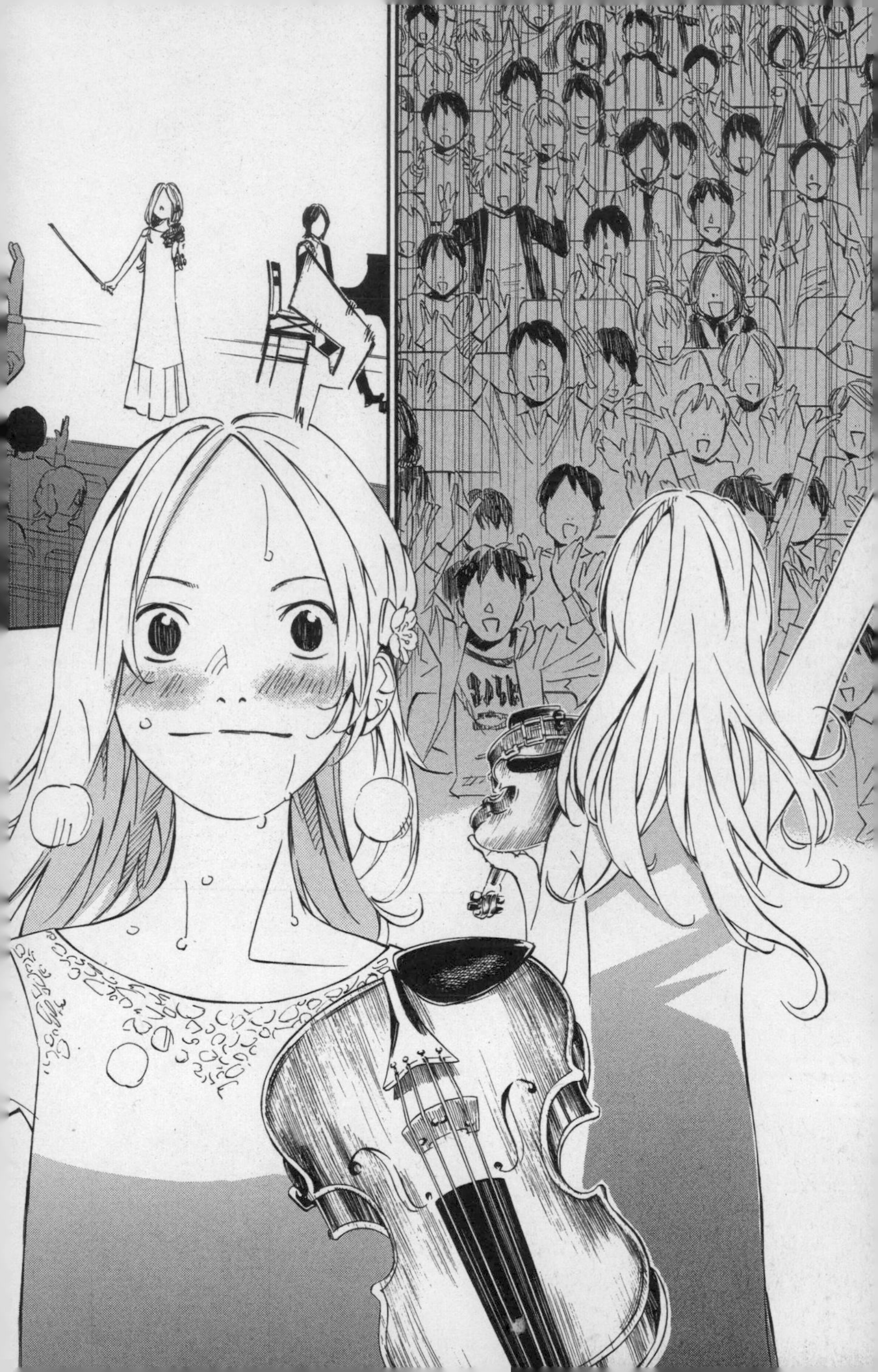

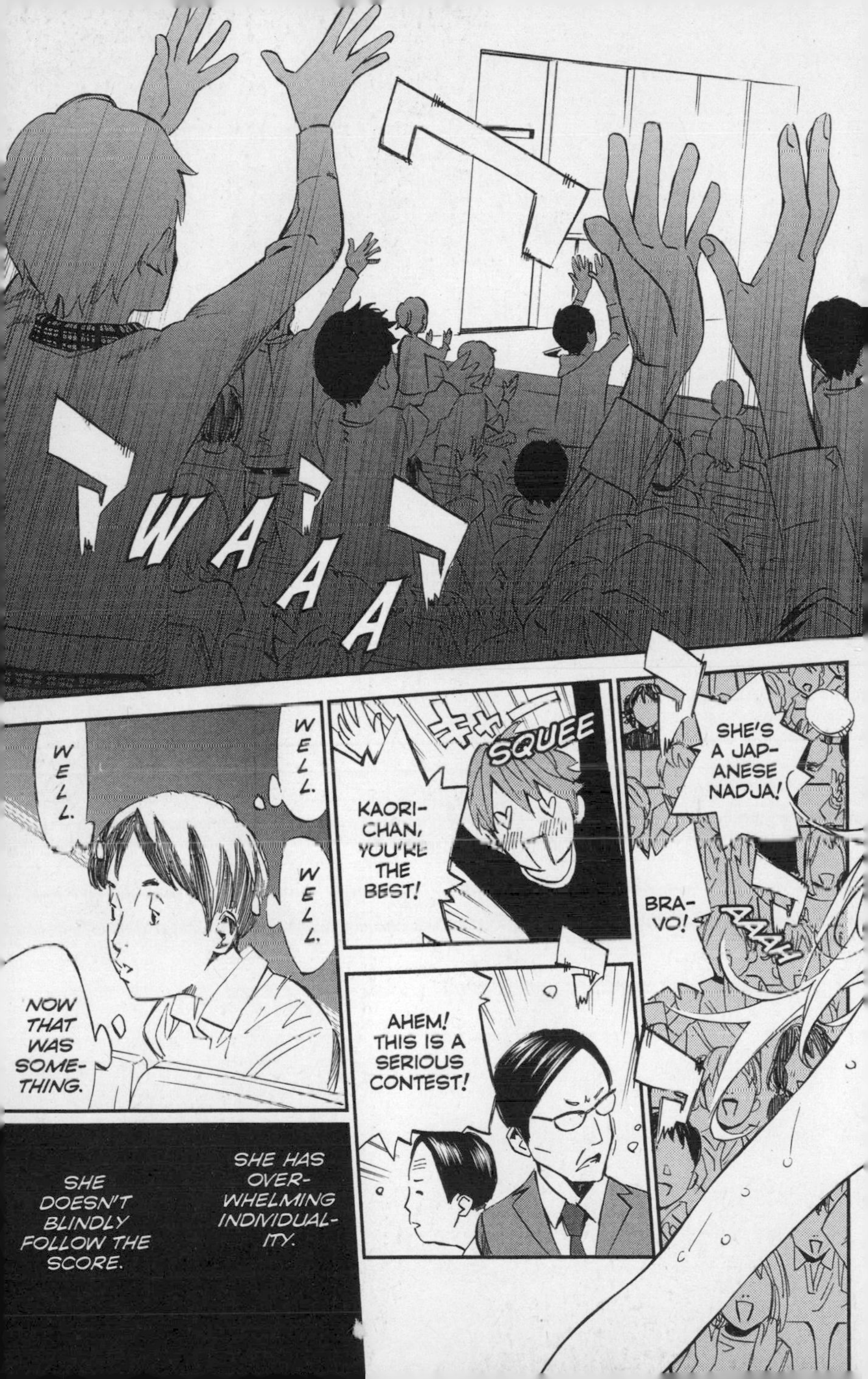
WAAAA
SHE'S A JAPANESE NADJA!
BRAVO!
AAAH
SQUEE
KAORI-CHAN, YOU'RE THE BEST!
WELL.
WELL.
WELL.
NOW THAT WAS SOMETHING.
AHEM! THIS IS A SERIOUS CONTEST!
SHE HAS OVERWHELMING INDIVIDUALITY.
SHE DOESN'T BLINDLY FOLLOW THE SCORE.

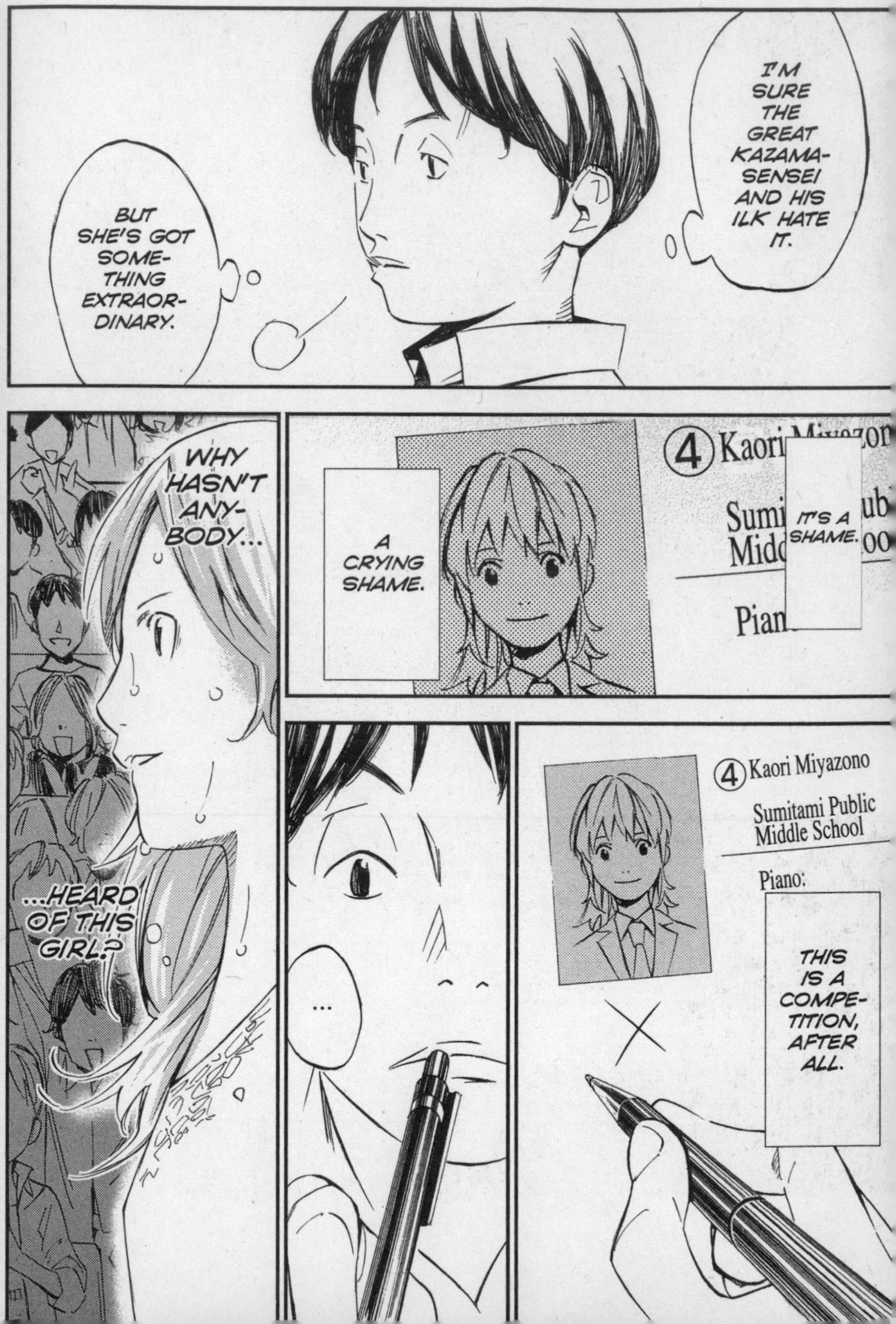
I'M SURE THE GREAT KAZAMA-SENSEI AND HIS ILK HATE IT.
BUT SHE'S GOT SOMETHING EXTRAORDINARY.
IT'S A SHAME.
A CRYING SHAME.
4 Kaori Miyazono
Sumitami Public Middle School
Piano:
THIS IS A COMPETITION, AFTER ALL.
...
WHY HASN'T ANYBODY...
...HEARD OF THIS GIRL?

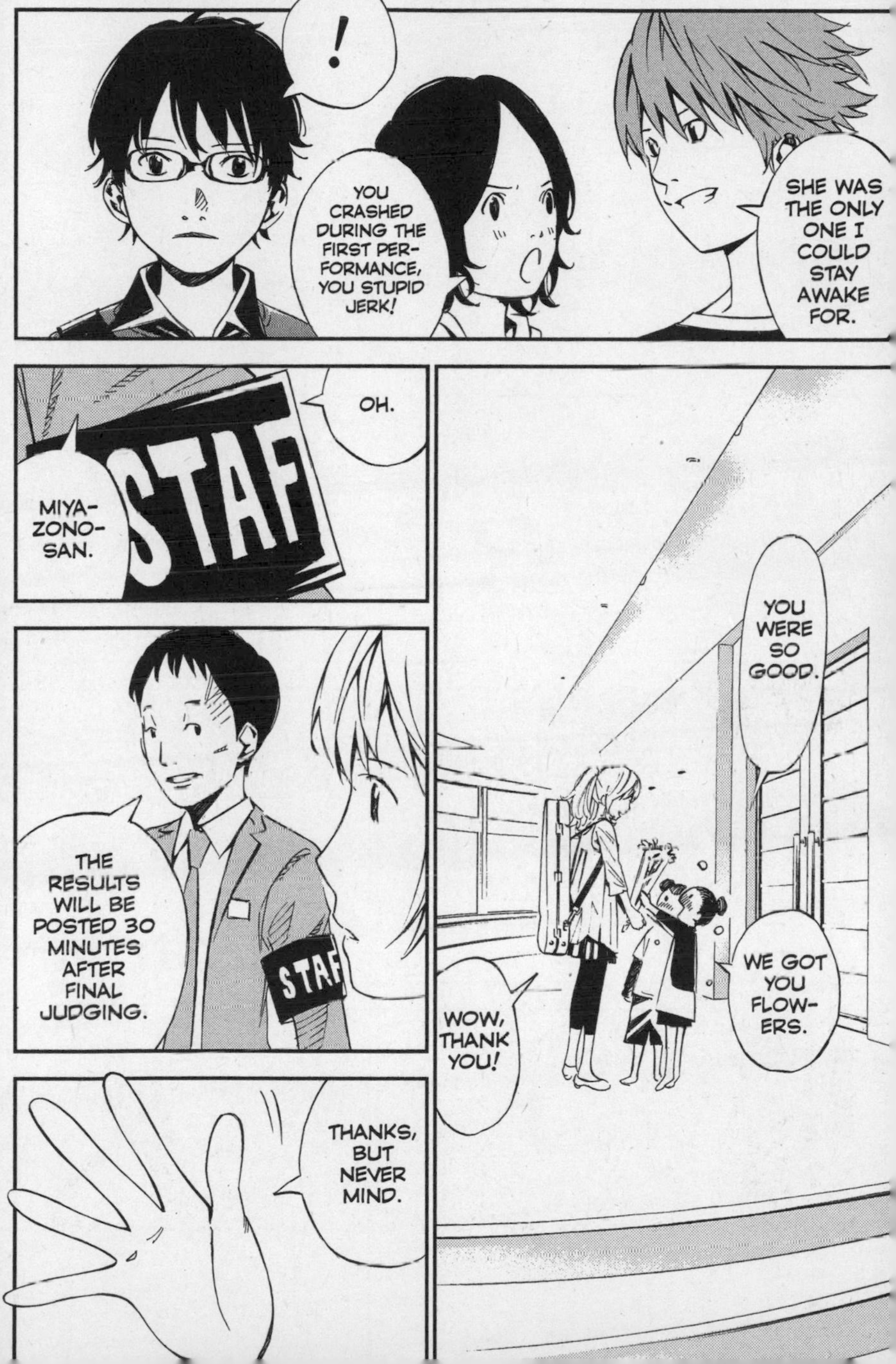
SHE WAS THE ONLY ONE I COULD STAY AWAKE FOR.
YOU CRASHED DURING THE FIRST PER-FORMANCE, YOU STUPID JERK!
!
YOU WERE SO GOOD.
WE GOT YOU FLOW-ERS.
WOW, THANK YOU!
OH.
STAF
MIYA-ZONO-SAN.
THE RESULTS WILL BE POSTED 30 MINUTES AFTER FINAL JUDGING.
STAF
THANKS, BUT NEVER MIND.

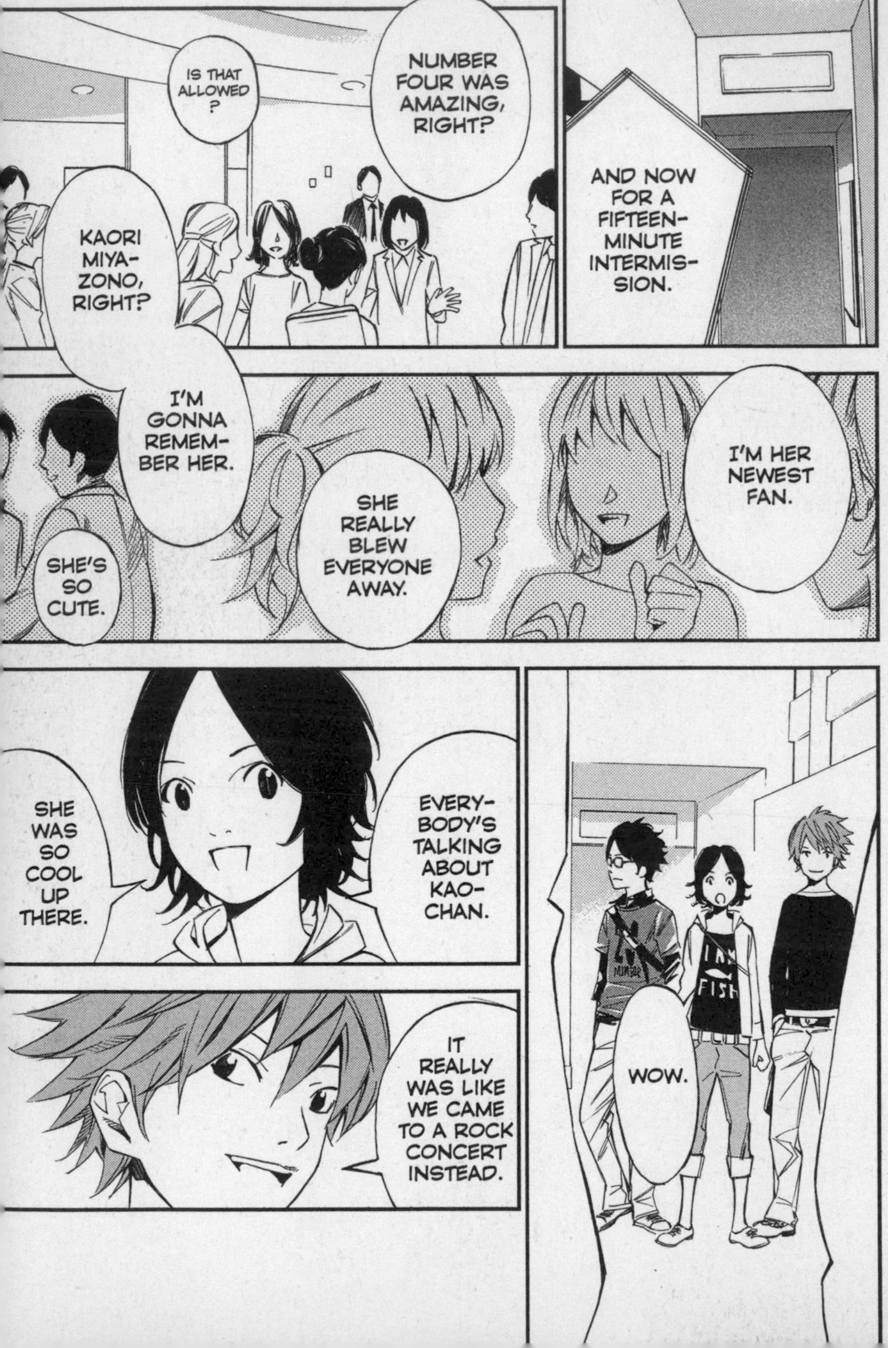
AND NOW FOR A FIFTEEN-MINUTE INTERMISSION.
NUMBER FOUR WAS AMAZING, RIGHT?
IS THAT ALLOWED?
KAORI MIYAZONO, RIGHT?
I'M HER NEWEST FAN.
SHE REALLY BLEW EVERYONE AWAY.
I'M GONNA REMEMBER HER.
SHE'S SO CUTE.
WOW.
EVERYBODY'S TALKING ABOUT KAO-CHAN.
SHE WAS SO COOL UP THERE.
IT REALLY WAS LIKE WE CAME TO A ROCK CONCERT INSTEAD.

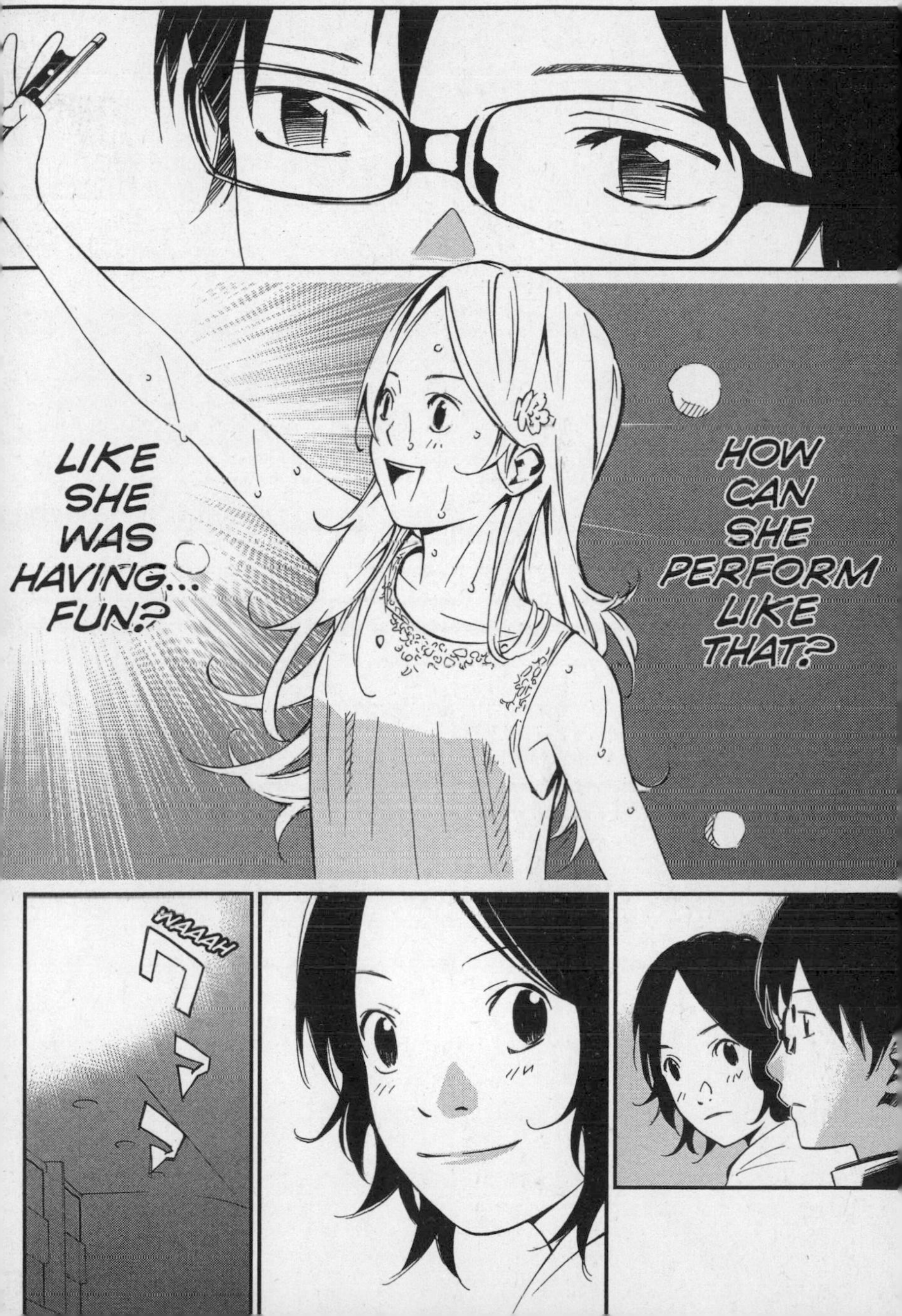
HOW CAN SHE PERFORM LIKE THAT?
LIKE SHE WAS HAVING... FUN?
WAAAH

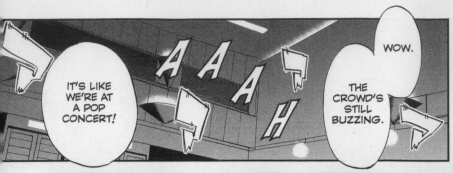

WOW.
THE CROWD'S STILL BUZZING.
AAAAH
IT'S LIKE WE'RE AT A POP CONCERT!
YOU THINK SHE'LL WIN?
HUH?
OH.
NO, SHE'S NOT GOING TO WIN. SHE WON'T EVEN PLACE.
SHE DID TOO MANY THINGS WRONG.
THE ONE THING YOU NEVER WANT TO DO IN A COMPETITION IS IGNORE THE SHEET MUSIC.
AWW, WHY?
EVERYBODY LOVED IT.
IT WOULD BE ONE THING IF THIS WERE A RECITAL, BUT YOU CAN'T DO THAT IN A COMPETITION.
BUT... I'M PRETTY SURE...
...THAT'S NOT WHAT SHE WAS AFTER ANYWAY...

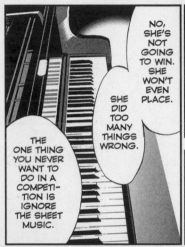

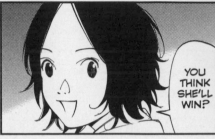

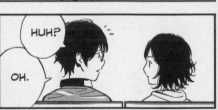

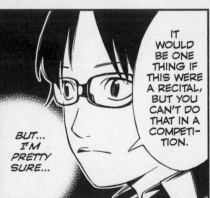

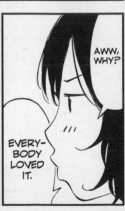

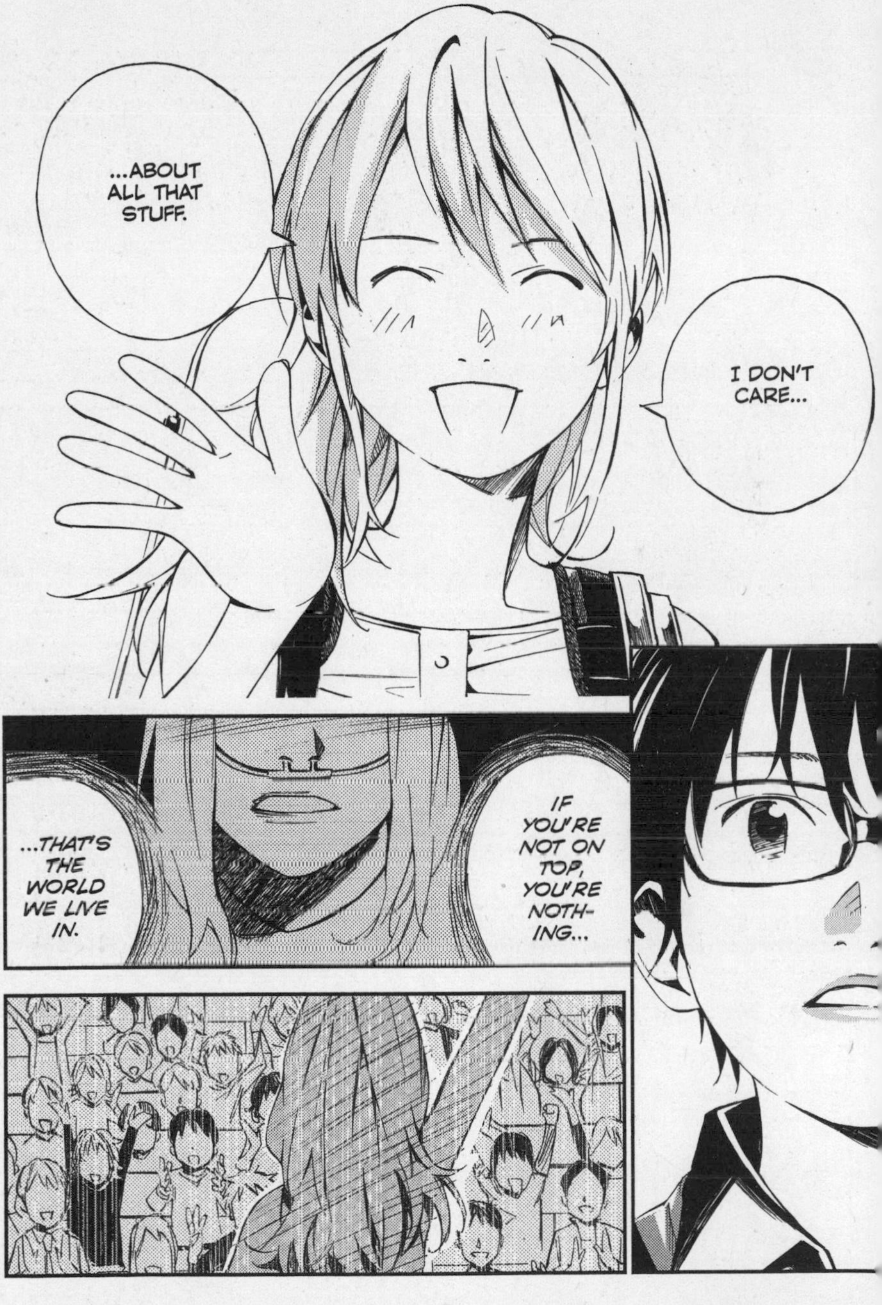
I DON'T CARE...
...ABOUT ALL THAT STUFF.
IF YOU'RE NOT ON TOP, YOU'RE NOTHING...
...THAT'S THE WORLD WE LIVE IN.

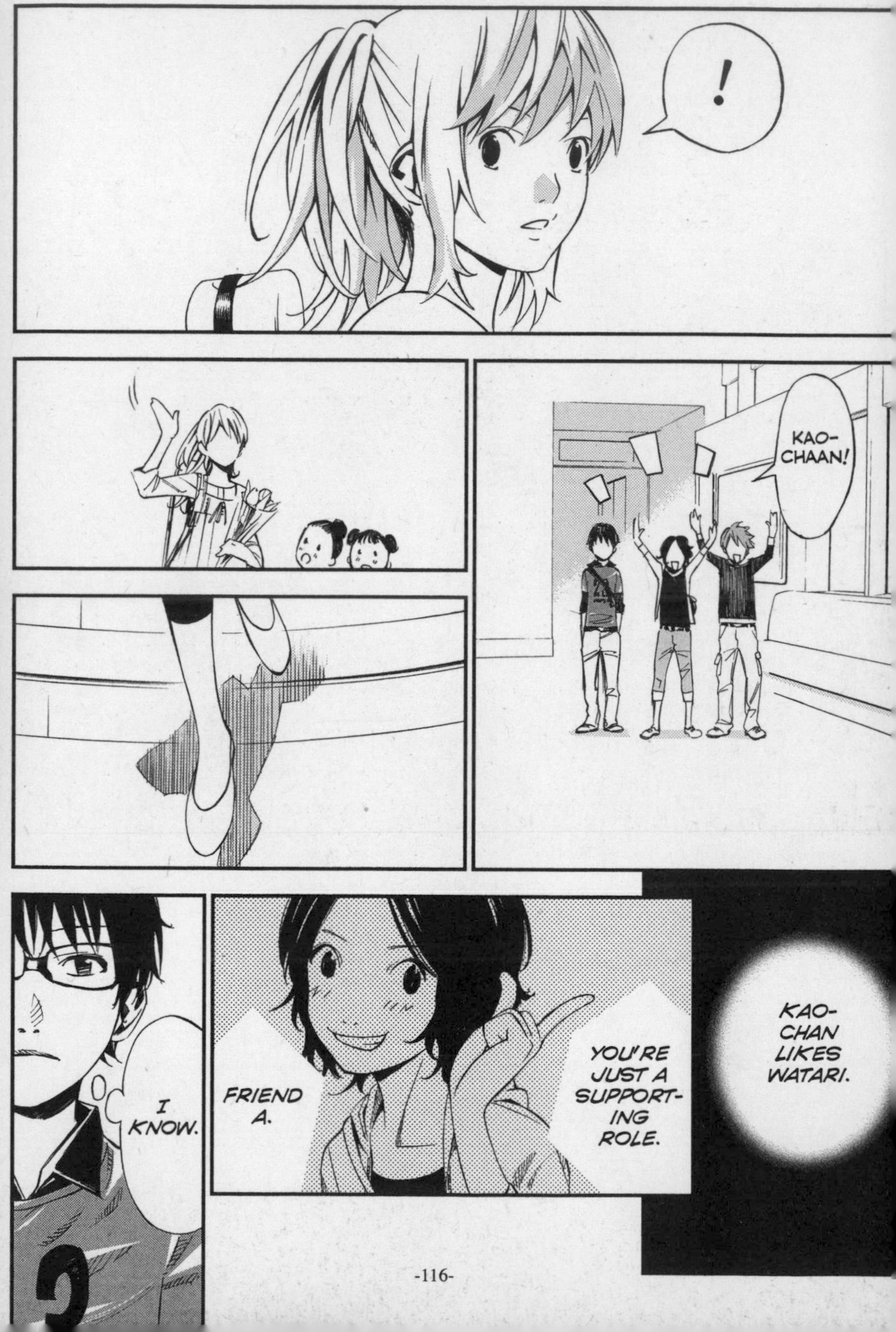
!
KAO-CHAAN!
KAO-CHAN LIKES WATARI.
YOU'RE JUST A SUPPORTING ROLE.
FRIEND A.
I KNOW.

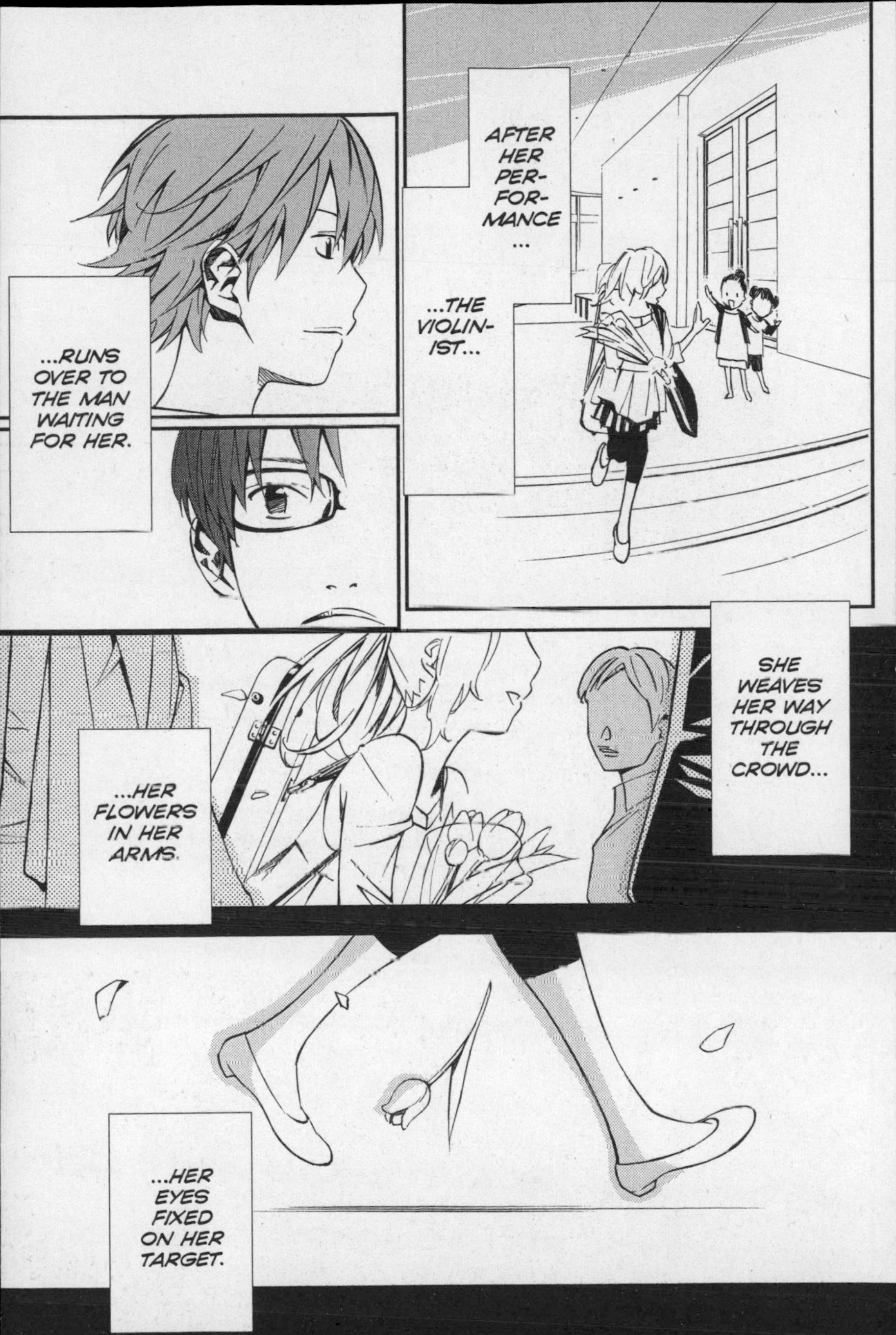
AFTER HER PER-FOR-MANCE...
...THE VIOLIN-IST...
...RUNS OVER TO THE MAN WAITING FOR HER.
SHE WEAVES HER WAY THROUGH THE CROWD...
...HER FLOWERS IN HER ARMS.
...HER EYES FIXED ON HER TARGET.

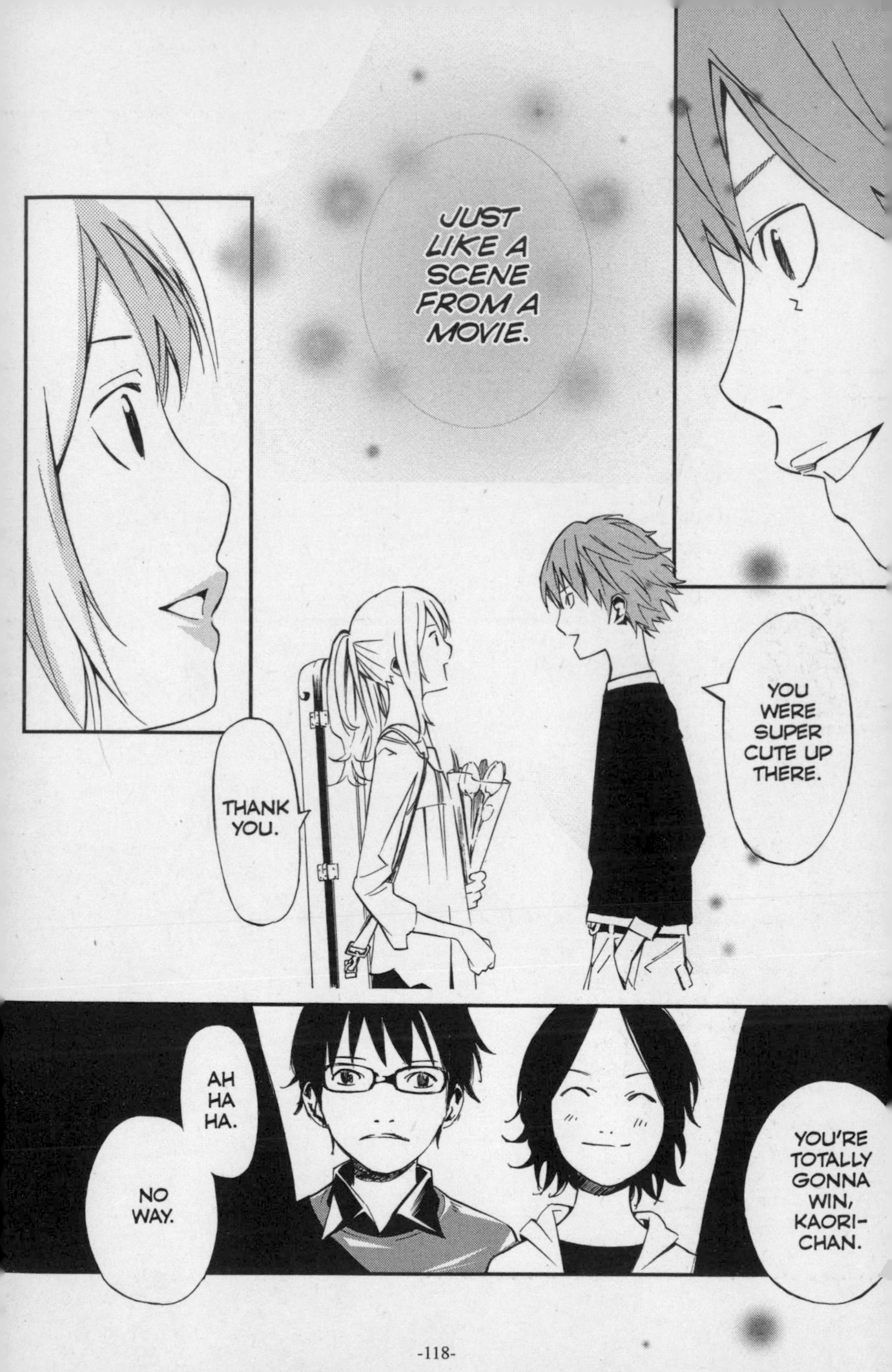
JUST LIKE A SCENE FROM A MOVIE.
YOU WERE SUPER CUTE UP THERE.
THANK YOU.
YOU'RE TOTALLY GONNA WIN, KAORI-CHAN.
AH HA HA.
NO WAY.

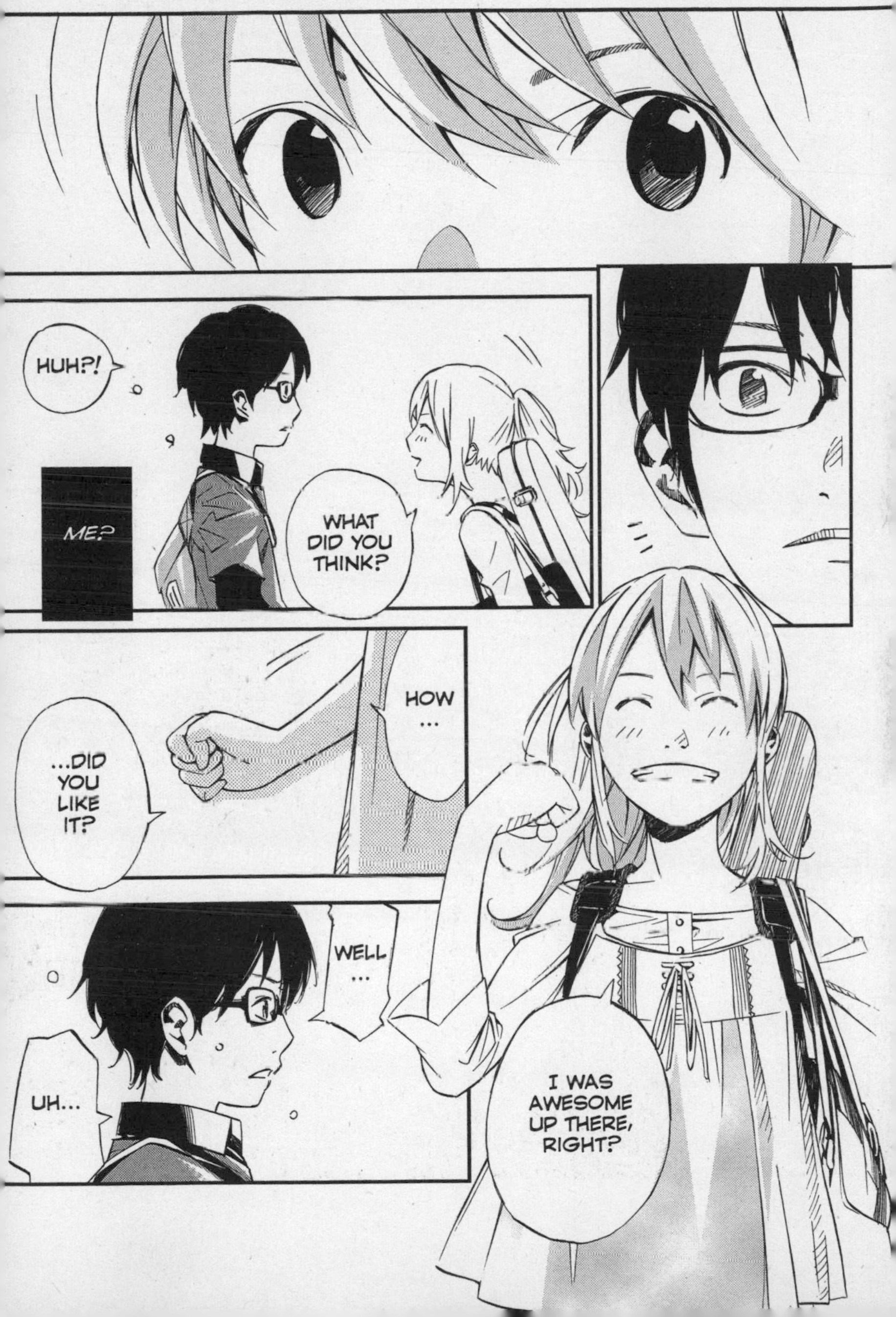
WHAT DID YOU THINK?
HUH?!
ME?
I WAS AWESOME UP THERE, RIGHT?
HOW ...
...DID YOU LIKE IT?
WELL ...
UH...

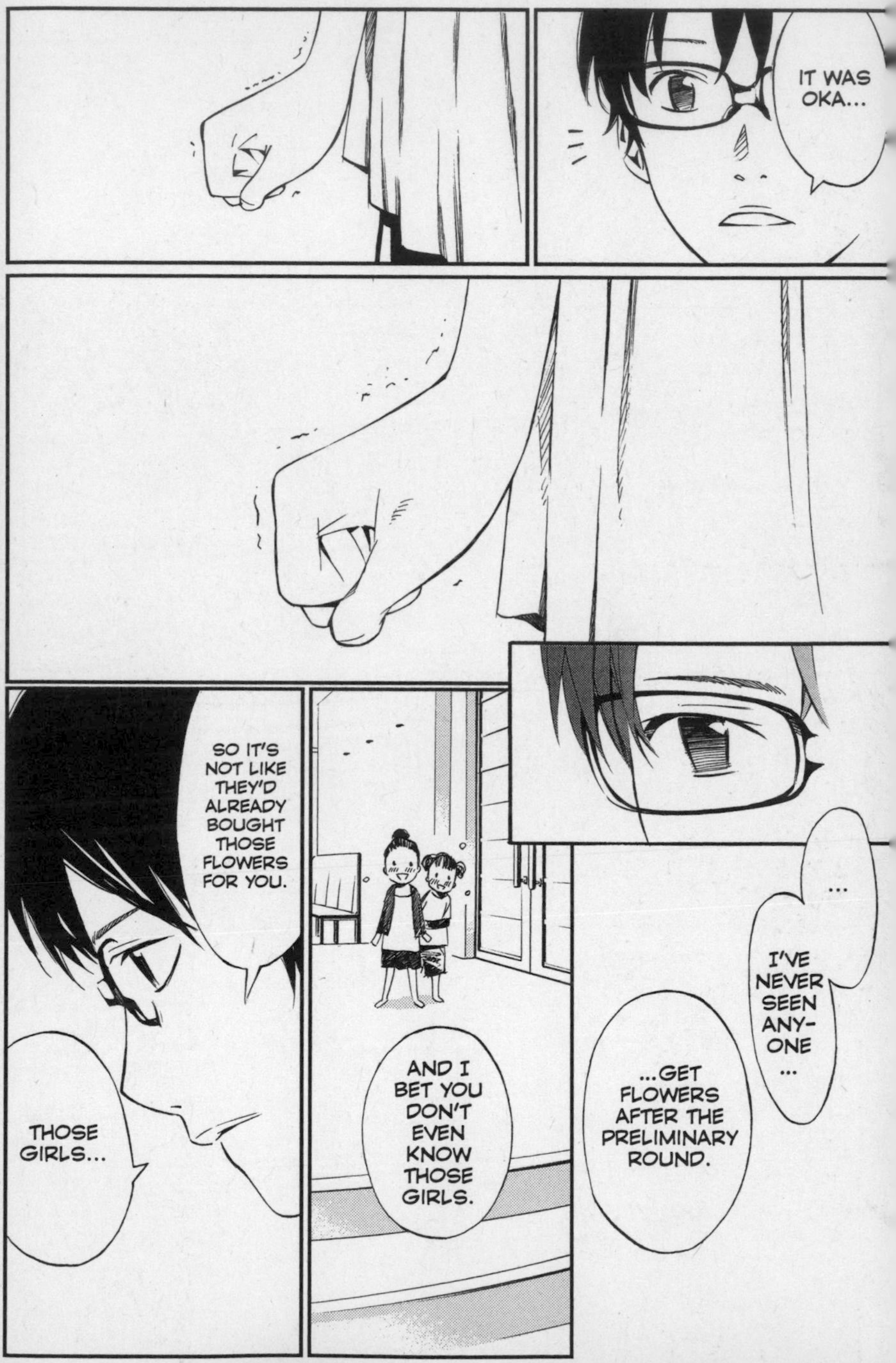
IT WAS OKA...
...
I'VE NEVER SEEN ANY-ONE...
...GET FLOWERS AFTER THE PRELIMINARY ROUND.
AND I BET YOU DON'T EVEN KNOW THOSE GIRLS.
SO IT'S NOT LIKE THEY'D ALREADY BOUGHT THOSE FLOWERS FOR YOU.
THOSE GIRLS...

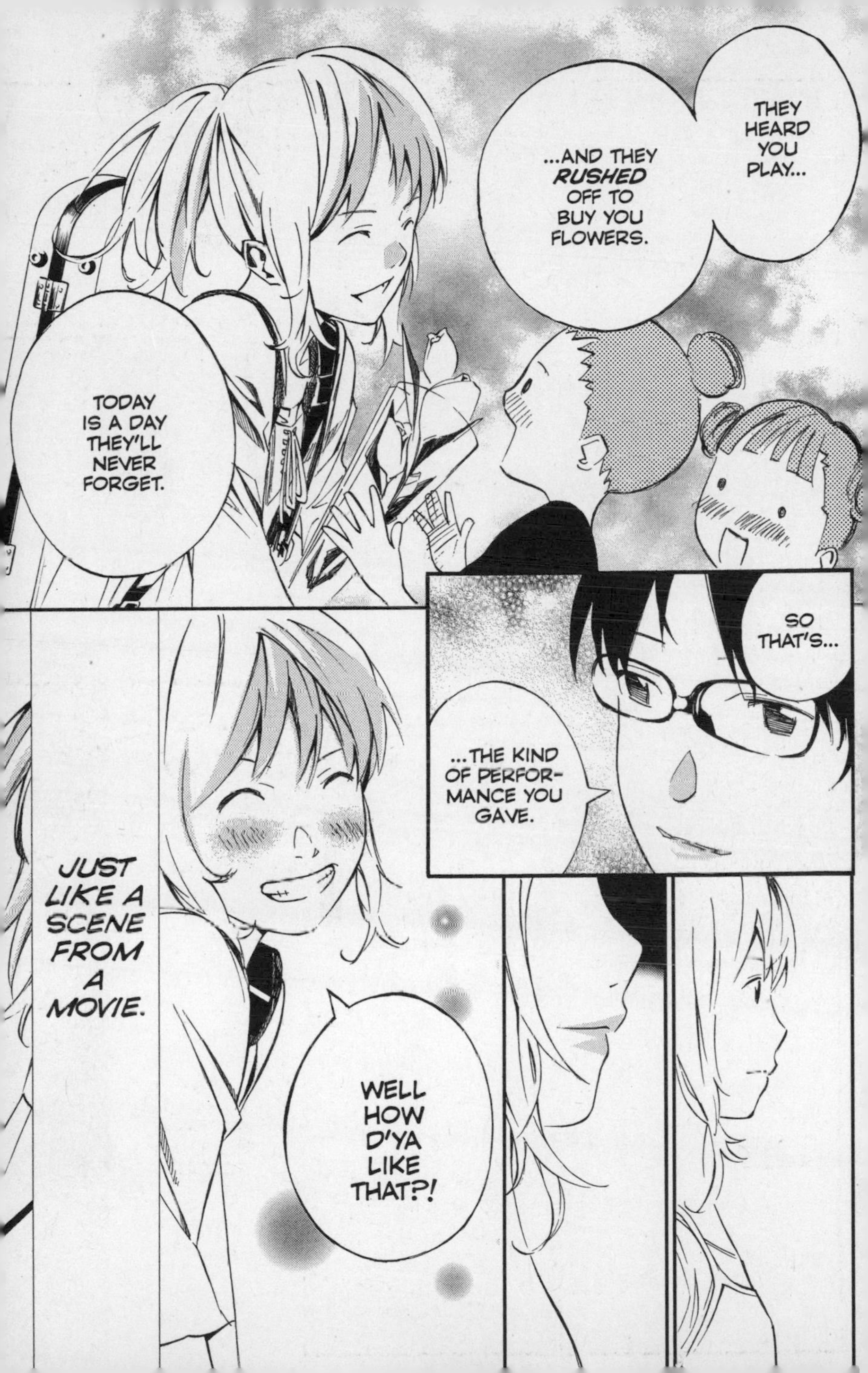
THEY HEARD YOU PLAY...
...AND THEY *RUSHED* OFF TO BUY YOU FLOWERS.
TODAY IS A DAY THEY'LL NEVER FORGET.
SO THAT'S...
...THE KIND OF PERFORMANCE YOU GAVE.
WELL HOW D'YA LIKE THAT?!
JUST LIKE A SCENE FROM A MOVIE.

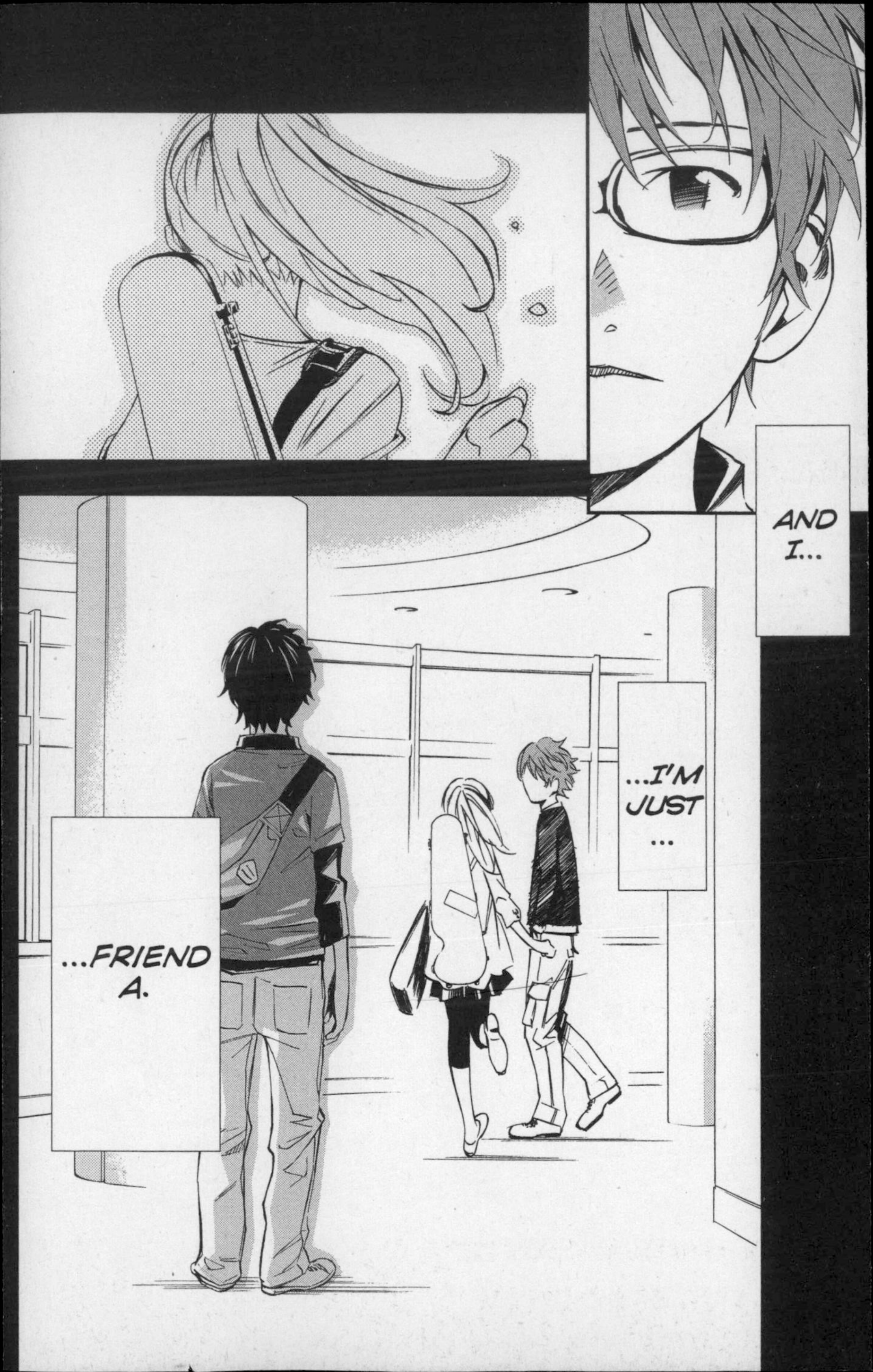
AND I...
...I'M JUST ...
...FRIEND A.

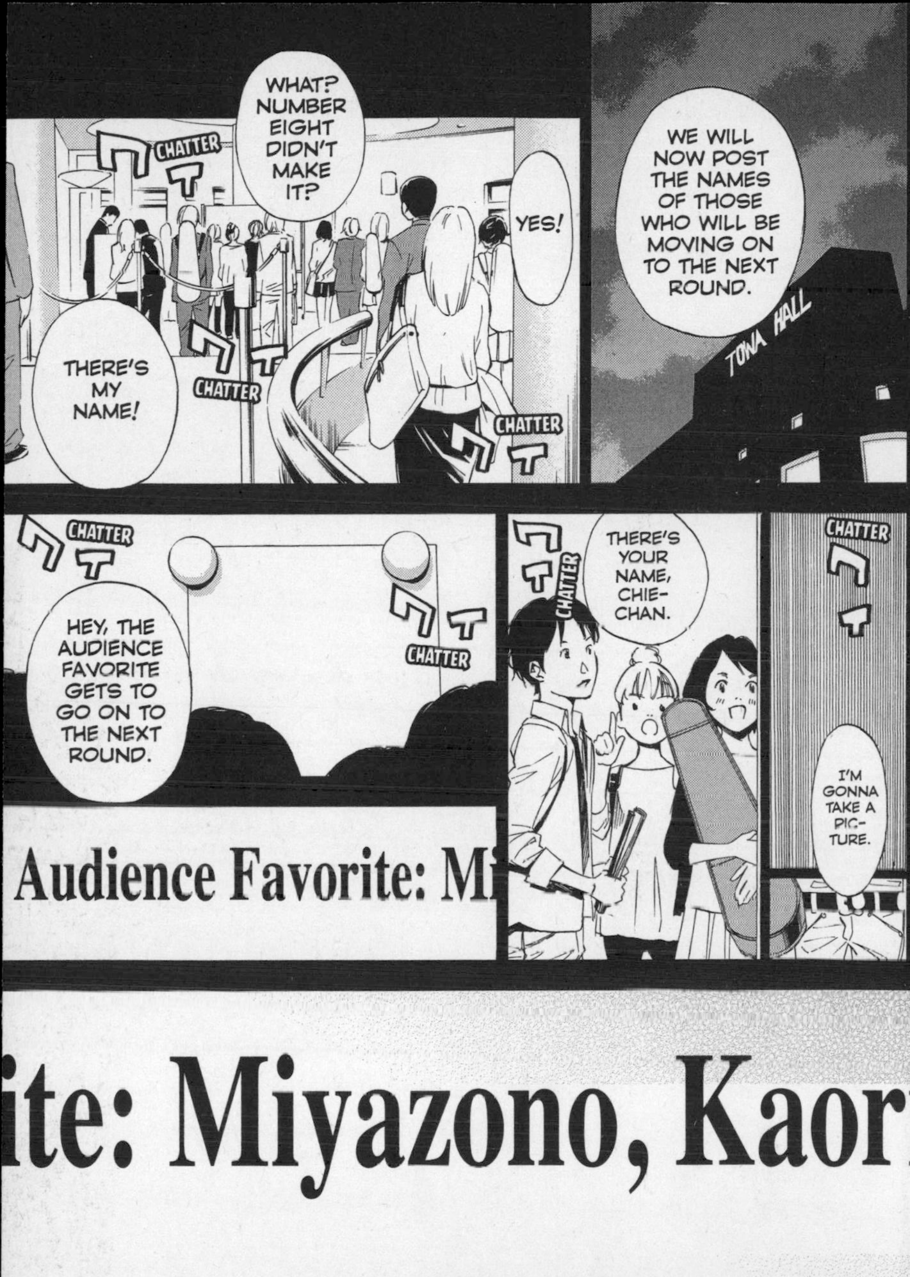
WE WILL NOW POST THE NAMES OF THOSE WHO WILL BE MOVING ON TO THE NEXT ROUND.
TONA HALL
YES!
WHAT? NUMBER EIGHT DIDN'T MAKE IT?
CHATTER
THERE'S MY NAME!
CHATTER
CHATTER
CHATTER
I'M GONNA TAKE A PIC-TURE.
THERE'S YOUR NAME, CHIE-CHAN.
CHATTER
CHATTER
CHATTER
HEY, THE AUDIENCE FAVORITE GETS TO GO ON TO THE NEXT ROUND.
Audience Favorite: Mi
ite: Miyazono, Kaor

The Love of a Violinist…The End

YOUR LIE IN APRIL FEATURED MUSIC

BEETHOVEN'S VIOLIN SONATA NO.9:
THE KREUTZER SONATA,
FIRST MOVEMENT

Of Beethoven's ten violin sonatas (compositions for violin and piano), this and his fifth, "Spring," are the most famous. Consisting of three movements, it is a long piece that, in full, lasts nearly half an hour.

"Kreutzer" is the name of the violinist to whom the piece was dedicated. However, due to various circumstances, the piece was never performed by Kreutzer himself.

The words "violin sonata" tend to give the impression that the piece features the violin while the piano is mere accompaniment, but in this piece, the two instruments are more equal. One might call it more of a double concerto. A high level of skill is required for both the piano and the violin, and the piece demands intense concentration and stamina.

Nevertheless, the sense of exhilaration that comes after playing it to the end is one that cannot be matched.

(Violinist Rieko Ikeda)

Watch it on Youtube
(Search for "Kodansha *Your Lie in April* Featured Music")

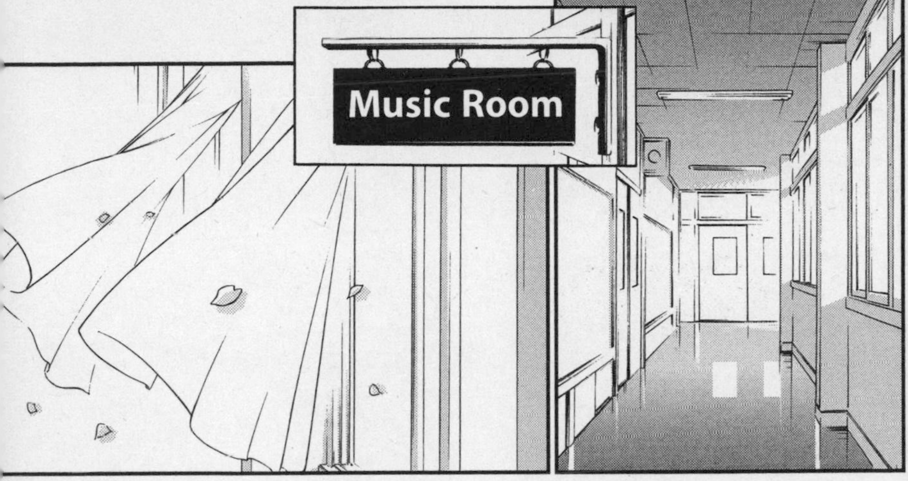
Music Room

Chapter 3: Black Cat

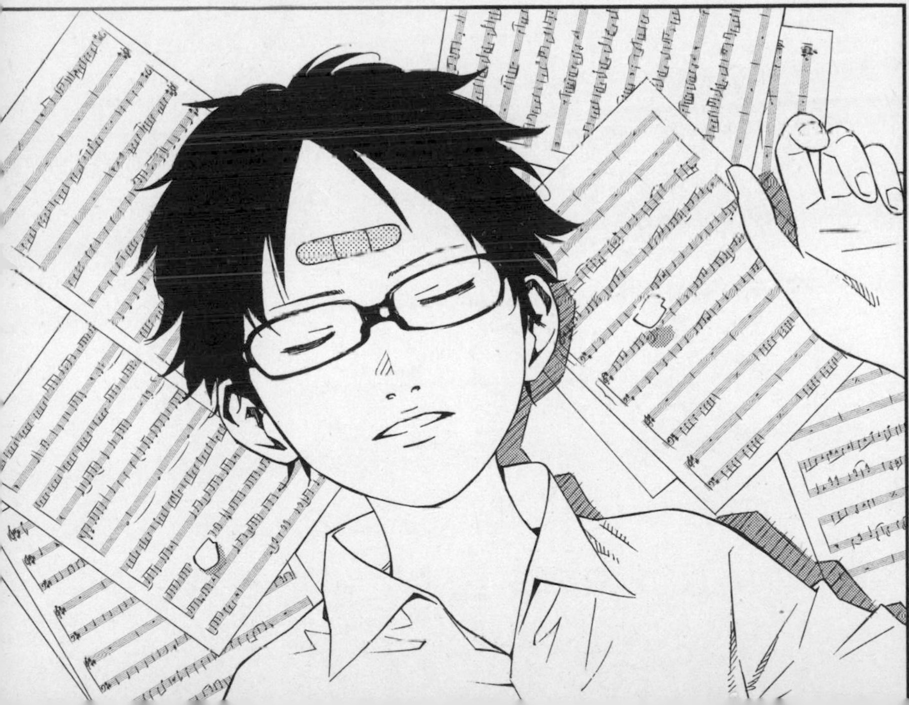

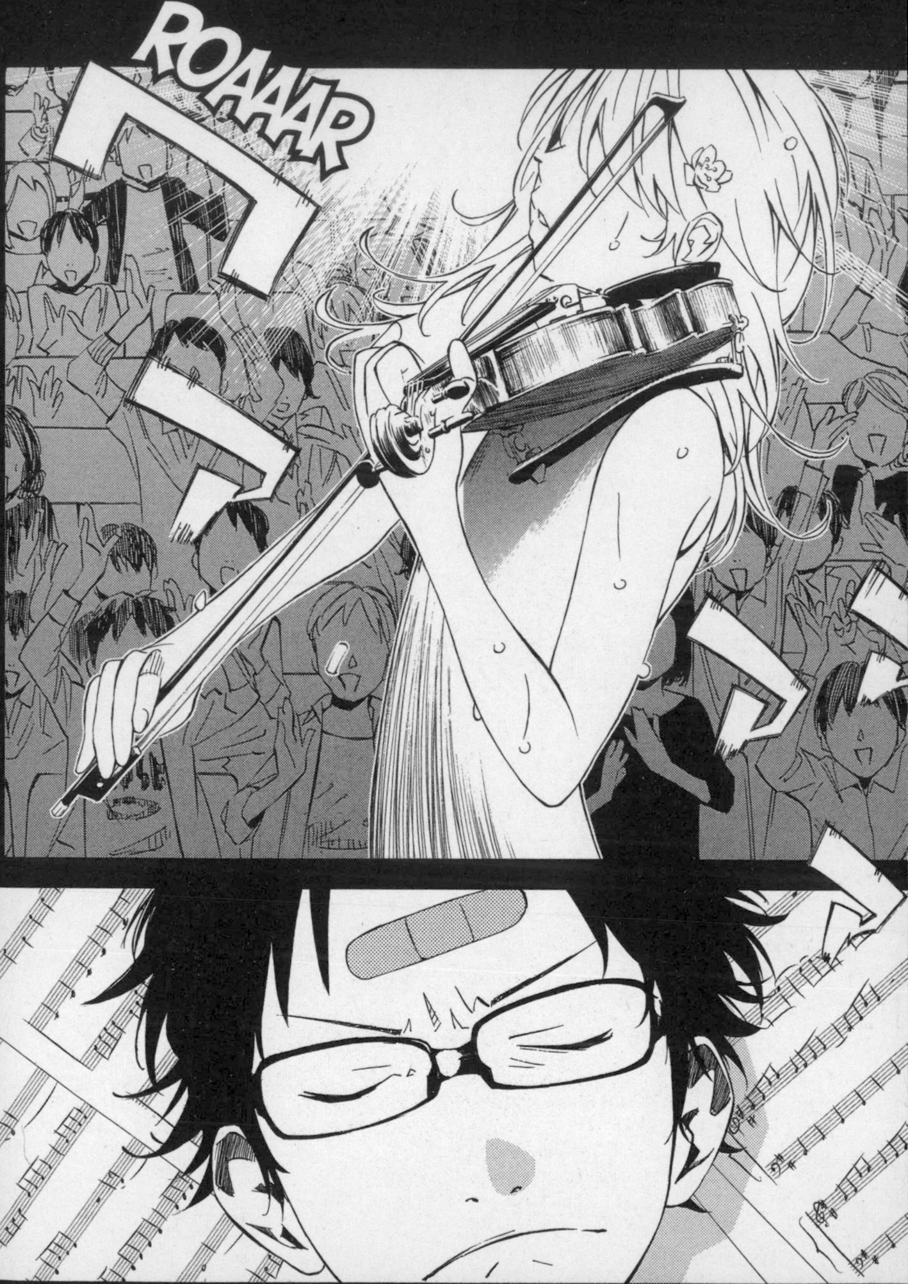
ROAAAR

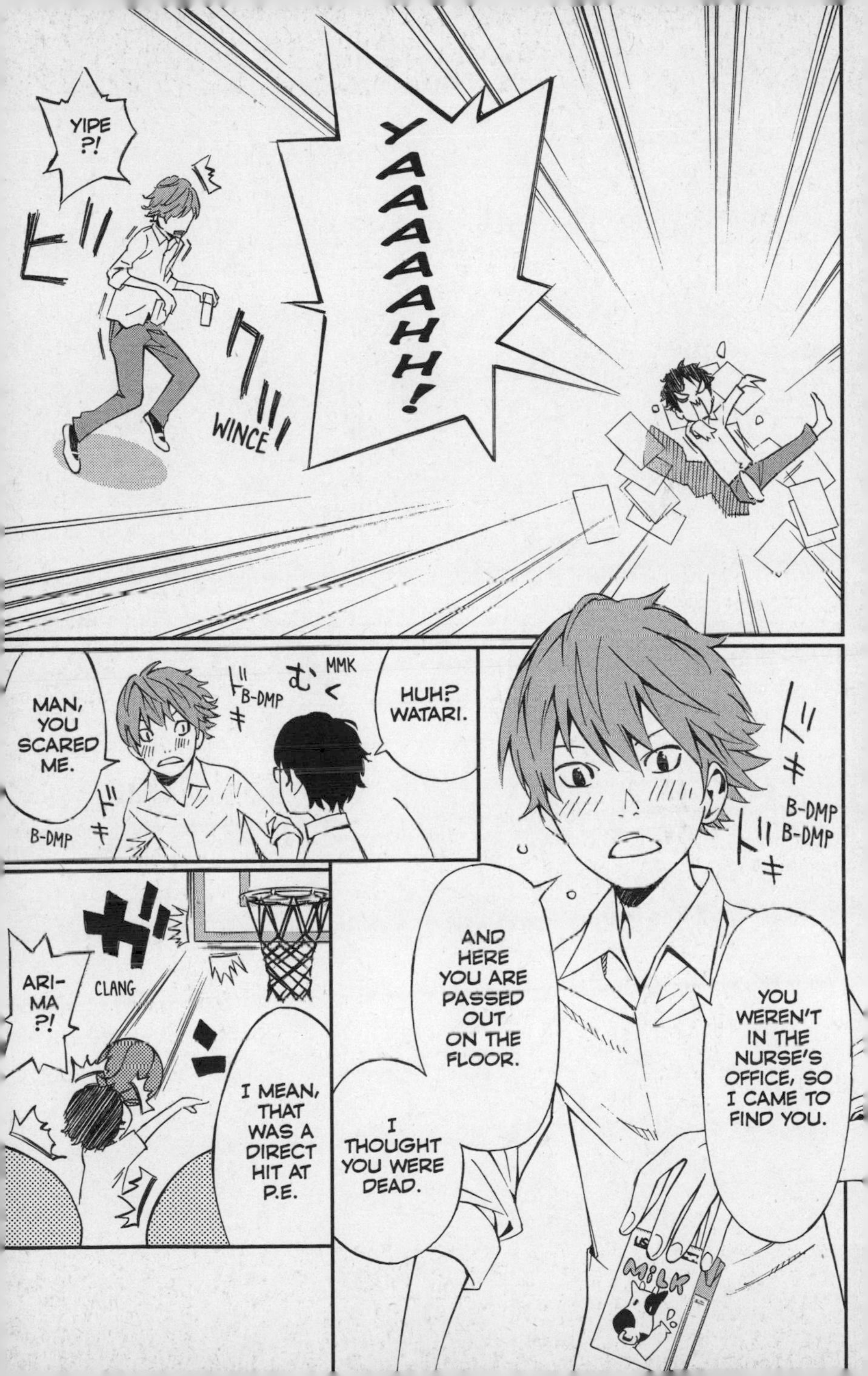
YAAAAAAH!
YIPE ?!
WINCE
B-DMP B-DMP
YOU WEREN'T IN THE NURSE'S OFFICE, SO I CAME TO FIND YOU.
AND HERE YOU ARE PASSED OUT ON THE FLOOR.
I THOUGHT YOU WERE DEAD.
I MEAN, THAT WAS A DIRECT HIT AT P.E.
MMK
HUH? WATARI.
B-DMP
MAN, YOU SCARED ME.
B-DMP
CLANG
ARI-MA ?!
MILK

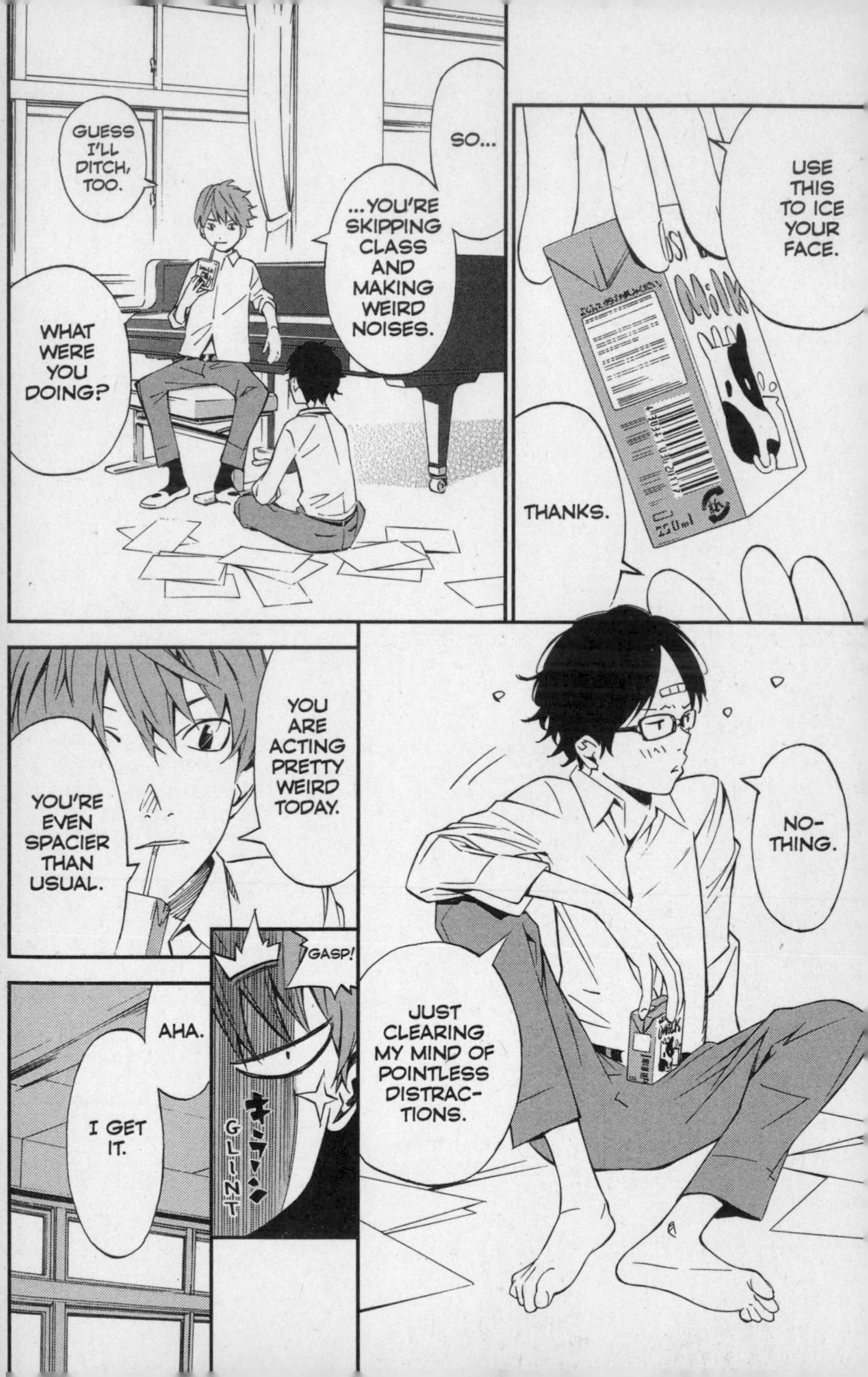
USE THIS TO ICE YOUR FACE.
THANKS.
SO...
...YOU'RE SKIPPING CLASS AND MAKING WEIRD NOISES.
GUESS I'LL DITCH, TOO.
WHAT WERE YOU DOING?
NO-THING.
JUST CLEARING MY MIND OF POINTLESS DISTRAC-TIONS.
YOU ARE ACTING PRETTY WEIRD TODAY.
YOU'RE EVEN SPACIER THAN USUAL.
GASP!
GLINT
AHA.
I GET IT.

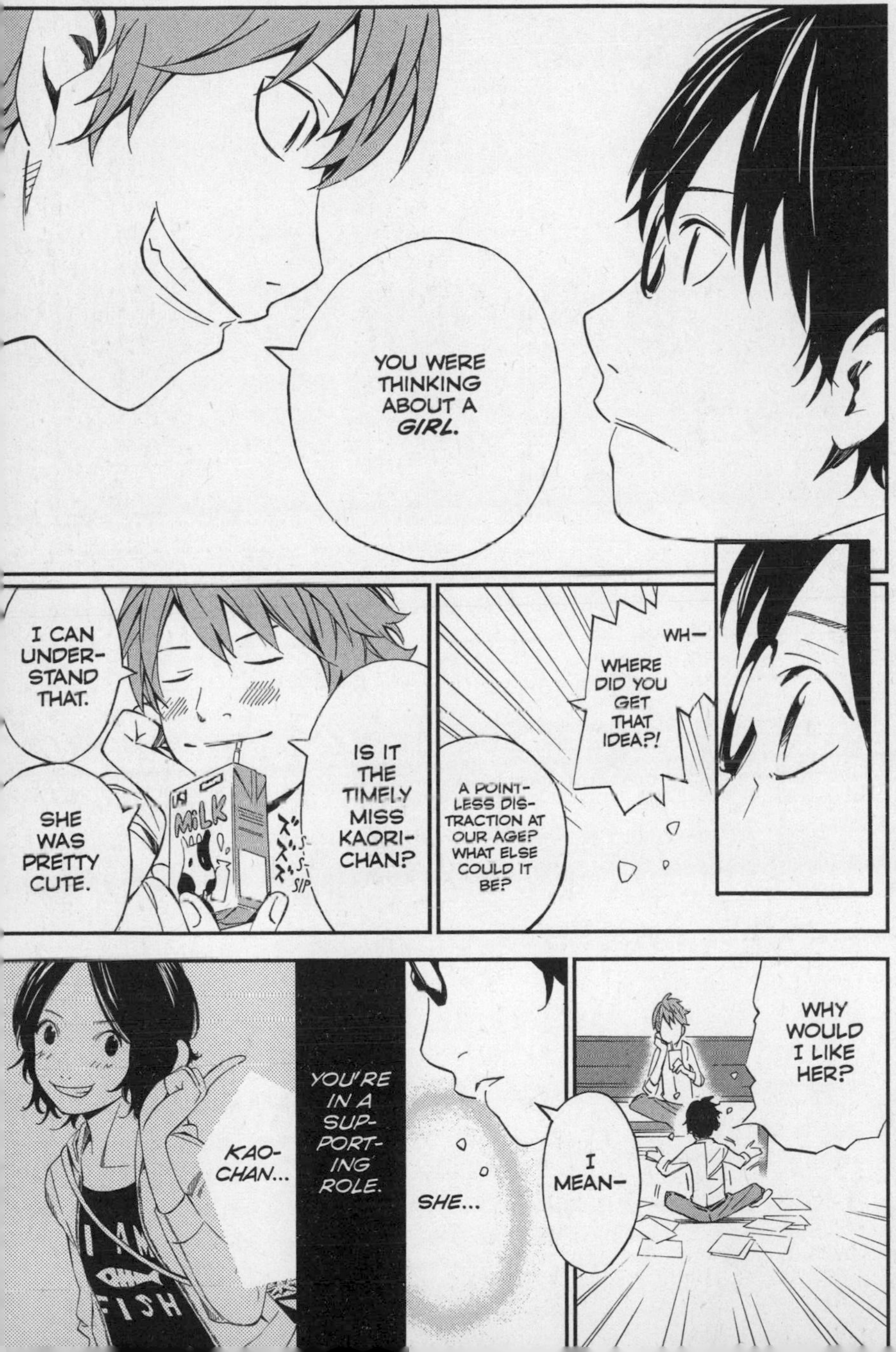
YOU WERE THINKING ABOUT A *GIRL.*
WH—
WHERE DID YOU GET THAT IDEA?!
A POINTLESS DISTRACTION AT OUR AGE? WHAT ELSE COULD IT BE?
IS IT THE TIMELY MISS KAORI-CHAN?
SIP
I CAN UNDERSTAND THAT.
SHE WAS PRETTY CUTE.
WHY WOULD I LIKE HER?
I MEAN—
SHE...
YOU'RE IN A SUPPORTING ROLE.
KAO-CHAN...

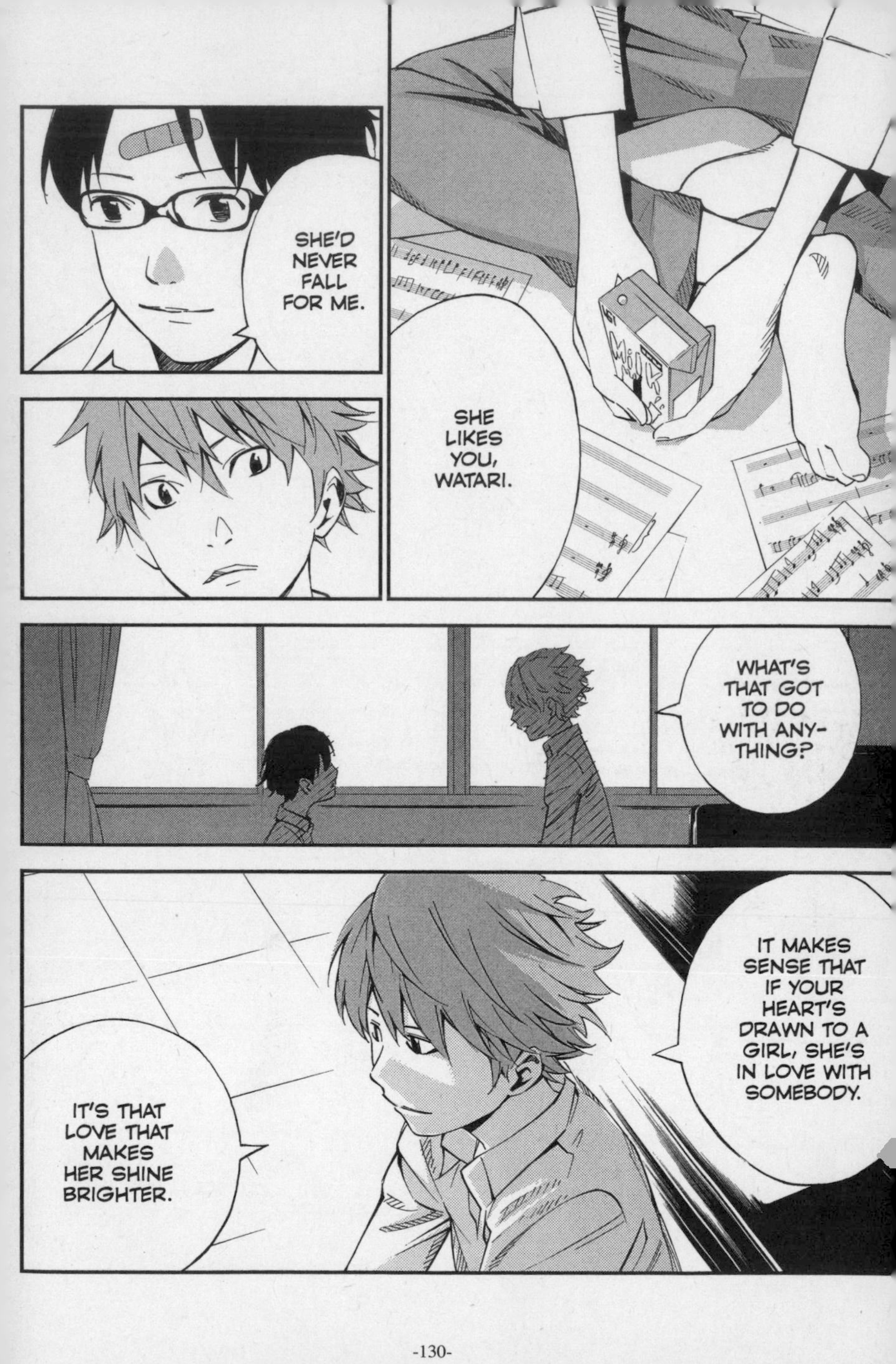
SHE LIKES YOU, WATARI.
SHE'D NEVER FALL FOR ME.
WHAT'S THAT GOT TO DO WITH ANY-THING?
IT MAKES SENSE THAT IF YOUR HEART'S DRAWN TO A GIRL, SHE'S IN LOVE WITH SOMEBODY.
IT'S THAT LOVE THAT MAKES HER SHINE BRIGHTER.

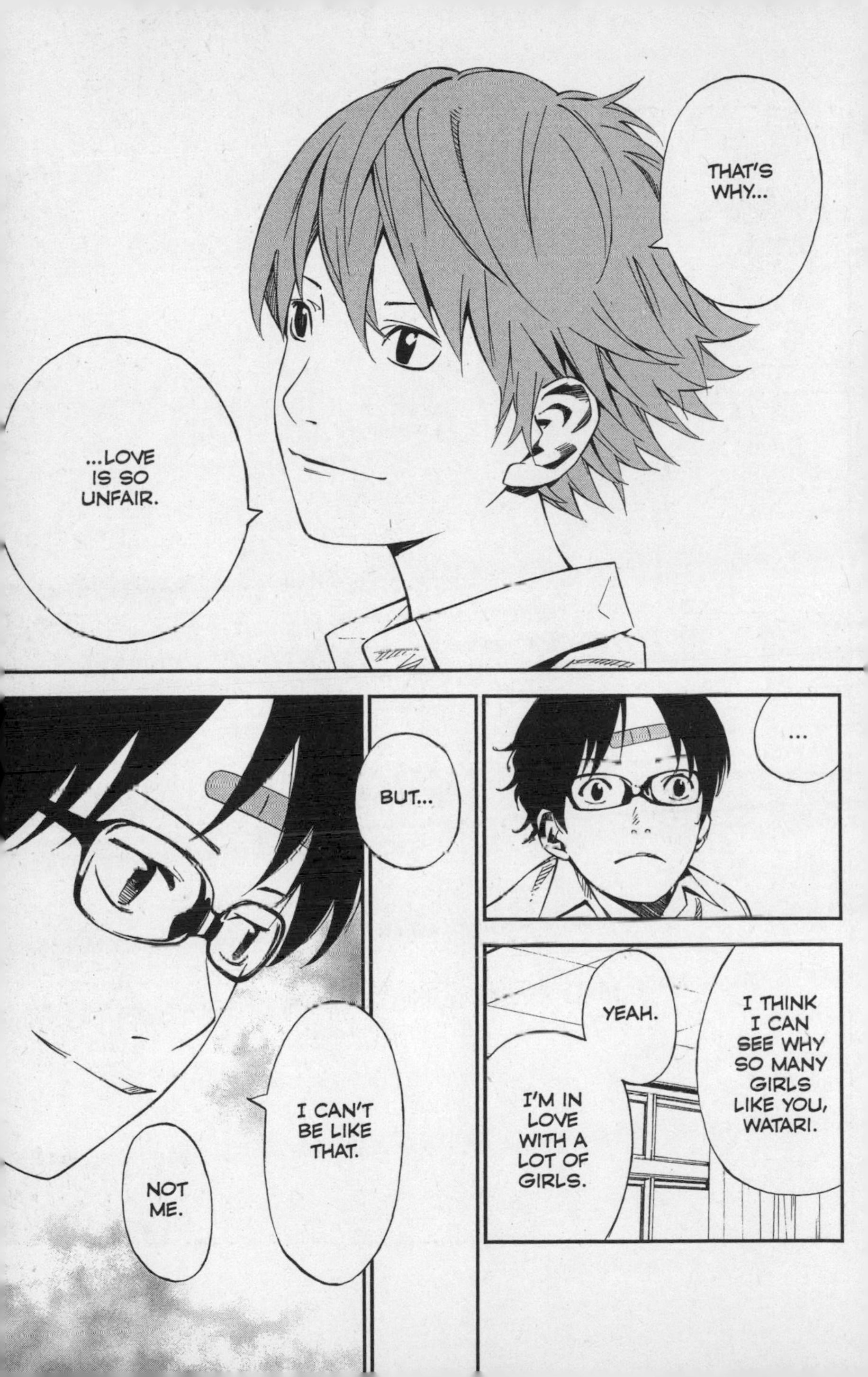
THAT'S WHY...
...LOVE IS SO UNFAIR.
...
I THINK I CAN SEE WHY SO MANY GIRLS LIKE YOU, WATARI.
YEAH.
I'M IN LOVE WITH A LOT OF GIRLS.
BUT...
I CAN'T BE LIKE THAT.
NOT ME.

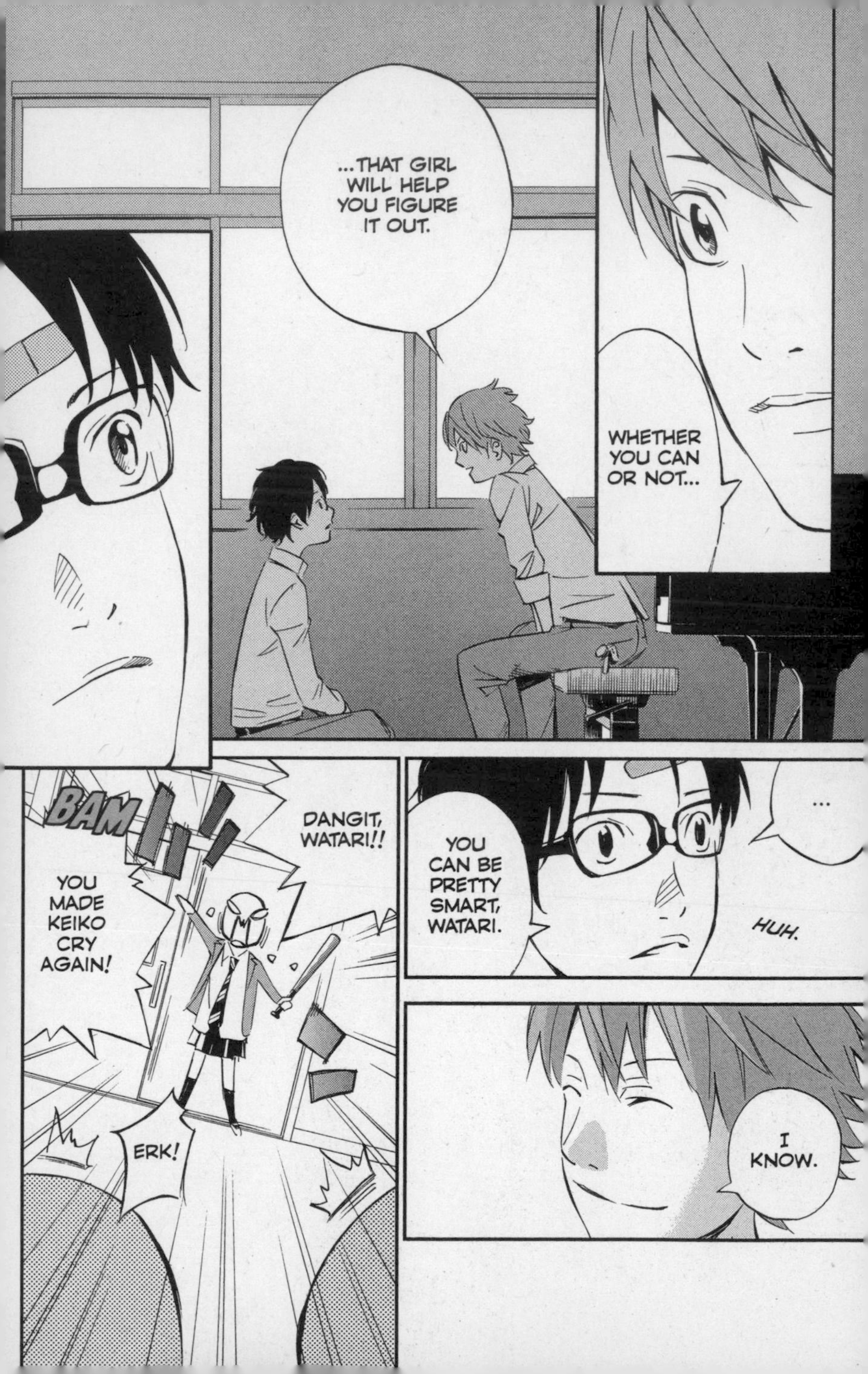
WHETHER YOU CAN OR NOT...
...THAT GIRL WILL HELP YOU FIGURE IT OUT.
...
YOU CAN BE PRETTY SMART, WATARI.
HUH.
I KNOW.
DANGIT, WATARI!!
BAM
YOU MADE KEIKO CRY AGAIN!
ERK!

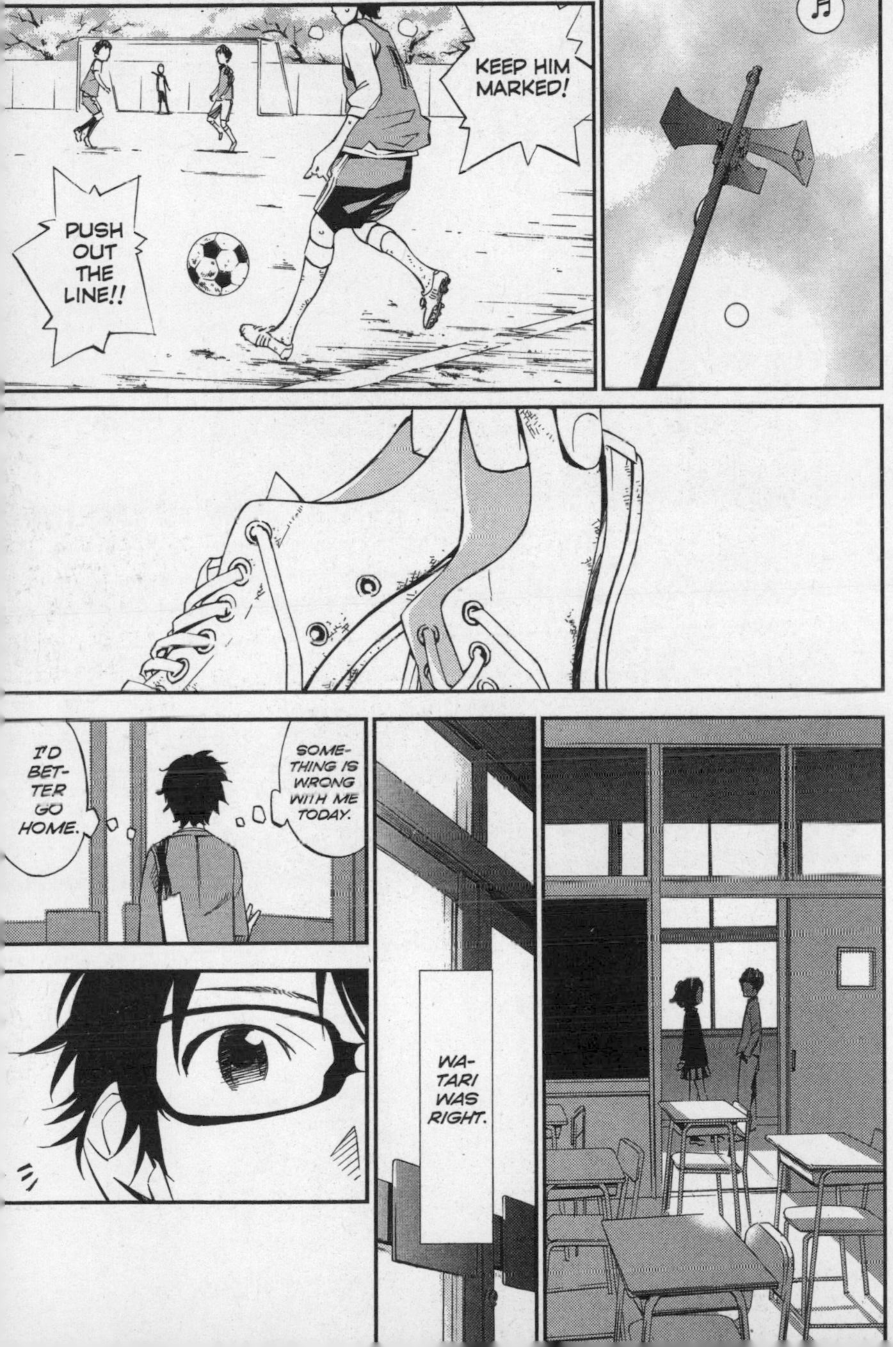
♬
KEEP HIM MARKED!
PUSH OUT THE LINE!!
WA-TARI WAS RIGHT.
SOME-THING IS WRONG WITH ME TODAY.
I'D BET-TER GO HOME.

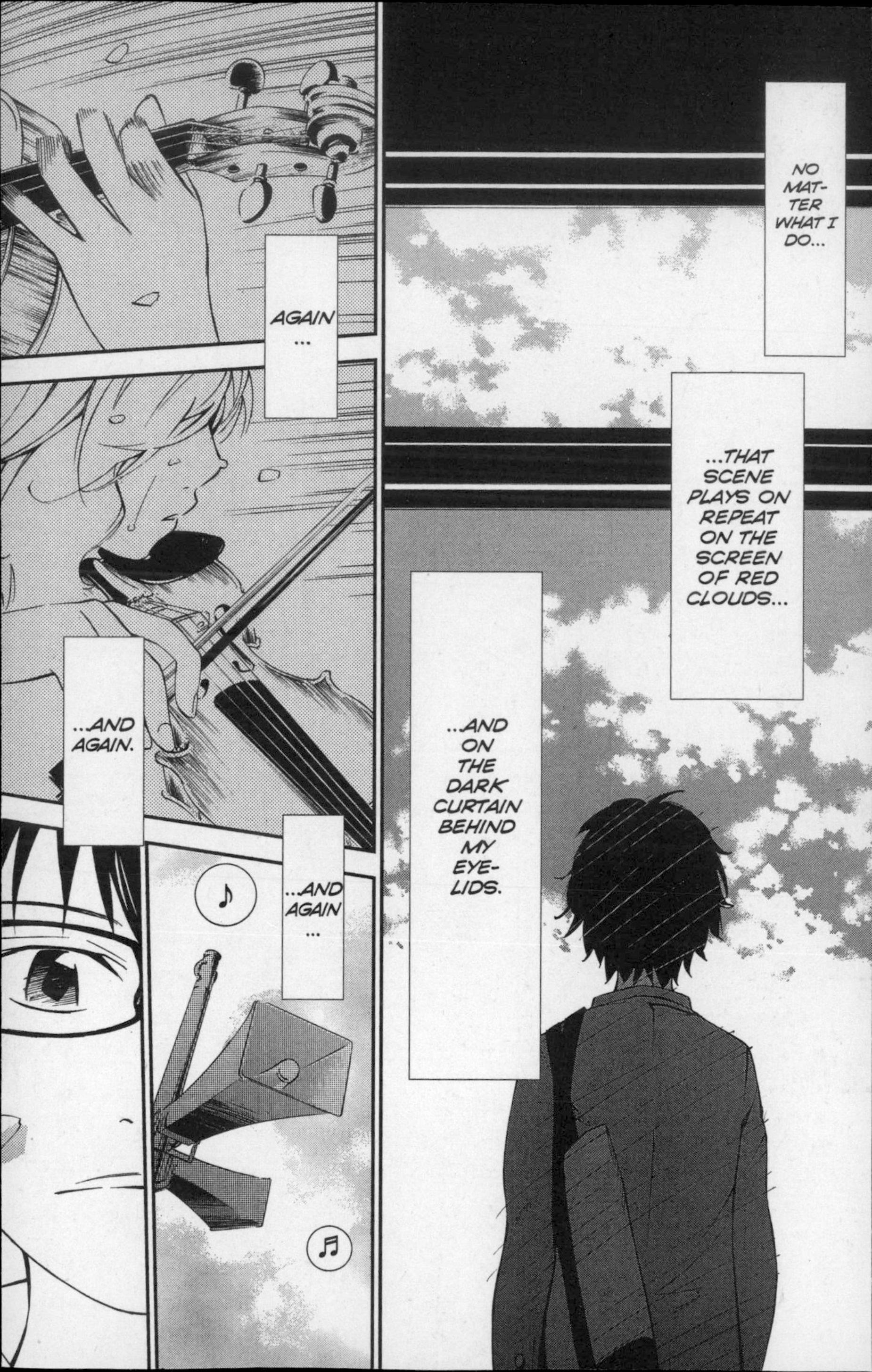
NO MAT-TER WHAT I DO...
...THAT SCENE PLAYS ON REPEAT ON THE SCREEN OF RED CLOUDS...
...AND ON THE DARK CURTAIN BEHIND MY EYE-LIDS.
AGAIN ...
...AND AGAIN.
...AND AGAIN ...

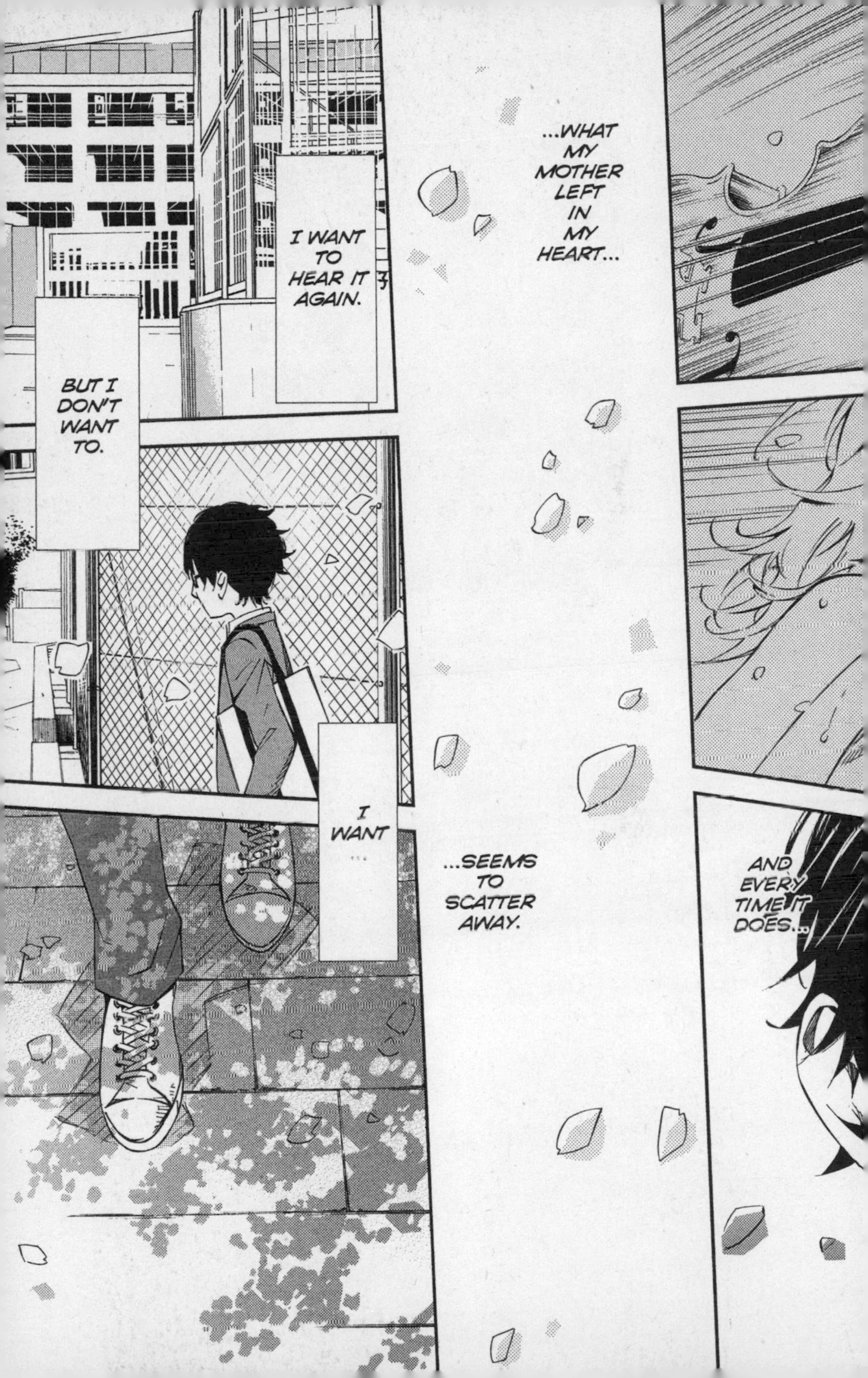
...WHAT MY MOTHER LEFT IN MY HEART...
...SEEMS TO SCATTER AWAY.
AND EVERY TIME IT DOES...
I WANT TO HEAR IT AGAIN.
BUT I DON'T WANT TO.
I WANT ...

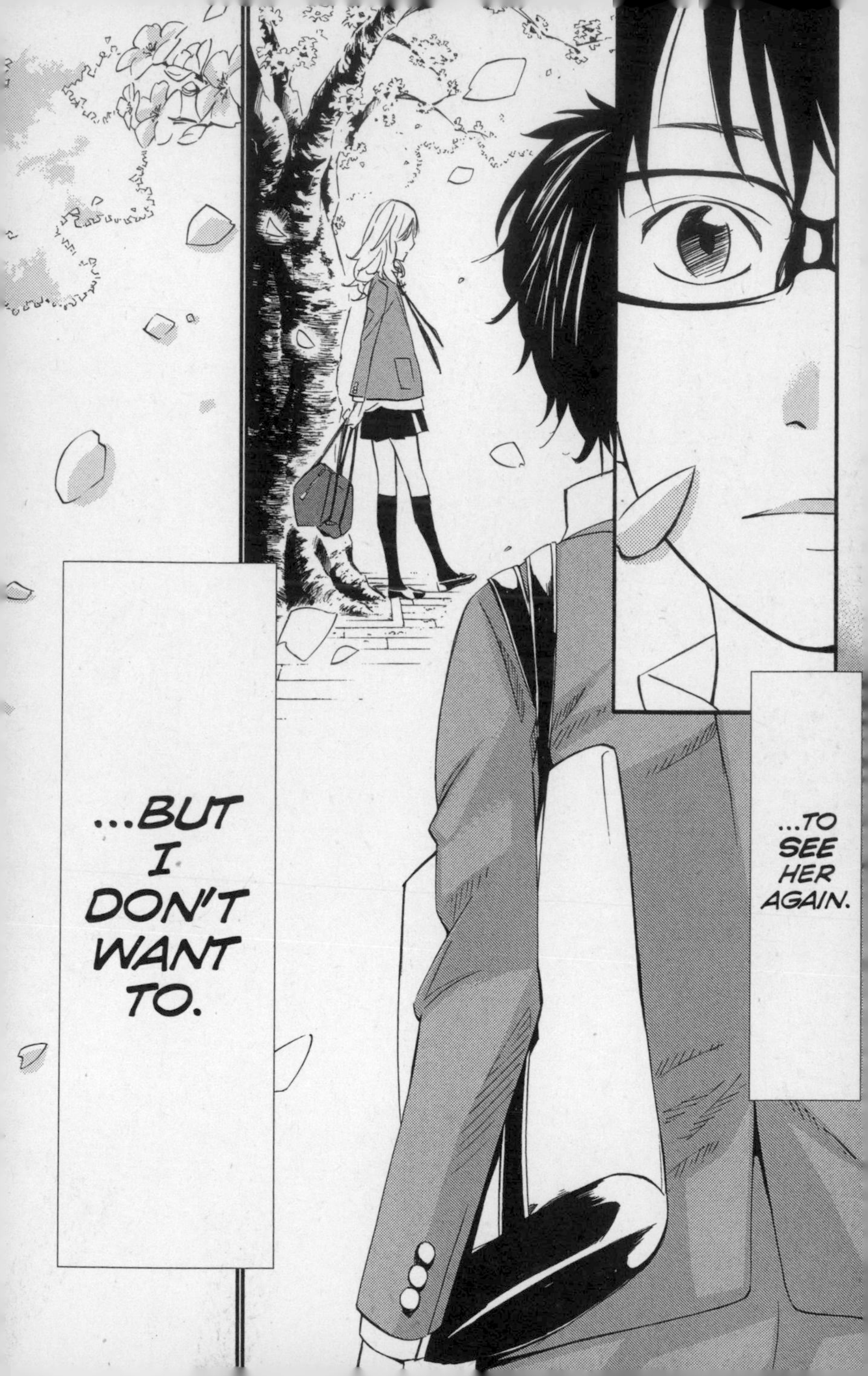
...TO SEE HER AGAIN.
...BUT I DON'T WANT TO.

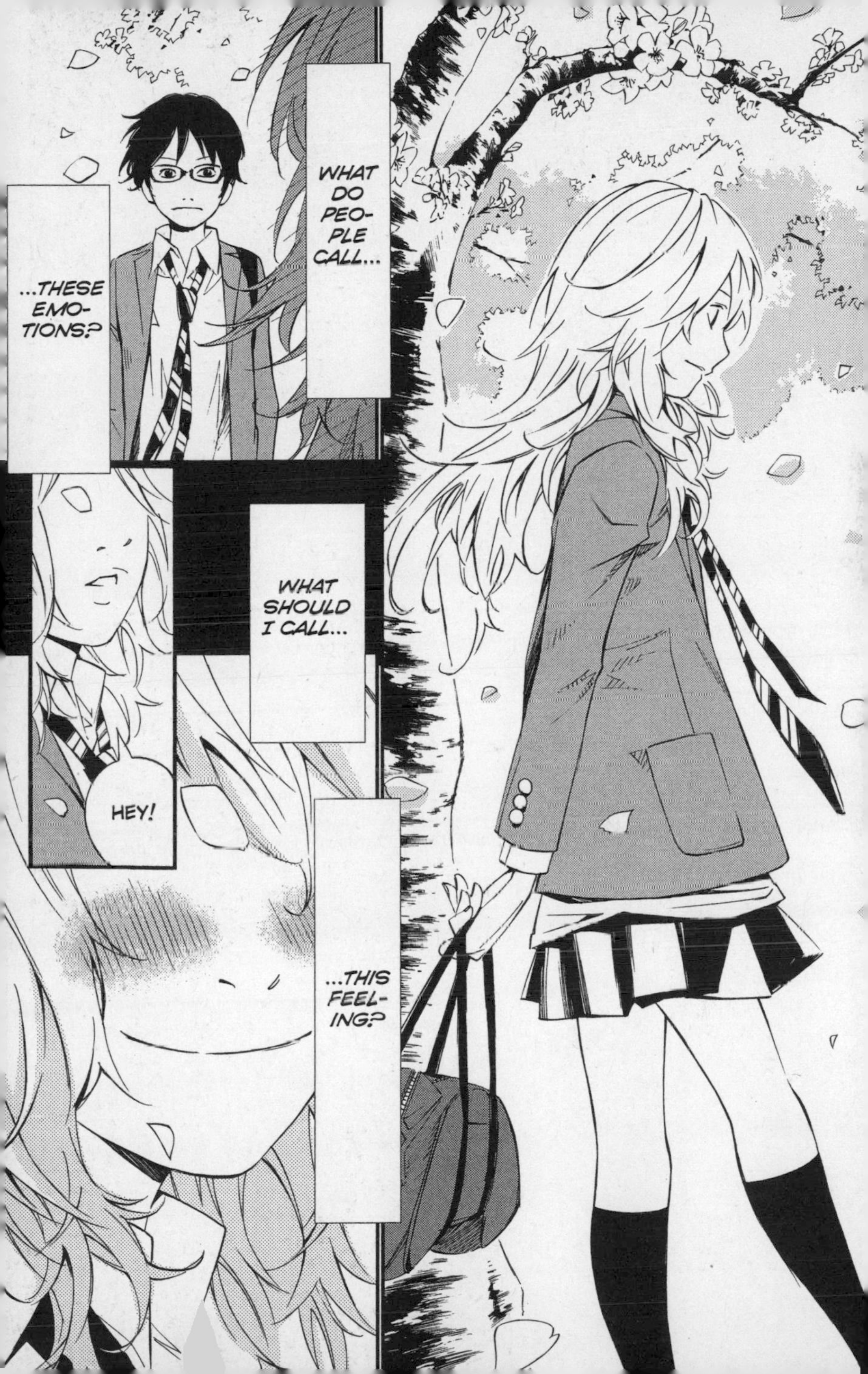
WHAT DO PEOPLE CALL...
...THESE EMOTIONS?
WHAT SHOULD I CALL...
HEY!
...THIS FEELING?

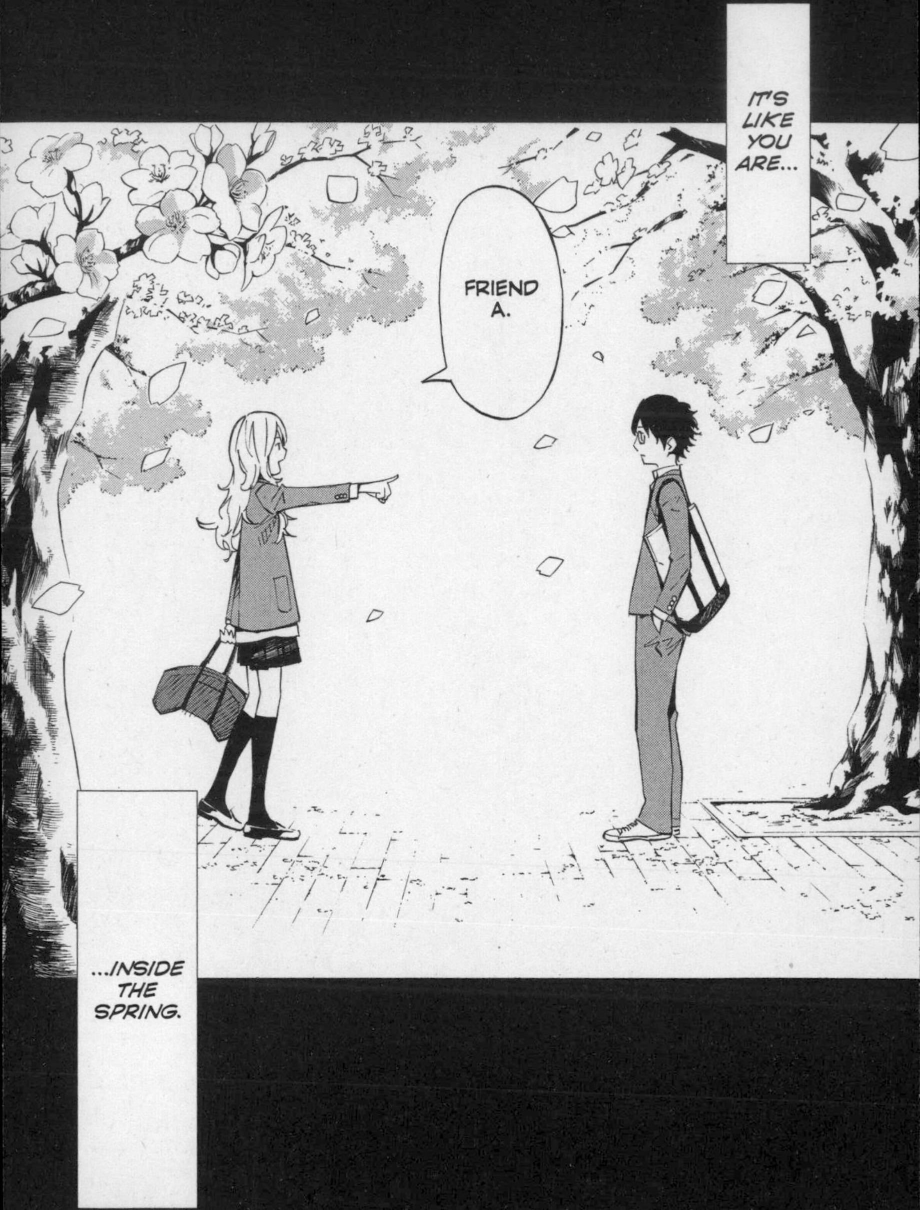
IT'S LIKE YOU ARE...
FRIEND A.
...INSIDE THE SPRING.

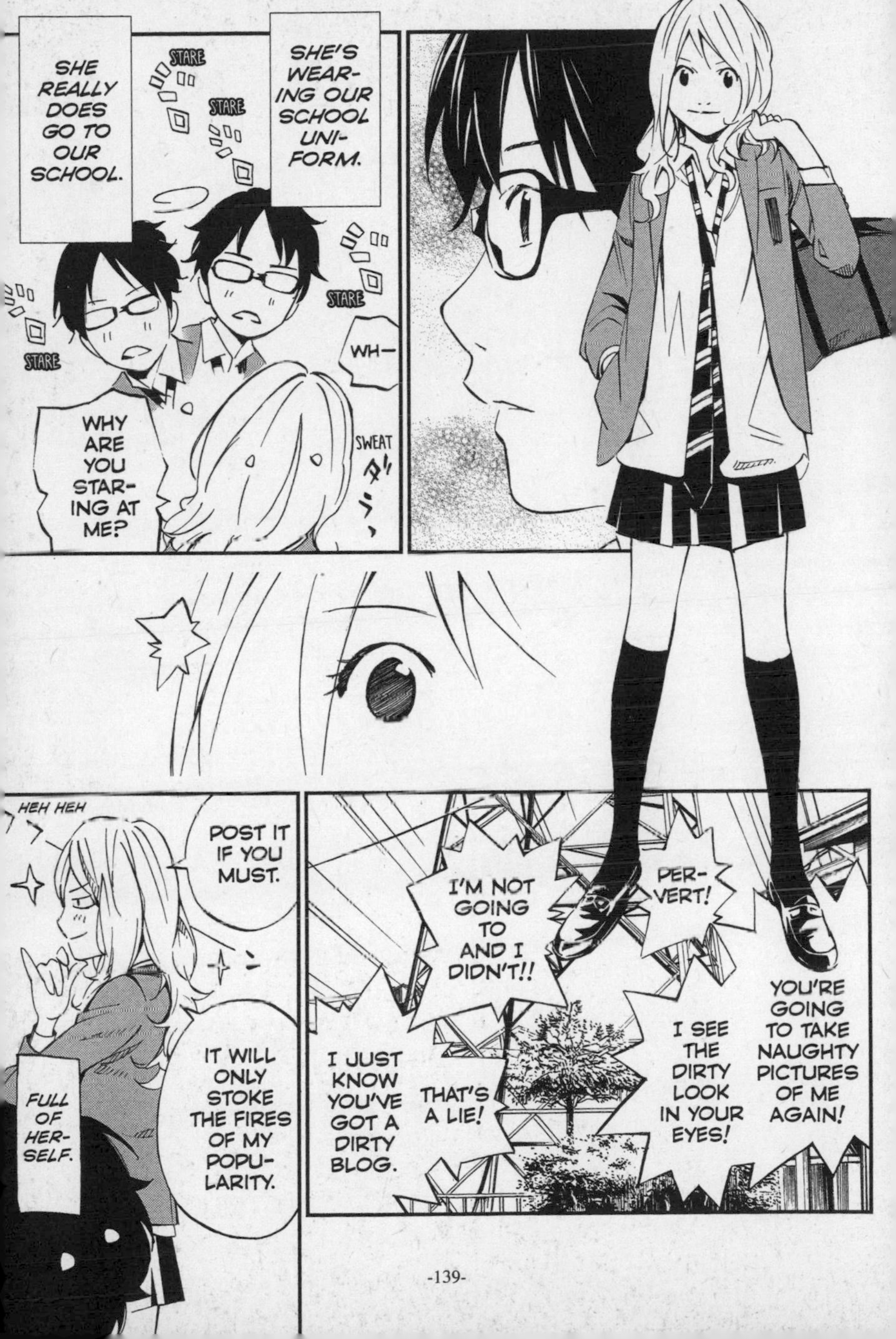
SHE'S WEARING OUR SCHOOL UNIFORM.
STARE
STARE
SHE REALLY DOES GO TO OUR SCHOOL.
STARE
STARE
WH—
WHY ARE YOU STARING AT ME?
SWEAT
YOU'RE GOING TO TAKE NAUGHTY PICTURES OF ME AGAIN!
I SEE THE DIRTY LOOK IN YOUR EYES!
PER-VERT!
I'M NOT GOING TO AND I DIDN'T!!
THAT'S A LIE!
I JUST KNOW YOU'VE GOT A DIRTY BLOG.
HEH HEH
POST IT IF YOU MUST.
IT WILL ONLY STOKE THE FIRES OF MY POPULARITY.
FULL OF HER-SELF.

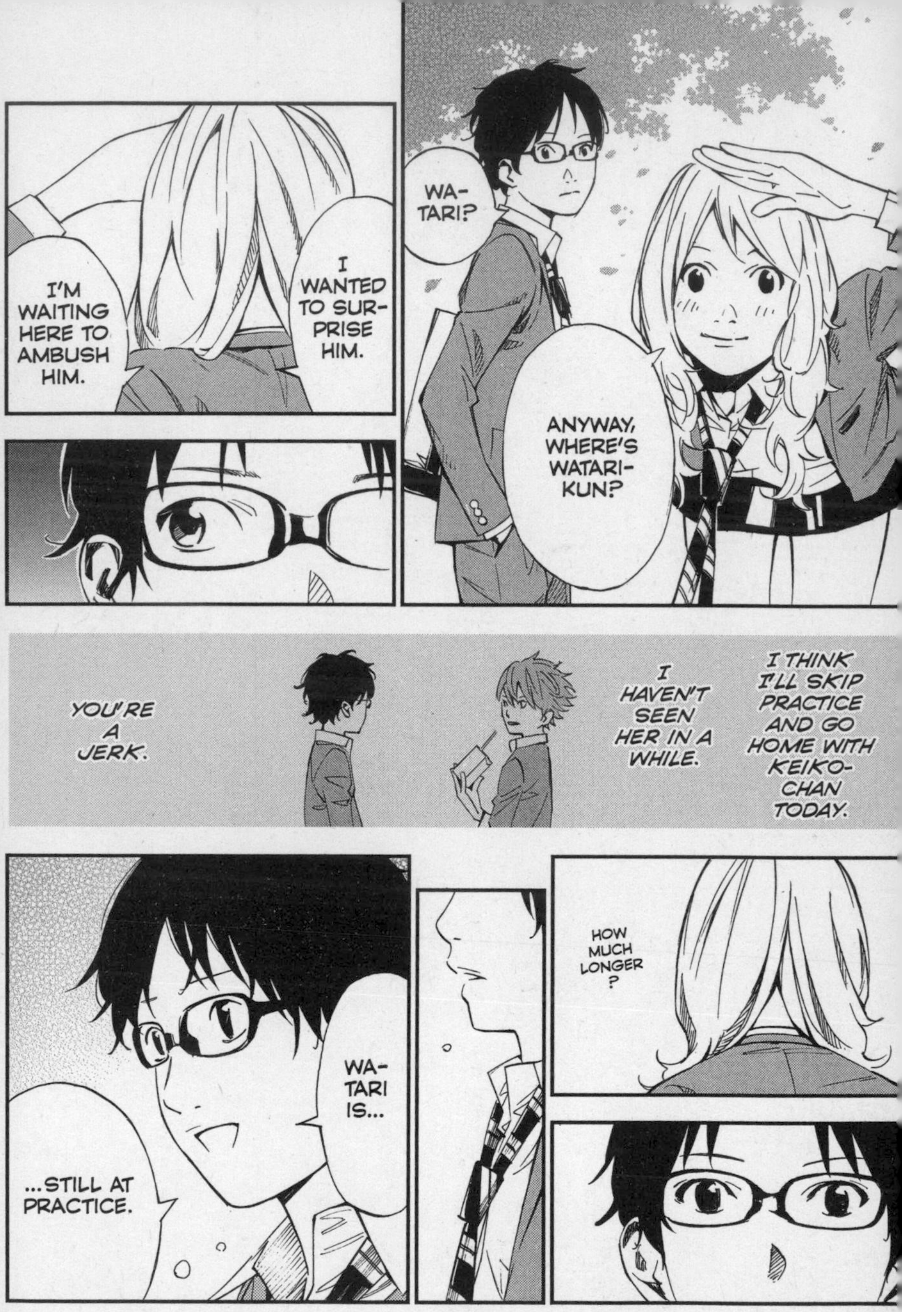
ANYWAY, WHERE'S WATARI-KUN?
WA-TARI?
I WANTED TO SUR-PRISE HIM.
I'M WAITING HERE TO AMBUSH HIM.
I THINK I'LL SKIP PRACTICE AND GO HOME WITH KEIKO-CHAN TODAY.
I HAVEN'T SEEN HER IN A WHILE.
YOU'RE A JERK.
HOW MUCH LONGER?
WA-TARI IS...
...STILL AT PRACTICE.

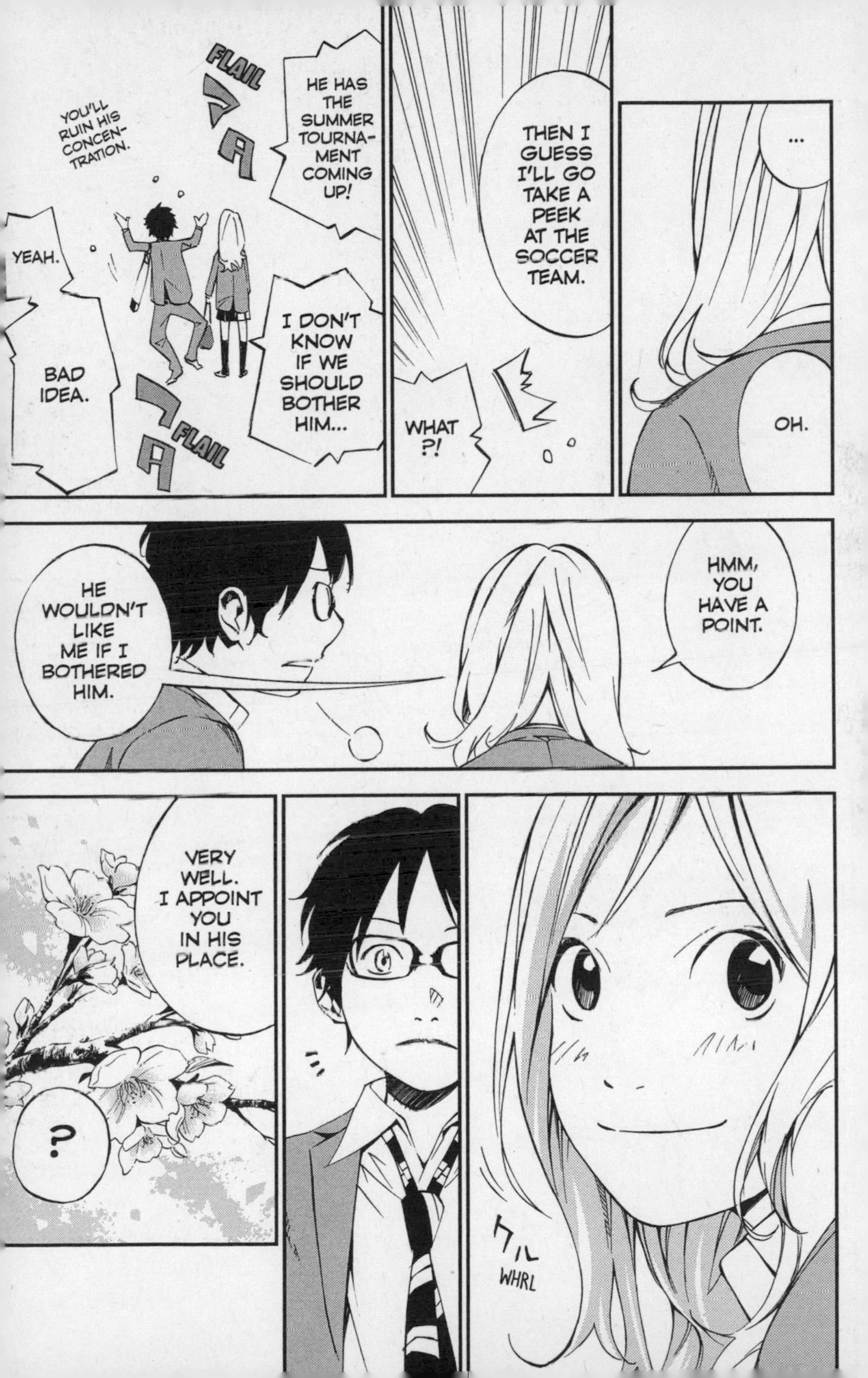
...
OH.
THEN I GUESS I'LL GO TAKE A PEEK AT THE SOCCER TEAM.
WHAT ?!
FLAIL
HE HAS THE SUMMER TOURNA-MENT COMING UP!
YOU'LL RUIN HIS CONCEN-TRATION.
I DON'T KNOW IF WE SHOULD BOTHER HIM...
YEAH.
BAD IDEA.
FLAIL
HMM, YOU HAVE A POINT.
HE WOULDN'T LIKE ME IF I BOTHERED HIM.
WHRL
VERY WELL. I APPOINT YOU IN HIS PLACE.
?

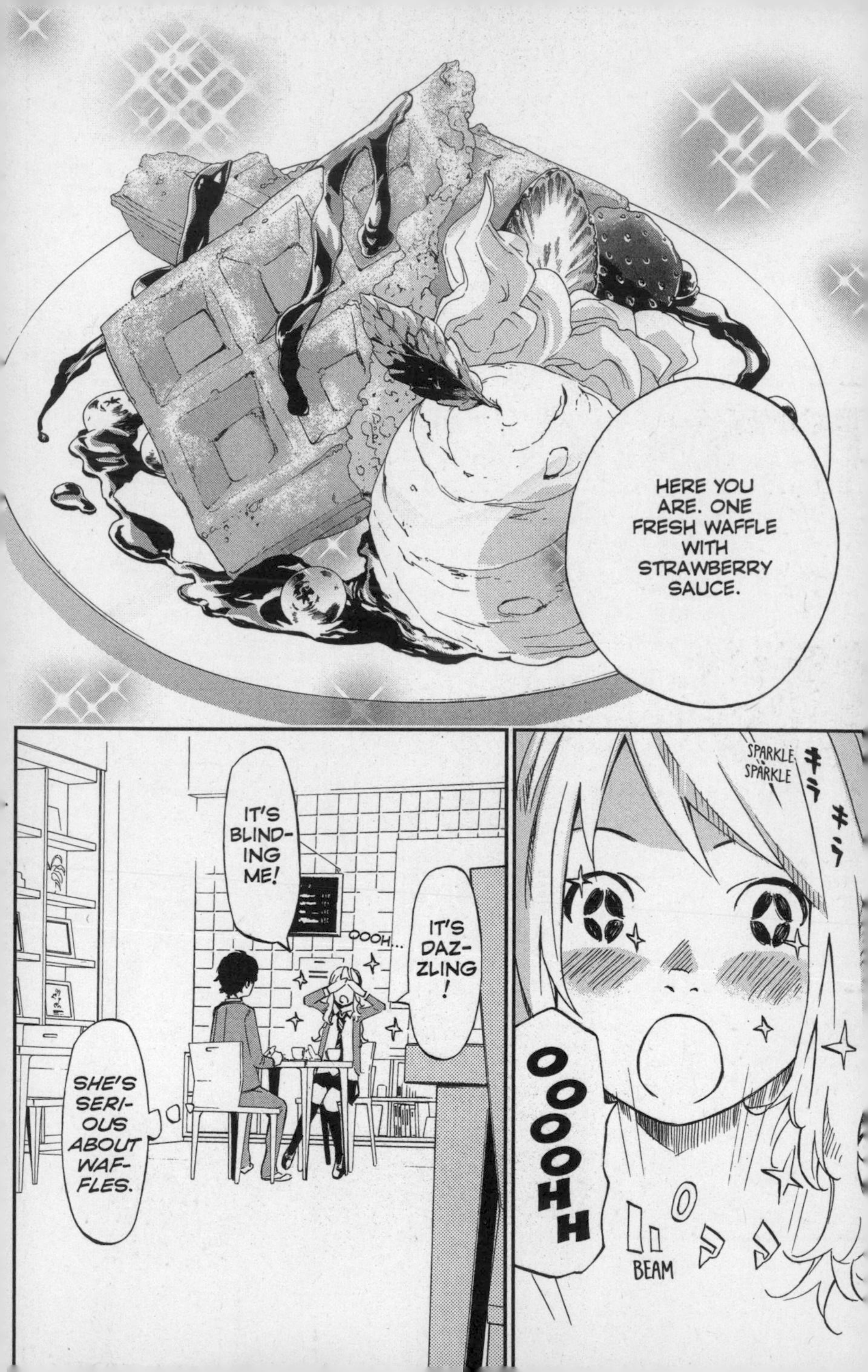
HERE YOU ARE. ONE FRESH WAFFLE WITH STRAWBERRY SAUCE.
SPARKLE SPARKLE
OOOOHH
BEAM
IT'S BLIND-ING ME!
IT'S DAZ-ZLING!
OOOH...
SHE'S SERI-OUS ABOUT WAF-FLES.

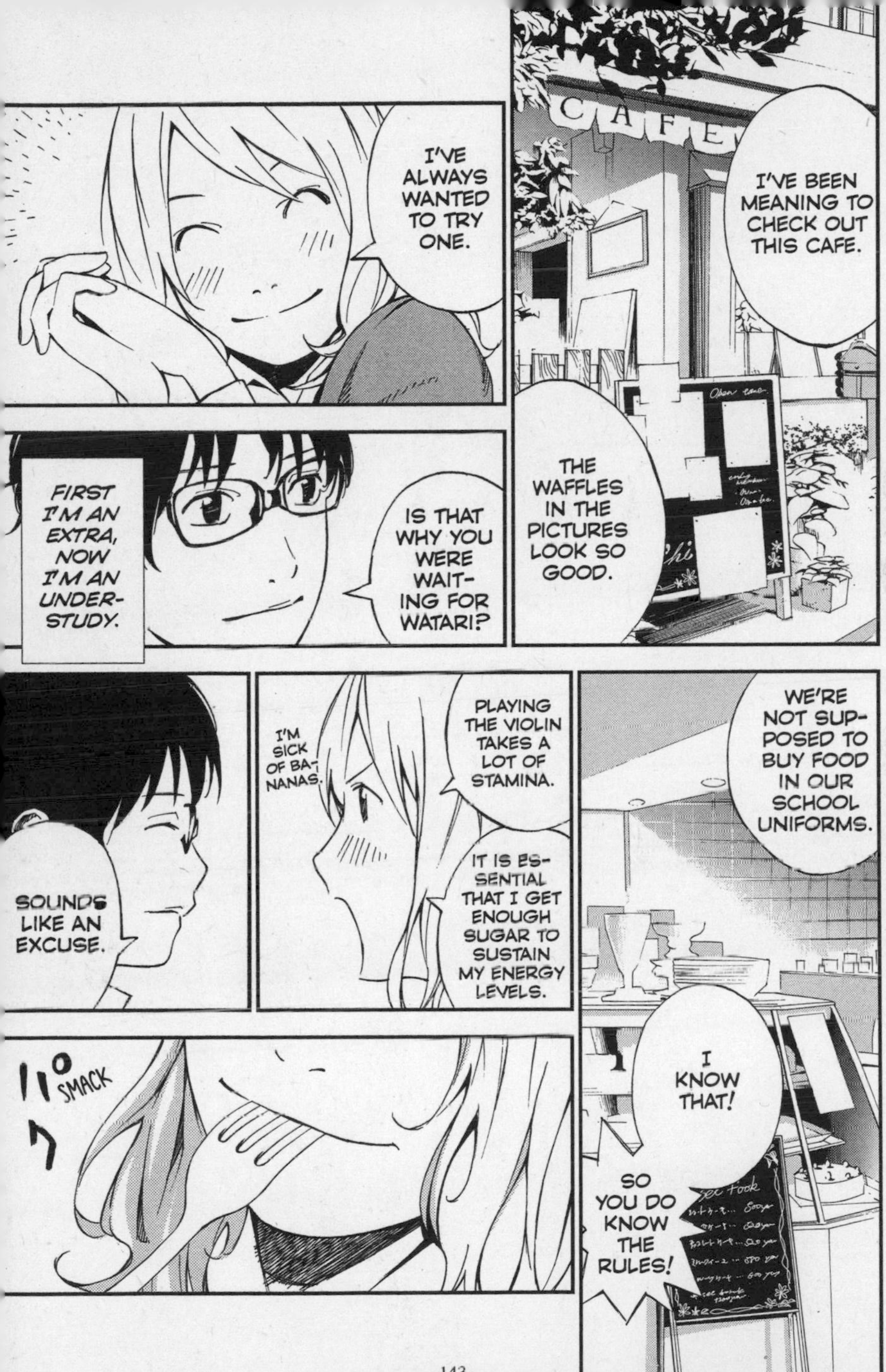
I'VE BEEN MEANING TO CHECK OUT THIS CAFE.
THE WAFFLES IN THE PICTURES LOOK SO GOOD.
CAFE
I'VE ALWAYS WANTED TO TRY ONE.
IS THAT WHY YOU WERE WAITING FOR WATARI?
FIRST I'M AN EXTRA, NOW I'M AN UNDERSTUDY.
WE'RE NOT SUPPOSED TO BUY FOOD IN OUR SCHOOL UNIFORMS.
I KNOW THAT!
SO YOU DO KNOW THE RULES!
PLAYING THE VIOLIN TAKES A LOT OF STAMINA.
I'M SICK OF BANANAS.
IT IS ESSENTIAL THAT I GET ENOUGH SUGAR TO SUSTAIN MY ENERGY LEVELS.
SOUNDS LIKE AN EXCUSE.
SMACK

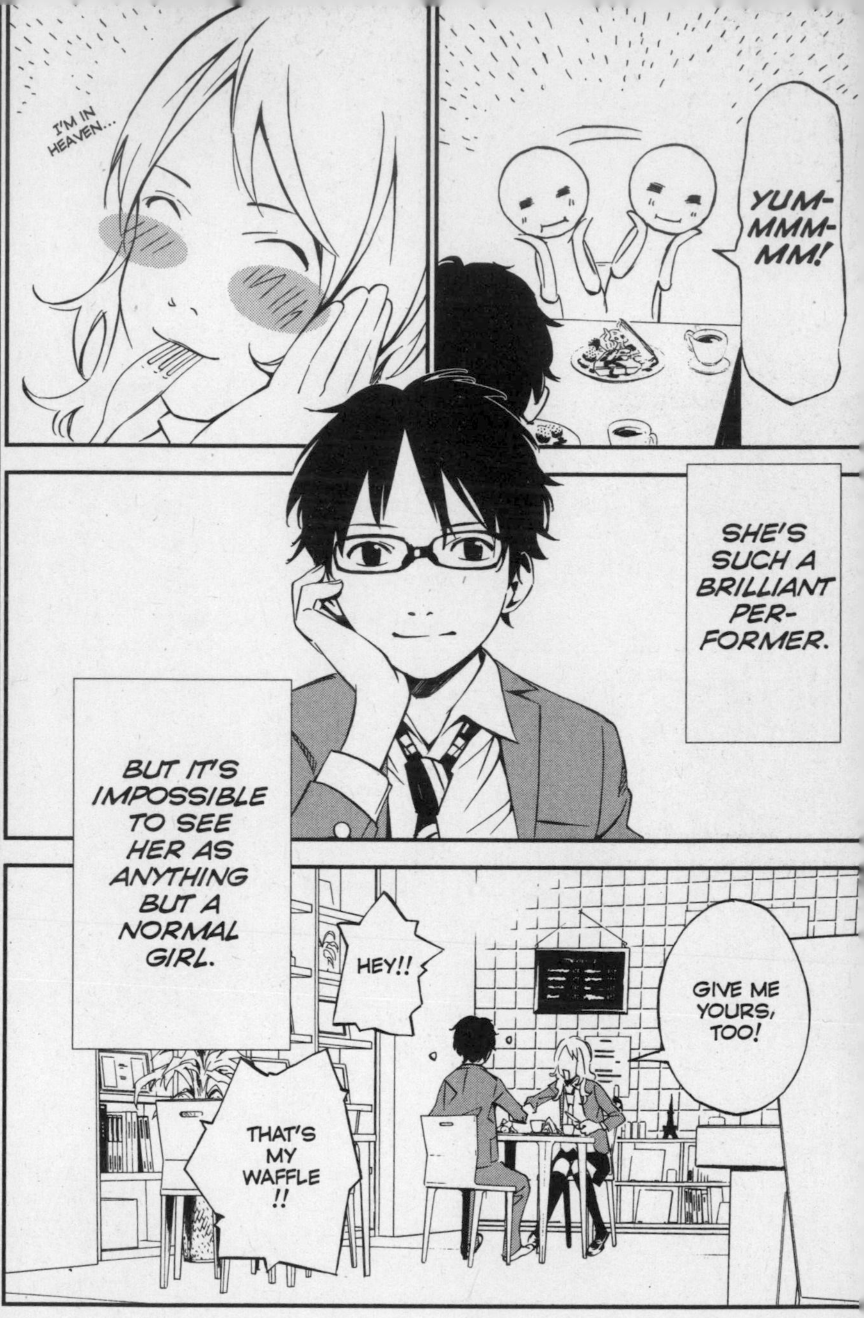
YUMMMMM-MM!
I'M IN HEAVEN...
SHE'S SUCH A BRILLIANT PERFORMER.
BUT IT'S IMPOSSIBLE TO SEE HER AS ANYTHING BUT A NORMAL GIRL.
GIVE ME YOURS, TOO!
HEY!!
THAT'S MY WAFFLE!!

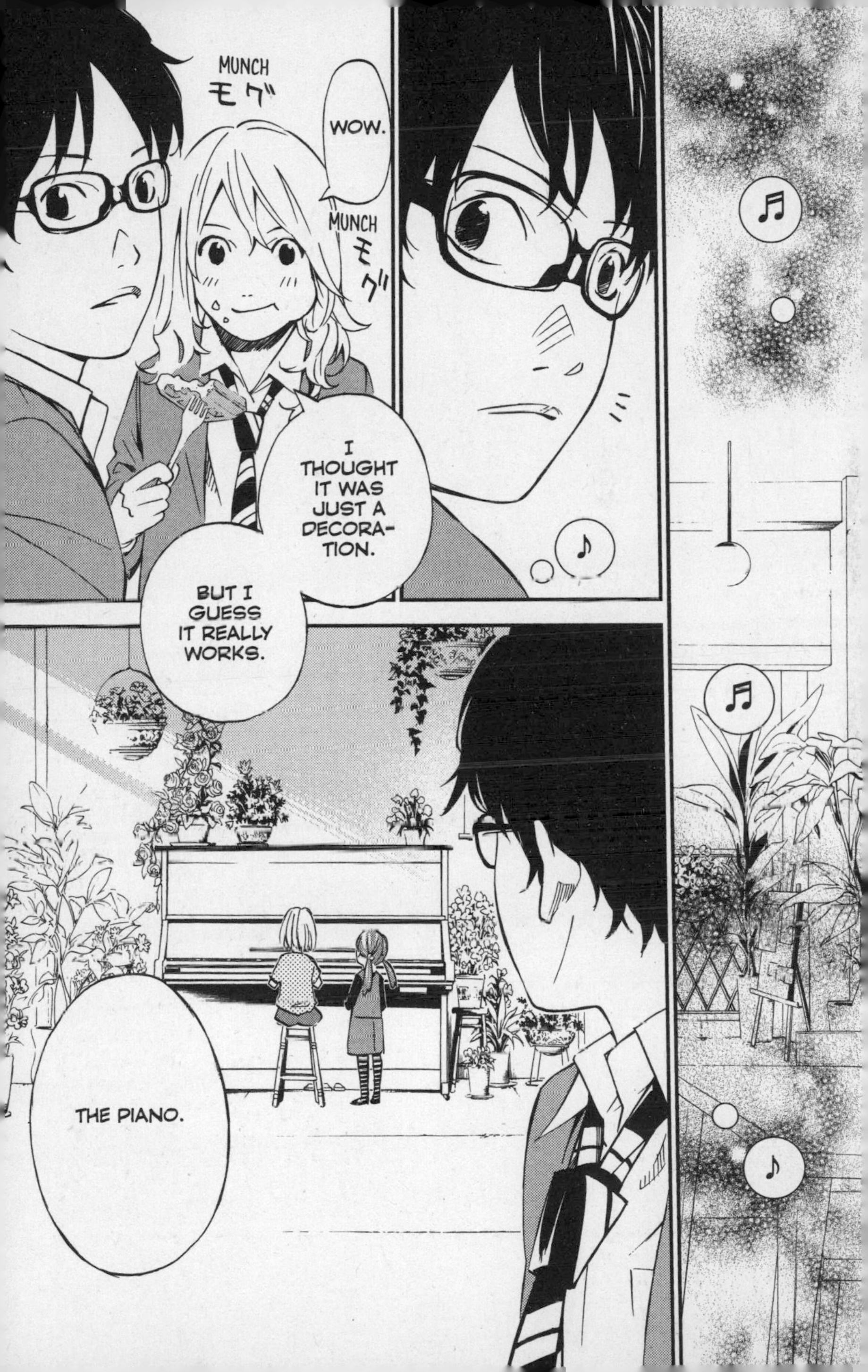
MUNCH
モグ
WOW.
MUNCH
モグ
I THOUGHT IT WAS JUST A DECORA-TION.
BUT I GUESS IT REALLY WORKS.
THE PIANO.

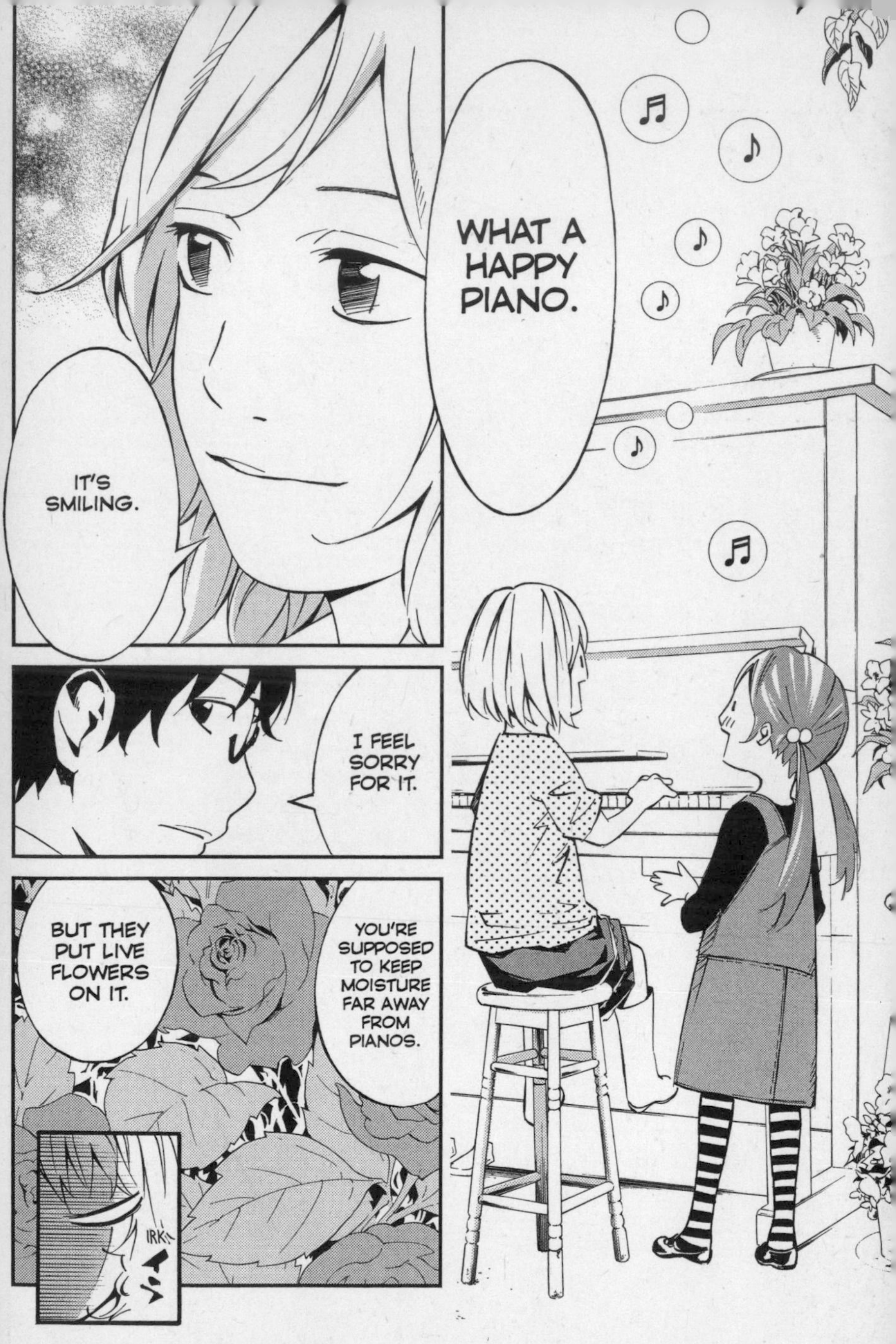
WHAT A HAPPY PIANO.
IT'S SMILING.
I FEEL SORRY FOR IT.
YOU'RE SUPPOSED TO KEEP MOISTURE FAR AWAY FROM PIANOS.
BUT THEY PUT LIVE FLOWERS ON IT.
IRK!

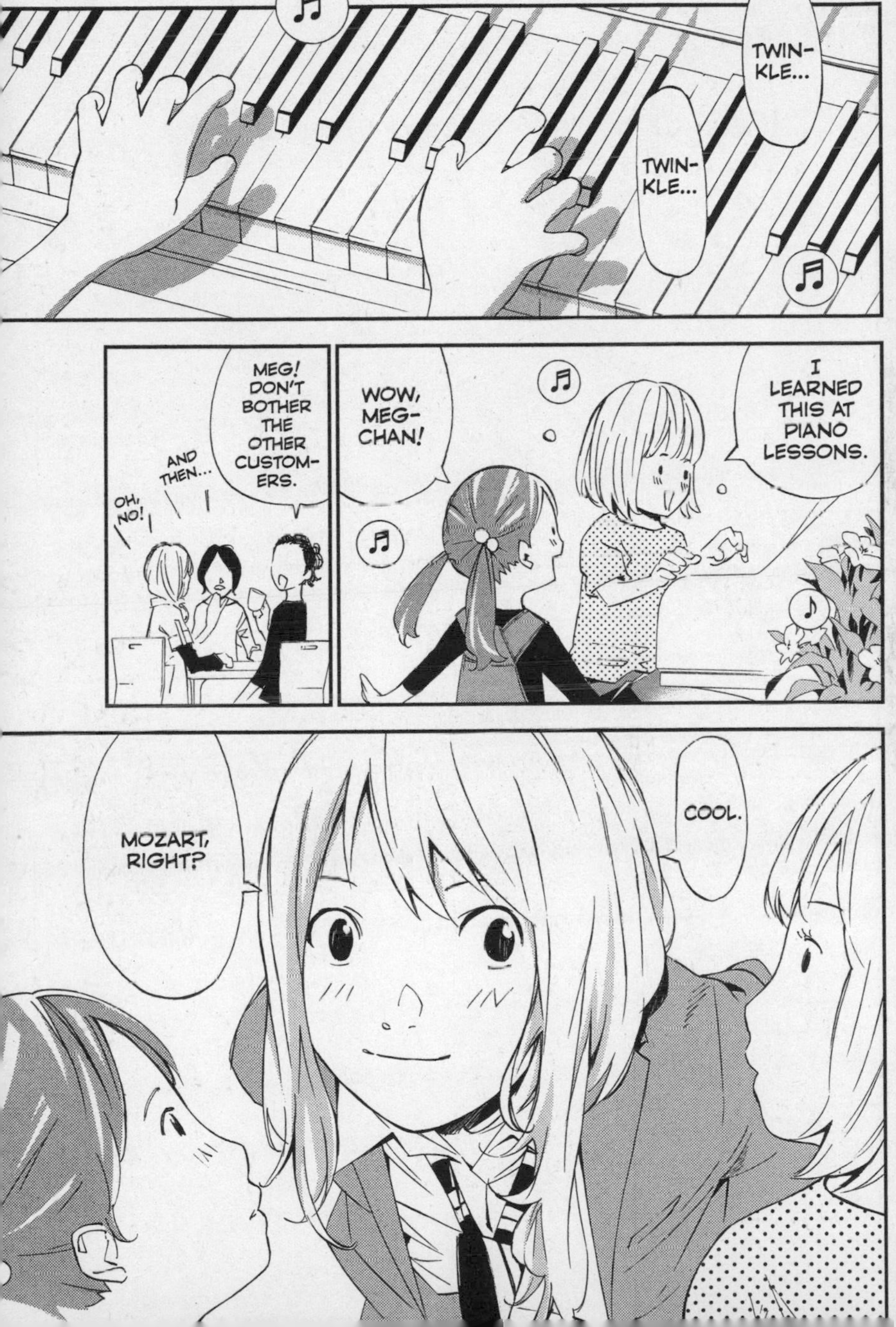
TWIN-KLE...
TWIN-KLE...
I LEARNED THIS AT PIANO LESSONS.
WOW, MEG-CHAN!
MEG! DON'T BOTHER THE OTHER CUSTOM-ERS.
AND THEN...
OH, NO!
COOL.
MOZART, RIGHT?

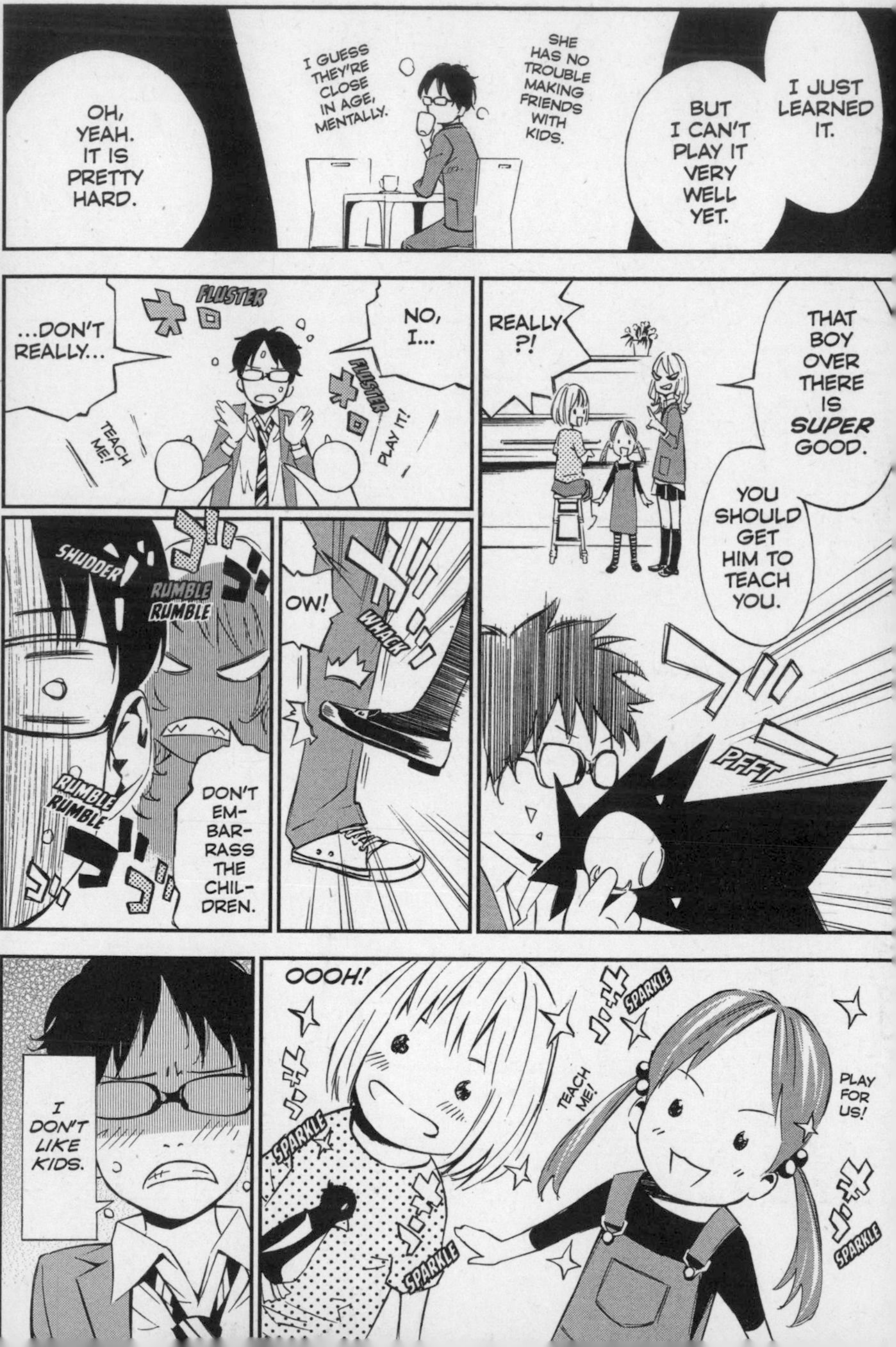
I JUST LEARNED IT.
BUT I CAN'T PLAY IT VERY WELL YET.
SHE HAS NO TROUBLE MAKING FRIENDS WITH KIDS.
I GUESS THEY'RE CLOSE IN AGE, MENTALLY.
OH, YEAH. IT IS PRETTY HARD.
THAT BOY OVER THERE IS SUPER GOOD.
REALLY?!
YOU SHOULD GET HIM TO TEACH YOU.
NO, I...
FLUSTER
FLUSTER
PLAY IT!
...DON'T REALLY...
TEACH ME!
PFFT
OW!
WHACK
SHUDDER
RUMBLE RUMBLE
DON'T EMBARRASS THE CHILDREN.
RUMBLE RUMBLE
SPARKLE
PLAY FOR US!
SPARKLE
OOOH!
TEACH ME!
SPARKLE
SPARKLE
I DON'T LIKE KIDS.

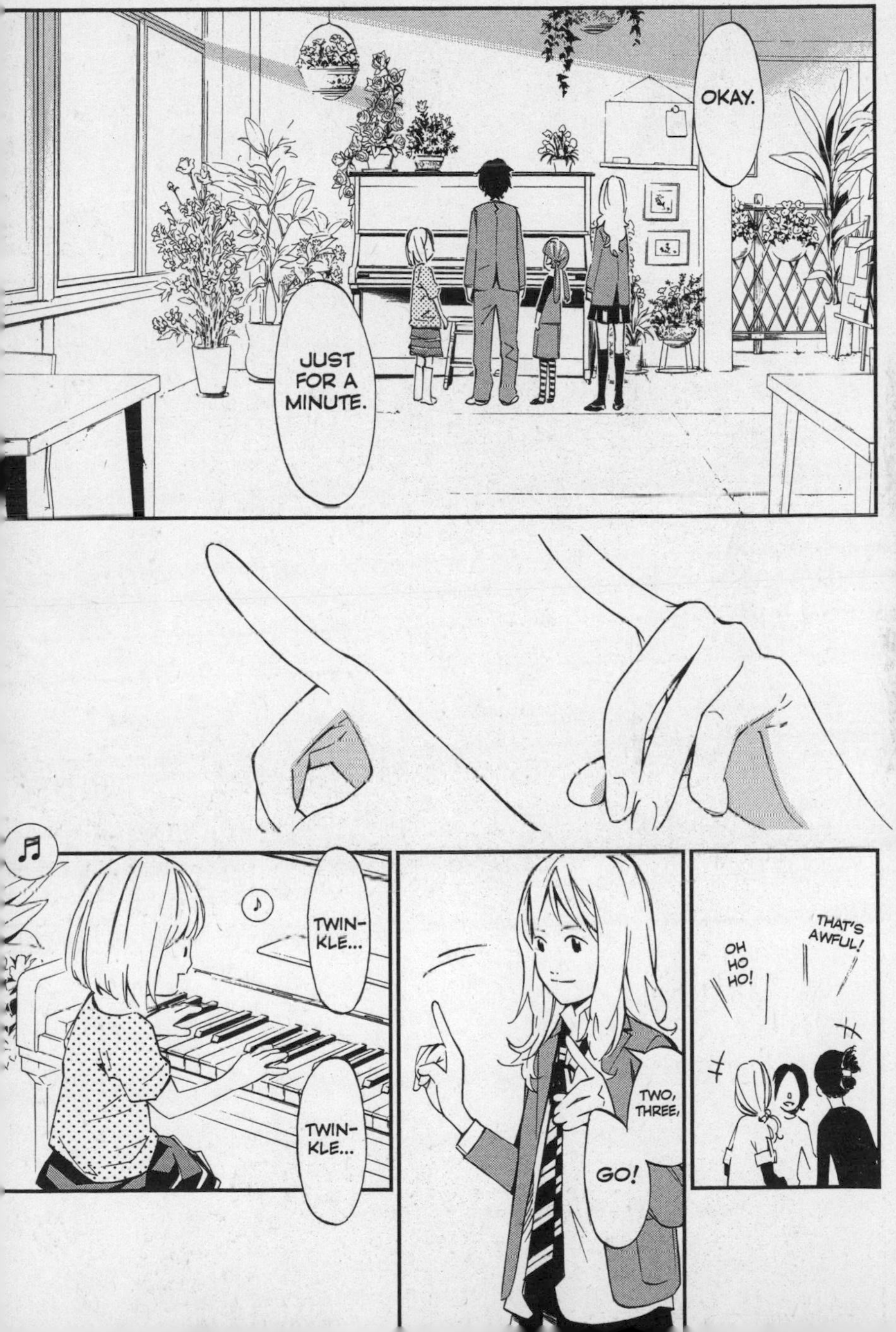
OKAY.
JUST FOR A MINUTE.
THAT'S AWFUL!
OH HO HO!
TWO, THREE,
GO!
TWIN-KLE...
TWIN-KLE...

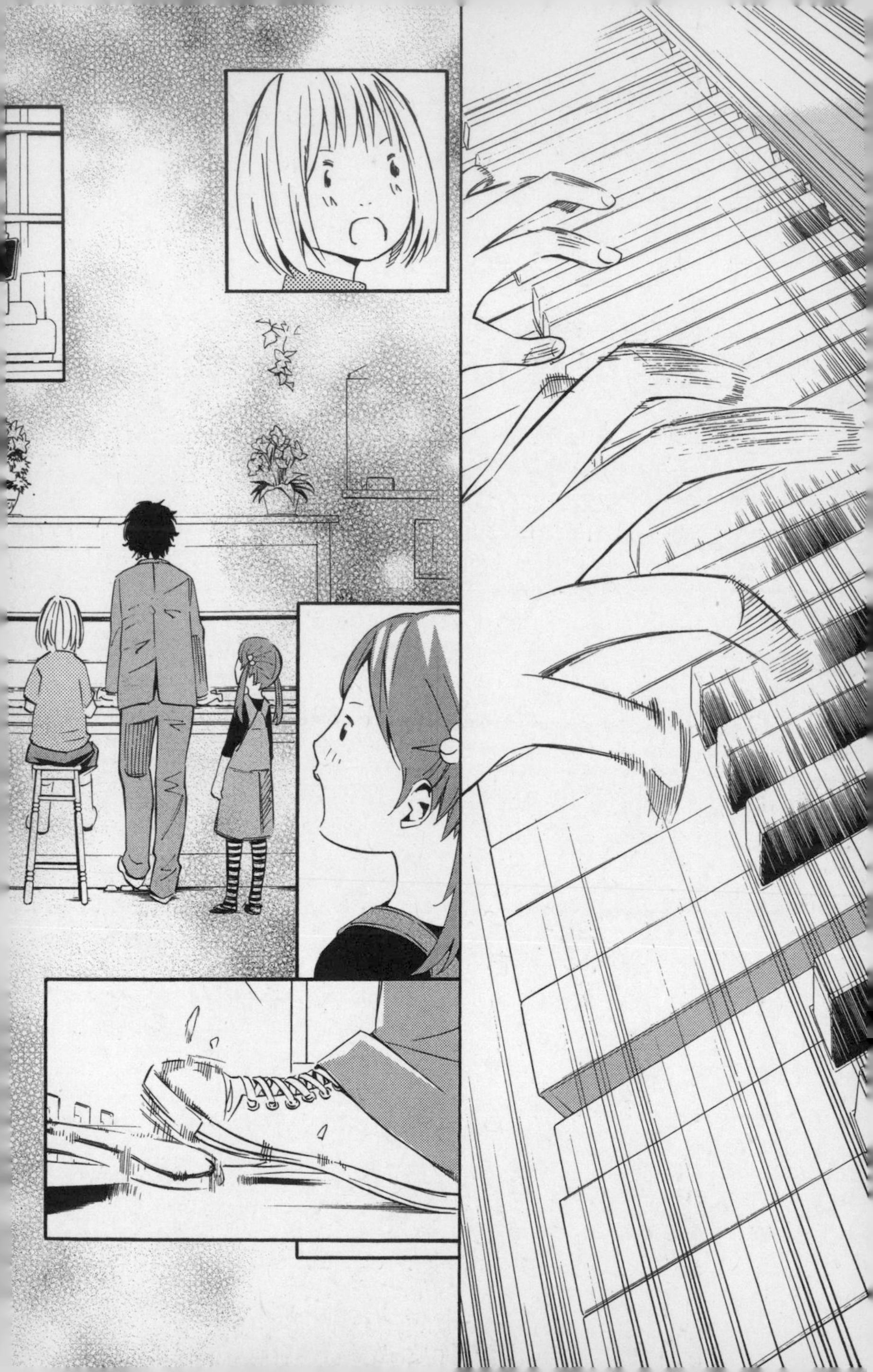

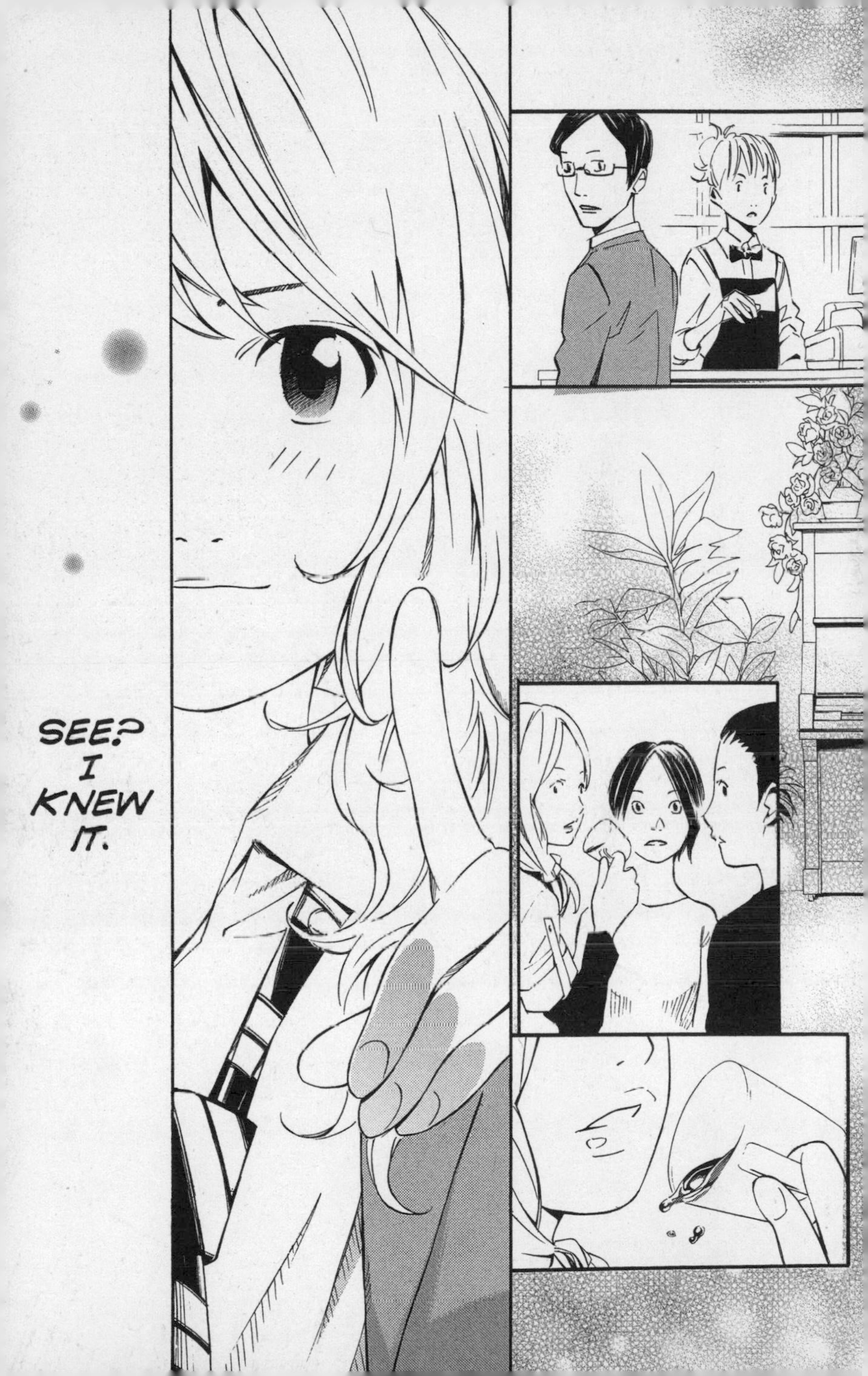
SEE? I KNEW IT.

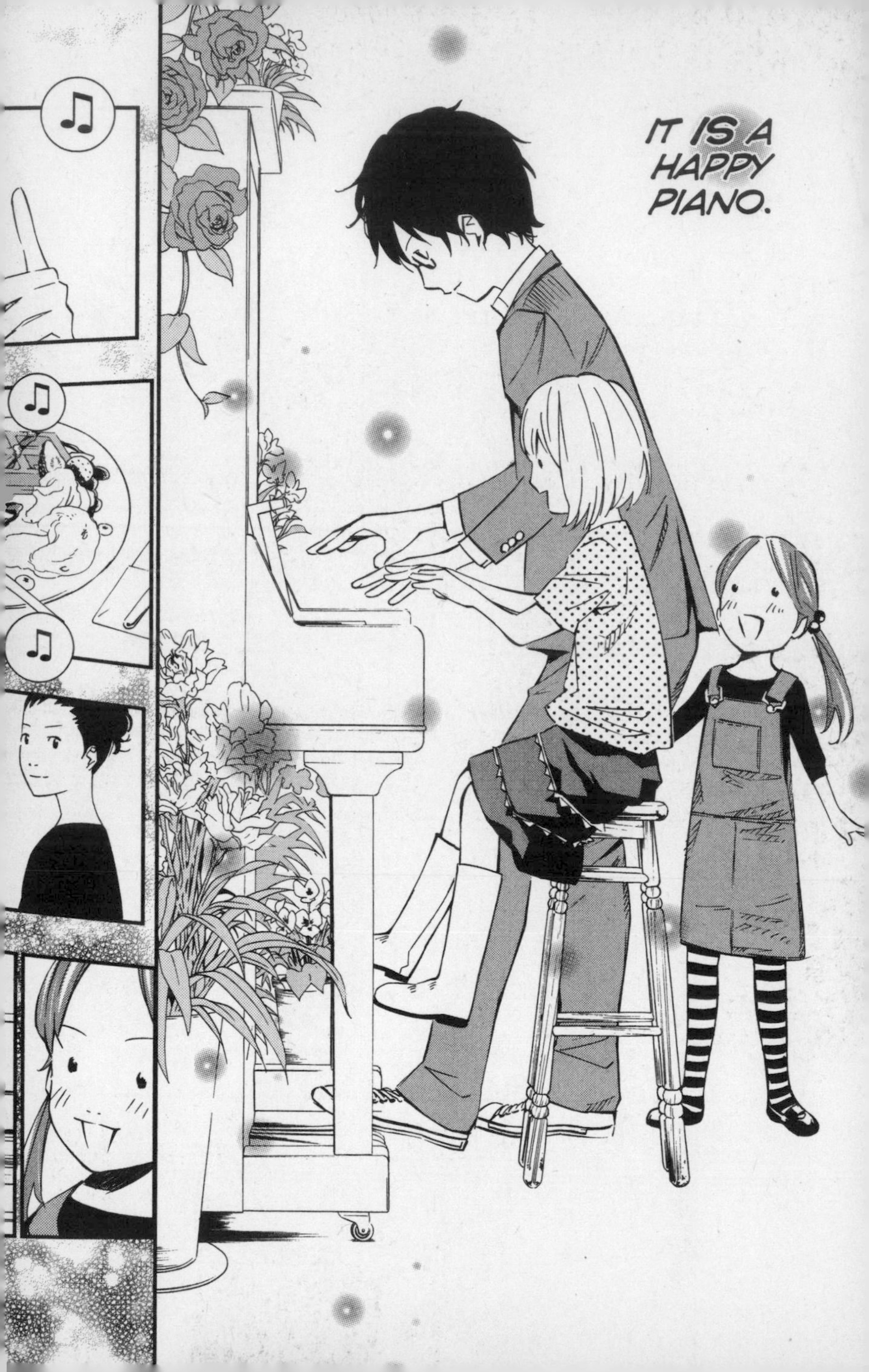
IT IS A HAPPY PIANO.

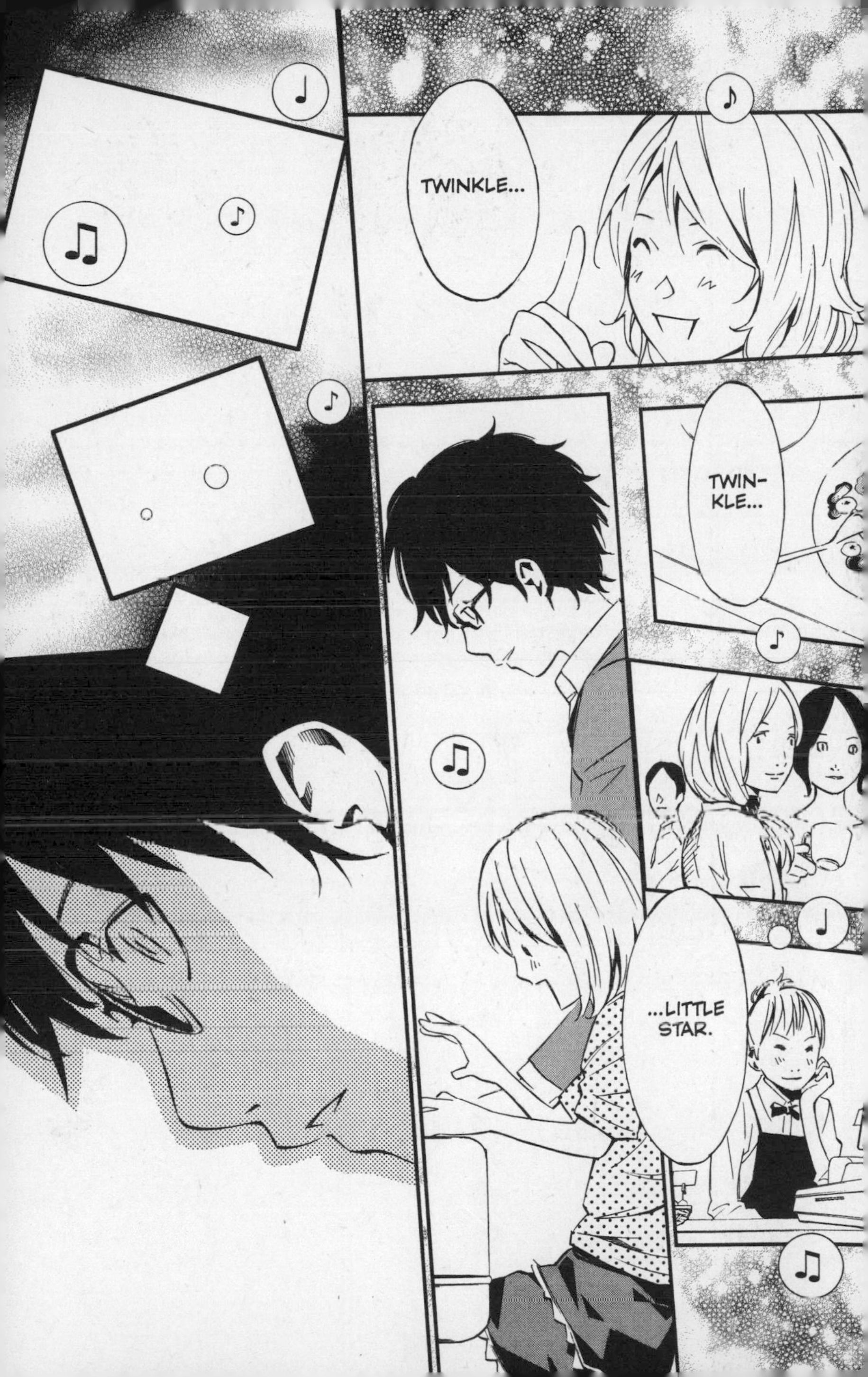
TWINKLE...
TWIN-
KLE...
...LITTLE
STAR.

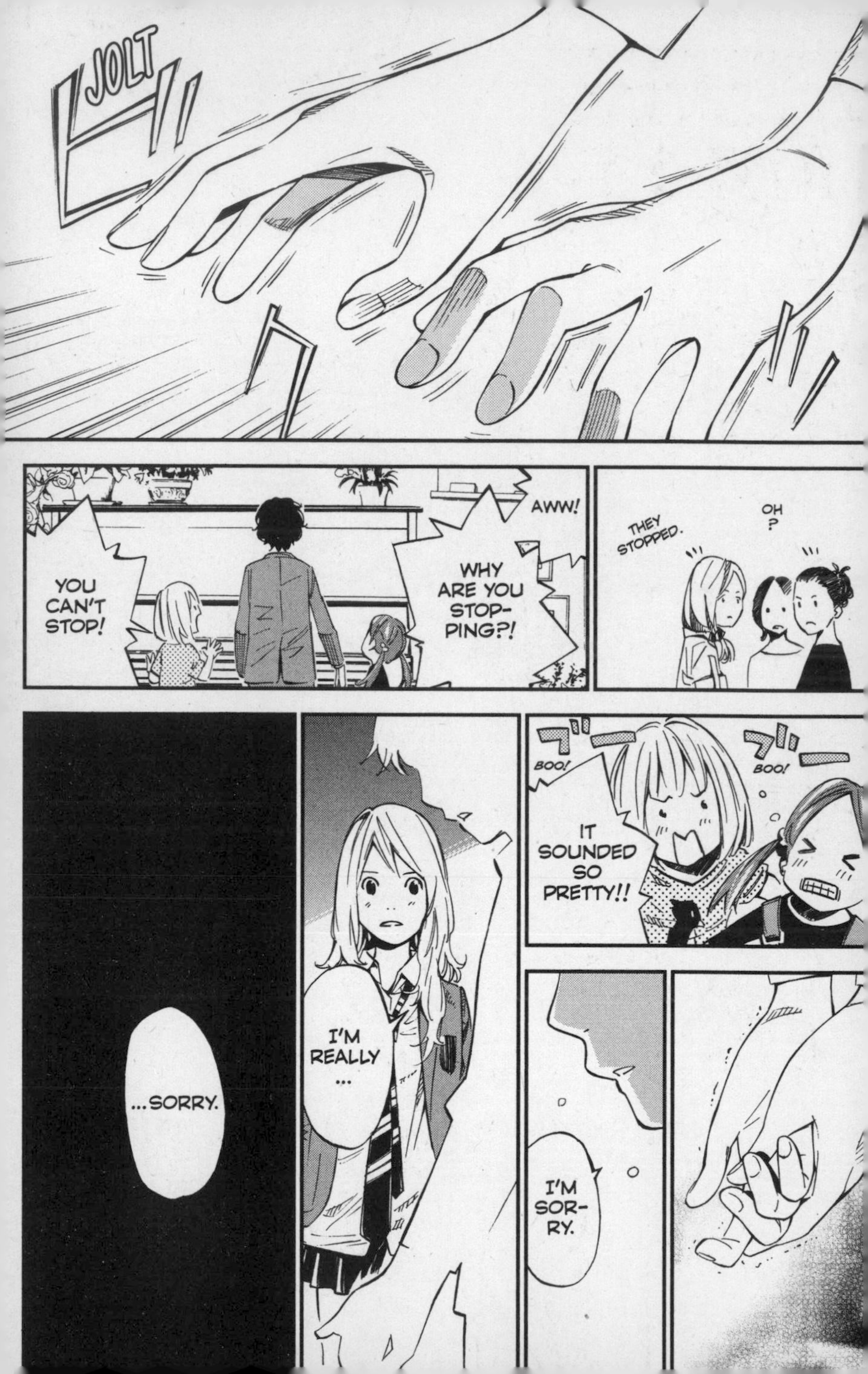
JOLT
OH?
THEY STOPPED.
AWW!
WHY ARE YOU STOP-PING?!
YOU CAN'T STOP!
BOO!
BOO!
IT SOUNDED SO PRETTY!!
I'M SOR-RY.
I'M REALLY ...
...SORRY.

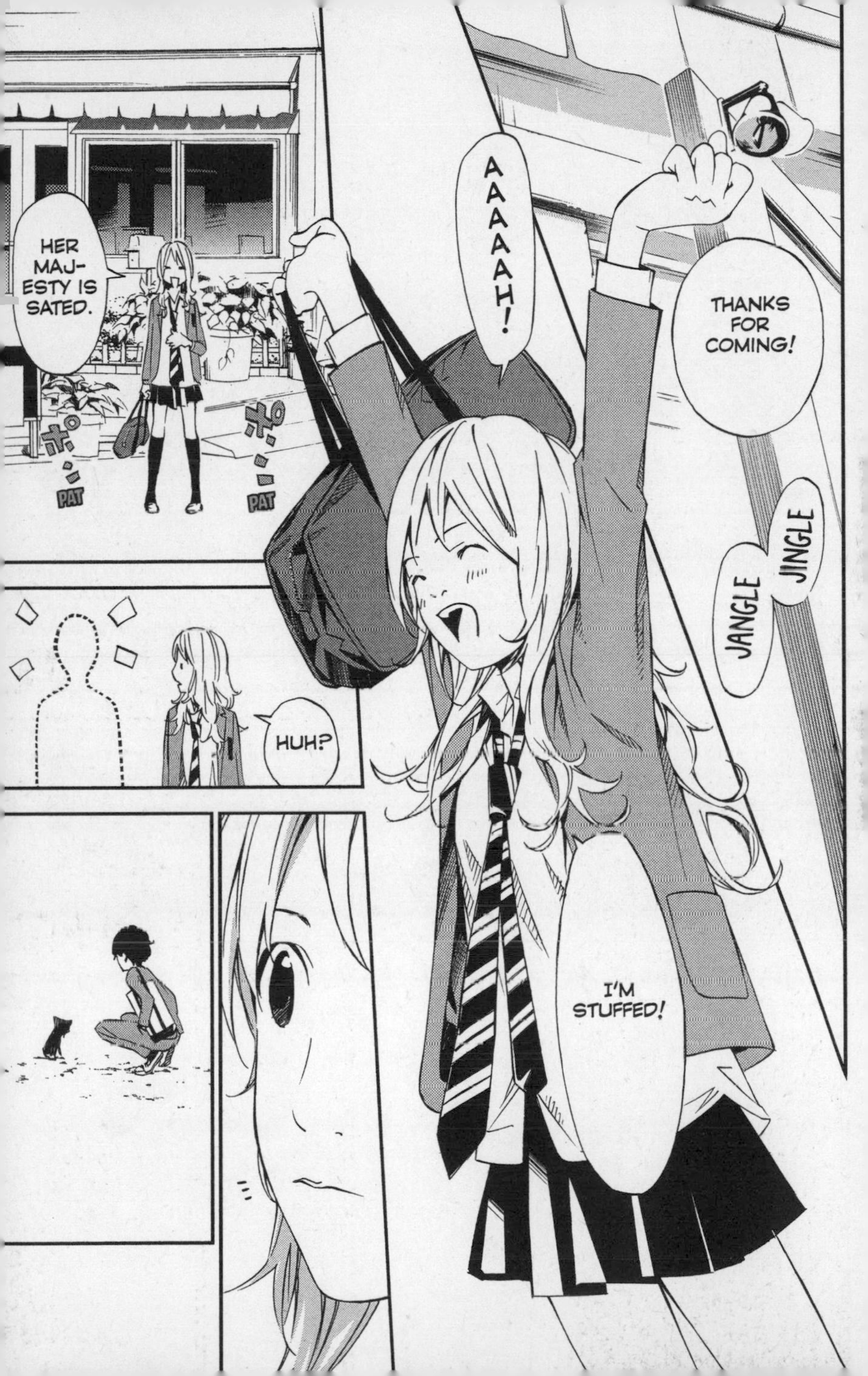
THANKS FOR COMING!
JANGLE JINGLE
AAAAAH!
I'M STUFFED!
HER MAJ-ESTY IS SATED.
PAT
PAT
HUH?

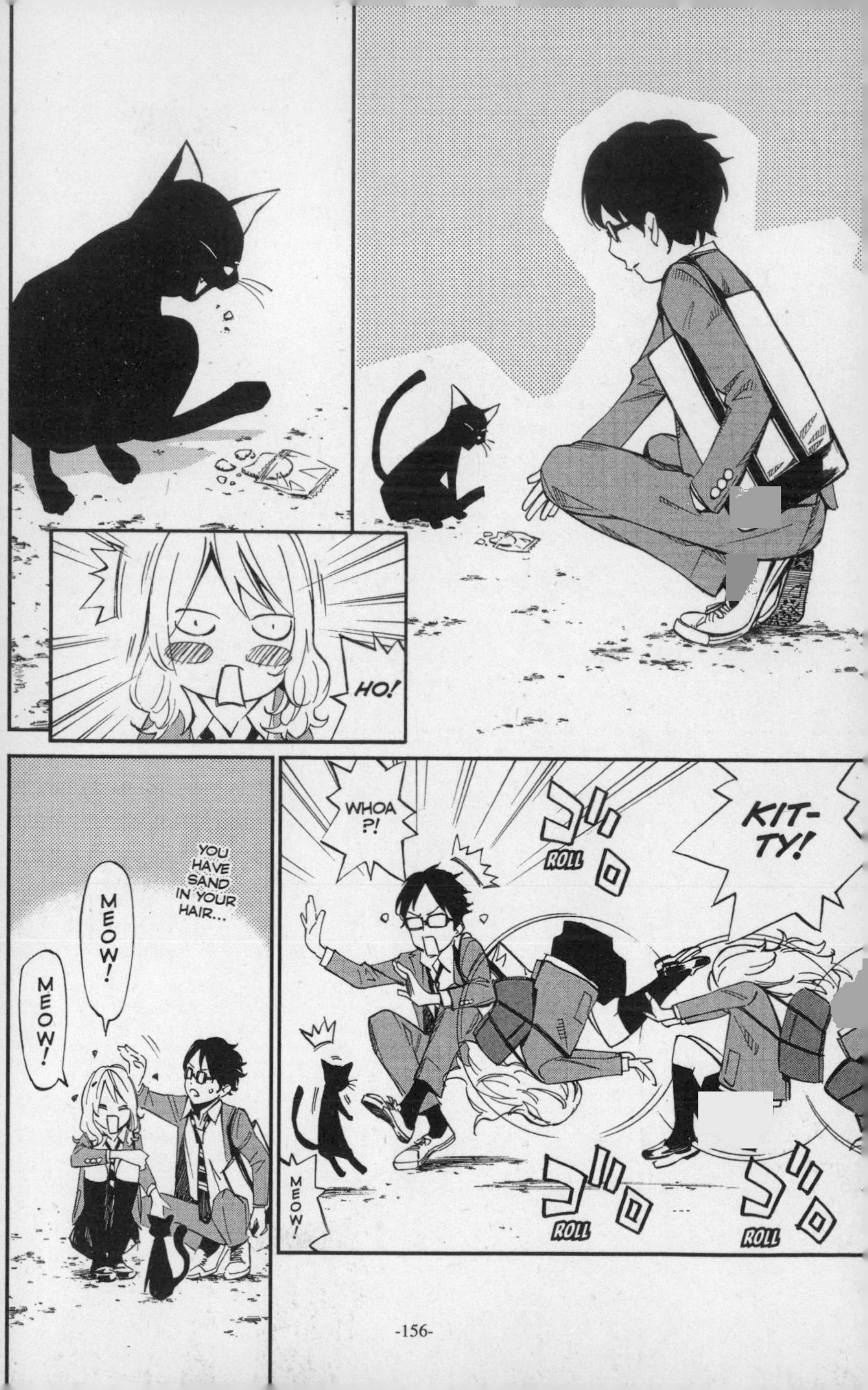
HO!
KIT-TY!
WHOA ?!
ROLL
ROLL
ROLL
MEOW!
YOU HAVE SAND IN YOUR HAIR...
MEOW!
MEOW!

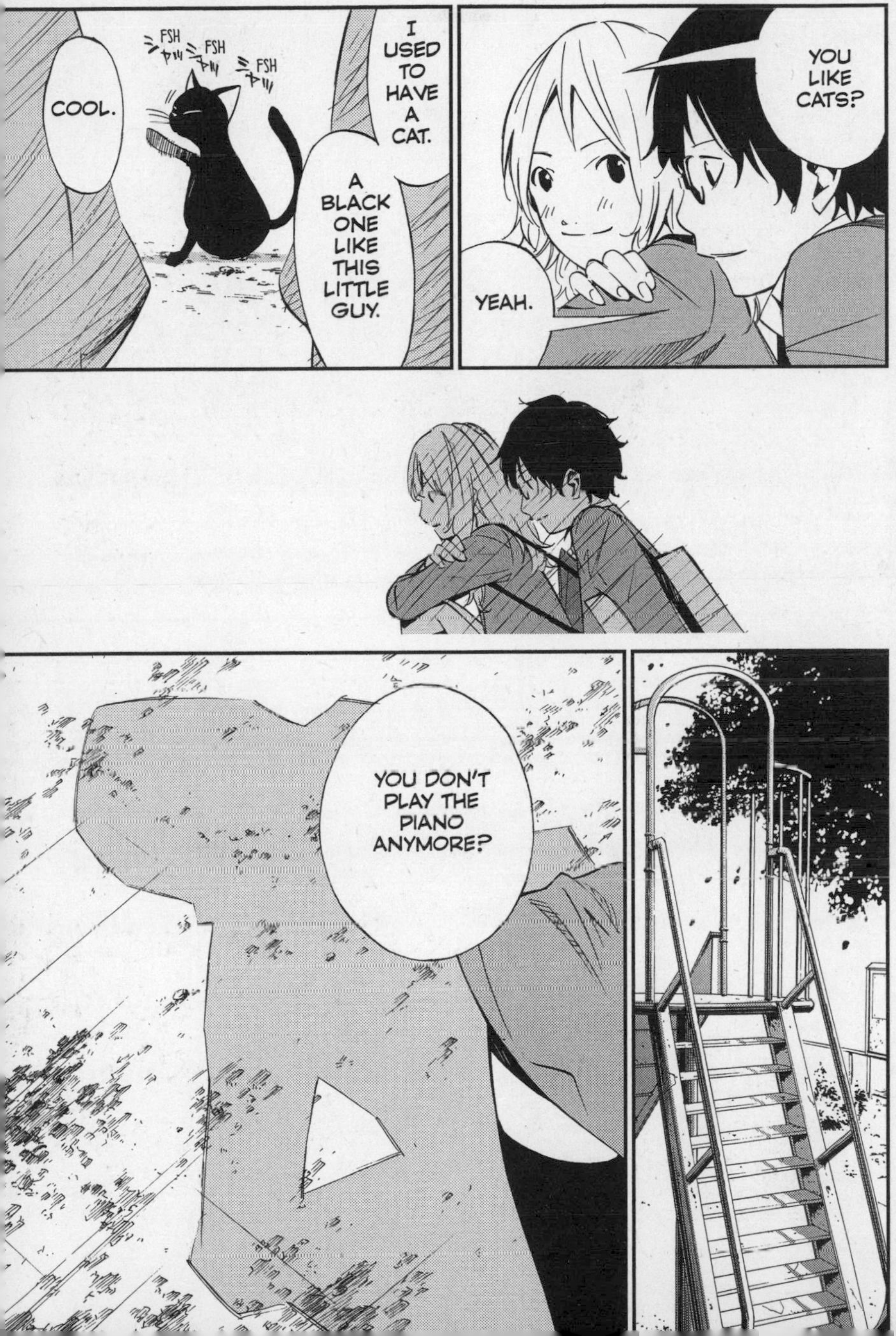
YOU LIKE CATS?
YEAH.
I USED TO HAVE A CAT.
A BLACK ONE LIKE THIS LITTLE GUY.
FSH
FSH
FSH
COOL.
YOU DON'T PLAY THE PIANO ANYMORE?

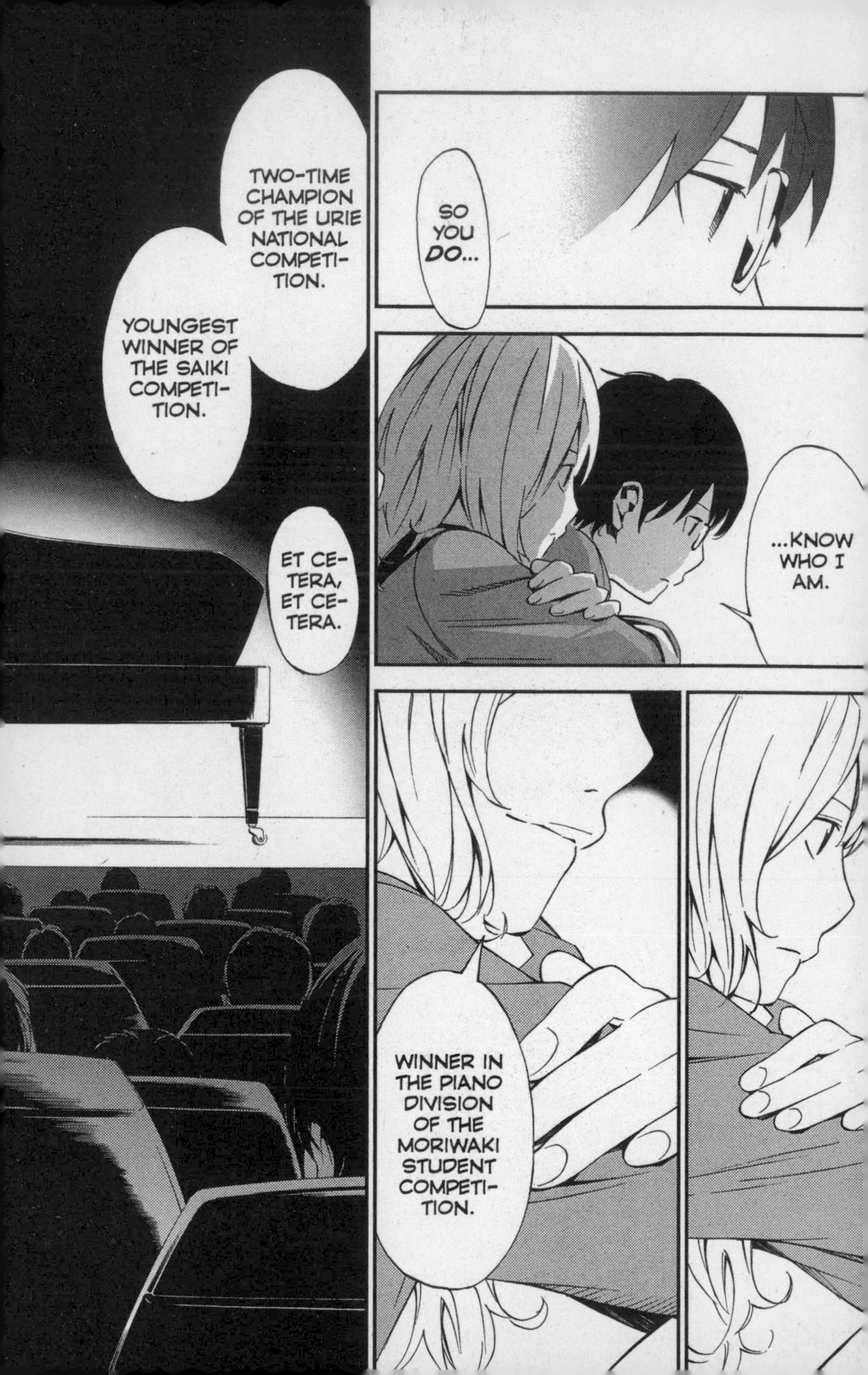
SO YOU DO...
...KNOW WHO I AM.
WINNER IN THE PIANO DIVISION OF THE MORIWAKI STUDENT COMPETI-TION.
TWO-TIME CHAMPION OF THE URIE NATIONAL COMPETI-TION.
YOUNGEST WINNER OF THE SAIKI COMPETI-TION.
ET CE-TERA, ET CE-TERA.

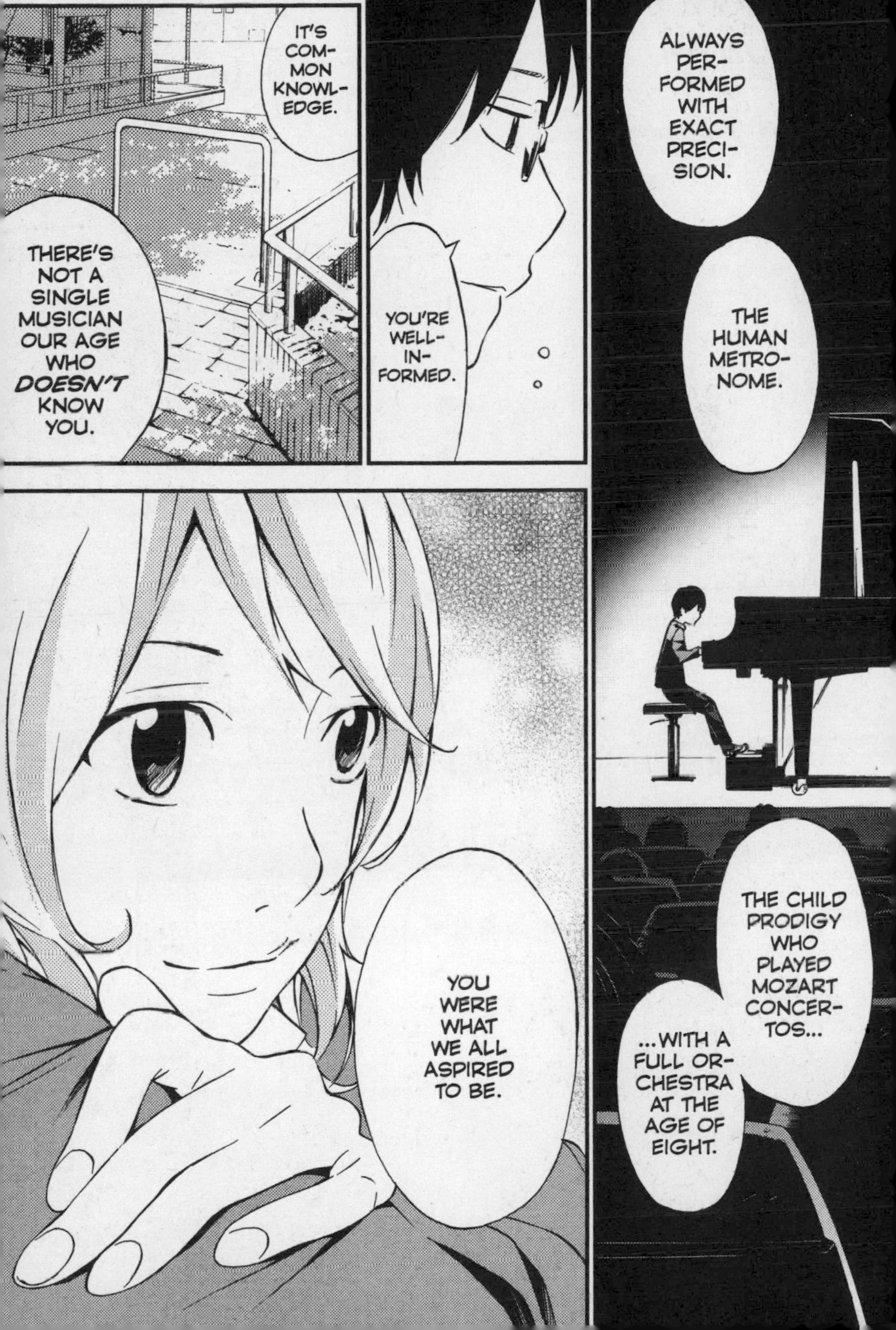
ALWAYS PER-FORMED WITH EXACT PRECI-SION.
THE HUMAN METRO-NOME.
THE CHILD PRODIGY WHO PLAYED MOZART CONCER-TOS...
...WITH A FULL OR-CHESTRA AT THE AGE OF EIGHT.
YOU'RE WELL-IN-FORMED.
IT'S COM-MON KNOWL-EDGE.
THERE'S NOT A SINGLE MUSICIAN OUR AGE WHO *DOESN'T* KNOW YOU.
YOU WERE WHAT WE ALL ASPIRED TO BE.

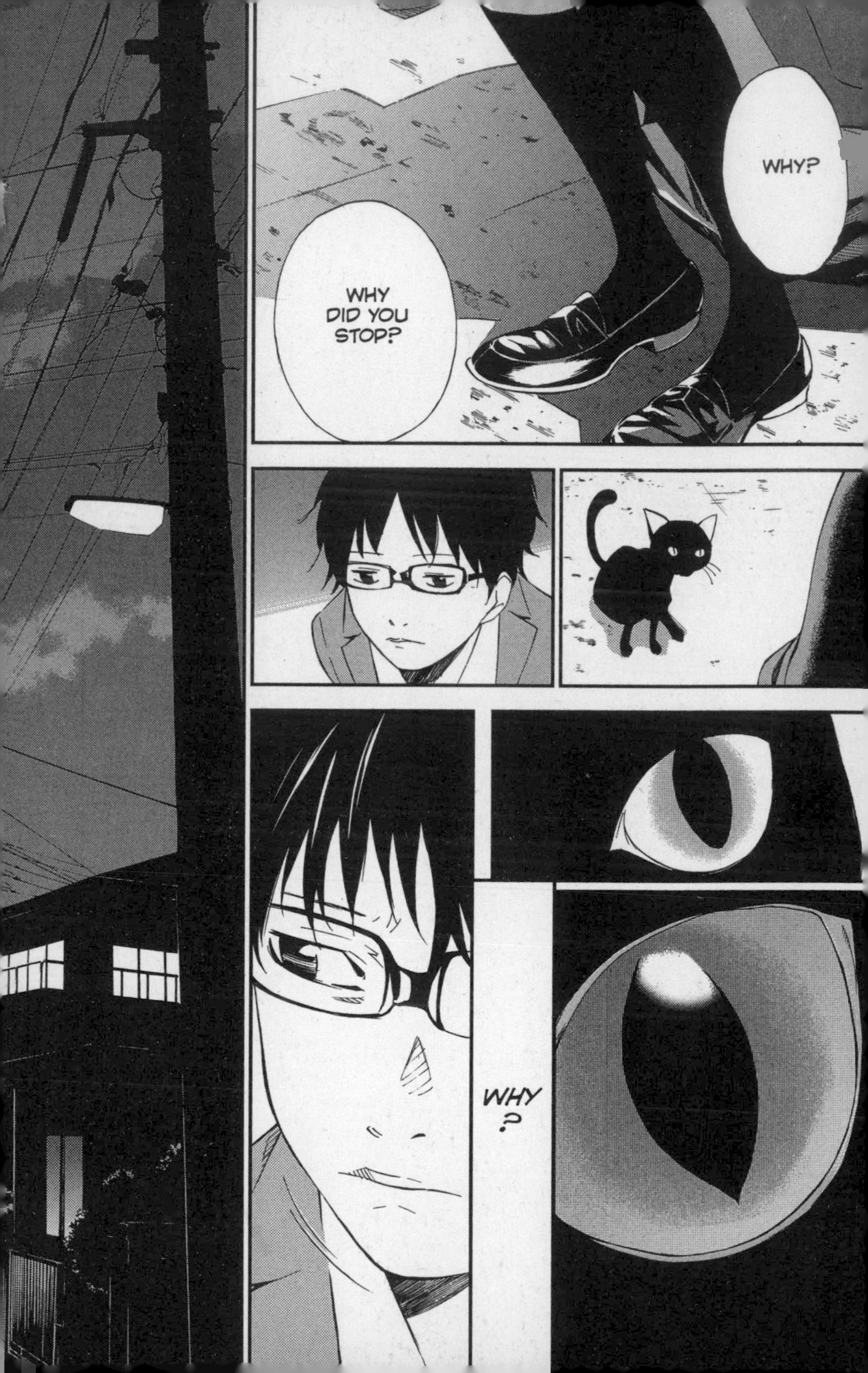
WHY?
WHY DID YOU STOP?
WHY ?

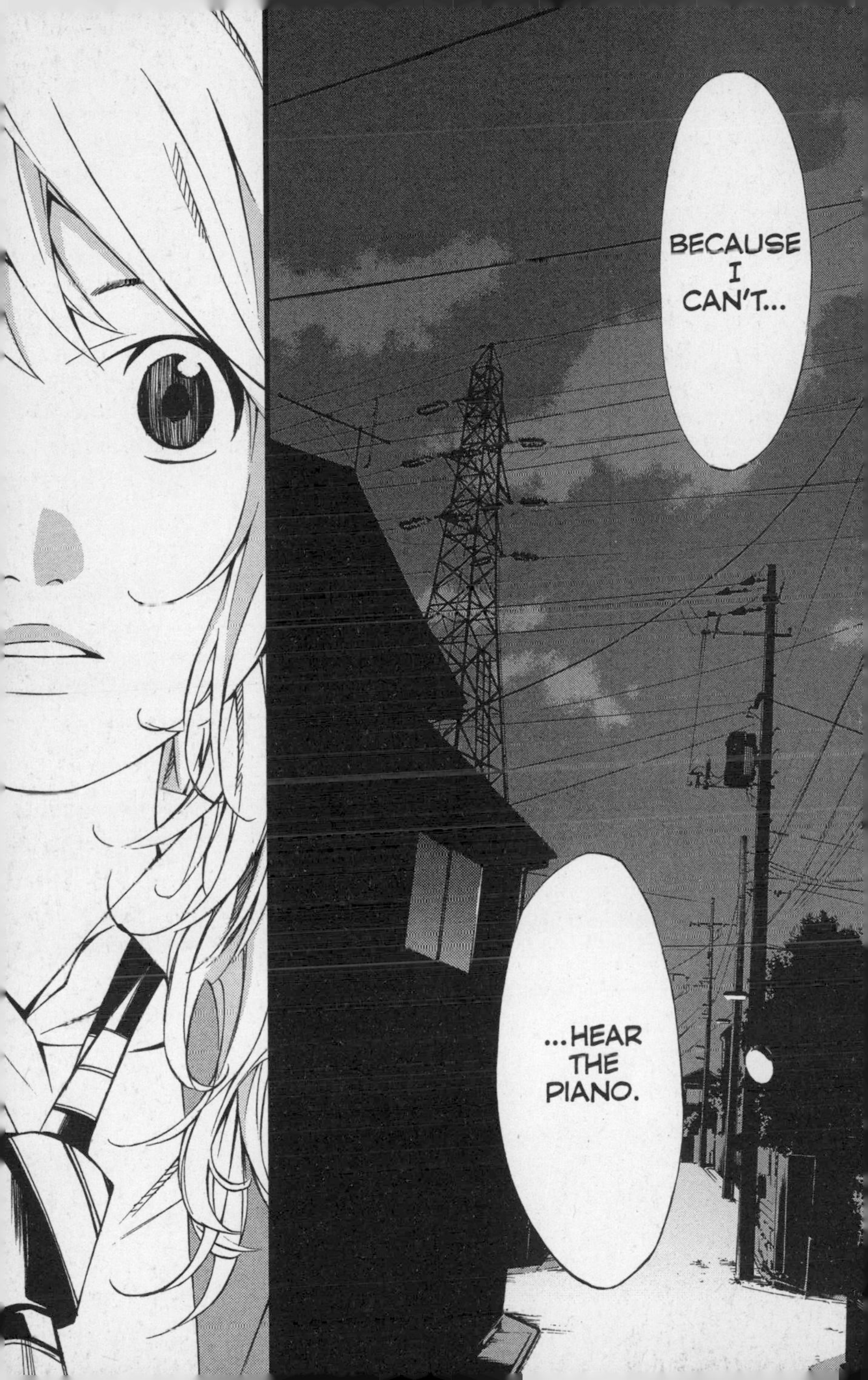
BECAUSE I CAN'T...
...HEAR THE PIANO.

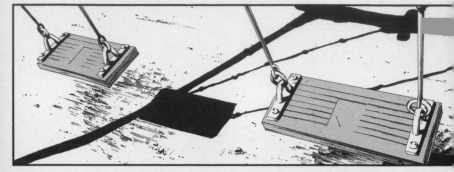

IT CAN HAPPEN TO ANYONE, RIGHT?

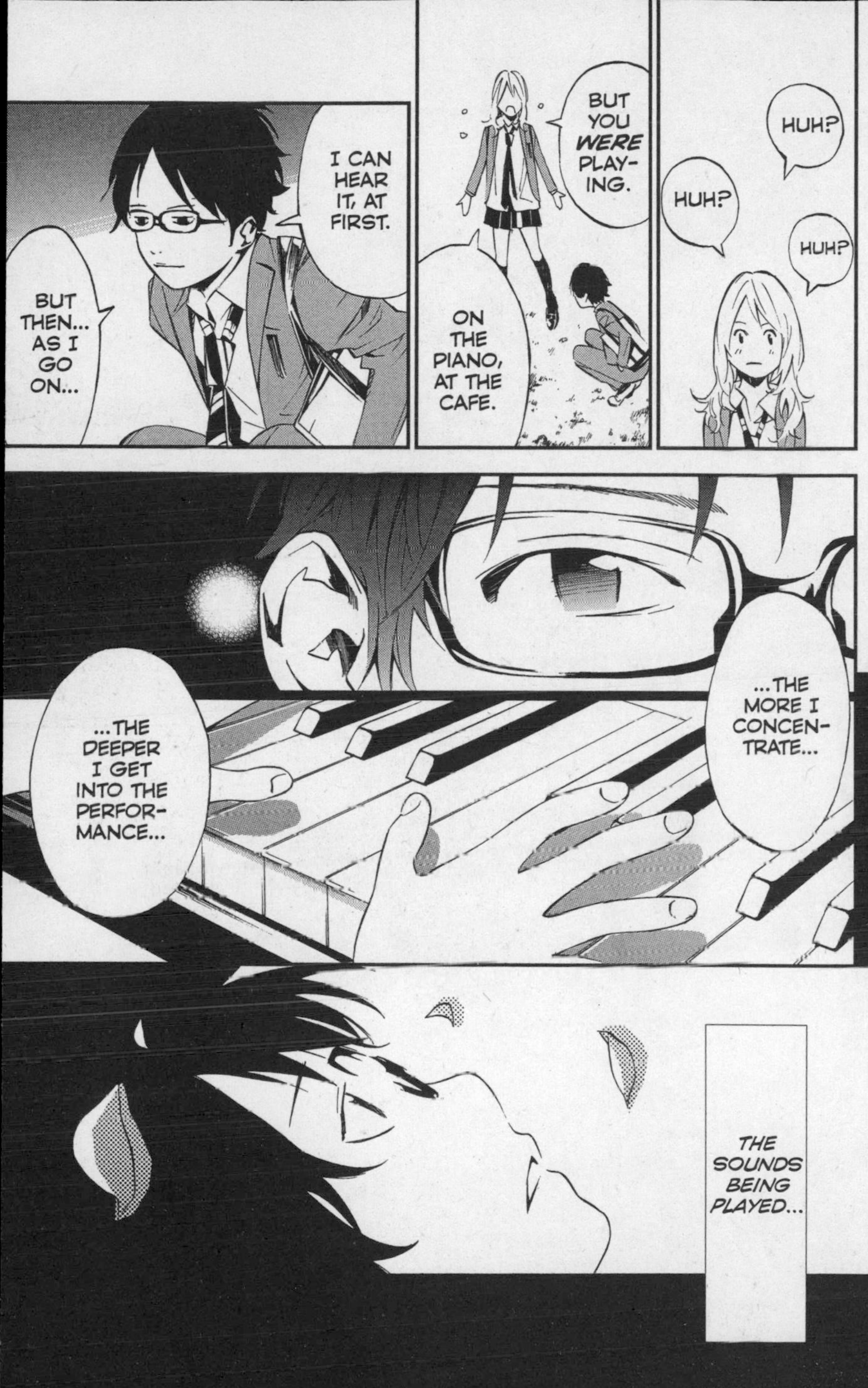
HUH?
HUH?
HUH?
BUT YOU *WERE* PLAYING.
ON THE PIANO, AT THE CAFE.
I CAN HEAR IT, AT FIRST.
BUT THEN... AS I GO ON...
...THE MORE I CONCENTRATE...
...THE DEEPER I GET INTO THE PERFORMANCE...
THE SOUNDS BEING PLAYED...

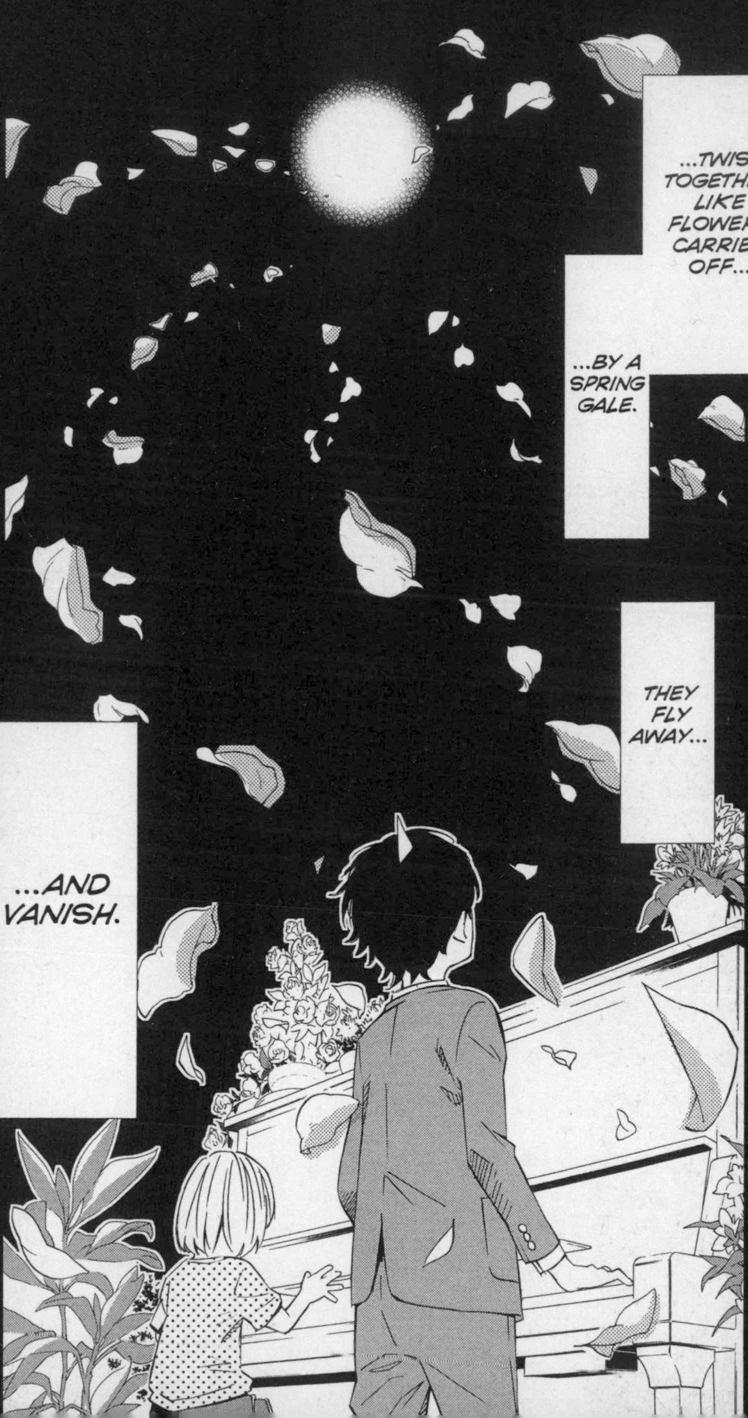
...TWIST TOGETHER LIKE FLOWERS CARRIED OFF...
...BY A SPRING GALE.
THEY FLY AWAY...
...AND VANISH.

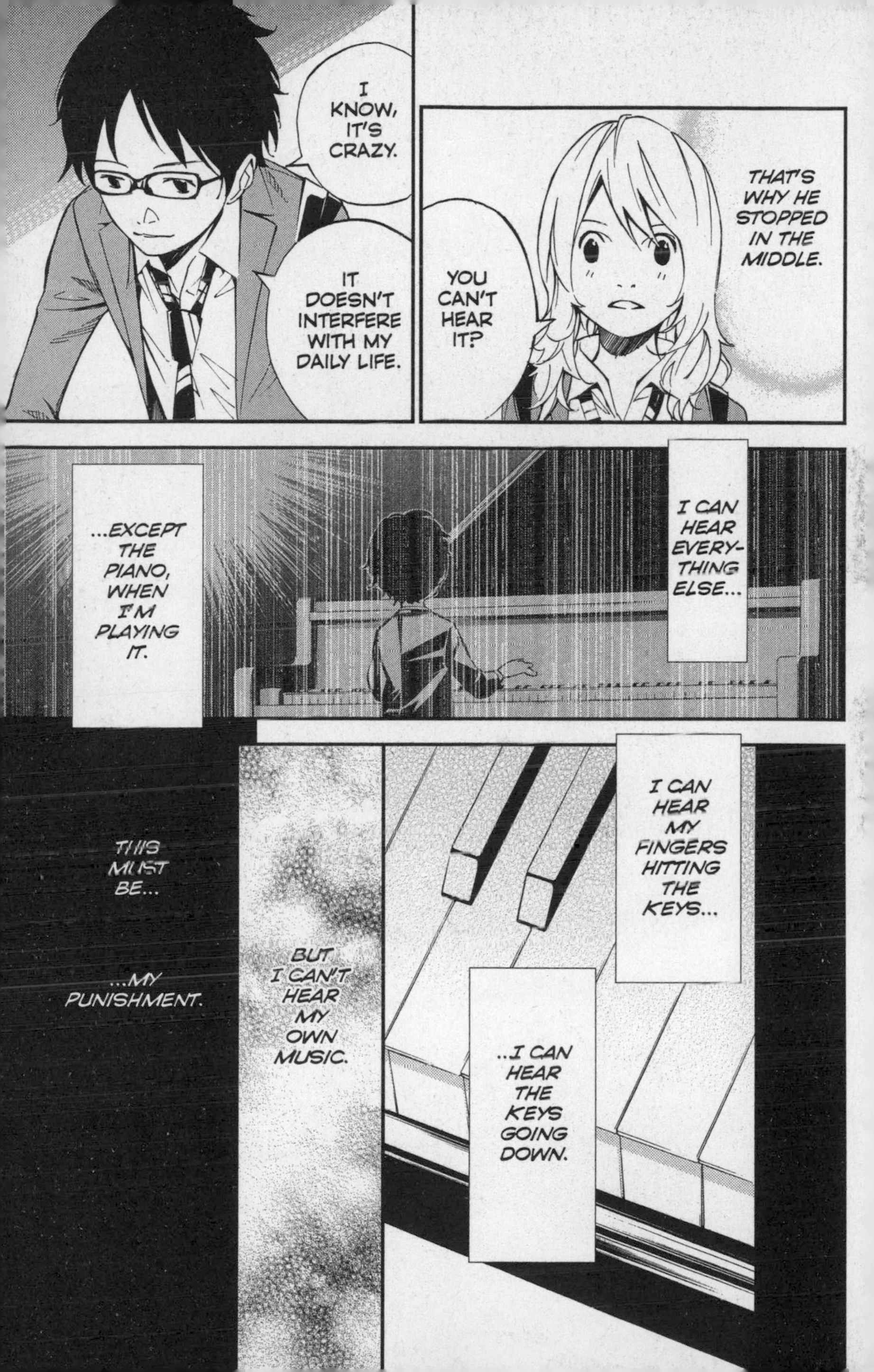
THAT'S WHY HE STOPPED IN THE MIDDLE.
YOU CAN'T HEAR IT?
I KNOW, IT'S CRAZY.
IT DOESN'T INTERFERE WITH MY DAILY LIFE.
I CAN HEAR EVERY-THING ELSE...
...EXCEPT THE PIANO, WHEN I'M PLAYING IT.
I CAN HEAR MY FINGERS HITTING THE KEYS...
...I CAN HEAR THE KEYS GOING DOWN.
BUT I CAN'T HEAR MY OWN MUSIC.
THIS MUST BE...
...MY PUNISHMENT.

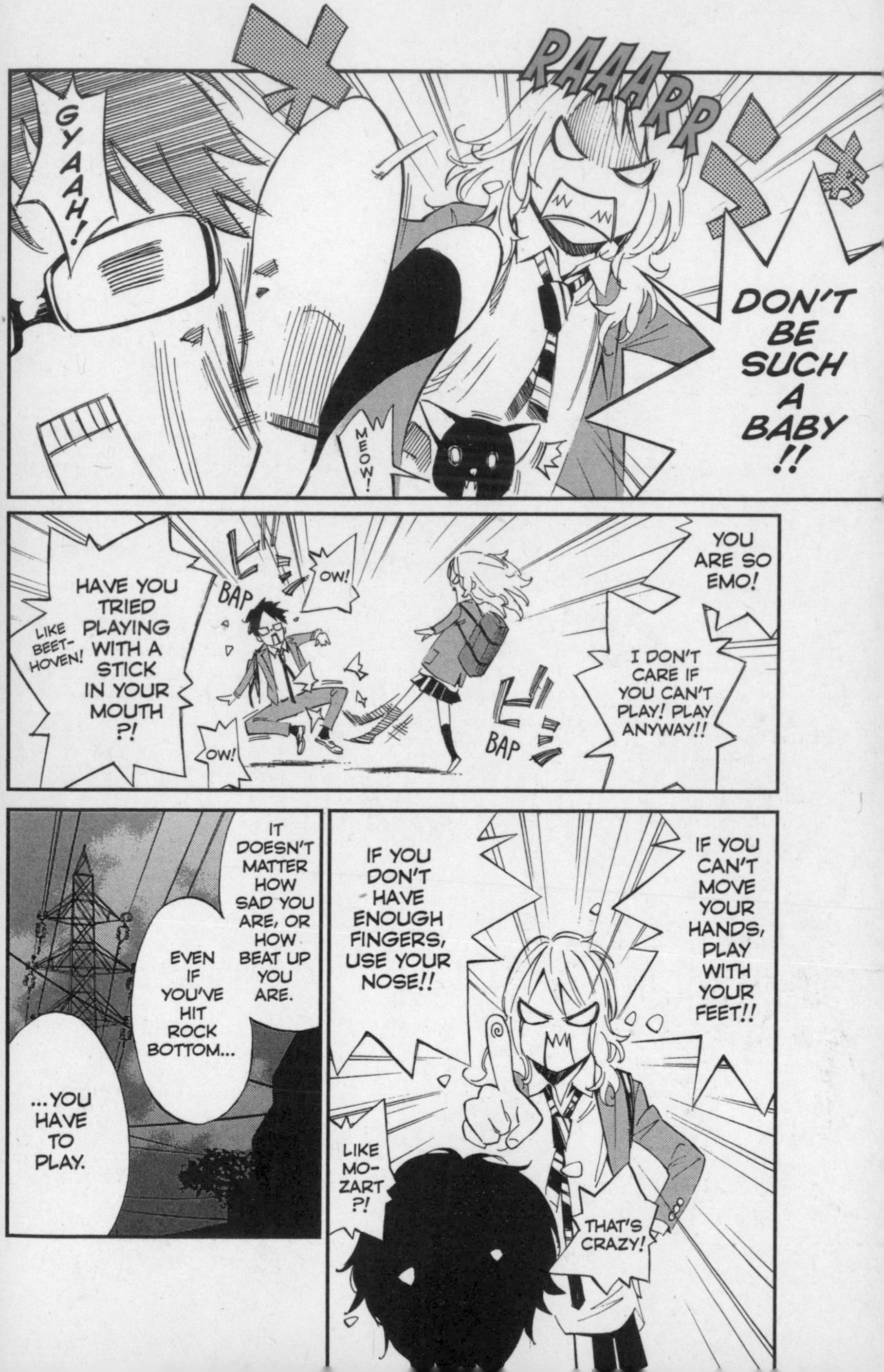
RAAAARR
DON'T BE SUCH A BABY!!
MEOW!
GYAAH!
YOU ARE SO EMO!
I DON'T CARE IF YOU CAN'T PLAY! PLAY ANYWAY!!
BAP
OW!
BAP
HAVE YOU TRIED PLAYING WITH A STICK IN YOUR MOUTH?!
LIKE BEETHOVEN!
OW!
IF YOU CAN'T MOVE YOUR HANDS, PLAY WITH YOUR FEET!!
IF YOU DON'T HAVE ENOUGH FINGERS, USE YOUR NOSE!!
THAT'S CRAZY!
LIKE MOZART?!
IT DOESN'T MATTER HOW SAD YOU ARE, OR HOW BEAT UP YOU ARE.
EVEN IF YOU'VE HIT ROCK BOTTOM...
...YOU HAVE TO PLAY.

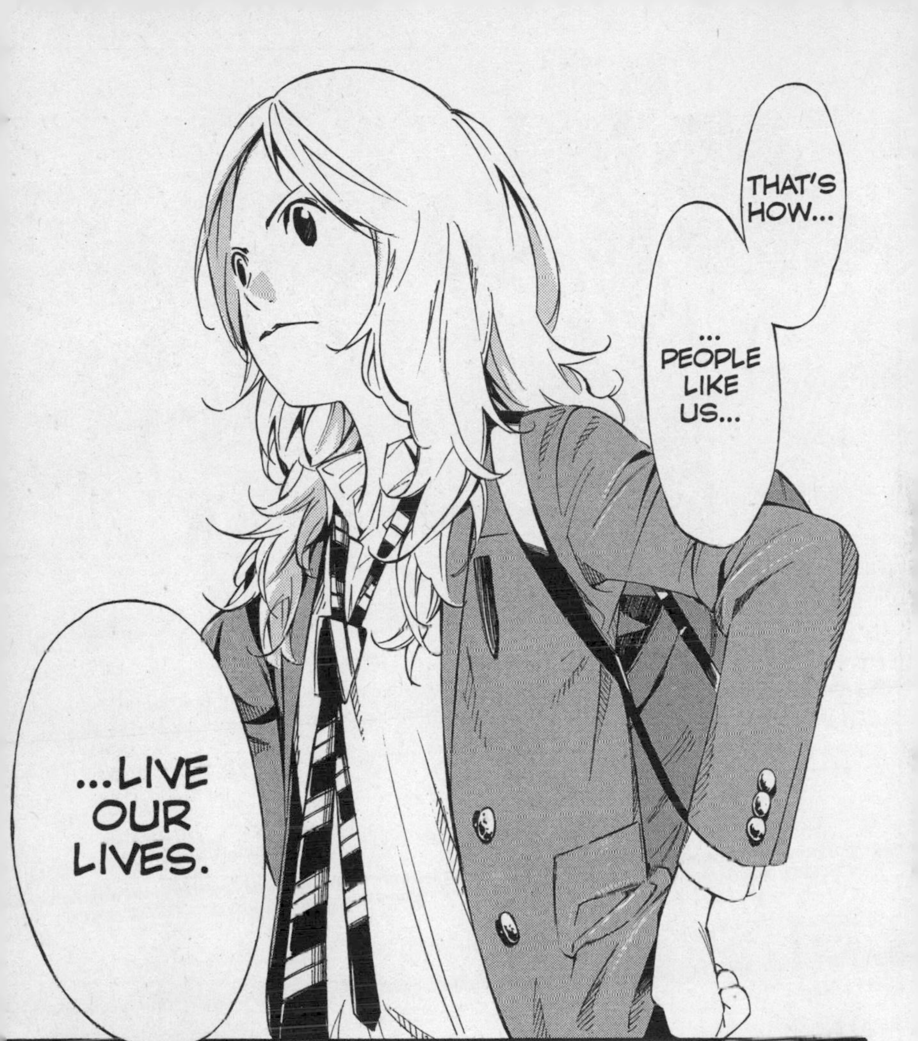
THAT'S HOW...
... PEOPLE LIKE US...
...LIVE OUR LIVES.
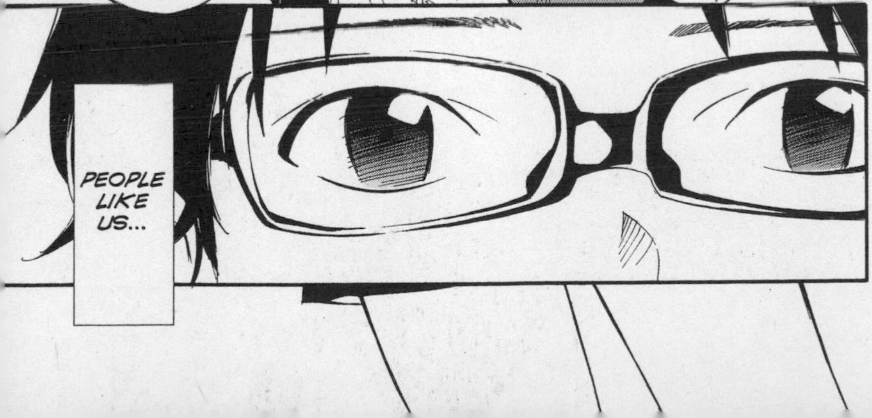
PEOPLE LIKE US...

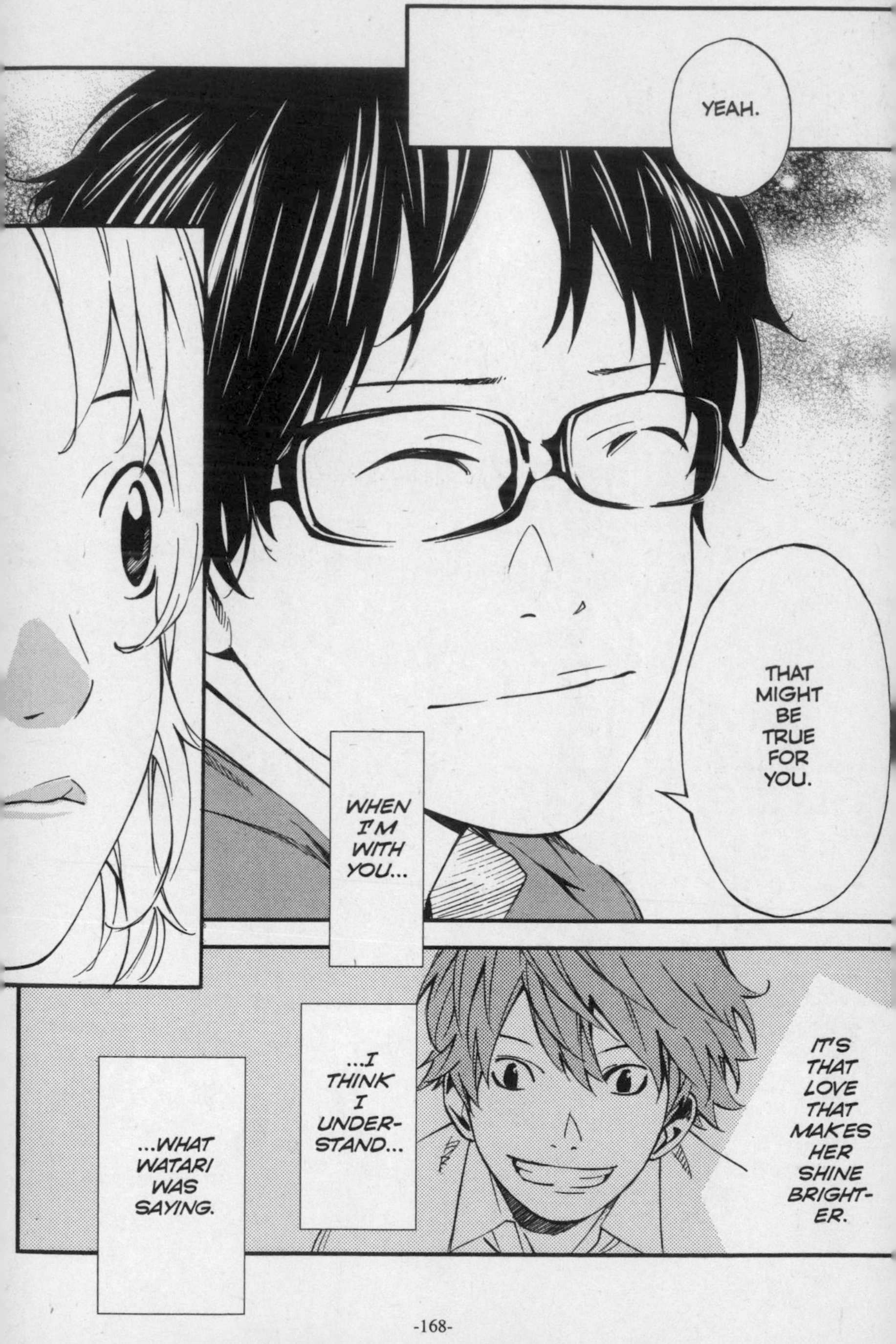
YEAH.
THAT MIGHT BE TRUE FOR YOU.
WHEN I'M WITH YOU...
IT'S THAT LOVE THAT MAKES HER SHINE BRIGHTER.
...I THINK I UNDERSTAND...
...WHAT WATARI WAS SAYING.

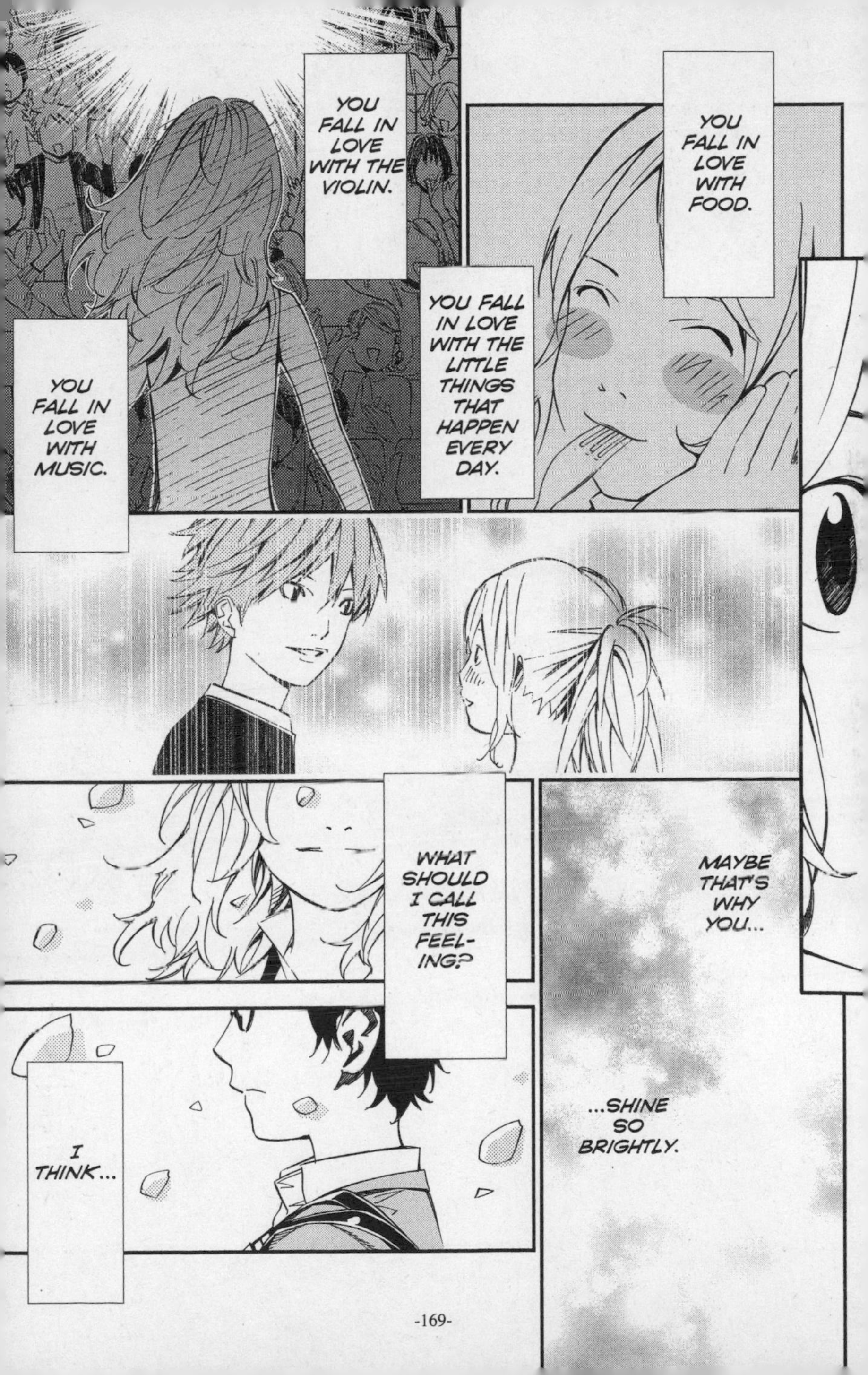
YOU FALL IN LOVE WITH FOOD.
YOU FALL IN LOVE WITH THE LITTLE THINGS THAT HAPPEN EVERY DAY.
YOU FALL IN LOVE WITH THE VIOLIN.
YOU FALL IN LOVE WITH MUSIC.
MAYBE THAT'S WHY YOU...
...SHINE SO BRIGHTLY.
WHAT SHOULD I CALL THIS FEEL-ING?
I THINK...

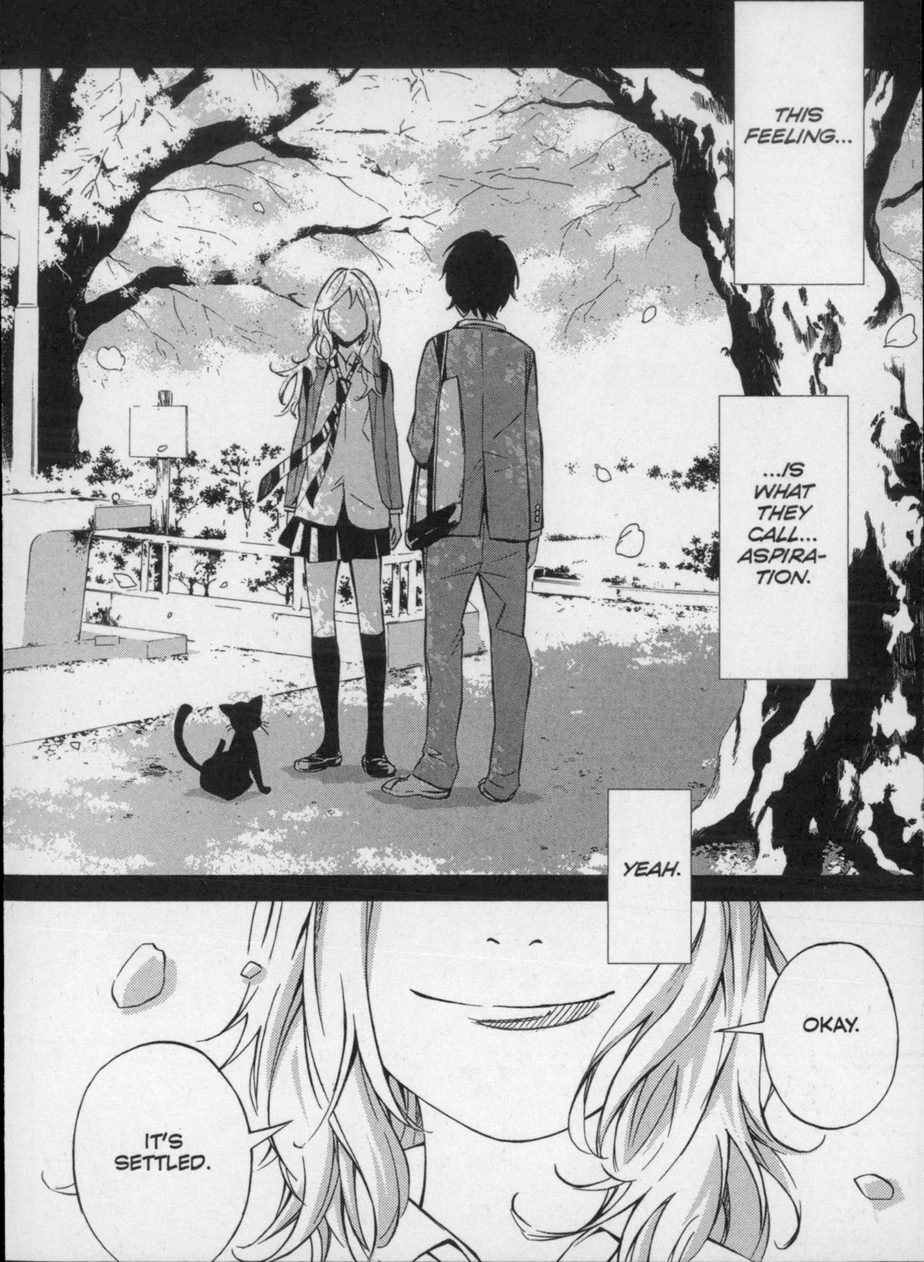
THIS FEELING...
...IS WHAT THEY CALL... ASPIRA-TION.
YEAH.
OKAY.
IT'S SETTLED.

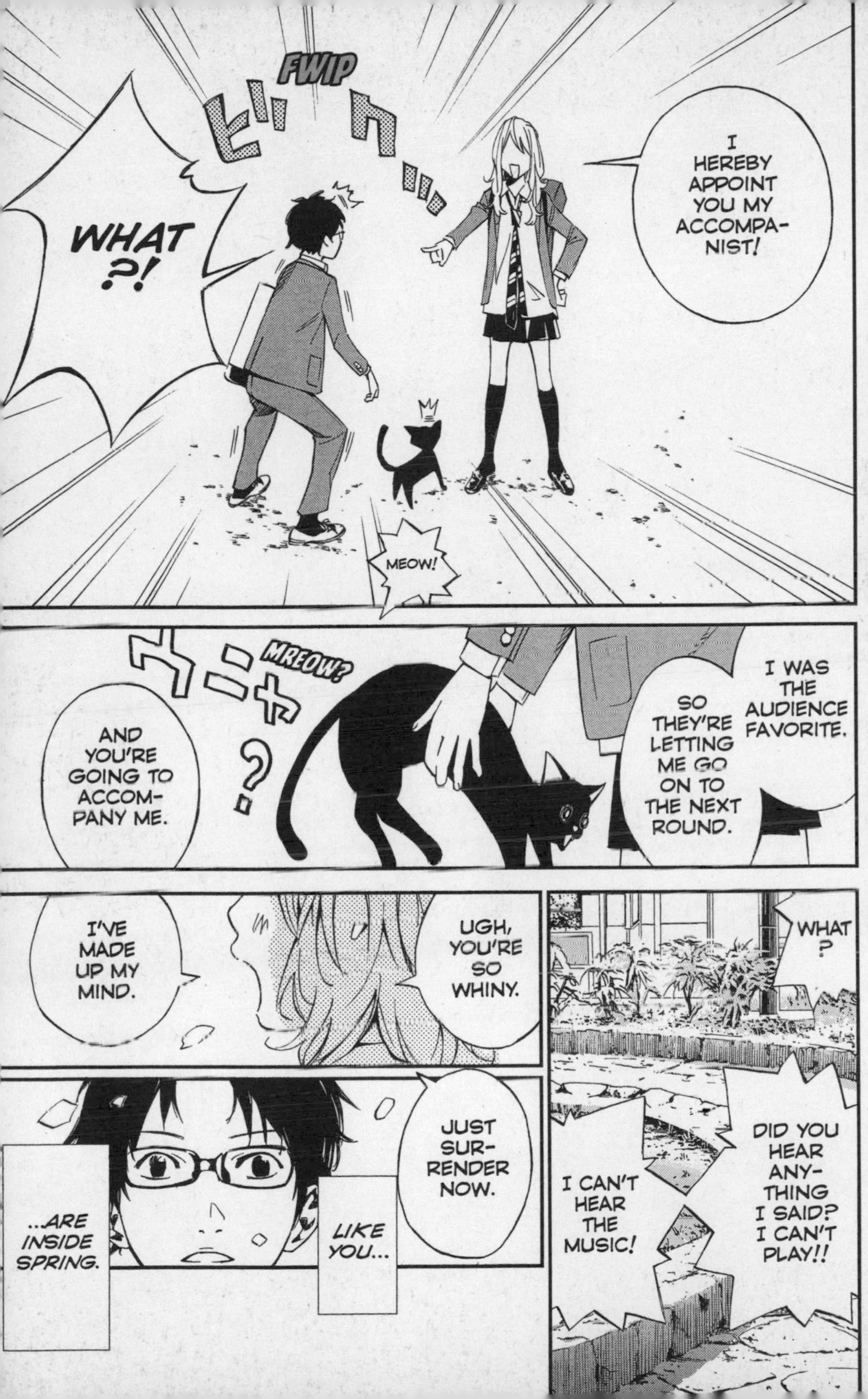
I HEREBY APPOINT YOU MY ACCOMPANIST!
FWIP
WHAT?!
MEOW!
I WAS THE AUDIENCE FAVORITE.
SO THEY'RE LETTING ME GO ON TO THE NEXT ROUND.
MREOW?
AND YOU'RE GOING TO ACCOMPANY ME.
?
WHAT?
DID YOU HEAR ANYTHING I SAID? I CAN'T PLAY!!
I CAN'T HEAR THE MUSIC!
UGH, YOU'RE SO WHINY.
I'VE MADE UP MY MIND.
JUST SURRENDER NOW.
LIKE YOU...
...ARE INSIDE SPRING.

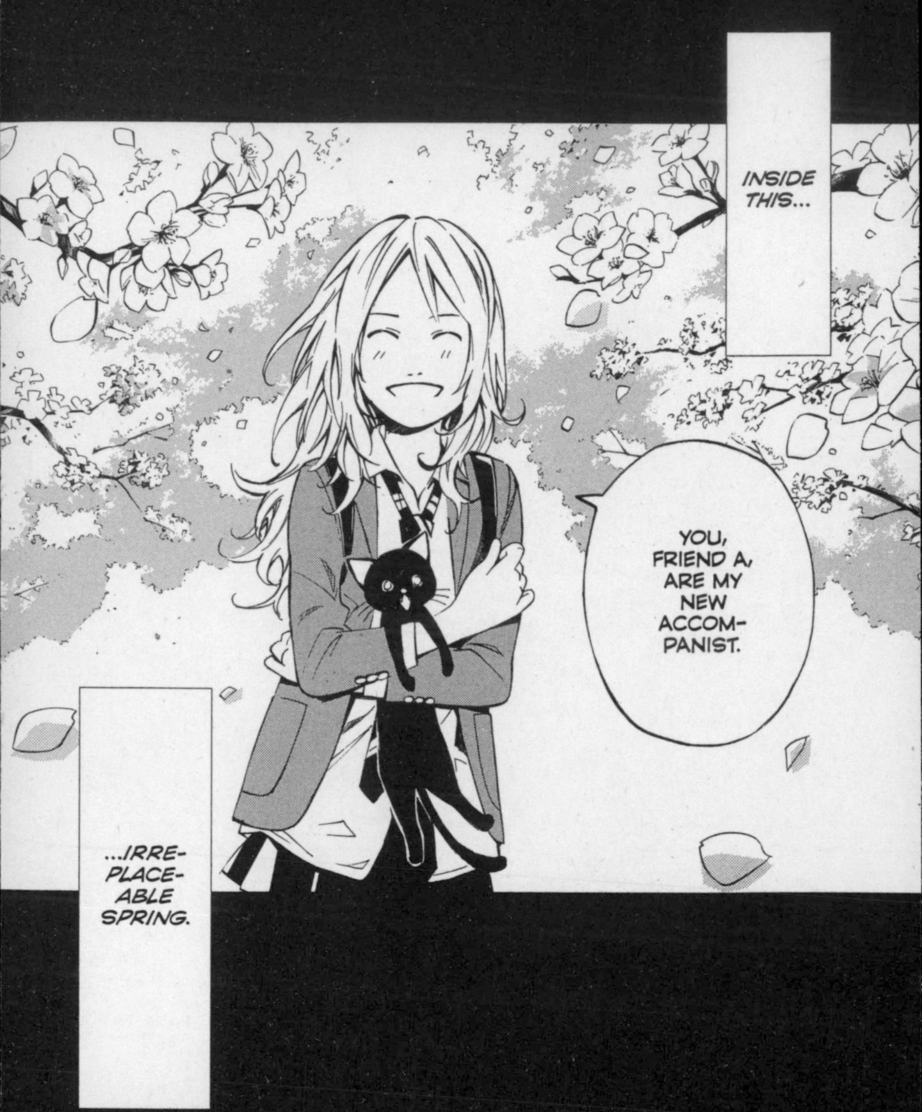
INSIDE THIS...
YOU, FRIEND A, ARE MY NEW ACCOMPANIST.
...IRREPLACEABLE SPRING.

I met the girl under full-bloomed cherry blossoms, and my fate has begun to change.

YOUR LIE IN APRIL FEATURED MUSIC

MOZART
VARIATIONS ON
"TWINKLE, TWINKLE, LITTLE STAR"

A piano piece consisting of twelve variations of a contemporary French folk melody that Mozart composed for the education of students.

In the manga, the children are playing the main melody (the one you're all familiar with: "Twinkle, Twinkle, Little Star"), and Kōsei plays the first of the twelve variations over it.

It may sound simple at first listen, but that's Mozart for you. Anyone who hears it will be amazed at what can be done with the melody, and that surprise and pleasure will fill the listener with joy.

Incidentally, the translation of the original title is, "Ah, Mother, If I Could Tell You."

(Violinist Rieko Ikeda)

Watch it on Youtube.
Search "Kodansha *Your Lie in April* featured music"

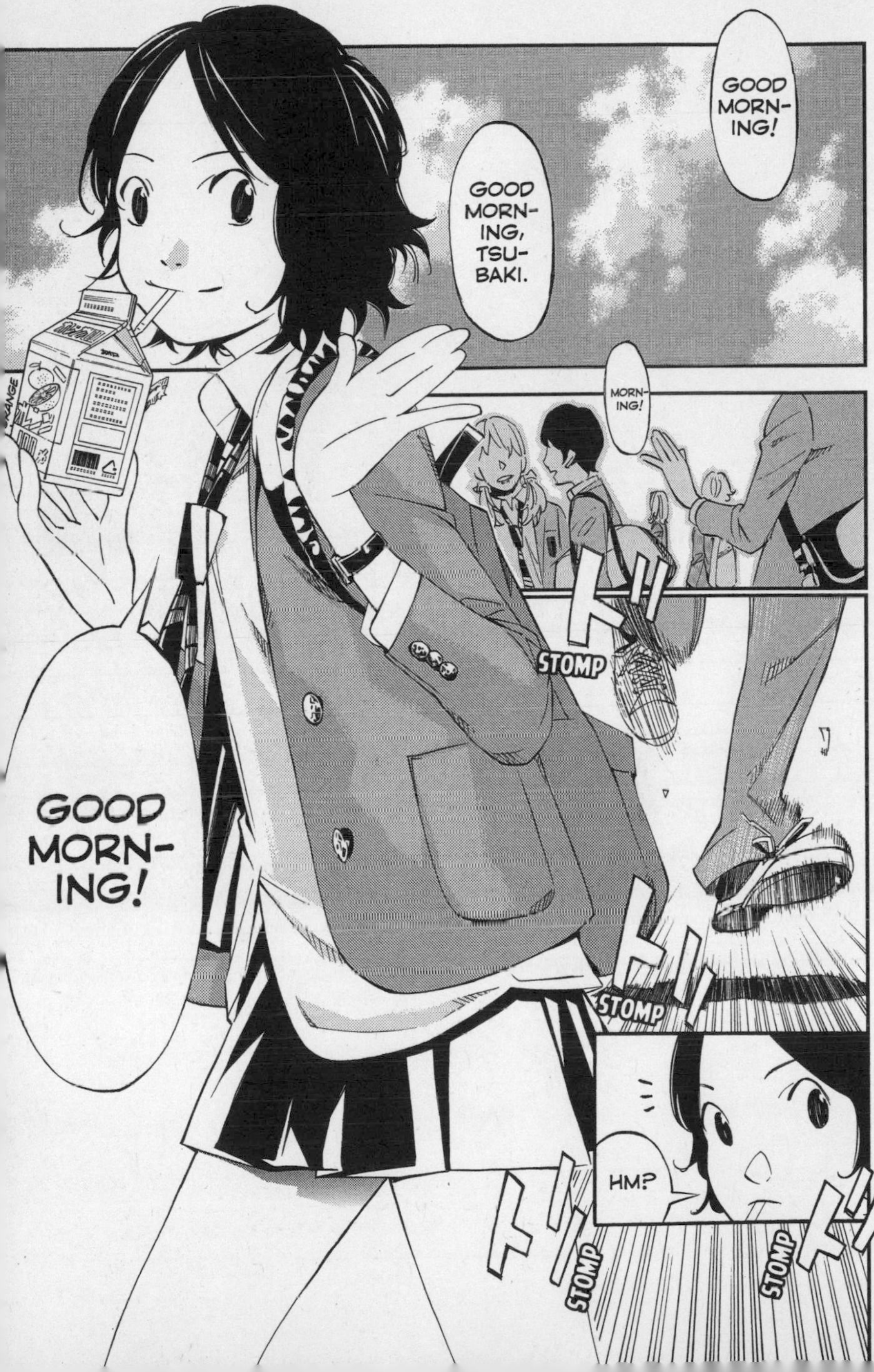
GOOD MORNING!
GOOD MORNING, TSUBAKI.
MORNING!
STOMP
STOMP
HM?
STOMP
STOMP
STOMP
GOOD MORNING!
ORANGE

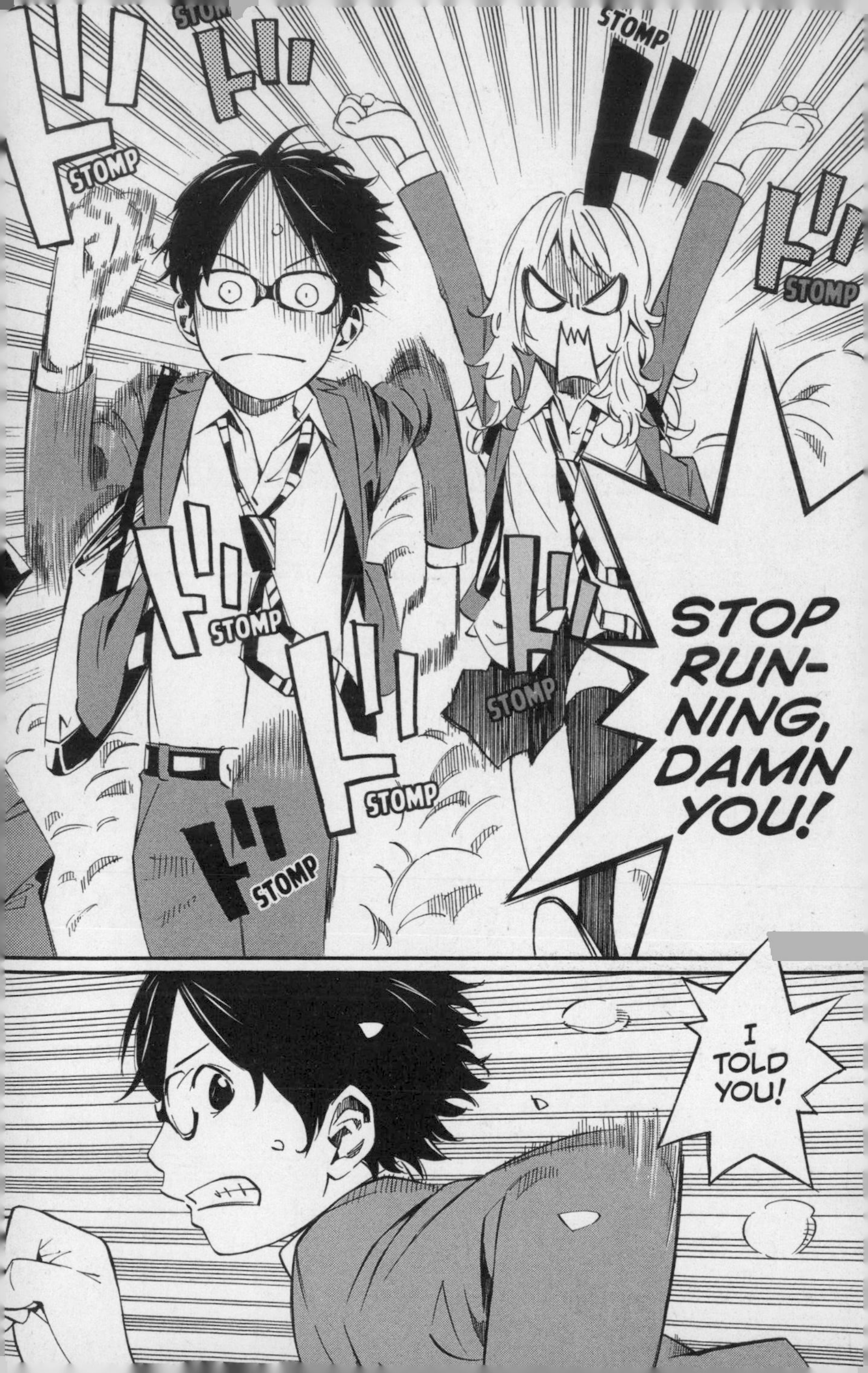
STOMP
STOMP
STOP RUN-NING, DAMN YOU!
STOMP
STOMP
STOMP
STOMP
STOMP
STOMP
I TOLD YOU!

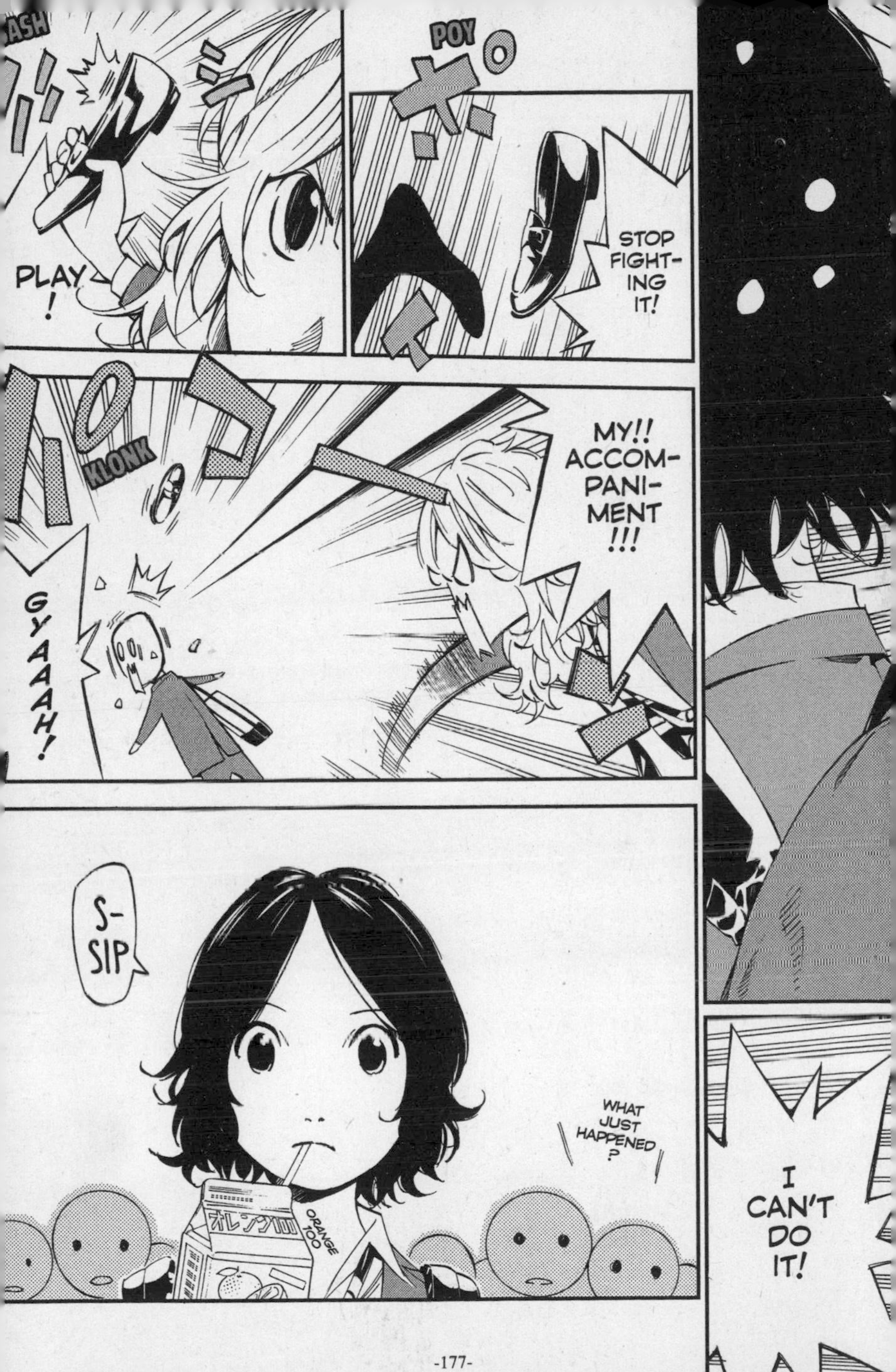
I CAN'T DO IT!
POY
STOP FIGHTING IT!
ASH
PLAY!
MY!! ACCOMPANIMENT!!!
KLONK
GYAAAAH!
WHAT JUST HAPPENED?
ORANGE 100
S-SIP

Chapter 4: Colorful

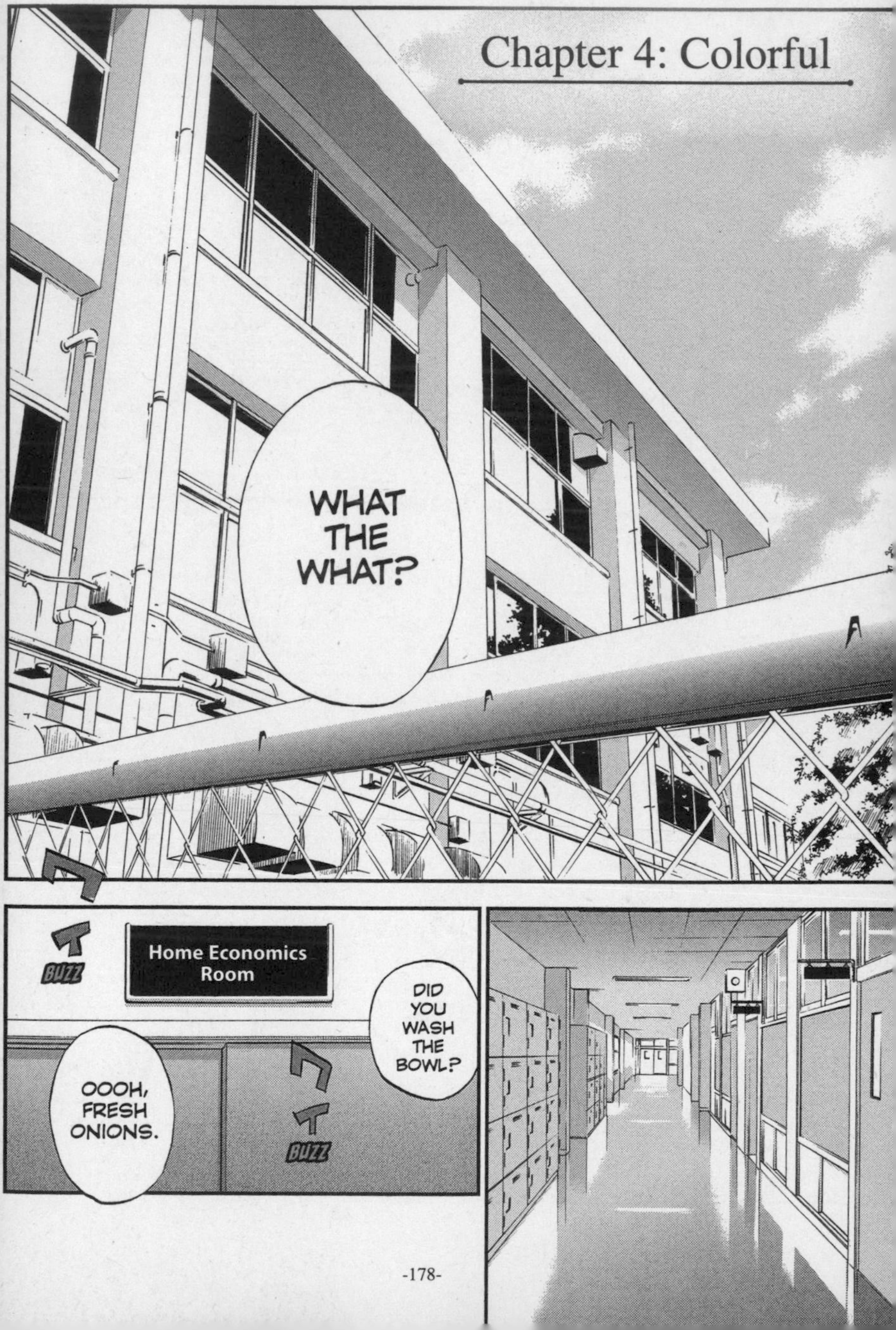
WHAT THE WHAT?
BUZZ
Home Economics Room
DID YOU WASH THE BOWL?
OOOH, FRESH ONIONS.
BUZZ

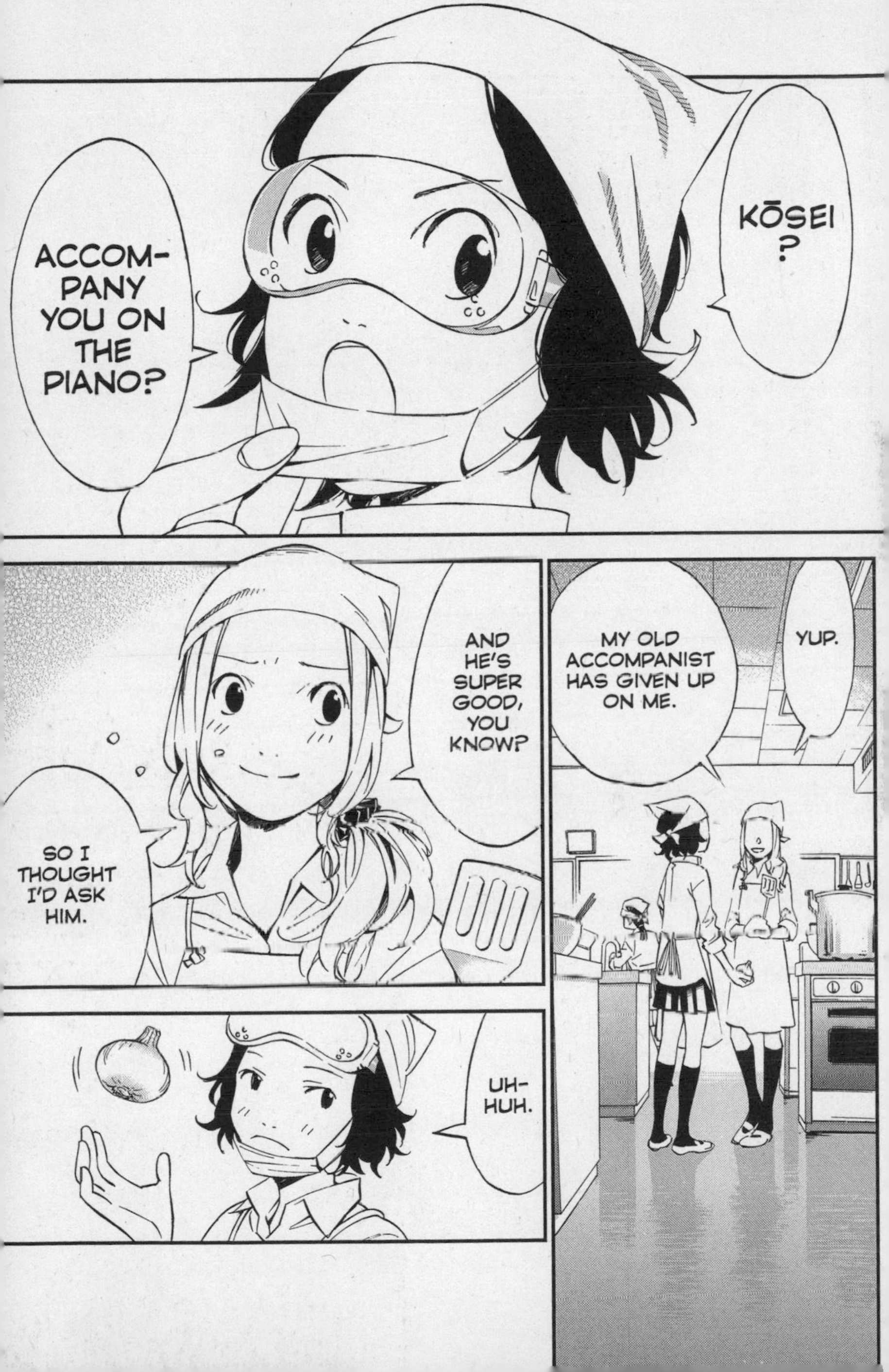
KŌSEI?
ACCOMPANY YOU ON THE PIANO?
YUP.
MY OLD ACCOMPANIST HAS GIVEN UP ON ME.
AND HE'S SUPER GOOD, YOU KNOW?
SO I THOUGHT I'D ASK HIM.
UH-HUH.

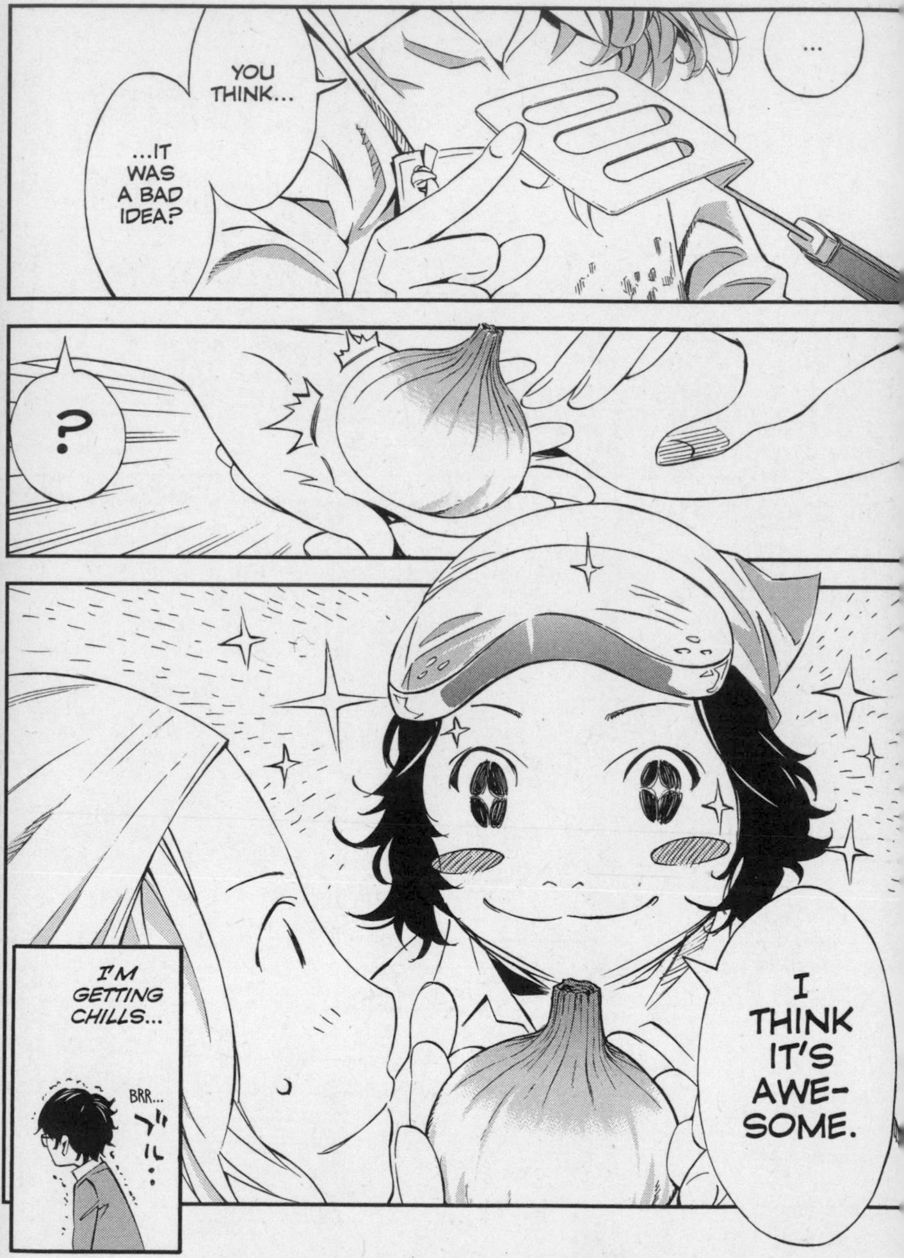
...
YOU THINK...
...IT WAS A BAD IDEA?
?
I THINK IT'S AWE-SOME.
I'M GETTING CHILLS...
BRR...
ブル…

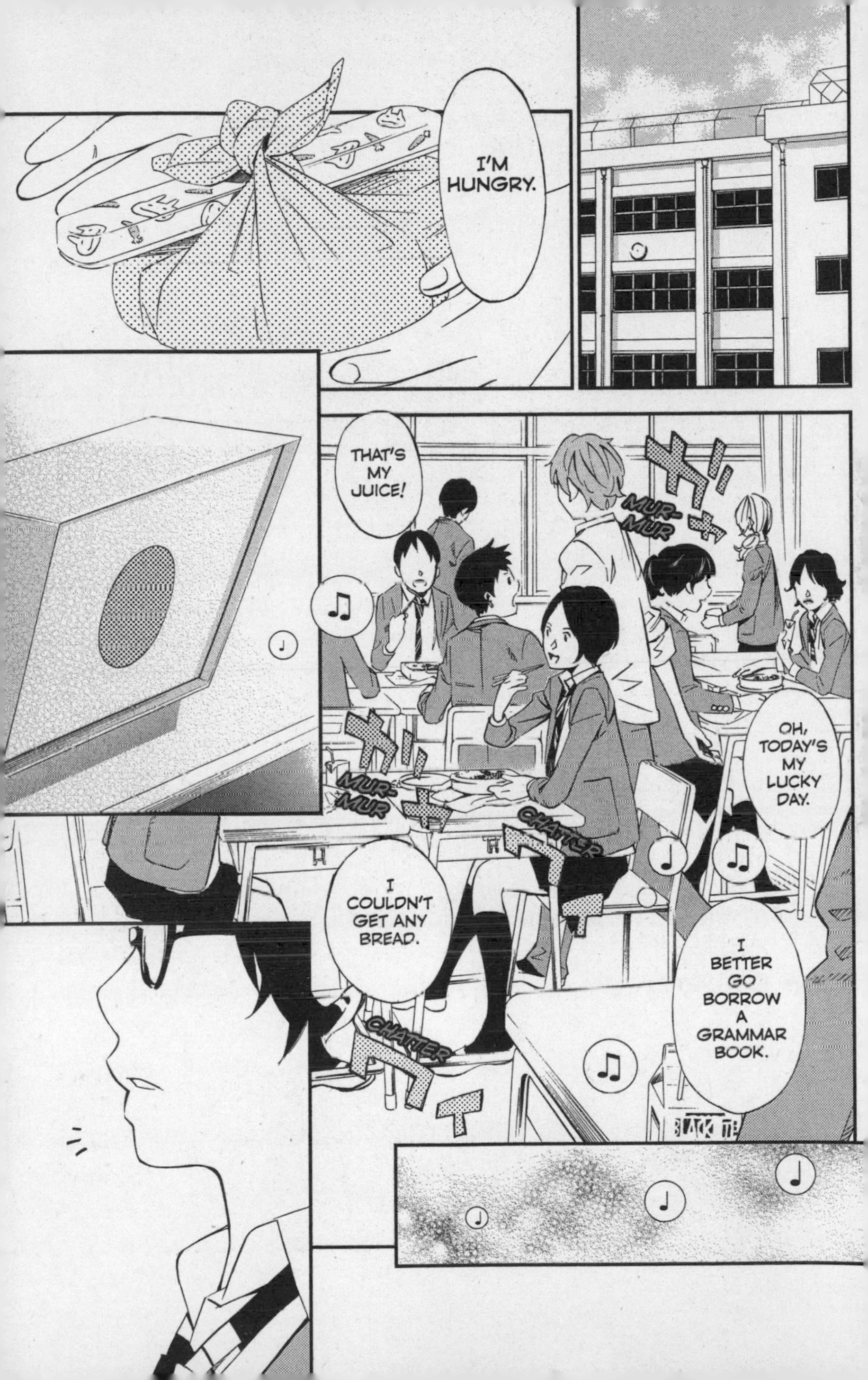
I'M HUNGRY.
MUR-MUR
OH, TODAY'S MY LUCKY DAY.
THAT'S MY JUICE!
MUR-MUR
CHATTER
I BETTER GO BORROW A GRAMMAR BOOK.
I COULDN'T GET ANY BREAD.
CHATTER

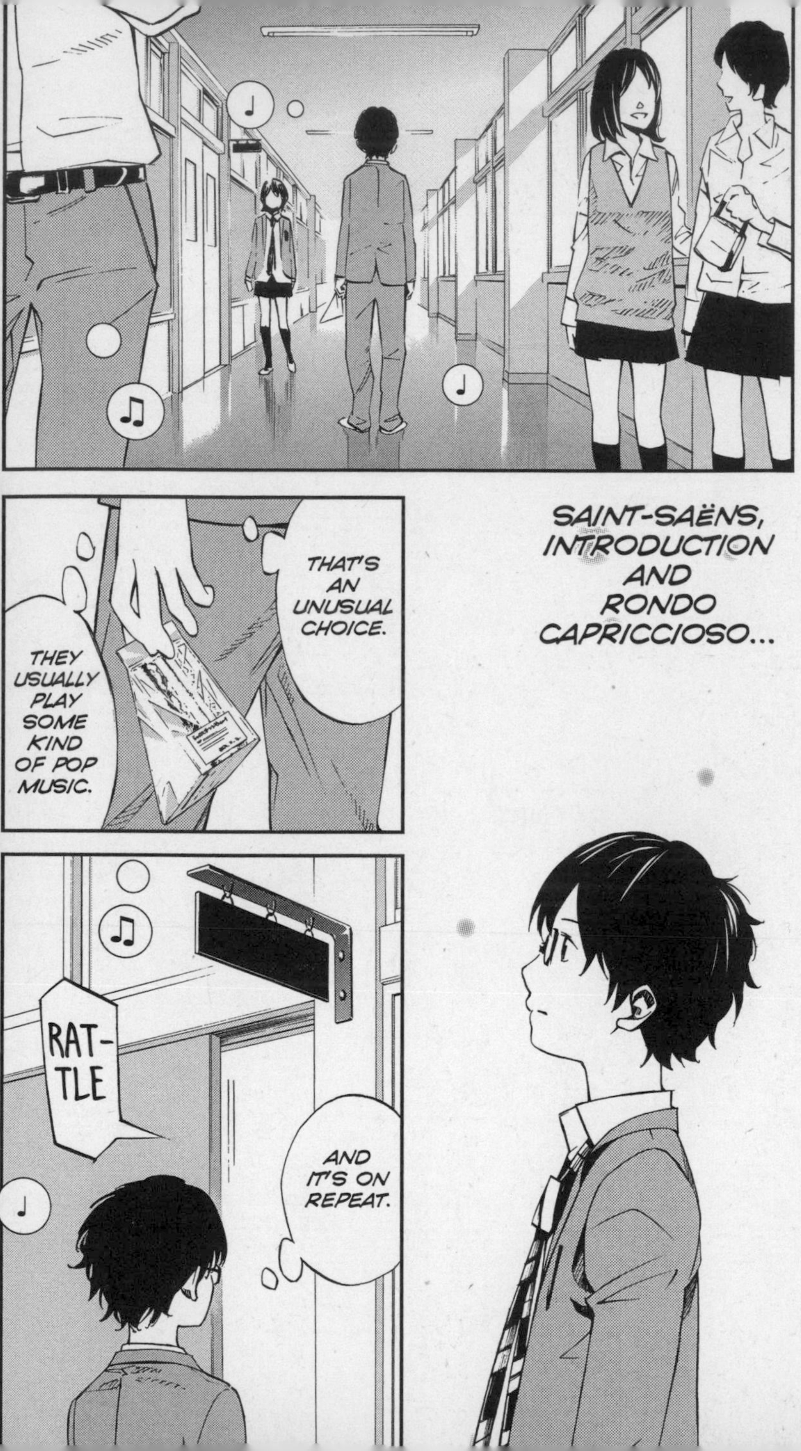
SAINT-SAËNS, INTRODUCTION AND RONDO CAPRICCIOSO...
THAT'S AN UNUSUAL CHOICE.
THEY USUALLY PLAY SOME KIND OF POP MUSIC.
RAT-TLE
AND IT'S ON REPEAT.

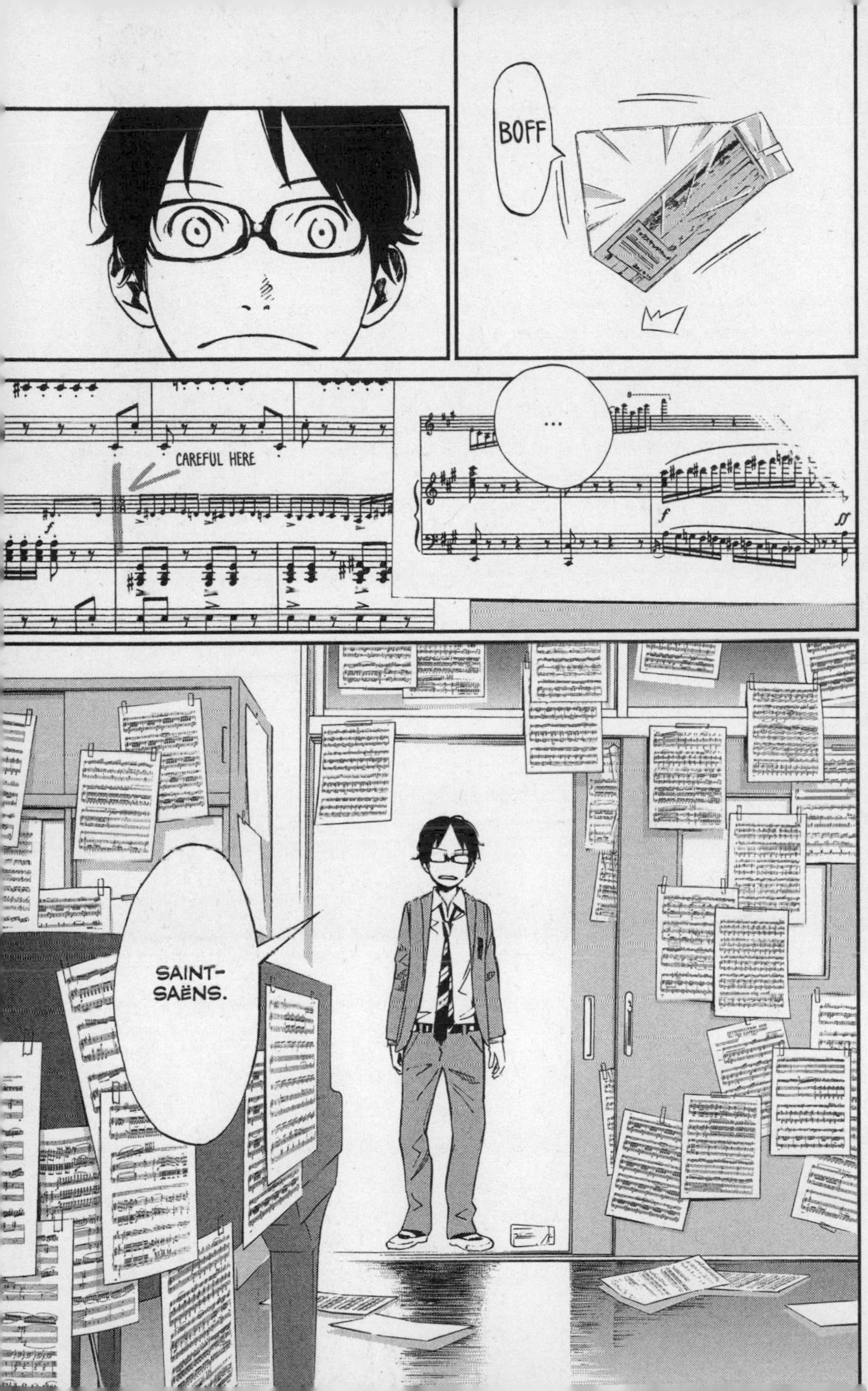
BOFF
...
CAREFUL HERE
SAINT-SAËNS.

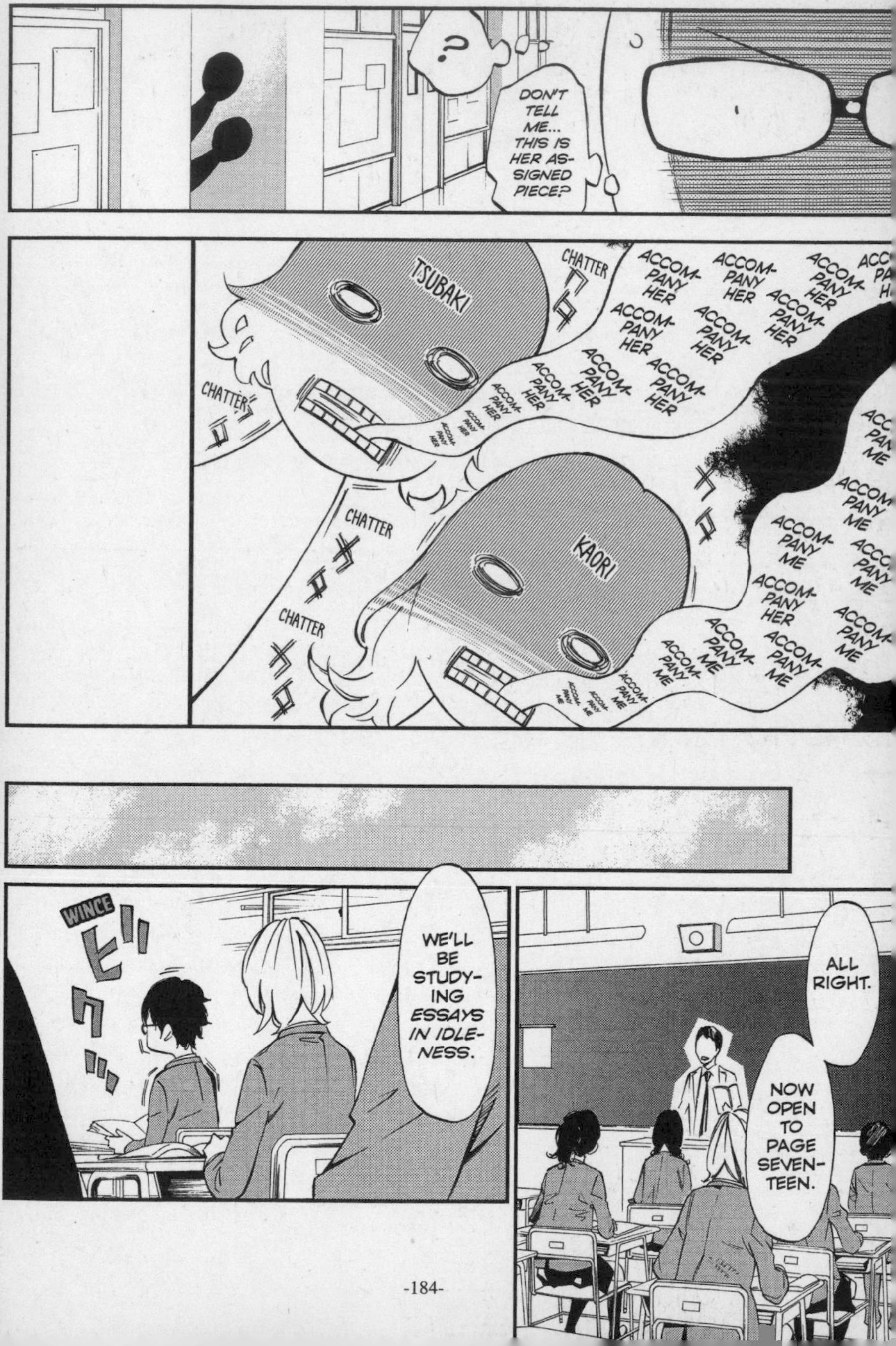
?
DON'T TELL ME... THIS IS HER ASSIGNED PIECE?
ACCOMPANY HER
ACCOMPANY HER
ACCOMPANY HER
ACCOMPANY HER
ACCOMPANY HER
ACCOMPANY HER
ACCOMPANY HER
ACCOMPANY HER
ACCOMPANY HER
ACCOMPANY HER
CHATTER
TSUBAKI
CHATTER
ACCOMPANY ME
ACCOMPANY ME
ACCOMPANY ME
ACCOMPANY ME
ACCOMPANY HER
ACCOMPANY ME
ACCOMPANY ME
ACCOMPANY ME
ACCOMPANY ME
ACCOMPANY ME
KAORI
CHATTER
CHATTER
ALL RIGHT.
NOW OPEN TO PAGE SEVENTEEN.
WE'LL BE STUDYING ESSAYS IN IDLENESS.
WINCE

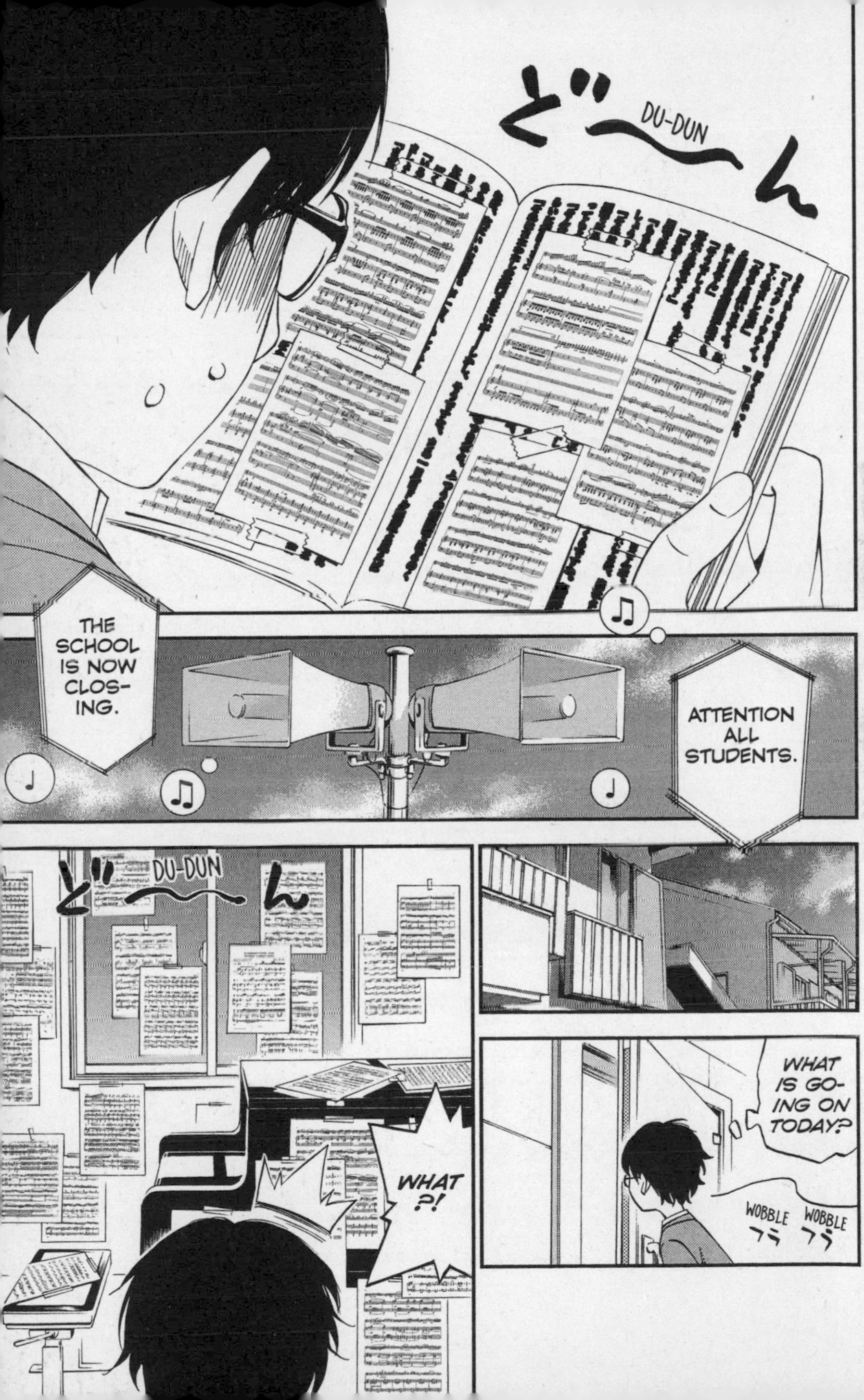

どーん
DU-DUN
ATTENTION ALL STUDENTS.
THE SCHOOL IS NOW CLOSING.
WHAT IS GOING ON TODAY?
WOBBLE
WOBBLE
どーん
DU-DUN
WHAT ?!

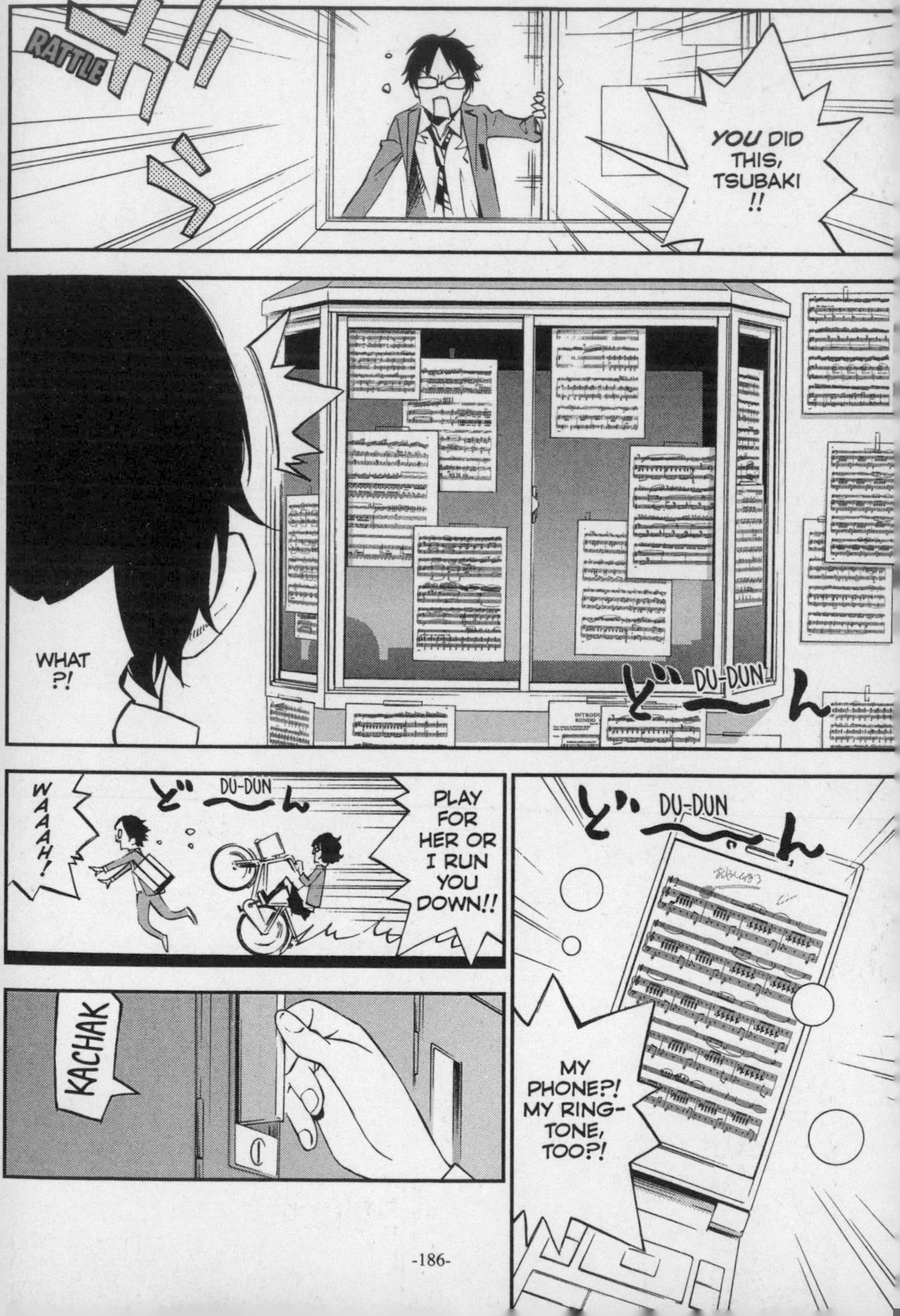
YOU DID THIS, TSUBAKI!!
RATTLE
DU-DUN
WHAT?!
DU-DUN
MY PHONE?! MY RING-TONE, TOO?!
PLAY FOR HER OR I RUN YOU DOWN!!
DU-DUN
WAAAH!
KACHAK

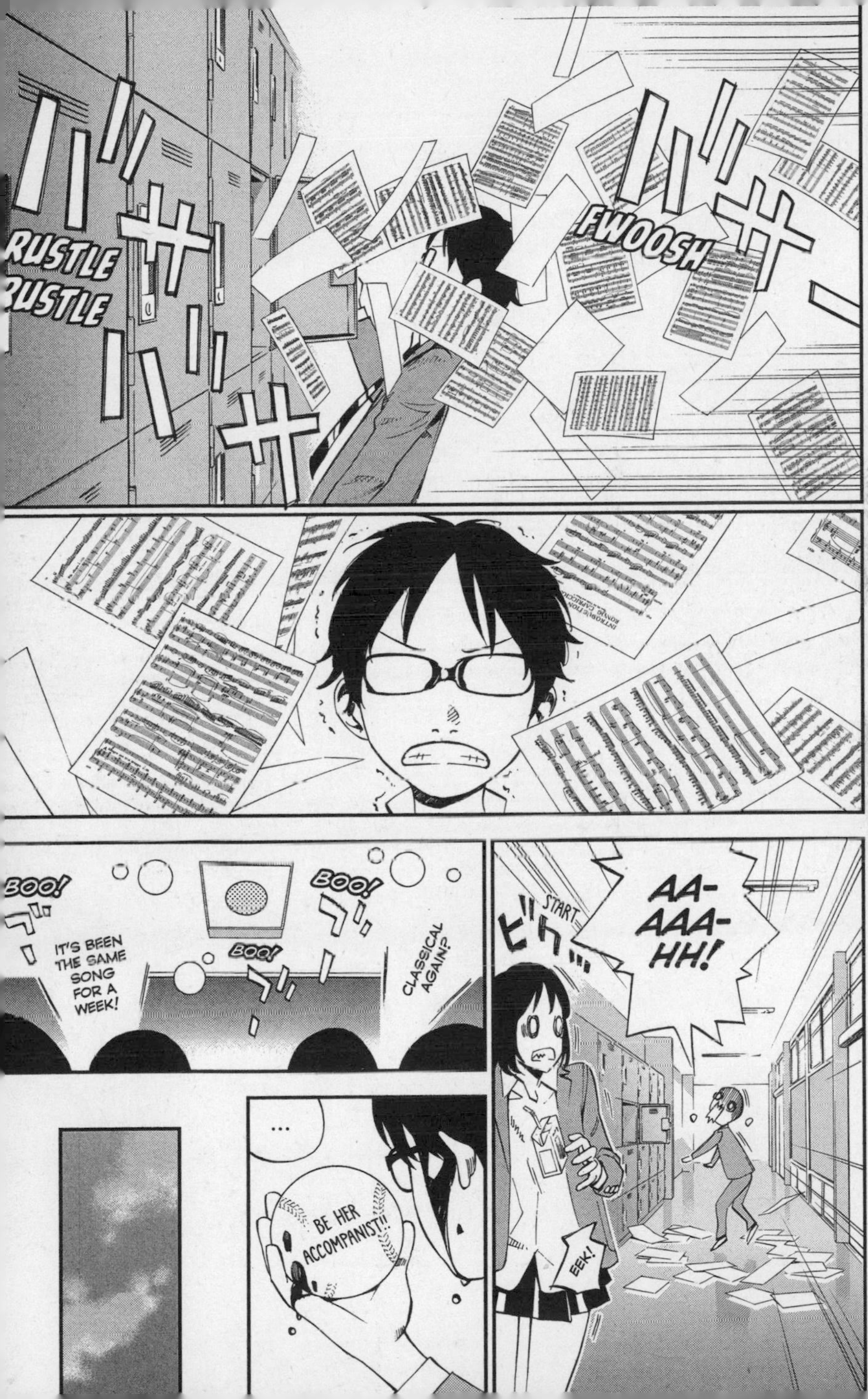
FWOOSH
RUSTLE RUSTLE
START
AA-AAA-HH!
EEK!
BOO!
CLASSICAL AGAIN?
BOO!
IT'S BEEN THE SAME SONG FOR A WEEK!
BOO!
...
BE HER ACCOMPANIST!!

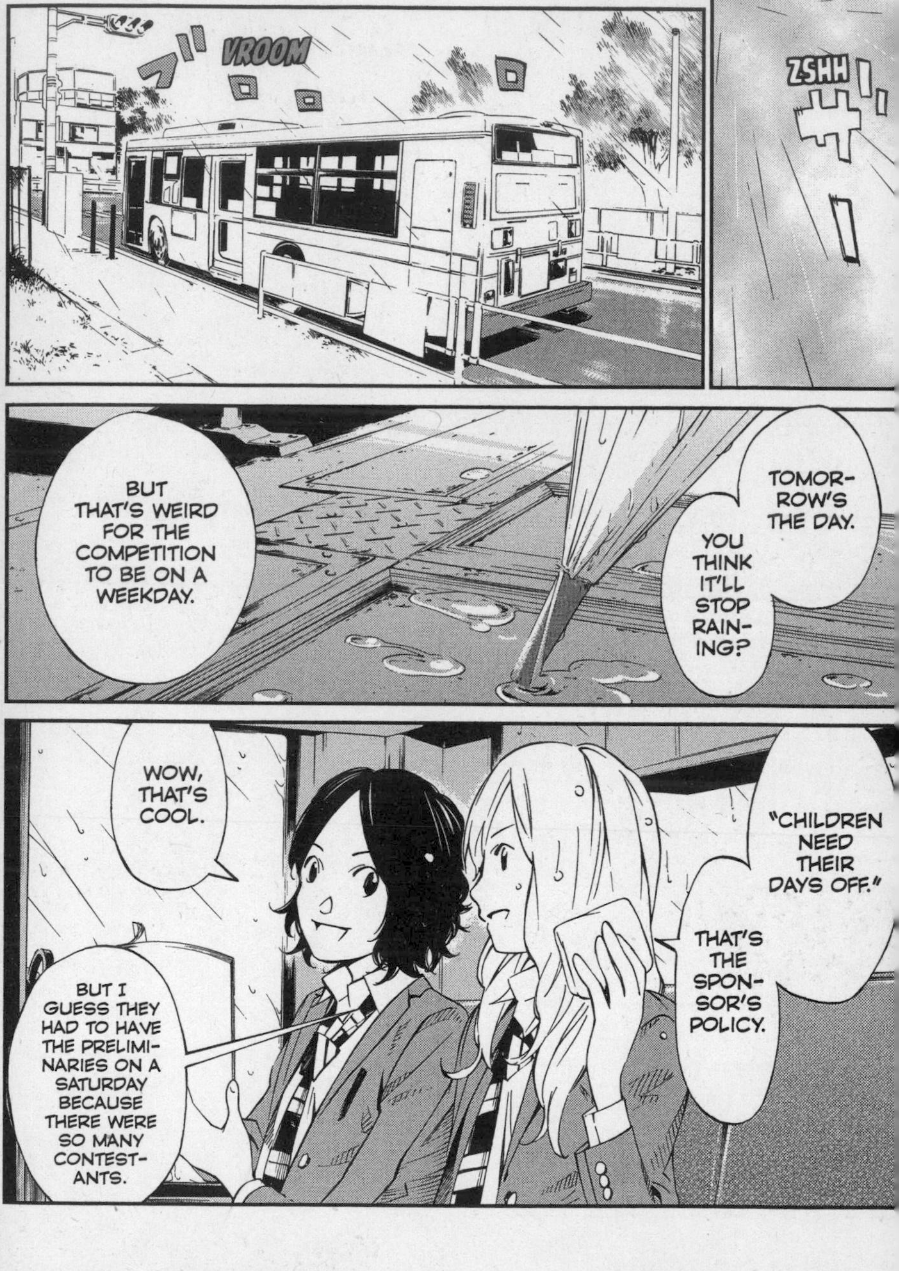
ZSHH
VROOM
TOMOR-ROW'S THE DAY.
YOU THINK IT'LL STOP RAIN-ING?
BUT THAT'S WEIRD FOR THE COMPETITION TO BE ON A WEEKDAY.
"CHILDREN NEED THEIR DAYS OFF."
THAT'S THE SPON-SOR'S POLICY.
WOW, THAT'S COOL.
BUT I GUESS THEY HAD TO HAVE THE PRELIMI-NARIES ON A SATURDAY BECAUSE THERE WERE SO MANY CONTEST-ANTS.

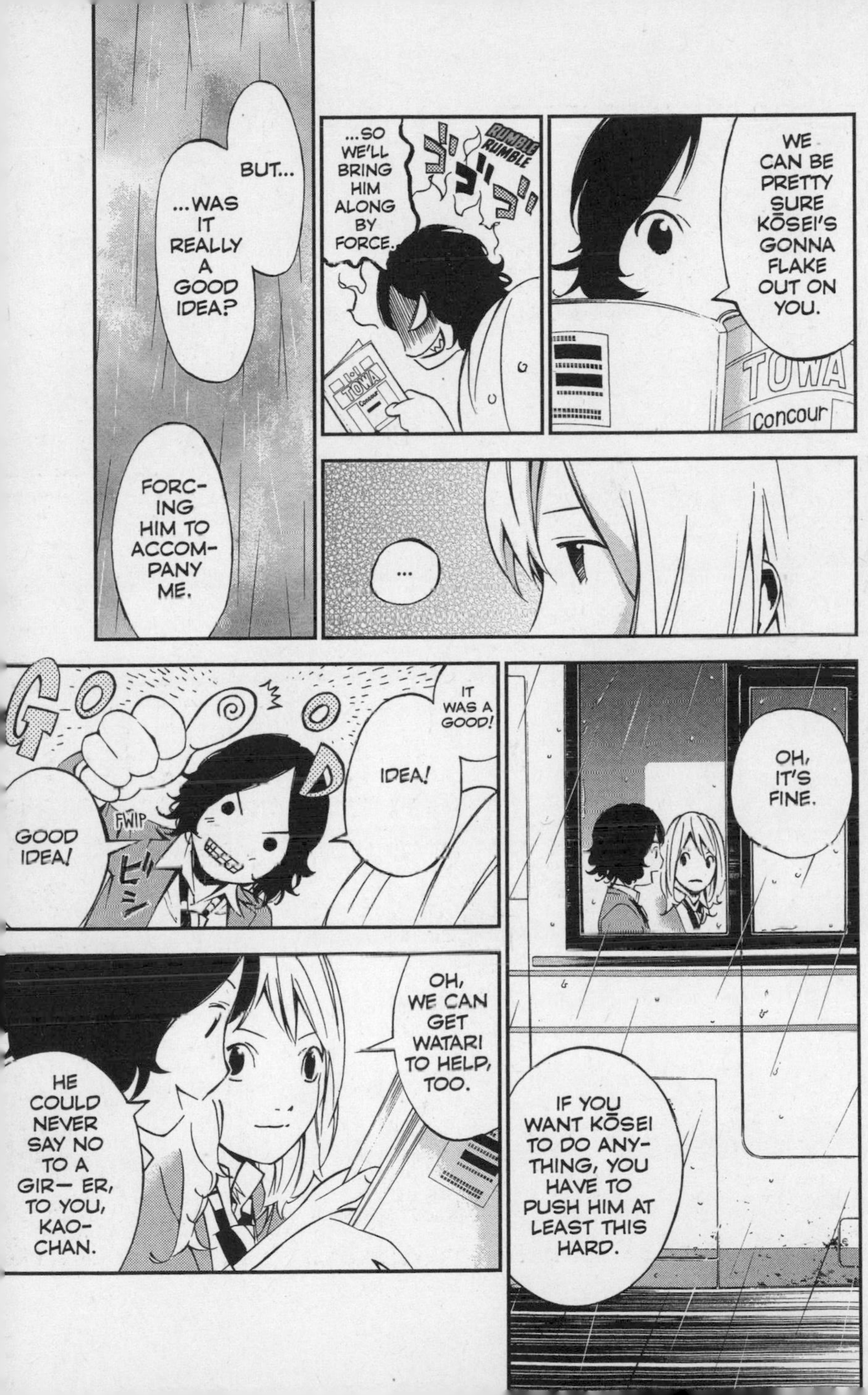
WE CAN BE PRETTY SURE KŌSEI'S GONNA FLAKE OUT ON YOU.
TOWA Concour
RUMBLE RUMBLE
...SO WE'LL BRING HIM ALONG BY FORCE.
...
BUT...
...WAS IT REALLY A GOOD IDEA?
FORCING HIM TO ACCOMPANY ME.
OH, IT'S FINE.
IF YOU WANT KŌSEI TO DO ANYTHING, YOU HAVE TO PUSH HIM AT LEAST THIS HARD.
IT WAS A GOOD!
IDEA!
FWIP
GOOD IDEA!
OH, WE CAN GET WATARI TO HELP, TOO.
HE COULD NEVER SAY NO TO A GIR— ER, TO YOU, KAO-CHAN.

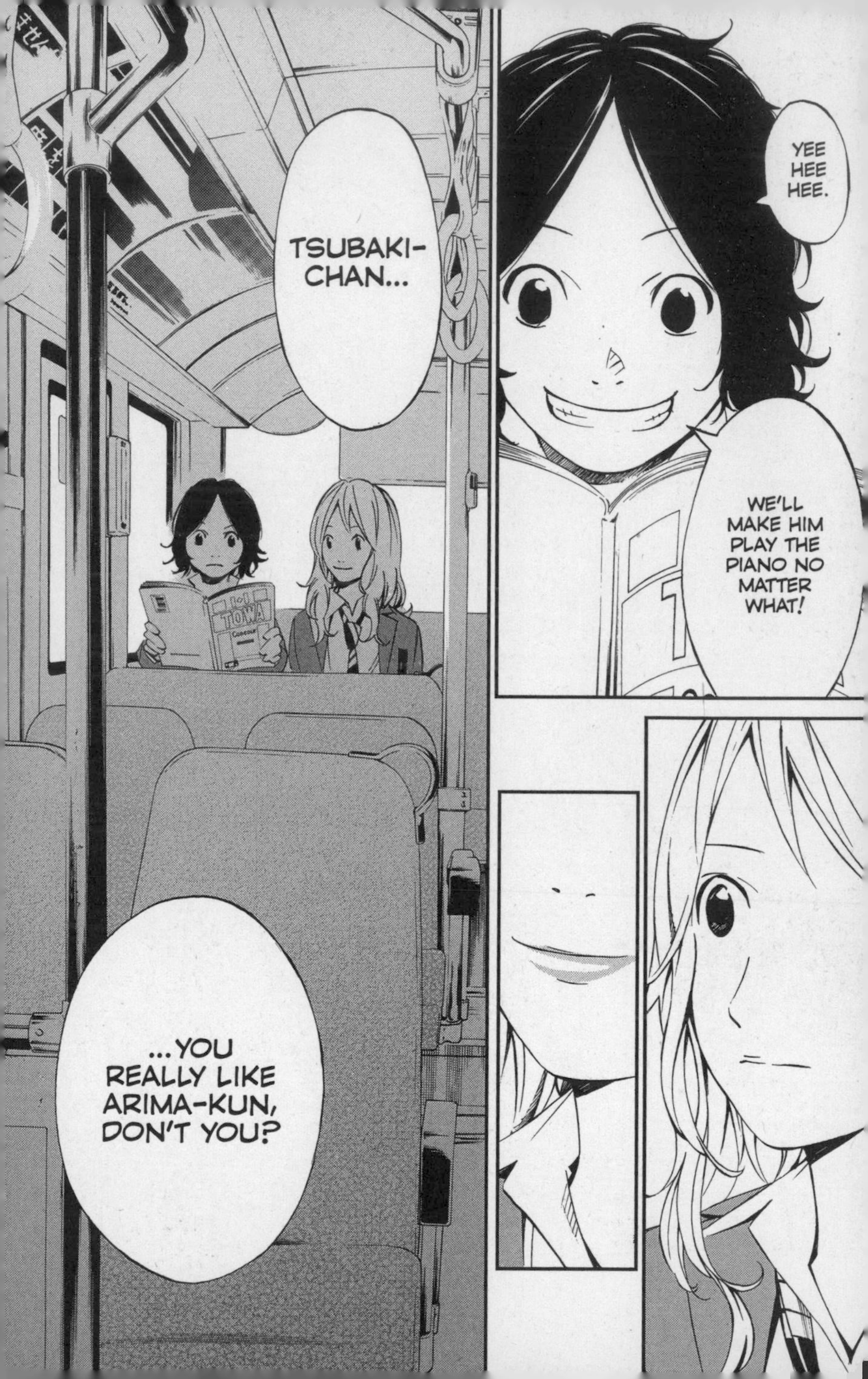
YEE HEE HEE.
WE'LL MAKE HIM PLAY THE PIANO NO MATTER WHAT!
TSUBAKI-CHAN...
...YOU REALLY LIKE ARIMA-KUN, DON'T YOU?

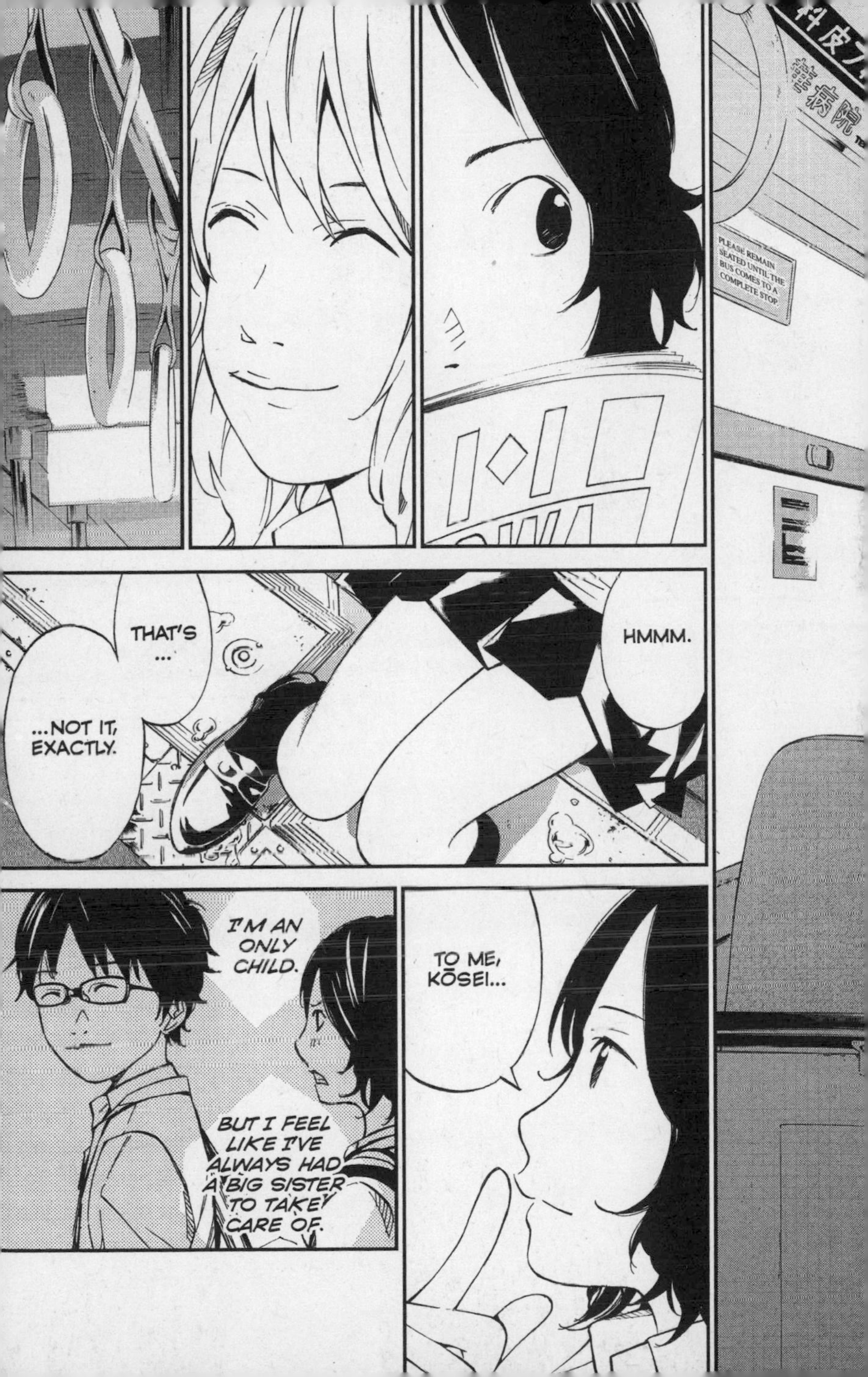
PLEASE REMAIN SEATED UNTIL THE BUS COMES TO A COMPLETE STOP
HMMM.
THAT'S ...
...NOT IT, EXACTLY.
TO ME, KŌSEI...
I'M AN ONLY CHILD.
BUT I FEEL LIKE I'VE ALWAYS HAD A BIG SISTER TO TAKE CARE OF.

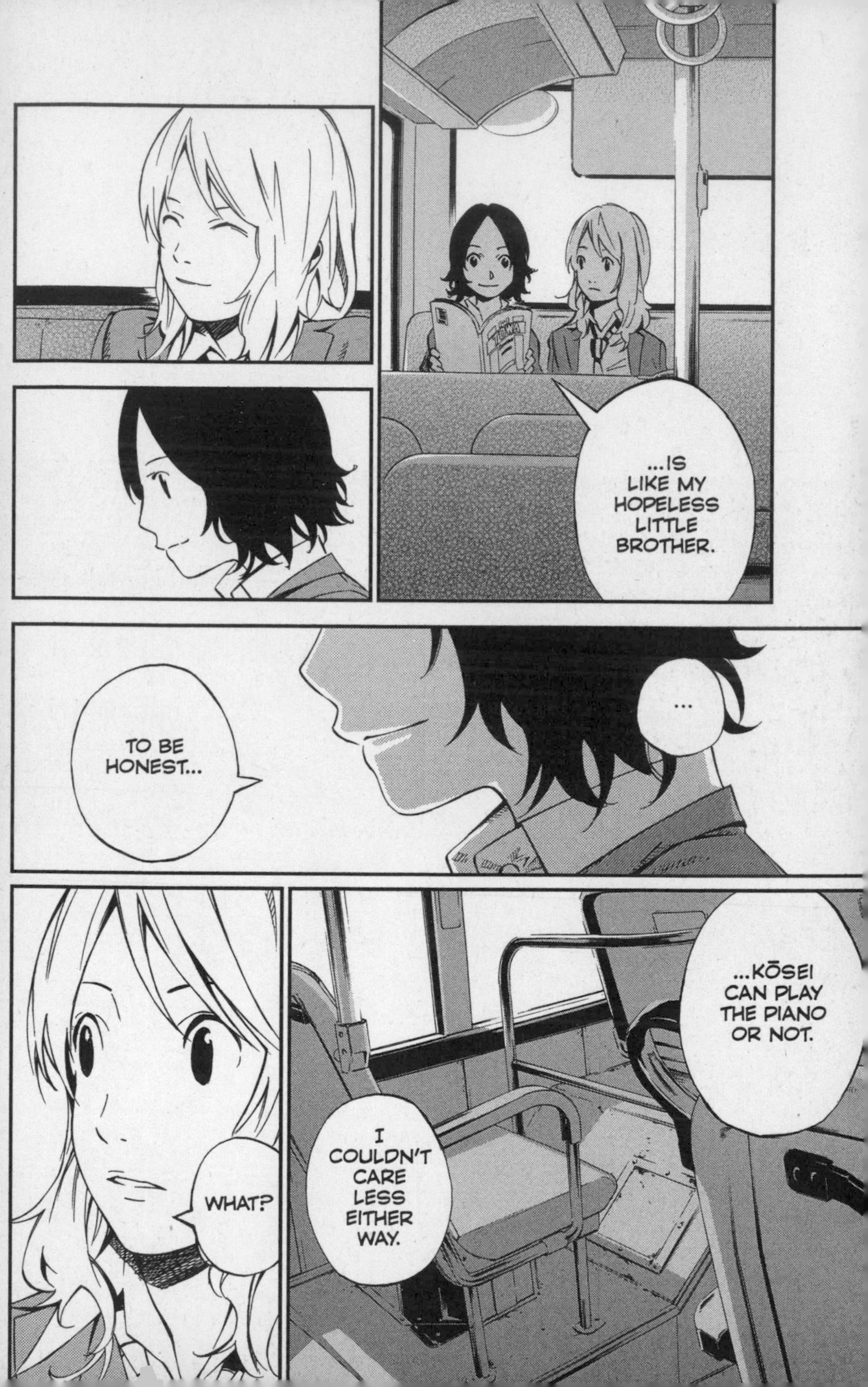
...IS LIKE MY HOPELESS LITTLE BROTHER.
...
TO BE HONEST...
...KŌSEI CAN PLAY THE PIANO OR NOT.
I COULDN'T CARE LESS EITHER WAY.
WHAT?

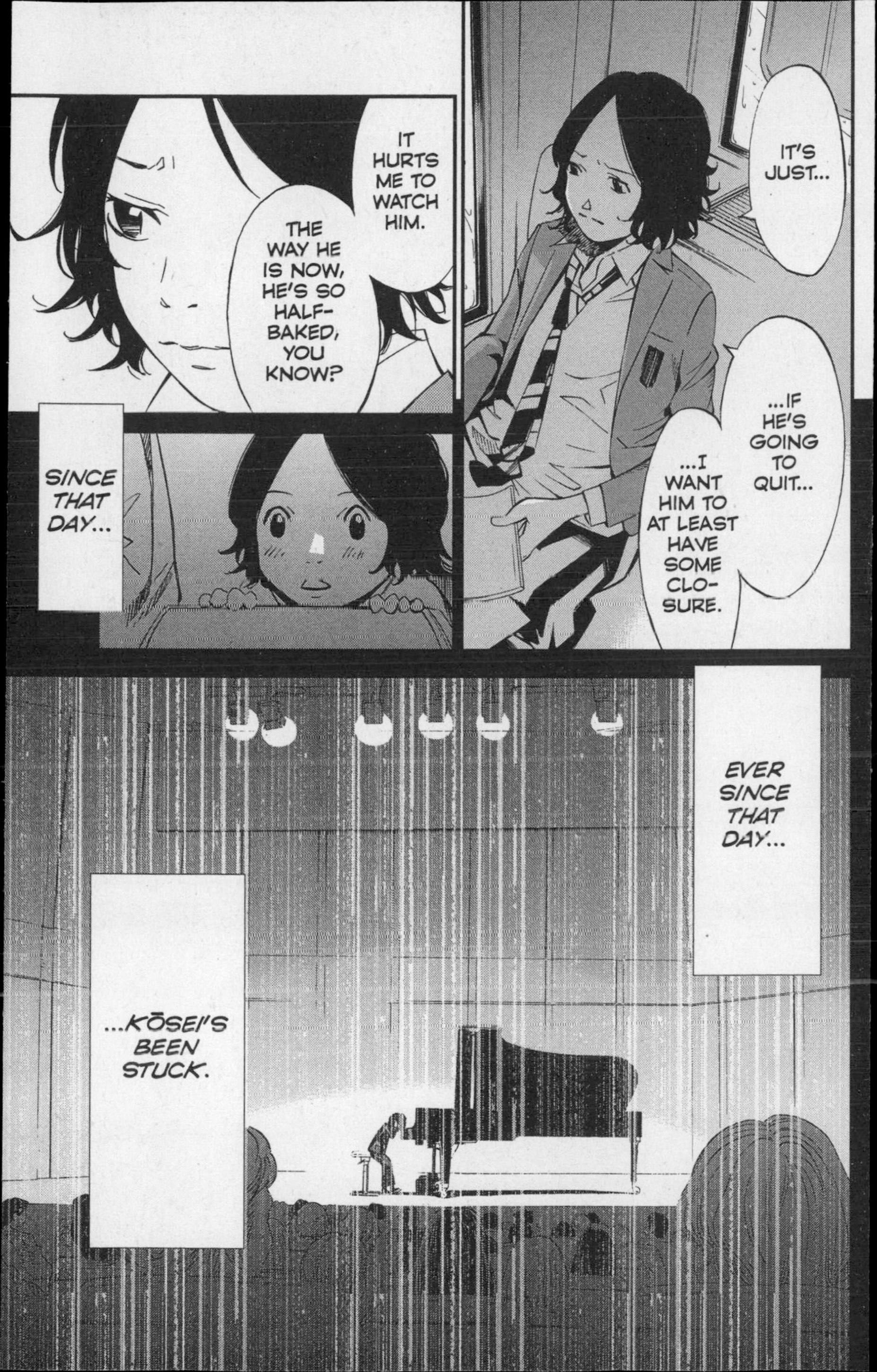
IT'S JUST...
...IF HE'S GOING TO QUIT...
...I WANT HIM TO AT LEAST HAVE SOME CLO-SURE.
IT HURTS ME TO WATCH HIM.
THE WAY HE IS NOW, HE'S SO HALF-BAKED, YOU KNOW?
SINCE THAT DAY...
EVER SINCE THAT DAY...
...KŌSEI'S BEEN STUCK.

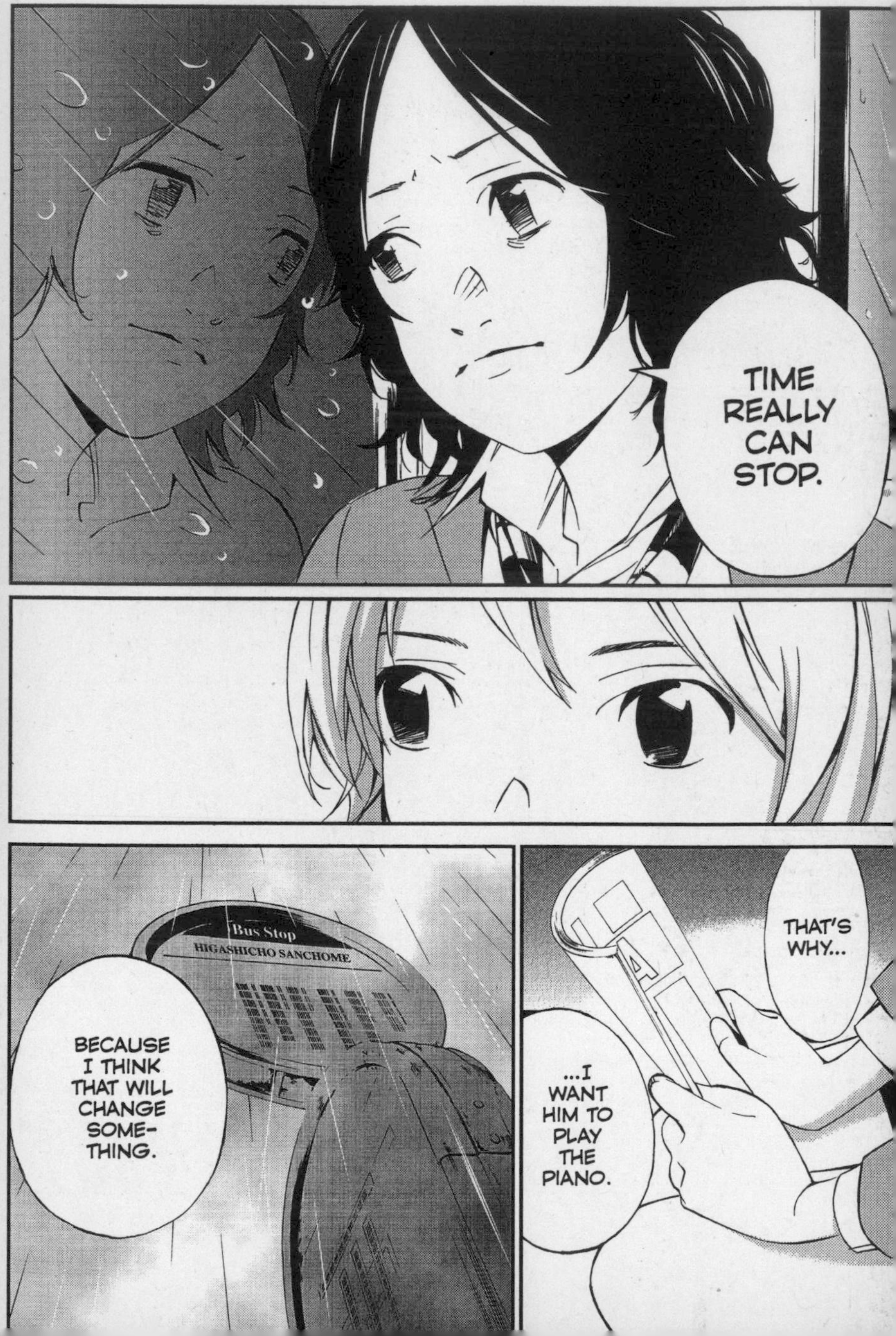
TIME REALLY CAN STOP.
THAT'S WHY...
...I WANT HIM TO PLAY THE PIANO.
Bus Stop
HIGASHICHO SANCHOME
BECAUSE I THINK THAT WILL CHANGE SOME-THING.

NEXT STOP, TOTSUHARA UNIVERSITY HOSPITAL.

.TOTSUHARA UNIVERSITY HOSPITAL.

STOP REQUESTED

PLEASE PUSH THIS BUTTON TO REQUE A ST

DING

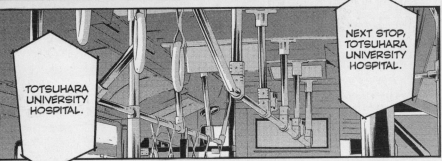

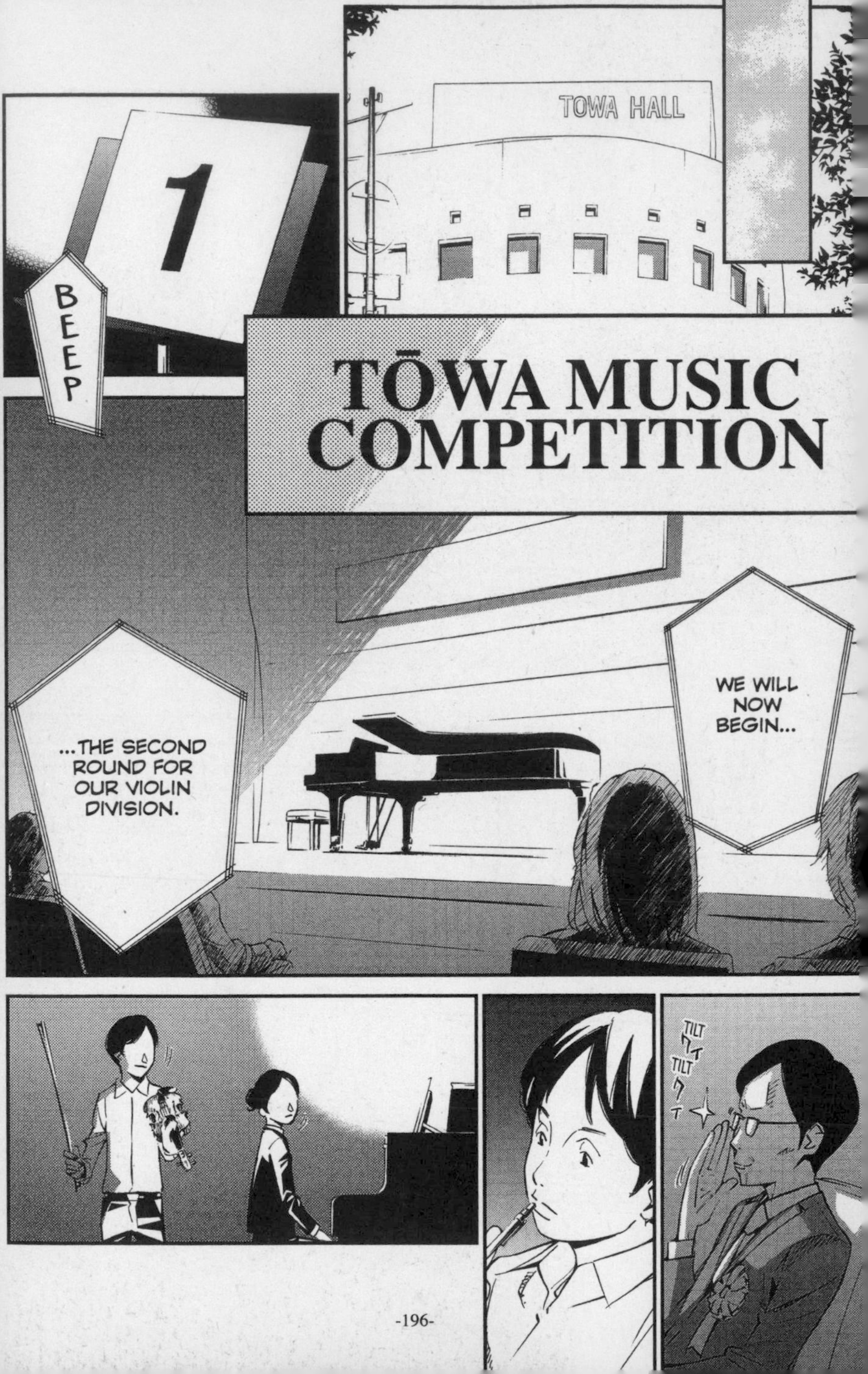
TOWA HALL
BEEP
TŌWA MUSIC COMPETITION
WE WILL NOW BEGIN...
...THE SECOND ROUND FOR OUR VIOLIN DIVISION.
TILT TILT

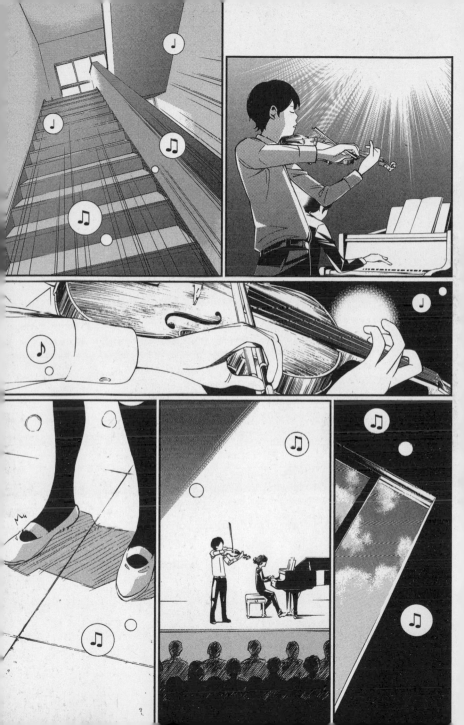

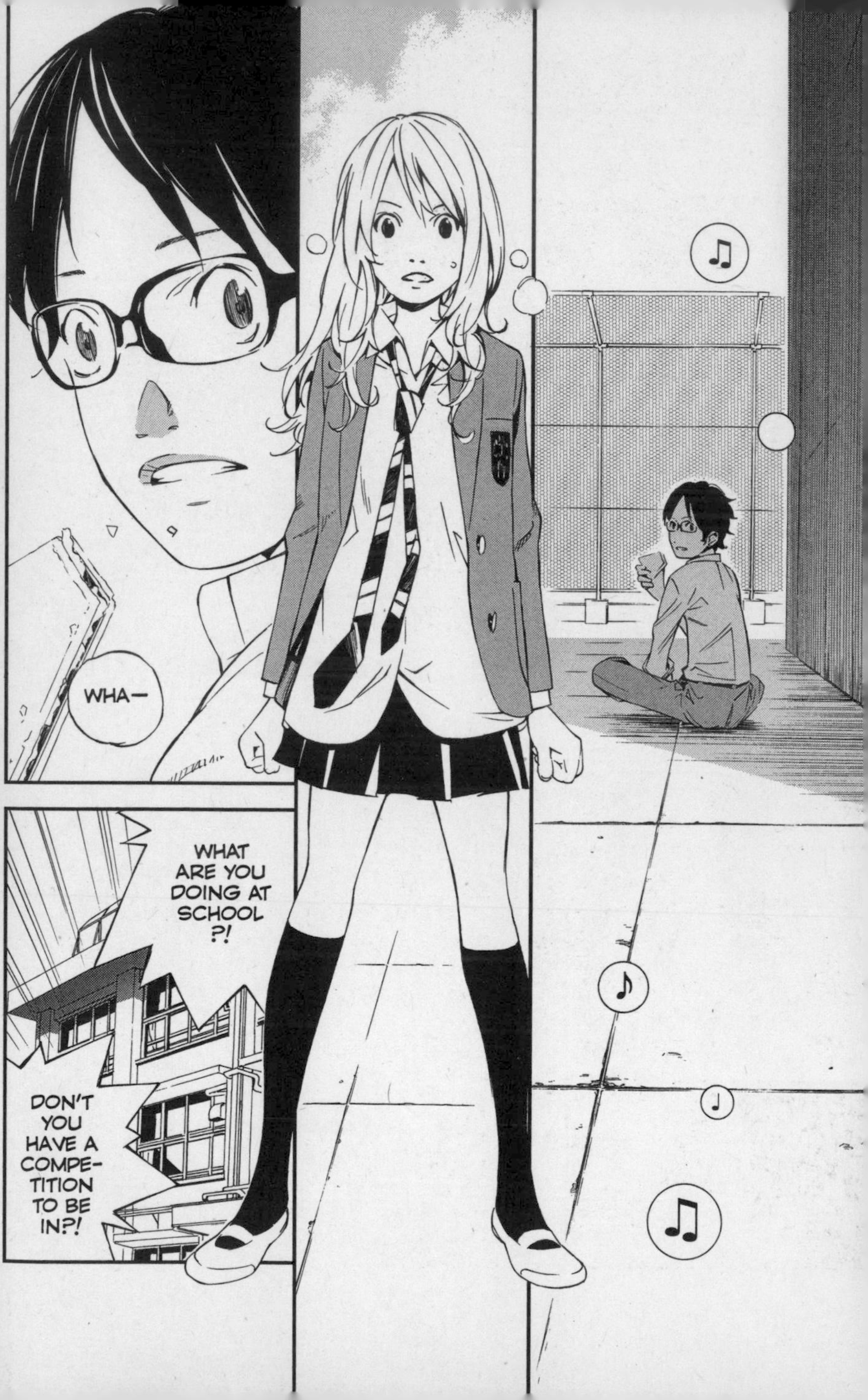
WHA—
WHAT ARE YOU DOING AT SCHOOL ?!
DON'T YOU HAVE A COMPETITION TO BE IN?!

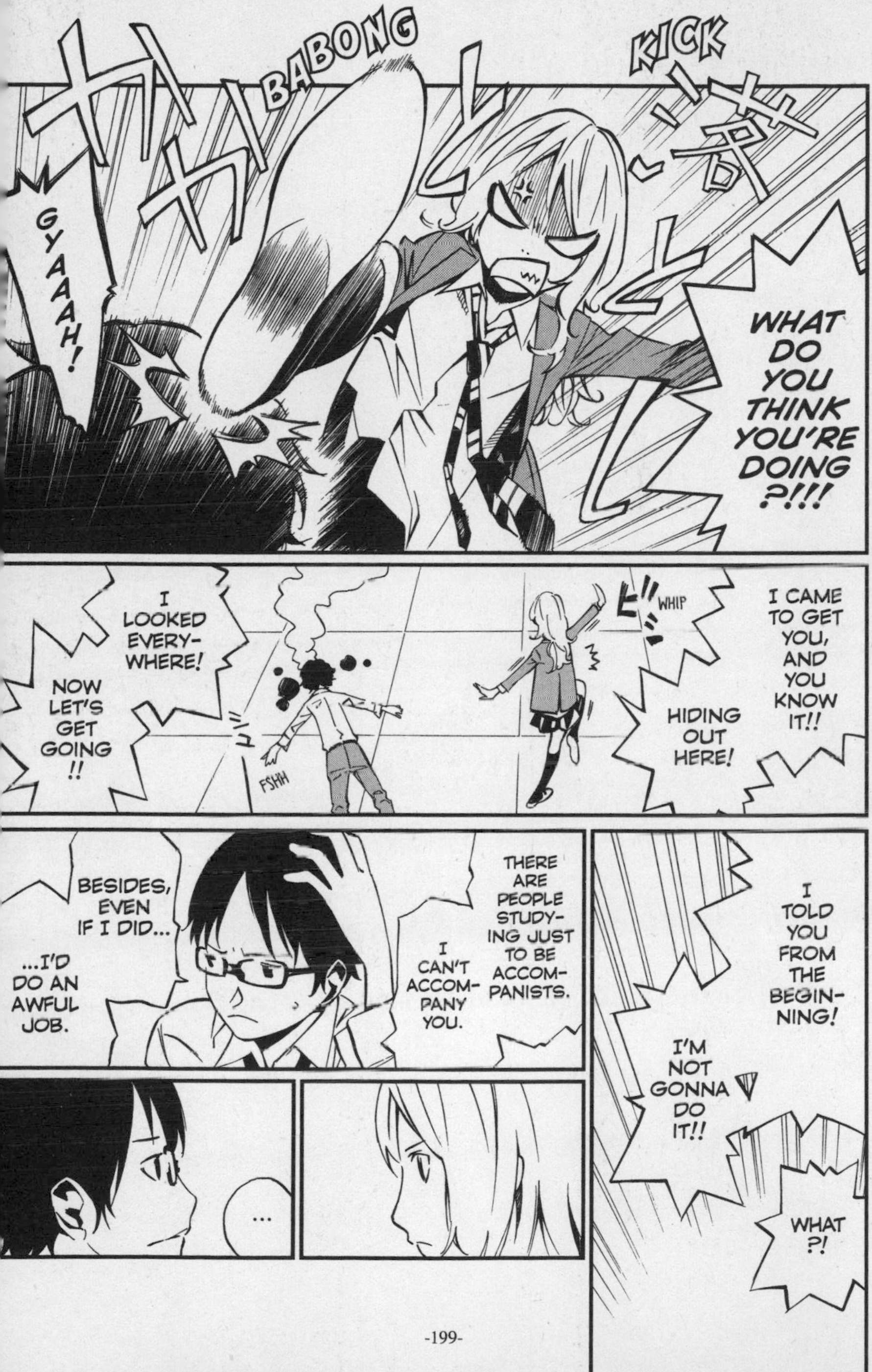
KICK
BABONG
WHAT DO YOU THINK YOU'RE DOING?!!!
GYAAAH!
I CAME TO GET YOU, AND YOU KNOW IT!!
WHIP
HIDING OUT HERE!
I LOOKED EVERY-WHERE!
NOW LET'S GET GOING!!
FSHH
I TOLD YOU FROM THE BEGIN-NING!
I'M NOT GONNA DO IT!!
WHAT?!
THERE ARE PEOPLE STUDY-ING JUST TO BE ACCOM-PANISTS.
I CAN'T ACCOM-PANY YOU.
BESIDES, EVEN IF I DID...
...I'D DO AN AWFUL JOB.
...

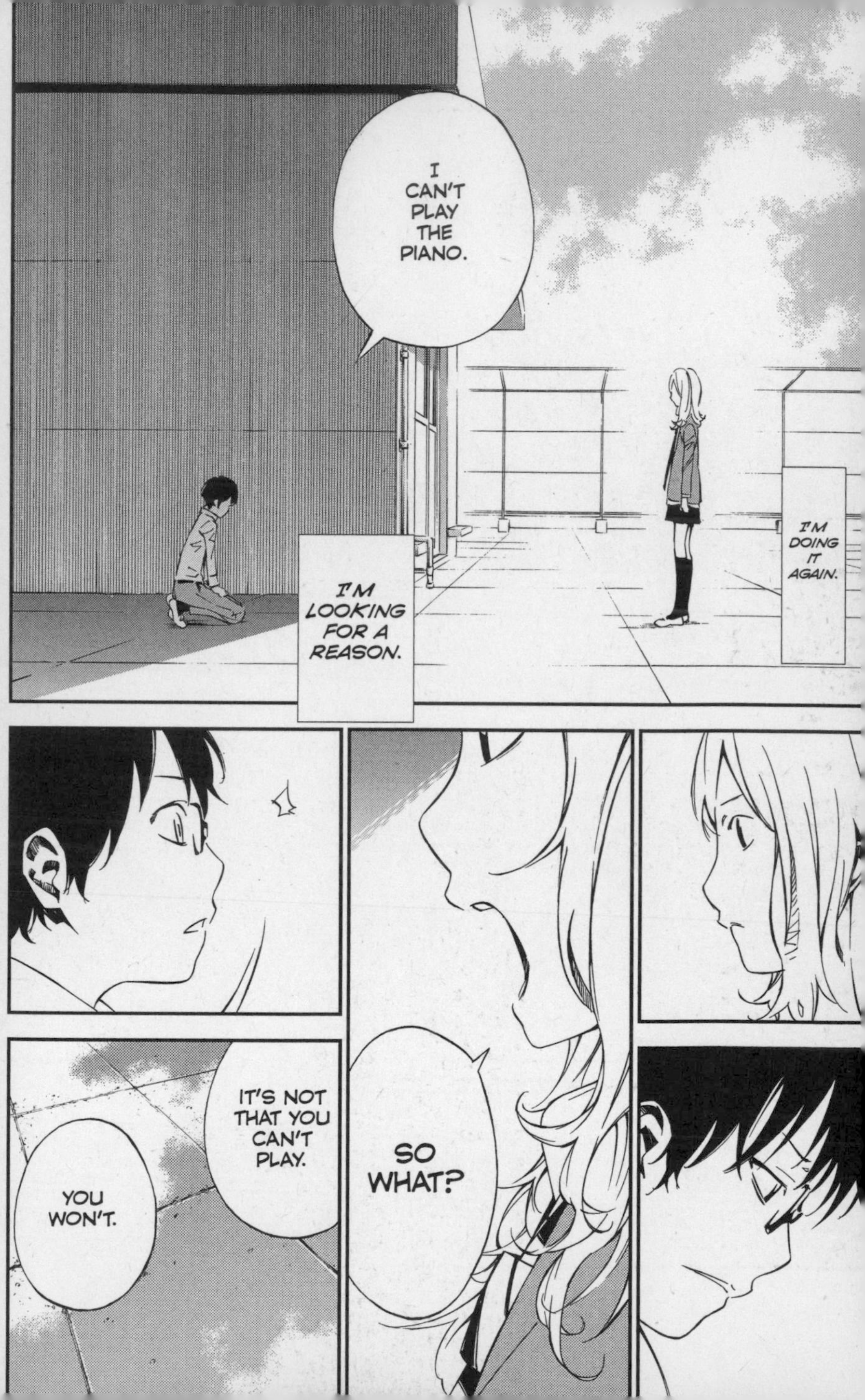

I CAN'T PLAY THE PIANO.
I'M DOING IT AGAIN.
I'M LOOKING FOR A REASON.
SO WHAT?
IT'S NOT THAT YOU CAN'T PLAY.
YOU WON'T.

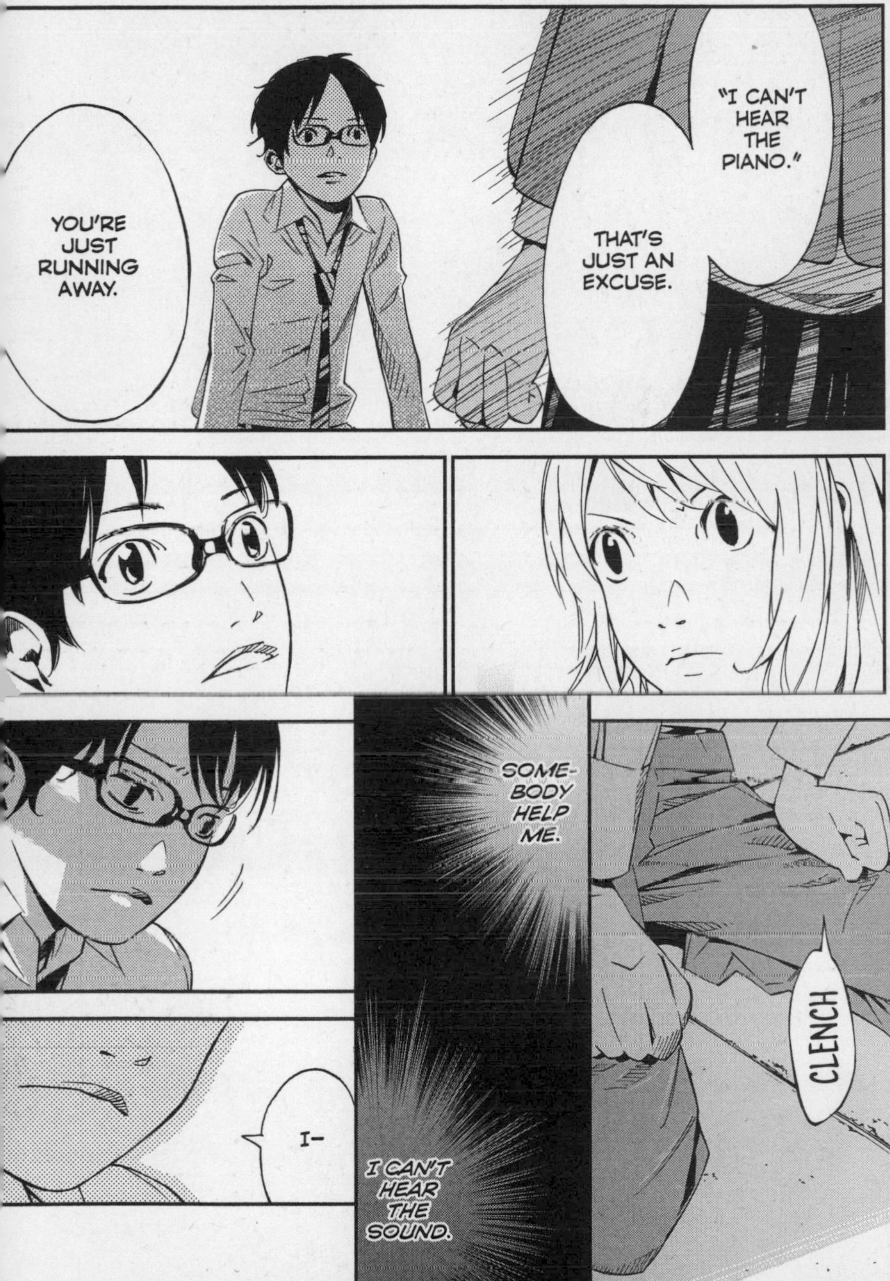
"I CAN'T HEAR THE PIANO."
THAT'S JUST AN EXCUSE.
YOU'RE JUST RUNNING AWAY.
CLENCH
SOME-BODY HELP ME.
I CAN'T HEAR THE SOUND.
I–

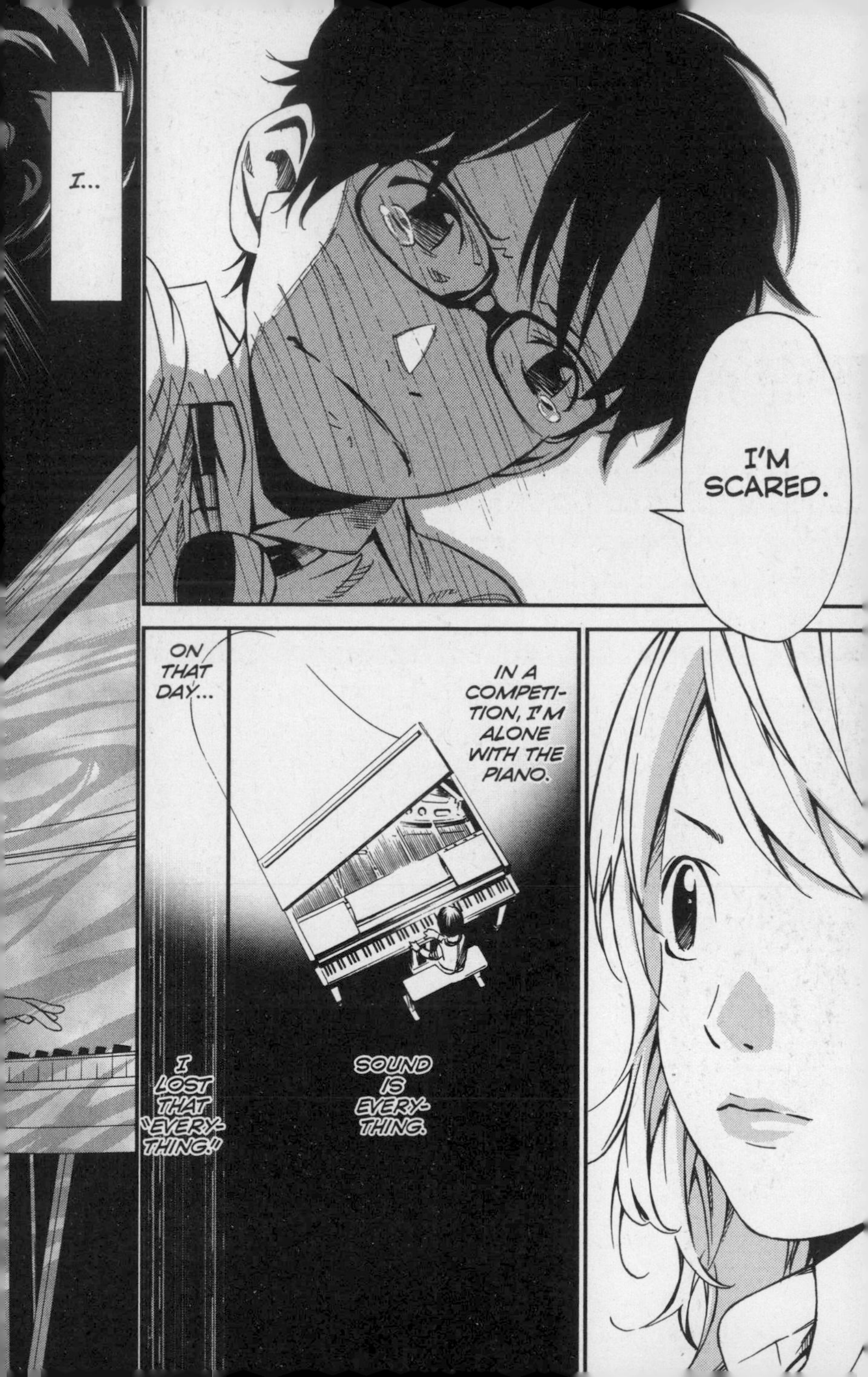
I'M SCARED.
IN A COMPETITION, I'M ALONE WITH THE PIANO.
SOUND IS EVERYTHING.
ON THAT DAY...
I LOST THAT "EVERYTHING."
I...

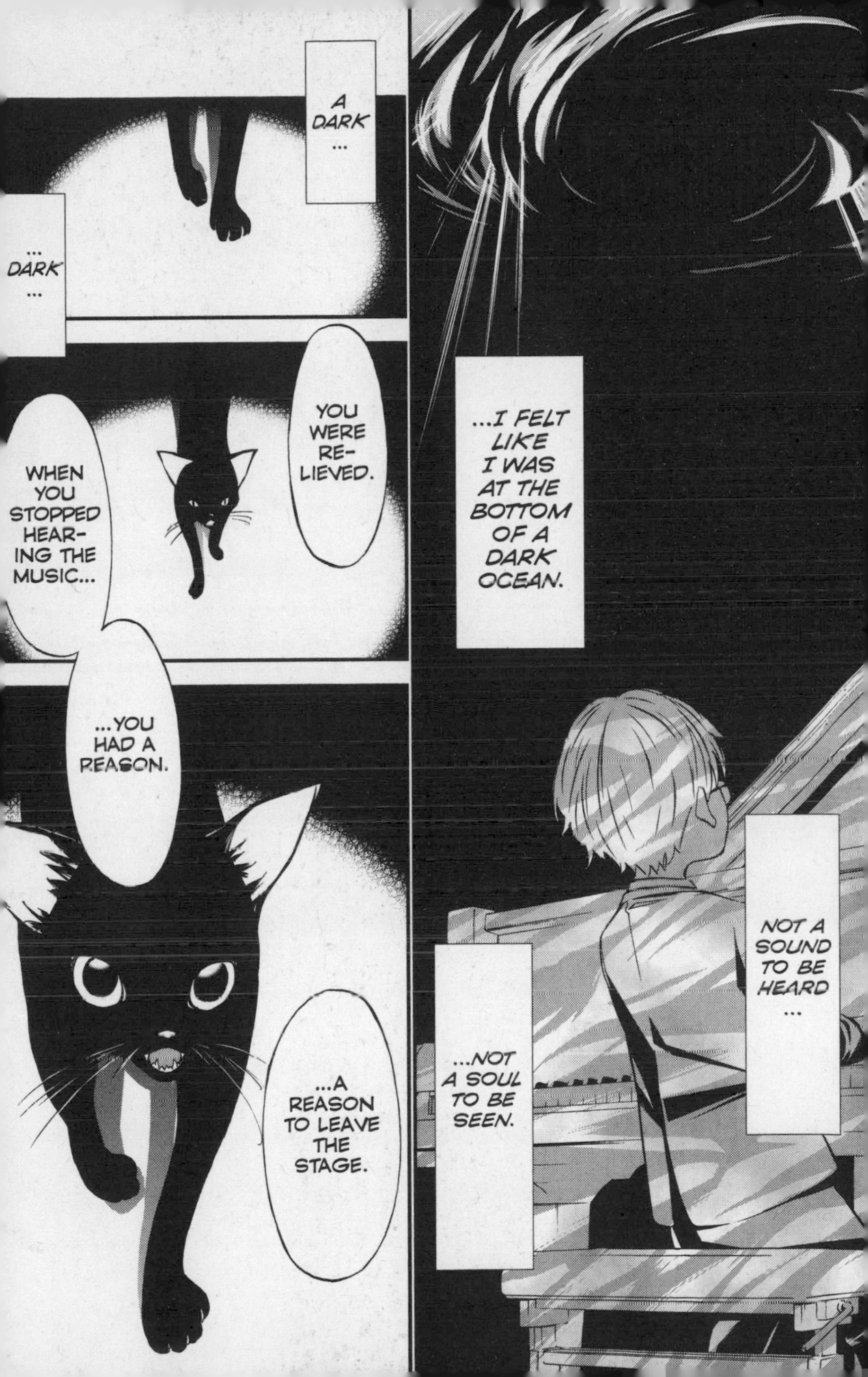
...I FELT LIKE I WAS AT THE BOTTOM OF A DARK OCEAN.
NOT A SOUND TO BE HEARD ...
...NOT A SOUL TO BE SEEN.
A DARK ...
... DARK ...
YOU WERE RE-LIEVED.
WHEN YOU STOPPED HEAR-ING THE MUSIC...
...YOU HAD A REASON.
...A REASON TO LEAVE THE STAGE.

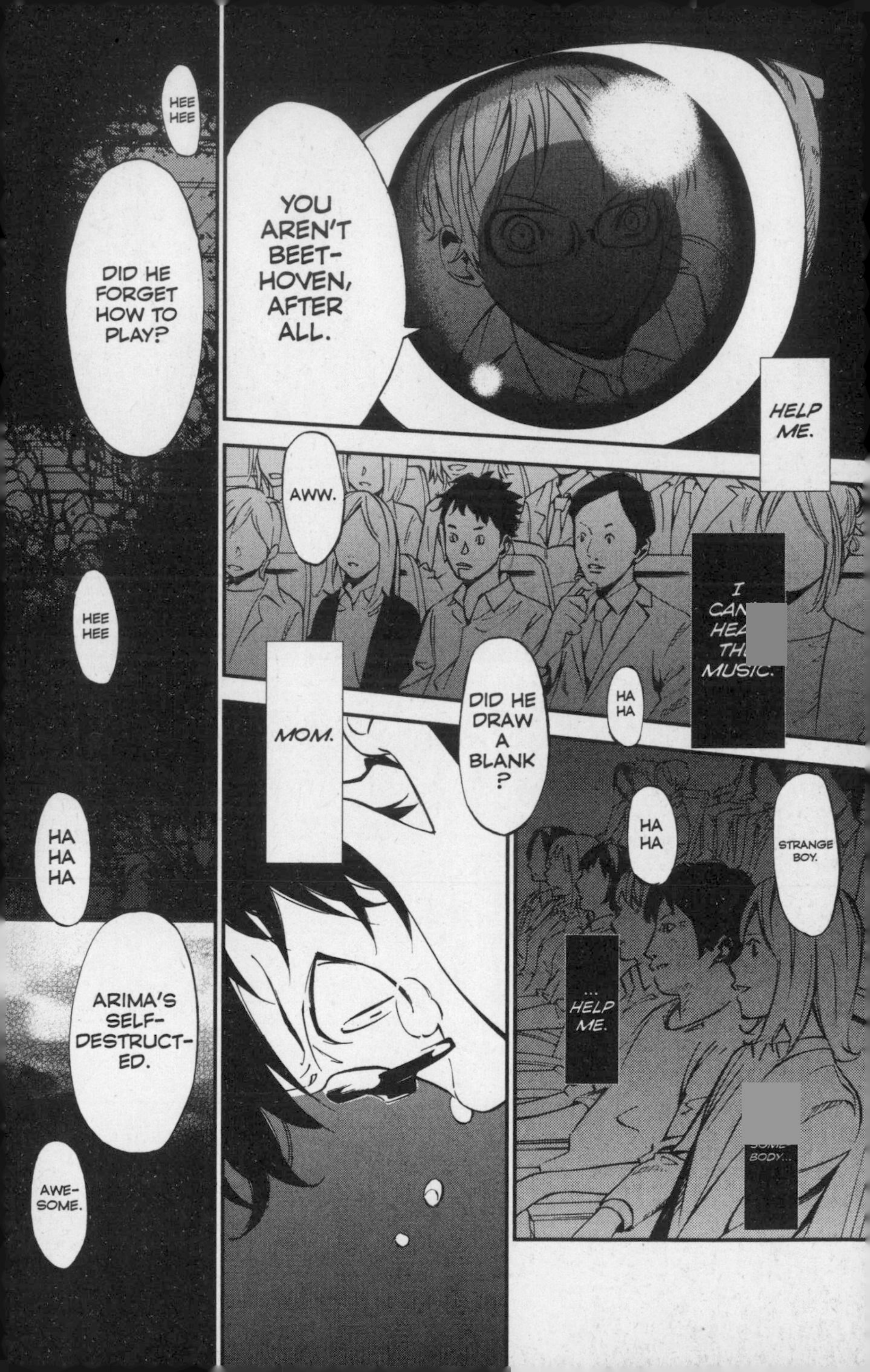
YOU AREN'T BEET-HOVEN, AFTER ALL.
HELP ME.
I CAN HEA TH MUSIC.
AWW.
HA HA
DID HE DRAW A BLANK?
MOM.
STRANGE BOY.
HA HA
...HELP ME.
BODY...
HEE HEE
DID HE FORGET HOW TO PLAY?
HEE HEE
HA HA HA
ARIMA'S SELF-DESTRUCT-ED.
AWE-SOME.

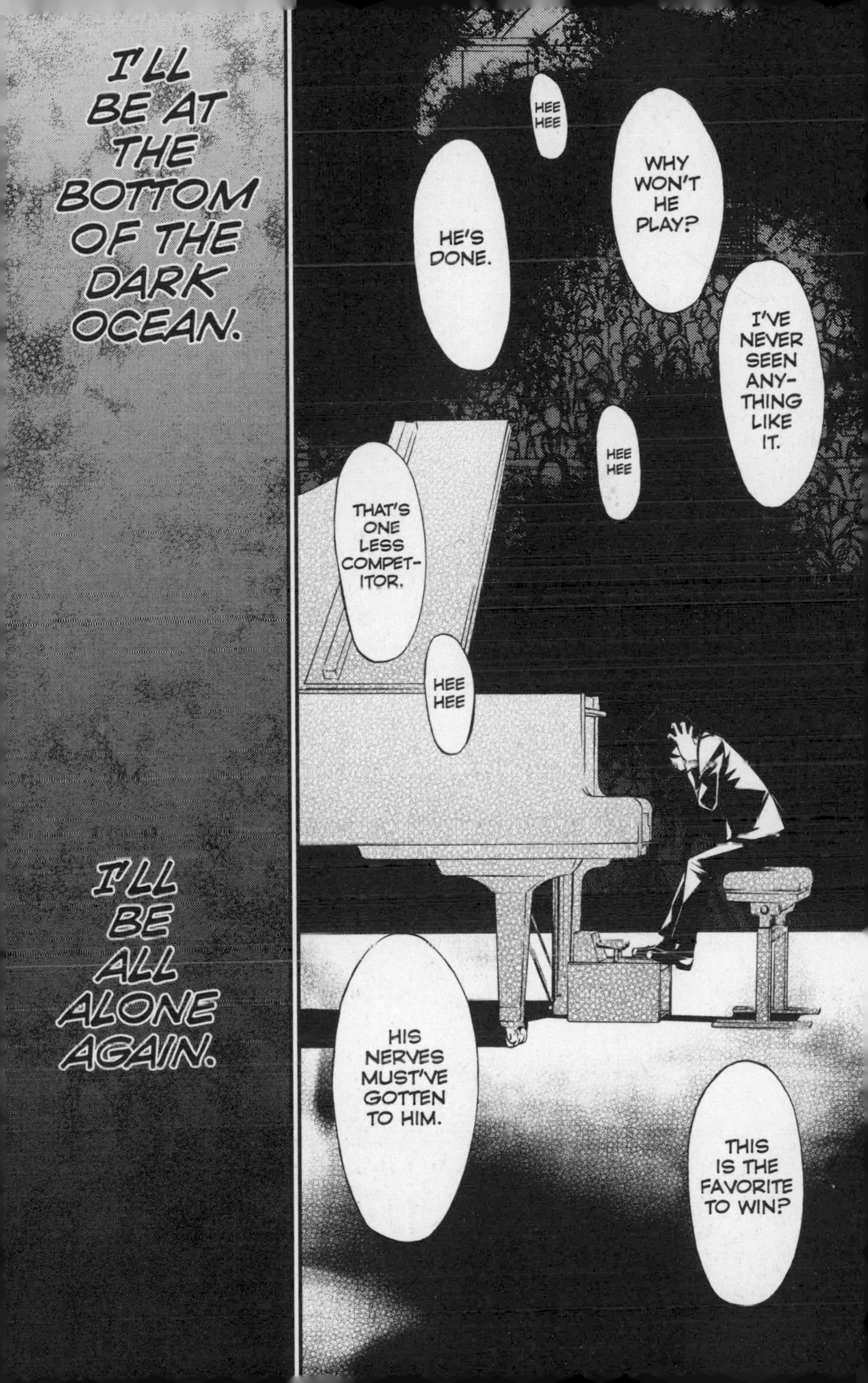
WHY WON'T HE PLAY?
HEE HEE
HE'S DONE.
I'VE NEVER SEEN ANYTHING LIKE IT.
HEE HEE
THAT'S ONE LESS COMPETITOR.
HEE HEE
THIS IS THE FAVORITE TO WIN?
HIS NERVES MUST'VE GOTTEN TO HIM.
I'LL BE AT THE BOTTOM OF THE DARK OCEAN.
I'LL BE ALL ALONE AGAIN.

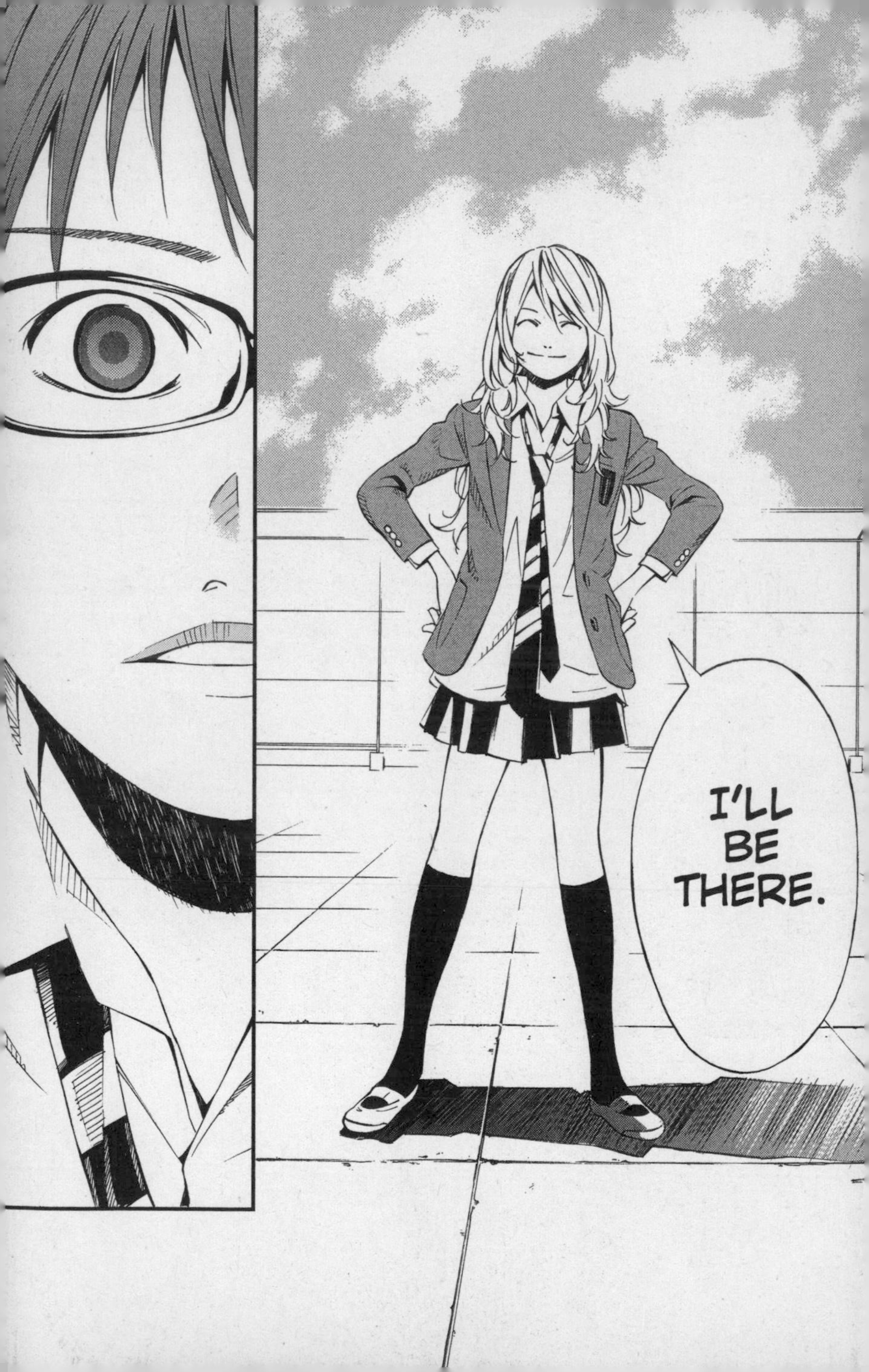
I'LL BE THERE.

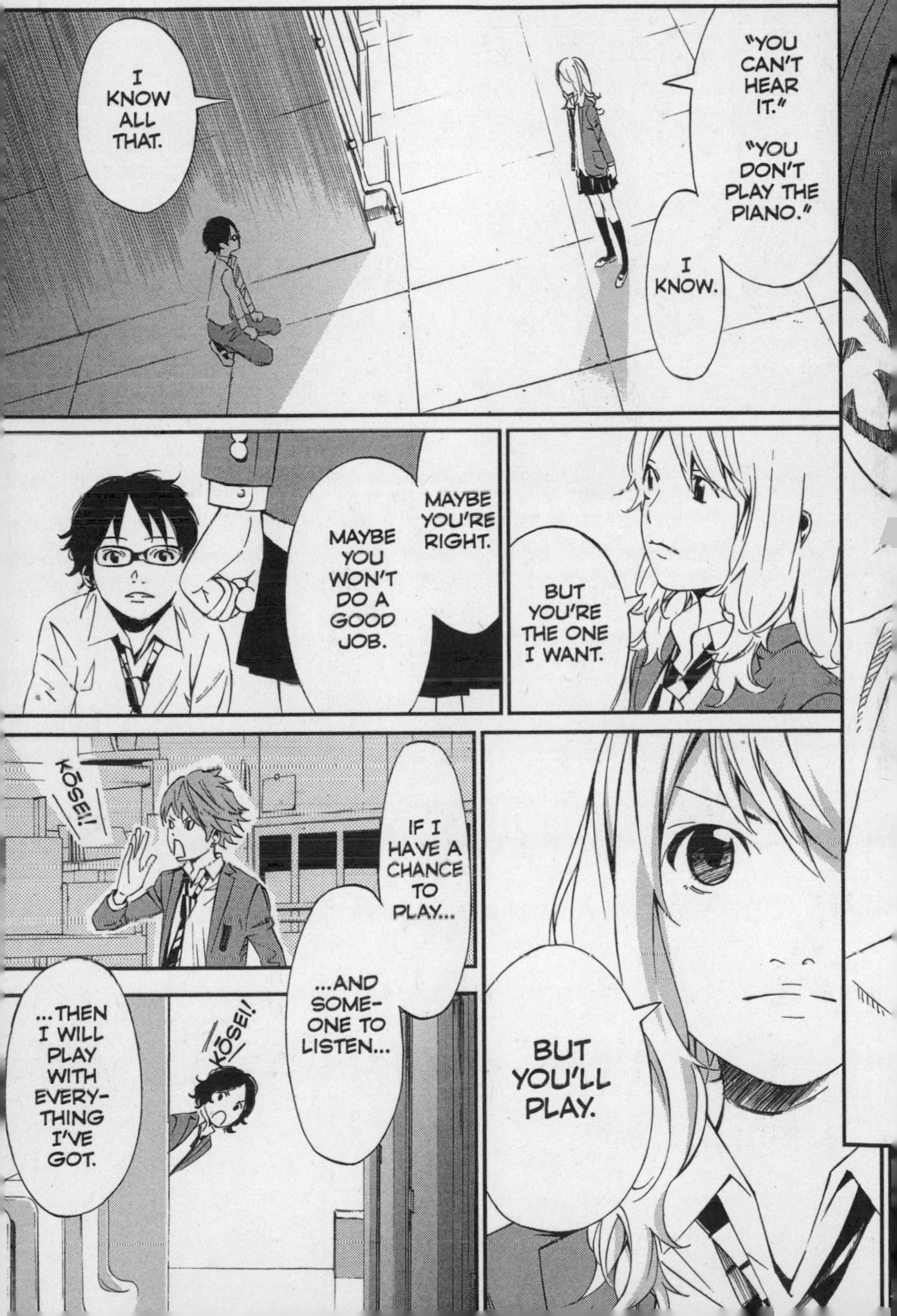
"YOU CAN'T HEAR IT." "YOU DON'T PLAY THE PIANO." I KNOW.
I KNOW ALL THAT.
BUT YOU'RE THE ONE I WANT.
MAYBE YOU'RE RIGHT. MAYBE YOU WON'T DO A GOOD JOB.
BUT YOU'LL PLAY.
IF I HAVE A CHANCE TO PLAY...
KŌSEI!!
...AND SOME-ONE TO LISTEN...
KŌSEI!
...THEN I WILL PLAY WITH EVERY-THING I'VE GOT.

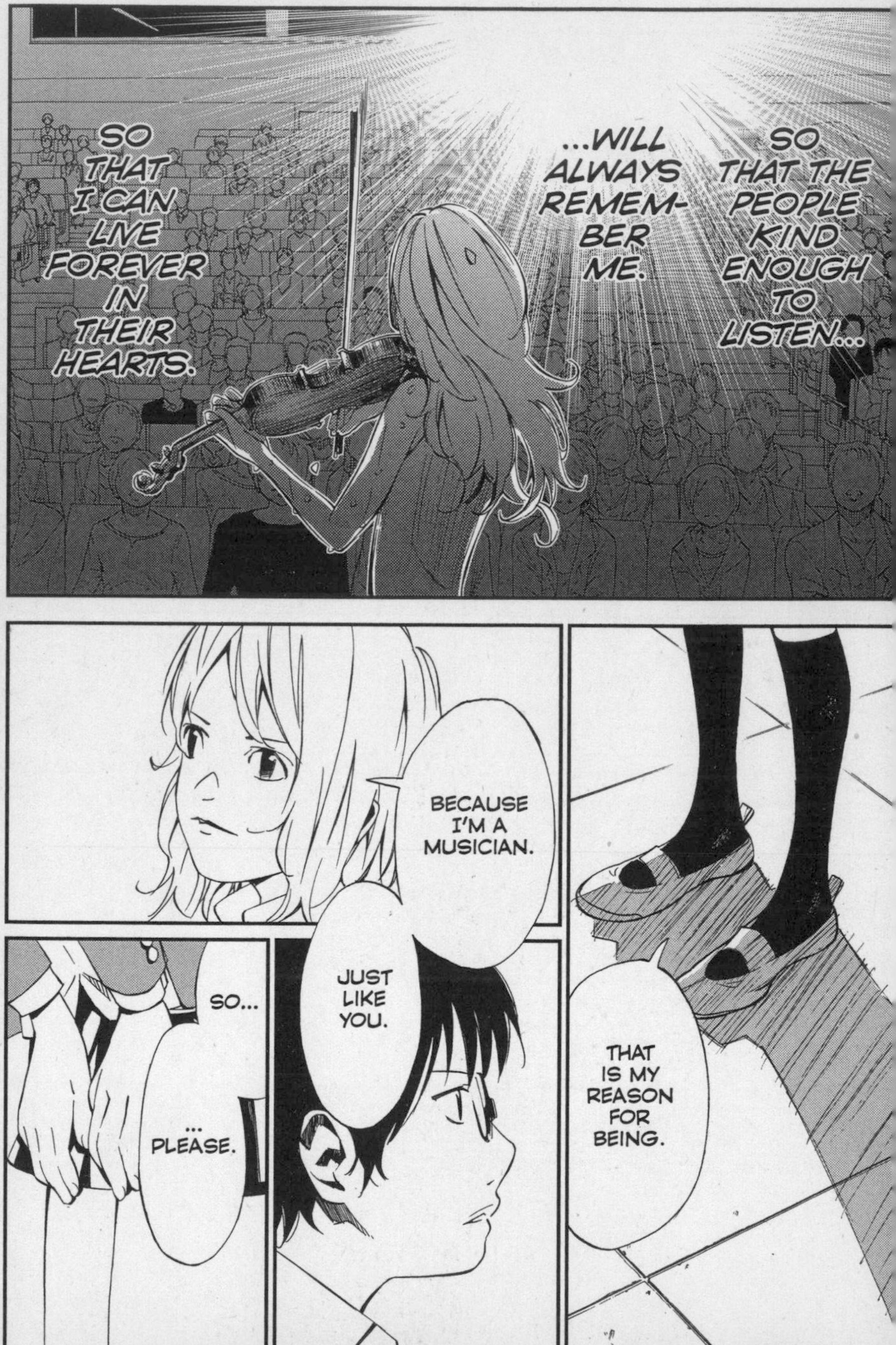
SO THAT THE PEOPLE KIND ENOUGH TO LISTEN...
...WILL ALWAYS REMEMBER ME.
SO THAT I CAN LIVE FOREVER IN THEIR HEARTS.
THAT IS MY REASON FOR BEING.
BECAUSE I'M A MUSICIAN.
JUST LIKE YOU.
SO...
...PLEASE.

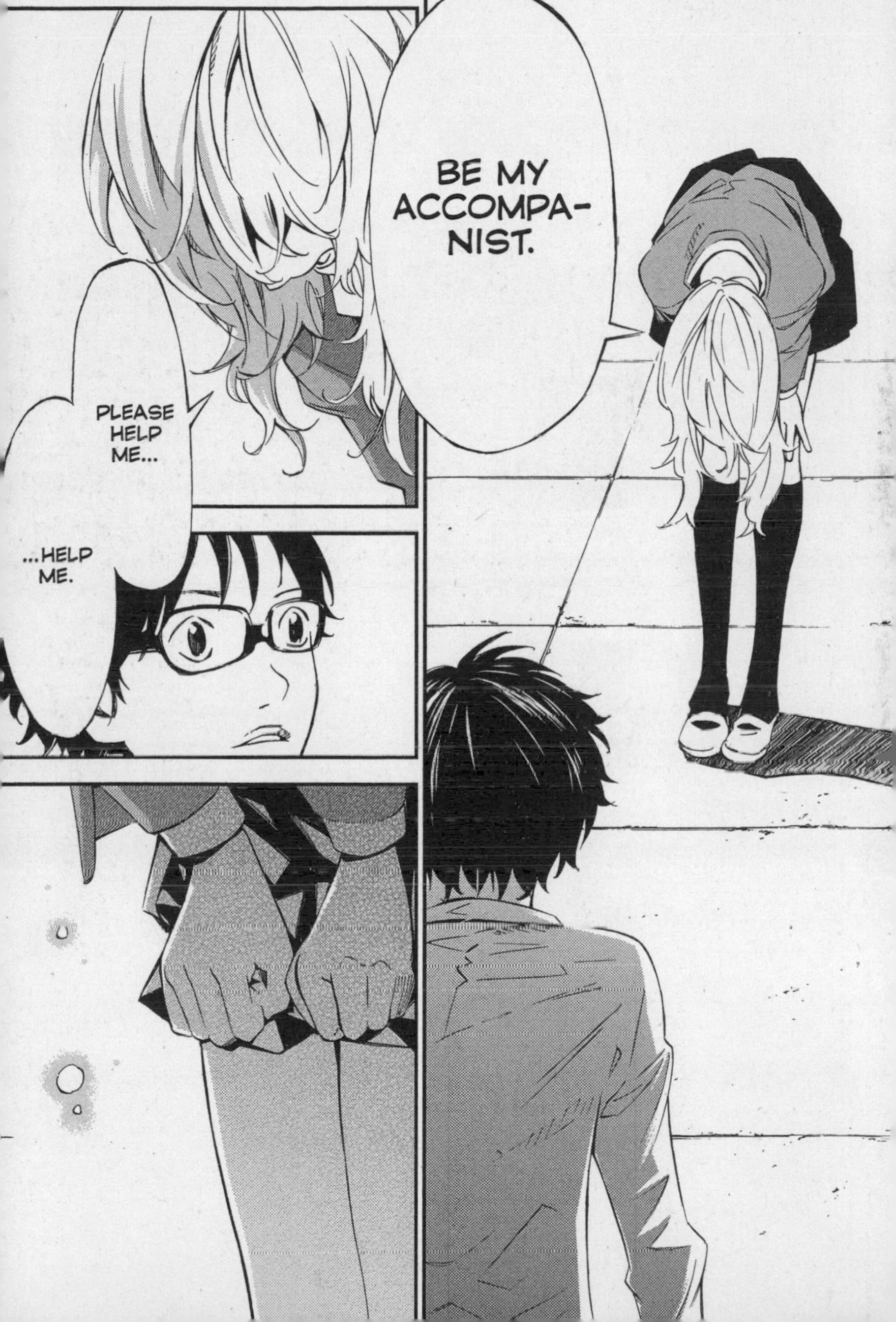
BE MY ACCOMPA-NIST.
PLEASE HELP ME...
...HELP ME.

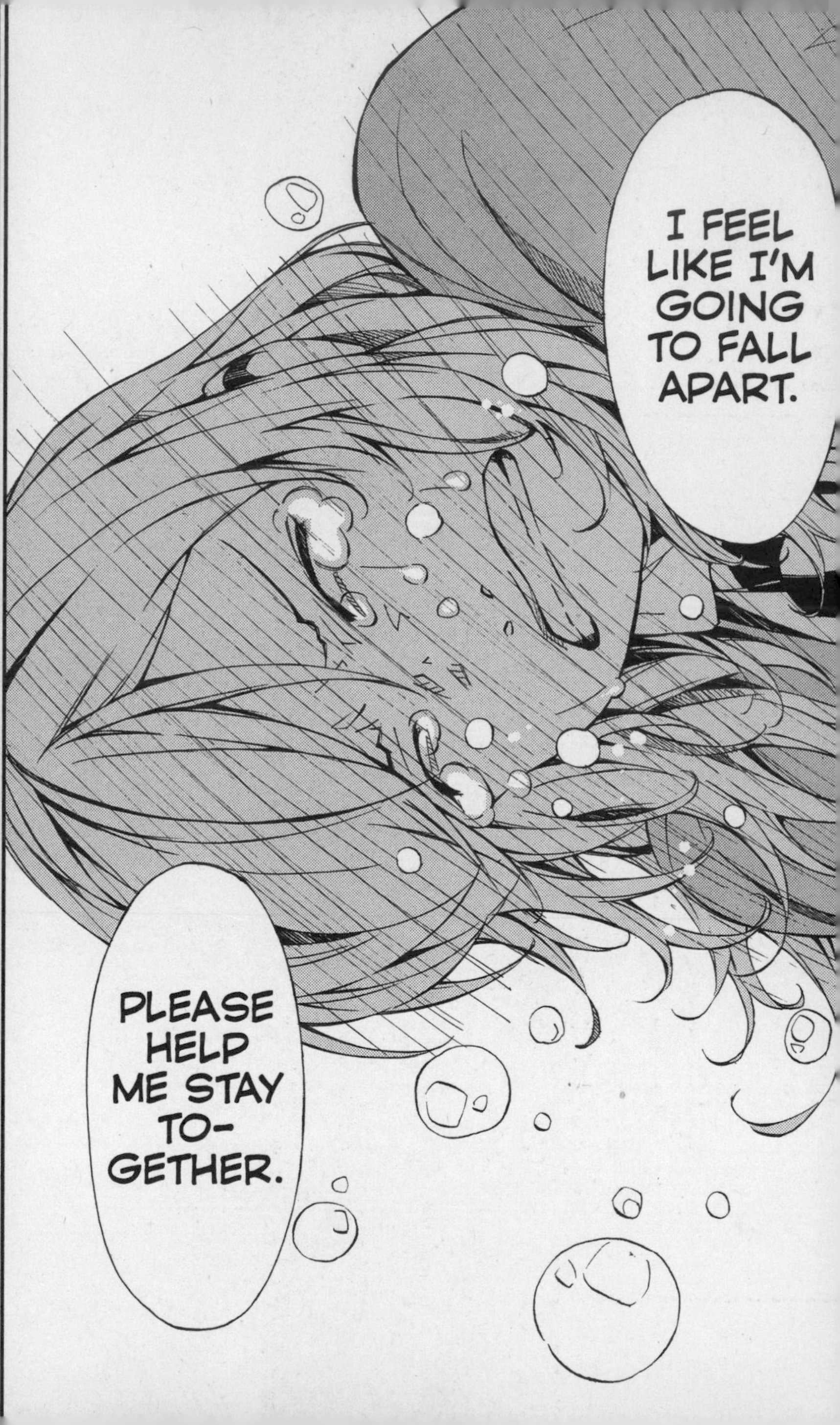
I FEEL LIKE I'M GOING TO FALL APART.
PLEASE HELP ME STAY TO-GETHER.

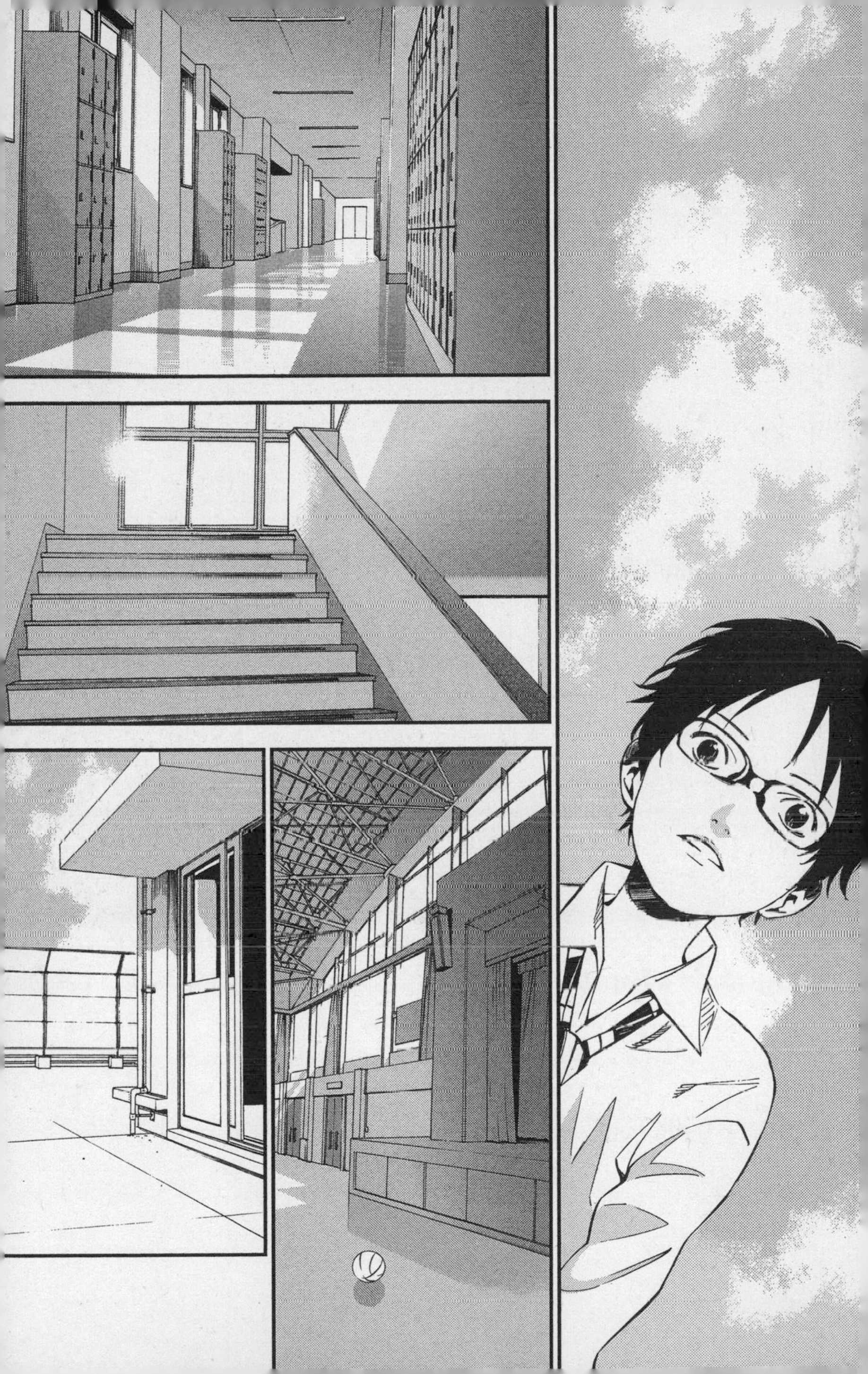

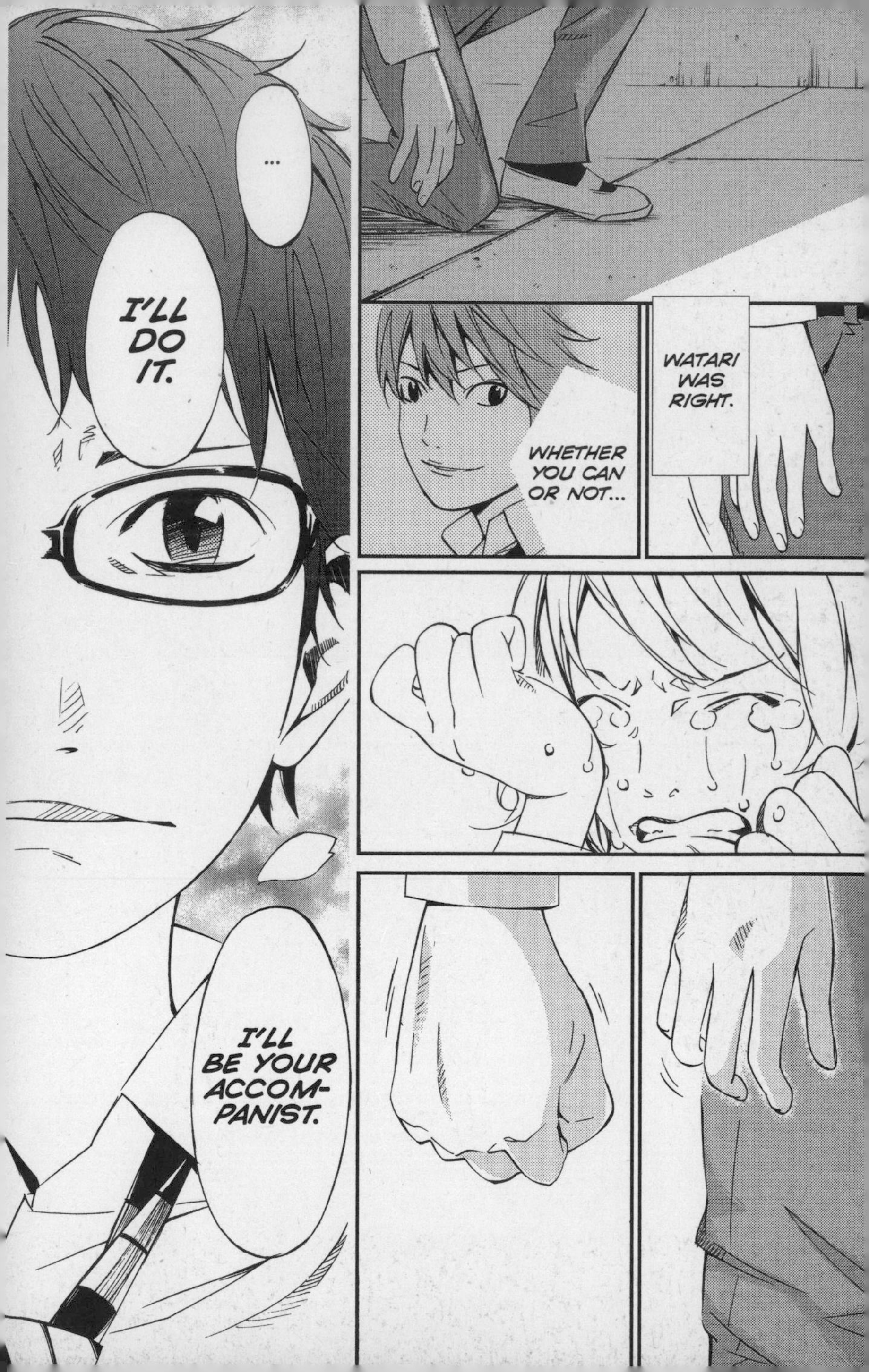
WATARI WAS RIGHT.
WHETHER YOU CAN OR NOT...
...
I'LL DO IT.
I'LL BE YOUR ACCOMPANIST.

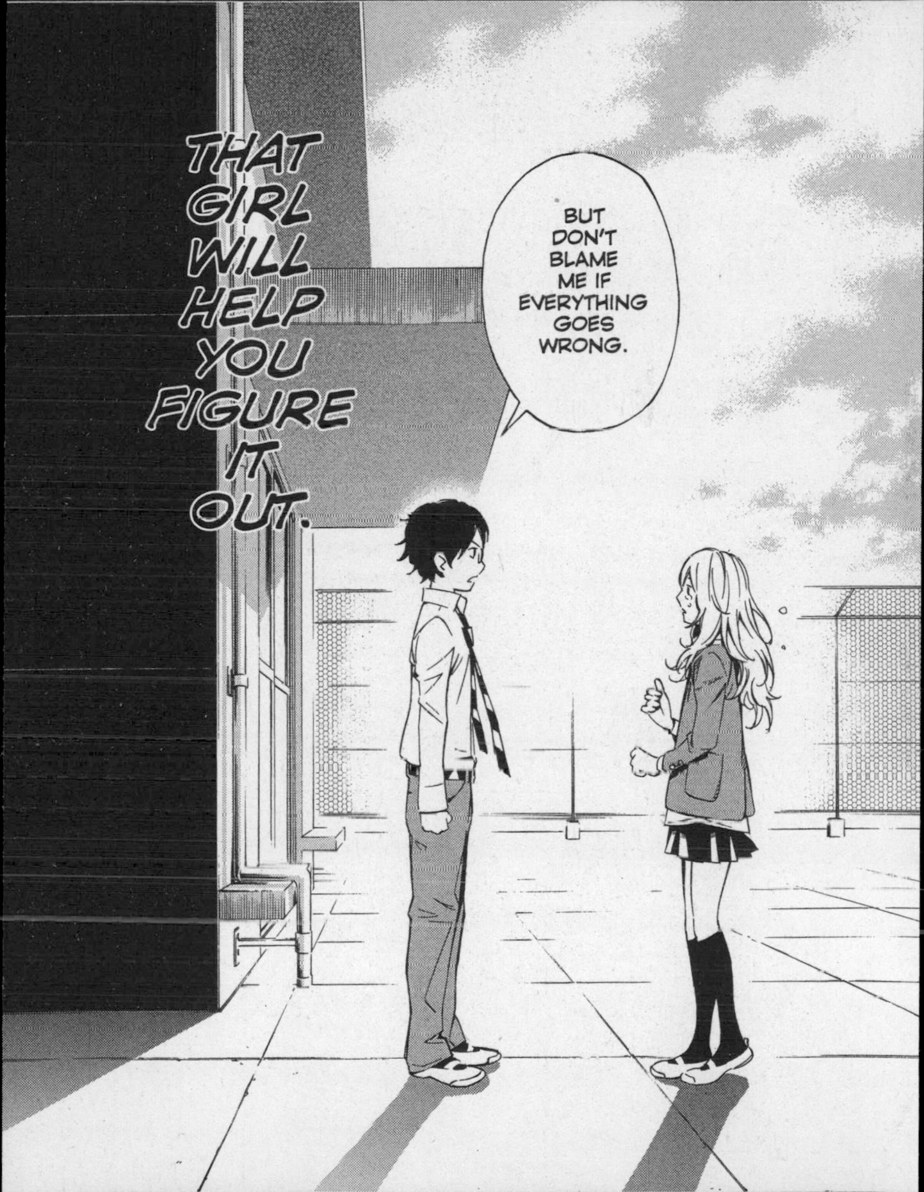
BUT DON'T BLAME ME IF EVERYTHING GOES WRONG.
THAT GIRL WILL HELP YOU FIGURE IT OUT.

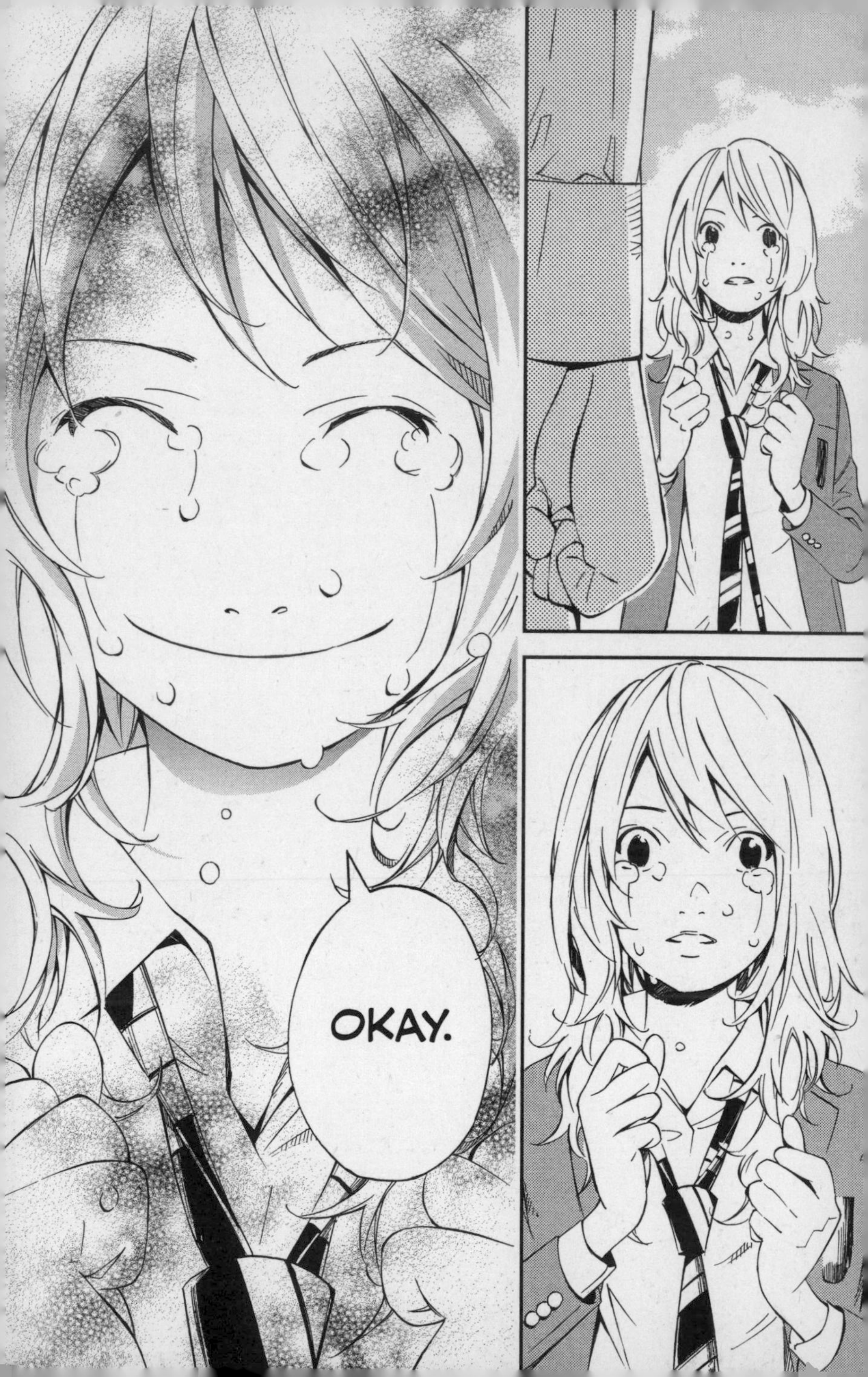
OKAY.

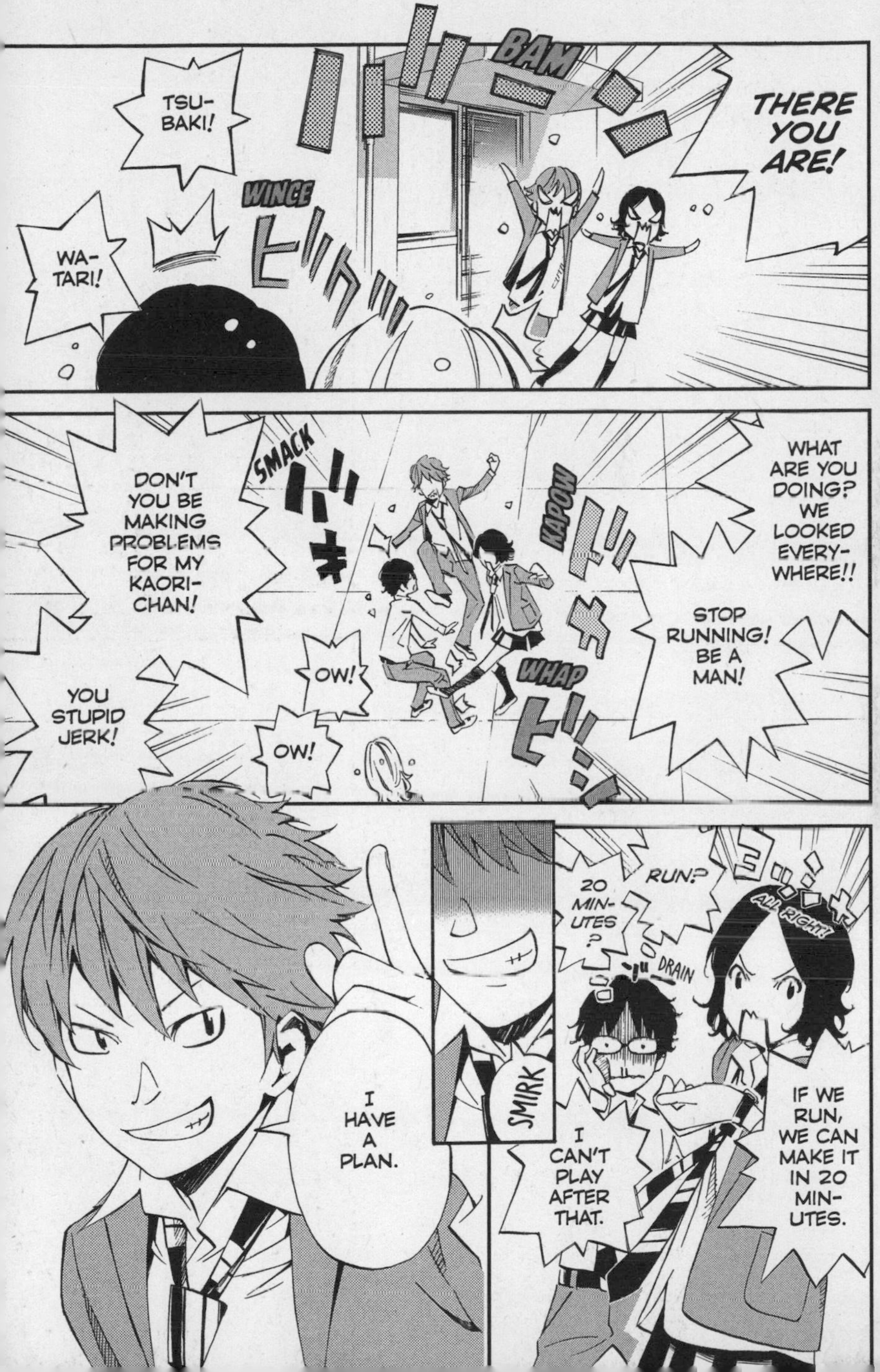
THERE YOU ARE!
BAM
TSU-BAKI!
WINCE
WA-TARI!
WHAT ARE YOU DOING? WE LOOKED EVERY-WHERE!!
KAPOW
STOP RUNNING! BE A MAN!
WHAP
SMACK
DON'T YOU BE MAKING PROBLEMS FOR MY KAORI-CHAN!
OW!
OW!
YOU STUPID JERK!
ALL RIGHT!
RUN?
20 MIN-UTES?
DRAIN
IF WE RUN, WE CAN MAKE IT IN 20 MIN-UTES.
I CAN'T PLAY AFTER THAT.
SMIRK
I HAVE A PLAN.

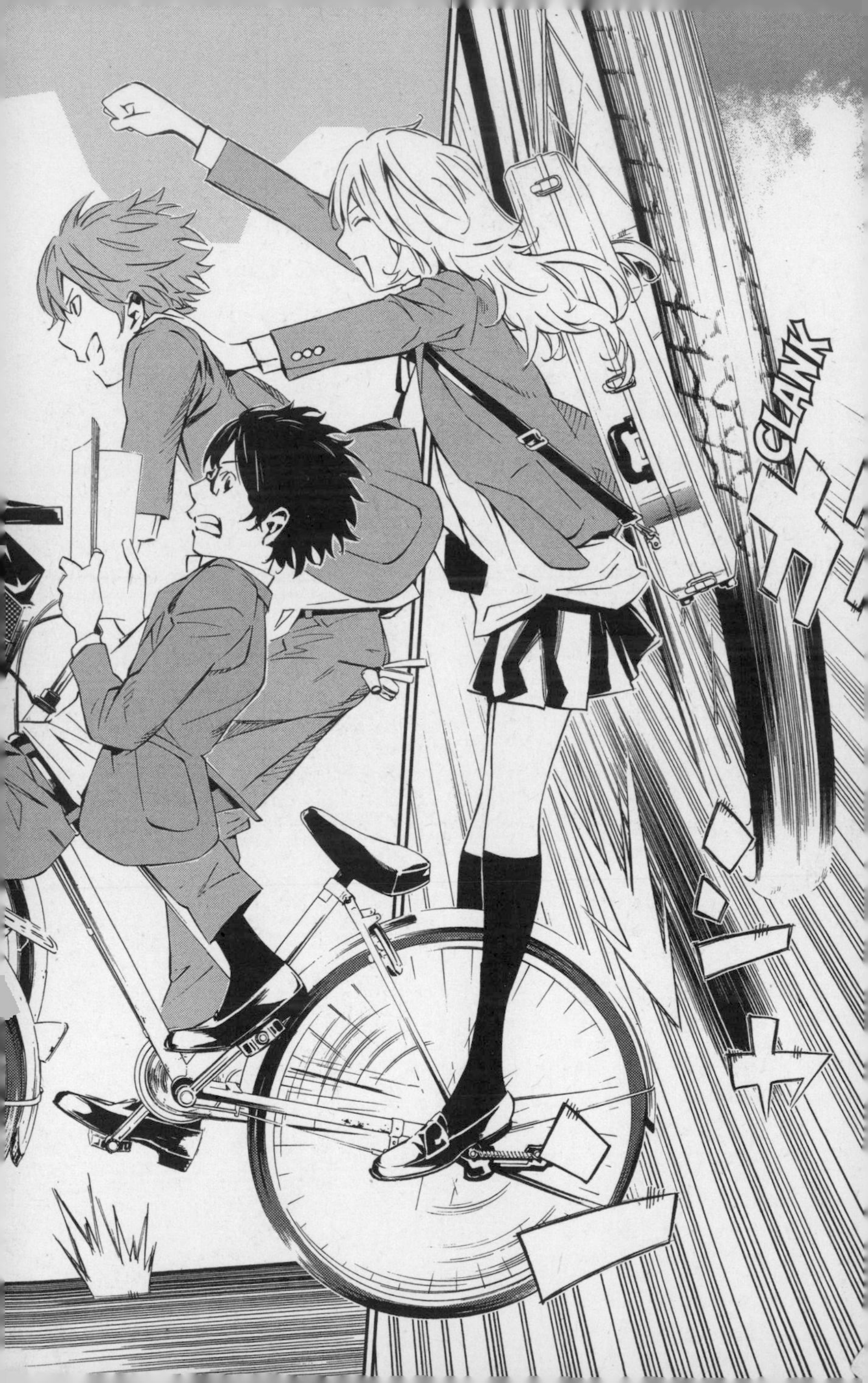
CLANK

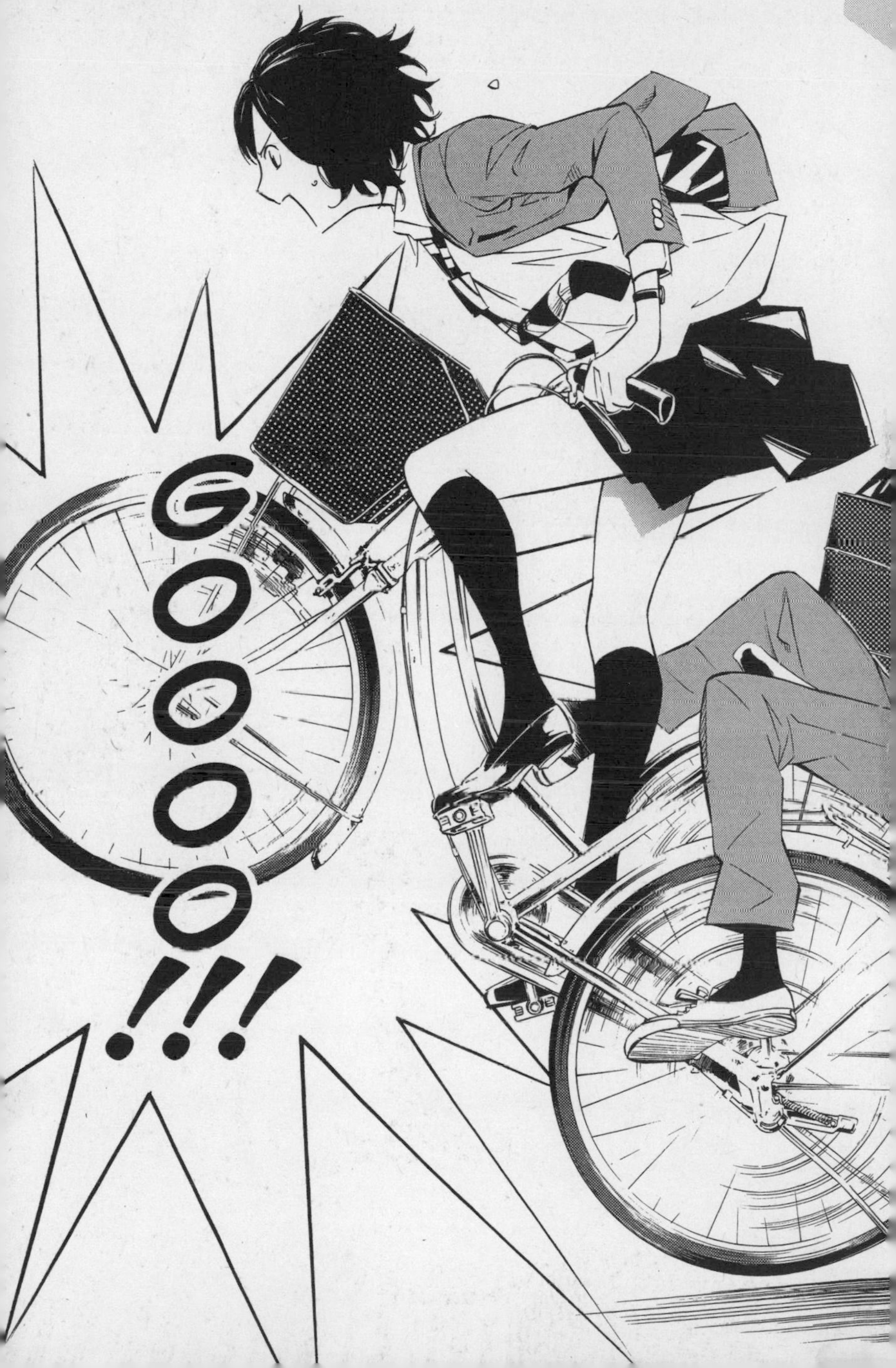
GOOOOO!!!

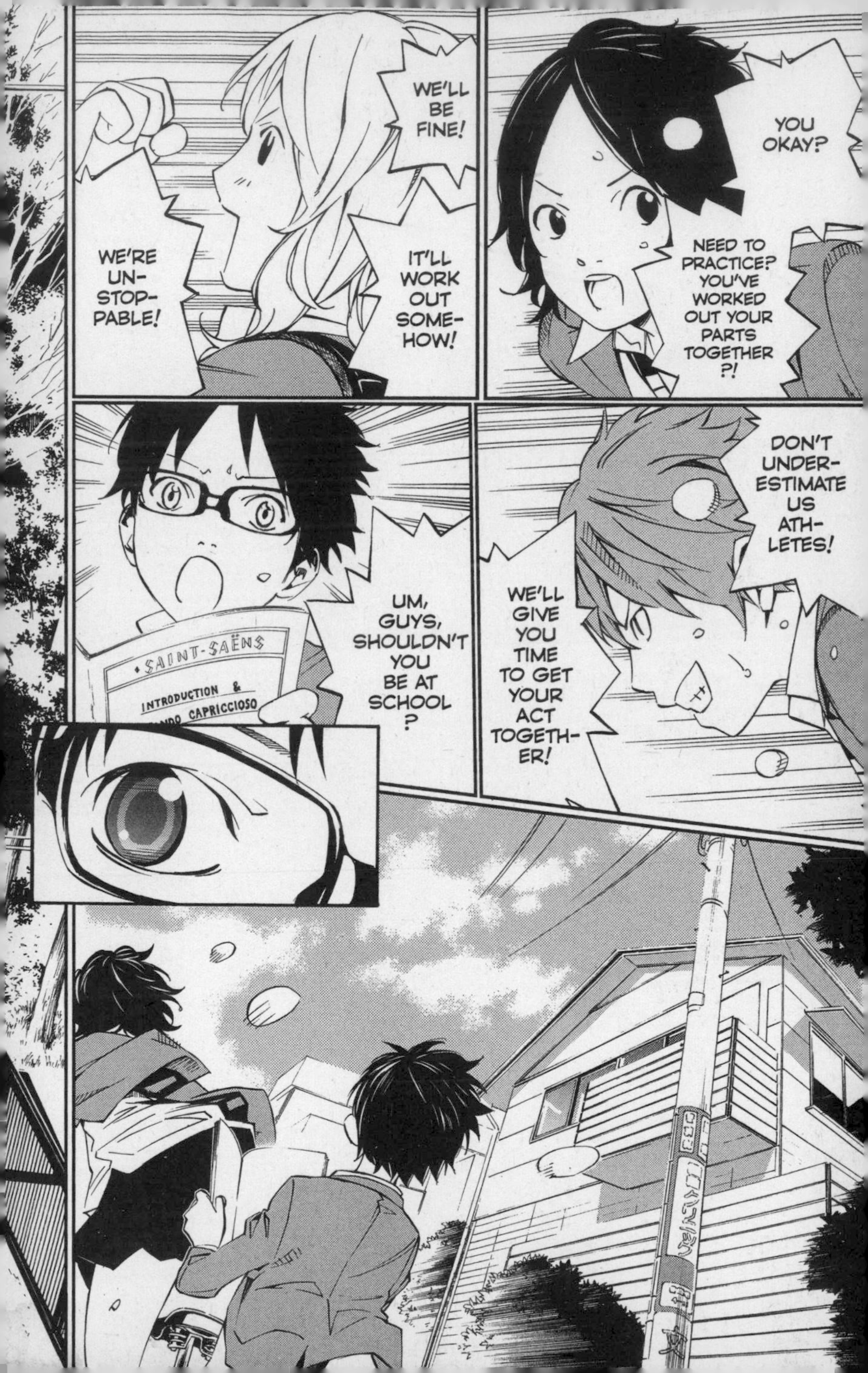
YOU OKAY?
NEED TO PRACTICE? YOU'VE WORKED OUT YOUR PARTS TOGETHER?!
WE'LL BE FINE!
IT'LL WORK OUT SOME-HOW!
WE'RE UN-STOP-PABLE!
DON'T UNDER-ESTIMATE US ATH-LETES!
WE'LL GIVE YOU TIME TO GET YOUR ACT TOGETH-ER!
UM, GUYS, SHOULDN'T YOU BE AT SCHOOL?
SAINT-SAËNS
INTRODUCTION &

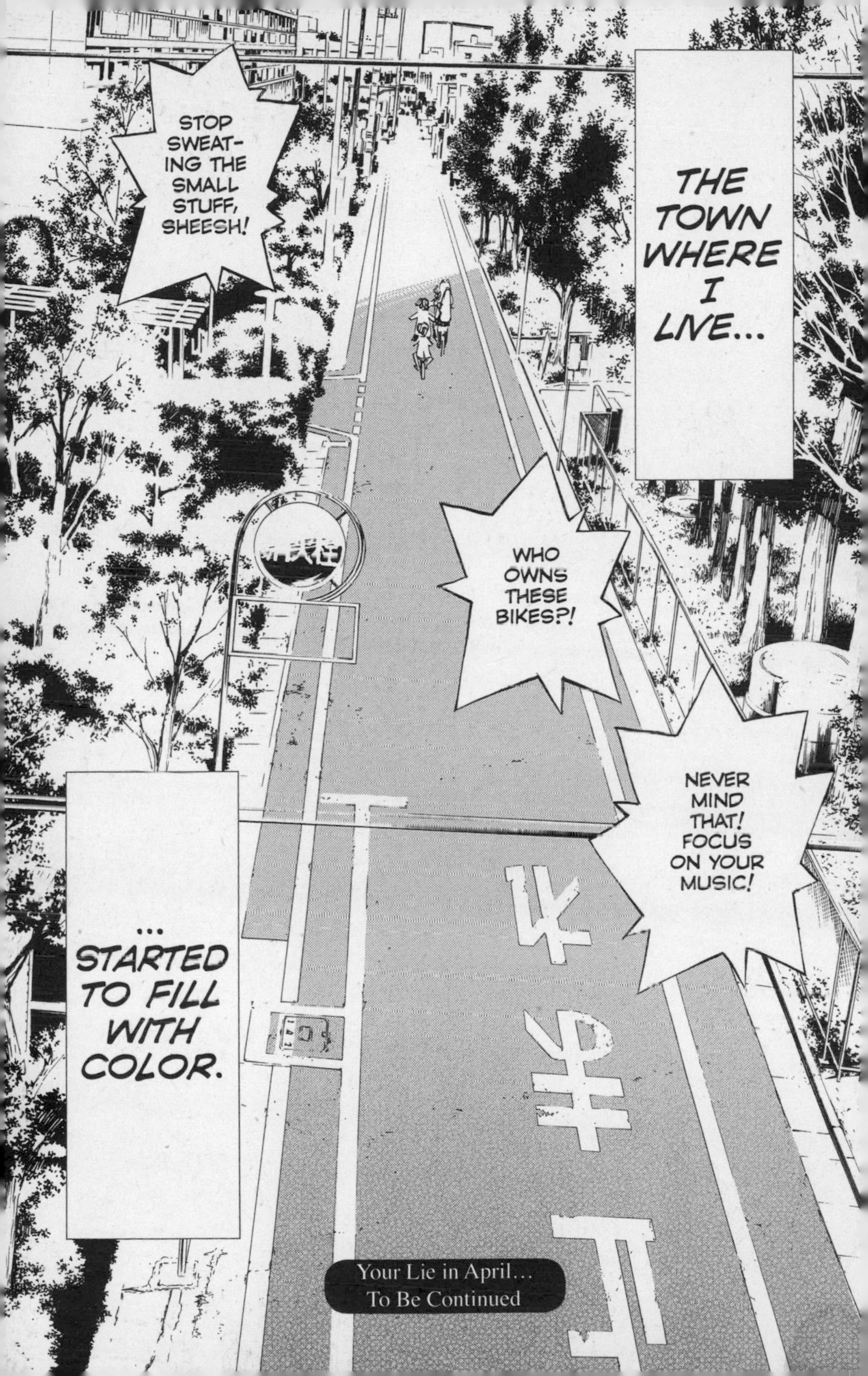
THE TOWN WHERE I LIVE...
STOP SWEATING THE SMALL STUFF, SHEESH!
WHO OWNS THESE BIKES?!
NEVER MIND THAT! FOCUS ON YOUR MUSIC!
...STARTED TO FILL WITH COLOR.
Your Lie in April... To Be Continued

Special Thanks:

AKINORI ŌSAWA

RIEKO IKEDA

KAORI YAMAZAKI

YOSHIHIRO KAMIYA

TOPPAN HALL

KAWAGUCHI LILIA

MUSIC HALL ANOANO

Translation Notes

Melodica, page 46

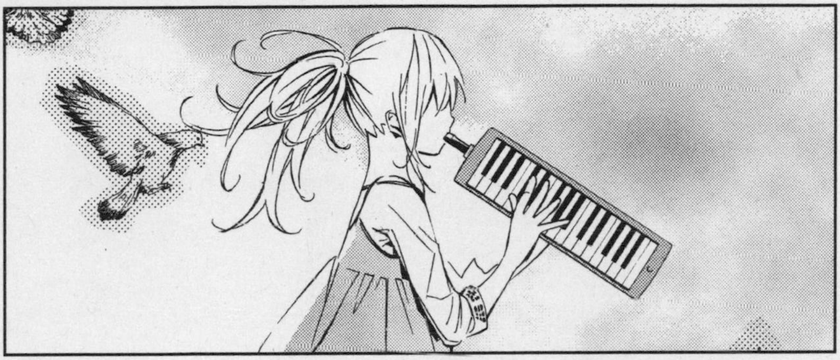

As you can see in the picture, a melodica (known in Japan as a pianica) is keyboard instrument that the musician blows into. It sounds something like a harmonica, and is popular in musical education. That being the case, it's something you might expect to be played by a someone in grade school, and not a serious musician.

Pazu, page 52

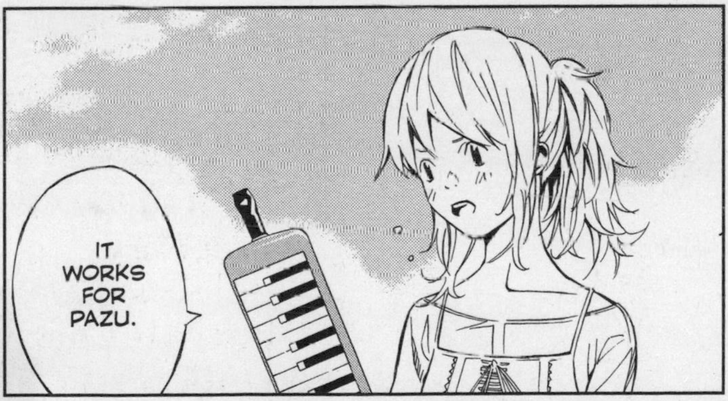
IT WORKS FOR PAZU.

Pazu is one of the main characters in the Studio Ghibli film, *Castle in the Sky*. Apparently the children are trying to replicate the scene where Pazu plays his trumpet while his pet doves fly around. Kōsei sees doves flying during the girl's solo, so it's possible that the children's complaint is referring to the end of the solo, when the doves are supposed gather back around the musician. Either that, or Kōsei is so moved by the music that he sees doves that aren't really there. Incidentally, in Japanese, the same word is used for dove and for pigeon, which is just as well, because doves and pigeons are in the same family of birds.

Kaori's pre-performance chant, page 94

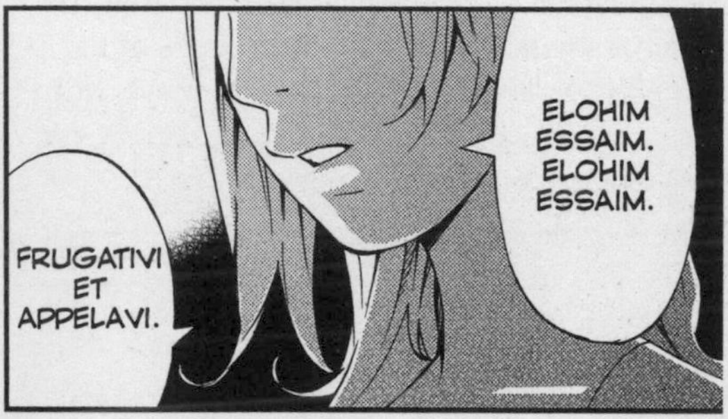
ELOHIM ESSAIM. ELOHIM ESSAIM.
FRUGATIVI ET APPELAVI.

This is a chant from the Red Dragon Grimoire, which contains spells for summoning demons. This particular incantation was famous enough to be used in manga series such as *Akuma-kun*, which is most likely where Kaori first read it. The first part is never translated into Japanese, which makes it difficult for Japanese-English translators to translate into English, but the second half means, roughly, "I seek and beseech thee."

The Japanese Nadja, page 109

This is a reference to the famous American violinist, Nadja Salerno-Sonnenberg, who is known for her wild, original playing.

Her Majesty is satisfied, page 155

In the Japanese version, Kaori uses the word *yo* for "I." This is a rather pompous first-person pronoun, and so the translators have decided to translate it as "Her Majesty."

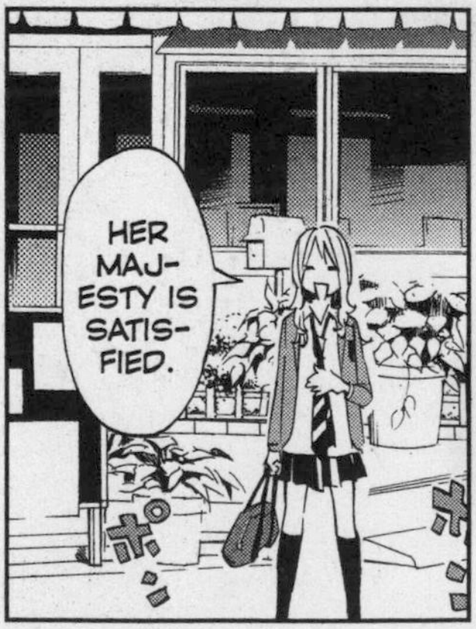
HER MAJ-ESTY IS SATIS-FIED.

Your Lie in April volume 1 is a work of fiction. Names, characters, places, and incidents are the products of the author's imagination or are used fictitiously. Any resemblance to actual events, locales, or persons, living or dead, is entirely coincidental.

A Kodansha Comics Trade Paperback Original

Published in the United States by Kodansha Comics, an imprint of Kodansha USA Publishing, LLC, New York.

Publication rights for this English edition arranged through Kodansha Ltd, Tokyo.

ISBN 978-1-63236-171-4

Special thanks:
Akinori Osawa, Rieko Ikeda, and Kaori Yamazaki

Printed in the United States of America.

www.kodanshacomics.com

9 8 7 6 5 4 3 2 1
Translation: Alethea and Athena Nibley
Lettering: Scott Brown
Editing: Ben Applegate
Kodansha Comics edition cover design by Phil Balsman

Beethoven and Mozart, page 166

Kaori's suggestions to help a pianist play despite difficulties come from historical anecdotes. One of the methods Beethoven used to help him through his hearing loss was to put a ruler in his mouth and touch it to his piano so he could feel the sound vibrations in his head even if he couldn't hear them. Mozart was a student of Haydn, who bet his students that no one could compose a piece of music he (Haydn) couldn't play on sight. Mozart took him up on this bet and wrote a simple piano piece that at one point required the musician to have a hand on each of the far ends of the keyboard, and at the same time play a note in the middle of the keyboard. When Haydn declared that no one could play such a piece, Mozart proved him wrong by using his long nose to play the middle note.

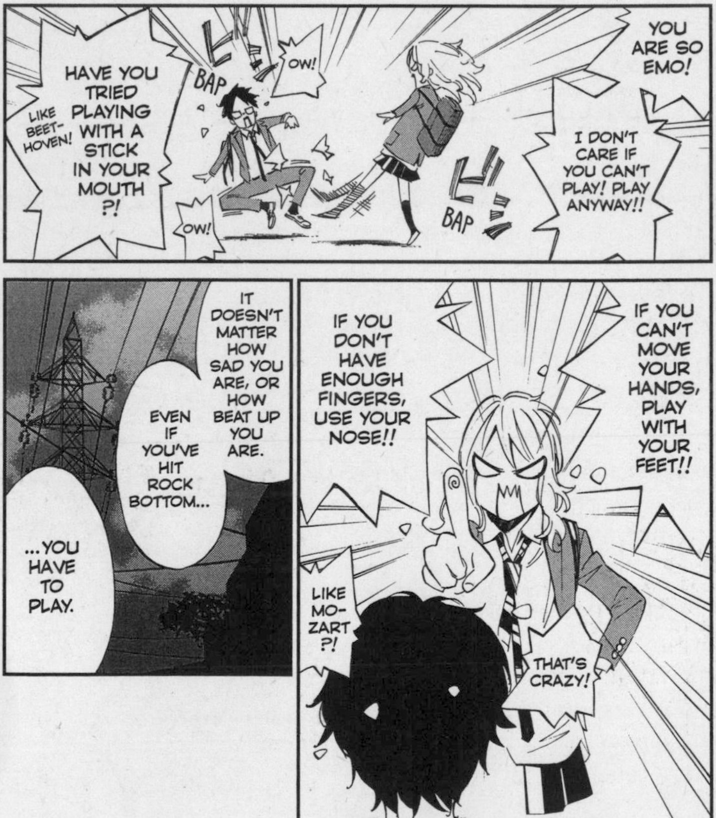
YOU ARE SO EMO!
I DON'T CARE IF YOU CAN'T PLAY! PLAY ANYWAY!!
BAP
OW!
BAP
HAVE YOU TRIED PLAYING WITH A STICK IN YOUR MOUTH?!
LIKE BEET-HOVEN!
OW!
IF YOU CAN'T MOVE YOUR HANDS, PLAY WITH YOUR FEET!!
IF YOU DON'T HAVE ENOUGH FINGERS, USE YOUR NOSE!!
THAT'S CRAZY!
LIKE MO-ZART?!
IT DOESN'T MATTER HOW SAD YOU ARE, OR HOW BEAT UP YOU ARE.
EVEN IF YOU'VE HIT ROCK BOTTOM...
...YOU HAVE TO PLAY.